English Spirituality

English Spirituality

An Outline of Ascetical Theology According to the English Pastoral Tradition

Martin Thornton

COWLEY PUBLICATIONS
Cambridge, Massachusetts

Previously published in Great Britain in 1963 by SPCK

International Standard Book Number: 0-936384-31-X paper
International Standard Book Number. 0-936384-38-7 cloth
Library of Congress: Number:86-6292

Cover photograph by Sarah Pfeiffer

Library of Congress
Cataloging-in-Publications Data
Thornton, Martin

English Spirituality

Reprint. Originally published: London : SPCK, 1963.

Bibliography: p.   Includes index

ISBN 0-936384-31-X (pbk.)—ISBN 0-936384-38-7

1. Asceticism. 2. Spirituality—England—History of
doctrines. 3. Spiritual Direction. 4. Pastoral
theology—Anglican Communion. 5. Anlican
Communion—Doctrines. 6. Pastoral theology—Church of
England. 7. Church of England—Doctrines. I. Title.

BV5031.2.T53 1986

248'.0942

86-6292

Cowley Publications
980 Memorial Drive
Cambridge, Massachusetts 02138

WITH AFFECTION
AND GRATITUDE TO
THE DEAN
FACULTY
STUDENTS AND
ALUMNI OF
THE GENERAL
THEOLOGICAL SEMINARY
NEW YORK

CONTENTS

PREFACE TO 1986 EDITION

WHEN THIS BOOK first appeared in 1963 a majority of reviewers, whether critical or otherwise, expressed dissatisfaction with its title, or rather with the single adjective which made up half of it. I was not surprised, since this one word had caused me more heartsearching than any of the other hundred and thirty thousand.

Is not "English" too narrow? Is it not suggestive of insularity, even a sort of spiritual jingoism? Should it not be "Anglican," pointing to a world-wide movement of which the Church of England is but a very small part? Indeed, is not the Church of England so enfeebled by its outmoded "establishment" as to be almost an insignificant joke as compared with Anglicanism in so many other parts of the globe? She may be sentimentally venerated as the Anglican matriarch by some of her daughters overseas, but great-grandmothers invariably suffer the risk of senility.

Since this reissue of *English Spirituality* has been largely initiated in America, the question is of new importance: would not *Anglican Spirituality* be more appropriate as a title? On further consideration, I still think not. "English" remains the more accurate term, for however much explanation is given—and the days of two page subtitles are happily past—however historically and theologically competent one's readers, Anglicanism still suggests a spiritual movement that began in the early seventeenth century. Theologically competent readers will know that we are concerned with a spiritual ethos traceable through the Fathers to the New Testament. Yet the erroneous first impression remains, and titles are concerned with first impressions.

As I hope the text makes clear, a specifically English spirituality is traceable to the influence and ascetical teaching of St Benedict and St Alselm. Twelfth-century England

became known as the "Land of the Benedictines," differing
from the Italian tradition in significant points, but one can
barely speak of Anglicanism at this juncture. The tradition
evolved out of such factors as the very English ancrene movement and the experiments of St Gilbert of Sempringham, but
it is still too early to discard the word "English." Or is it
admissible to describe our renowned fourteenth-century
school—Hilton, Julian and Rolle—as Anglican? In a somewhat speculative vein I have argued that one possibly might,
yet all Christian ascetical studies, from whatever denomina-
tional source, refer to this school as English, as they might
speak of the Spanish Carmelites or the German Dominicans.
Ironically it is the term Anglican, despite its growth over five
continents, that really risks the charge of narrow insularity.
Perhaps we may conclude this somewhat verbose pedantry by
saying that as ascetical theology, the Anglican grew out of
the English.

   In the present spiritual and theological climate, two
decades is a long time; new questions, or old questions in a
new form, have arisen since the first appearance of *English
Spirituality*. During this period ecumenicism has expanded to
the extent of bursting Christian boundaries with a growing
interest in the teaching and technique of eastern religion.
So should we continue to talk of specific schools of prayer at
all? Is not this itself narrow and parochial? Or should we
rather develop the idea of the schools being related to each
other instead of seeing each one as isolated and autonomous?
It is this approach that I seem to have pursued, almost subconsciously, in *Spiritual Direction*, published by Cowley-
SPCK in 1984. I suspect that the comparative success of this
book has prompted the publishers to reissue *English Spirituality*, since in a curiously roundabout way the latter forms
a sequel to *Spiritual Direction* more than twenty years later.
There I suggest a four-fold source for spiritual guidance to
consist of studies of biblical and patristic theology, moral
theology, ascetical theology, and finally an examination of
the primary schools of prayer—precisely what *English Spiri-*

tuality purports to do. Whatever the shortcomings of either volume, they seem to go well enough together and form a whole, but with the 1963 book completing that of 1984.

A further characteristic of this period is a continuing emphasis on synthesis at the expense of analysis, not only in theology but in its allied disciplines. Modern theological studies become more thematic and less departmental. For instance, whereas biblical commentary was once a matter of verse-by-verse, chapter-by-chapter exposition, it now tends to deal with the prominant themes throughout particular books of the Bible. The concern is for a single gospel rather than a series of isolated clauses; it is not a question of what Romans, chapter 1, verse 1, then 2, then 3, actually "means", but rather what is St Paul's composite message? What is he getting at all the time? So too with doctrine. The creeds present the great themes of the faith—the Trinity, the Incarnation, Christology, the Atonement—in living and pastoral terms, rather than as a series of metaphysical statements to be "believed," or accepted or assented to. It is significant that we now talk of "systematic" rather than "dogmatic" theology.

So with psychology, and therefore its relevance to Christology. In the 1920s, F.R. Tennant wrote of the "psychologist's fallacy," a veiled anti-Freudian insistence on the unity of human being which cannot be split up into isolated "faculties." So modern Christology stresses the whole living Christ, to be encountered and known as sacred humanity, not as Chalcedonian categories; as an integrated being, risen and glorified, rather than as a psychological jig-saw puzzle.

Behind this wide movement lies a change from substantive to existential thought, from metaphysical understanding or explanation to experience, from intellection to feeling, from objectivity to empiricism. All of this has its influence on contemporary spirituality. For we aim to live the whole faith as whole people, to love rather than to understand, to know God in simple, non-discursive contemplation rather than to meditate systematically on his attributes. We are not

so much engaged in a search for meaning as an exploration
into the divine activity and how we know, experience and
love it. So contemplative silence tends to replace the older
Anglican verbosity of the seventeenth century and the Book
of Common Prayer, where petition is apt to turn into a
theological lecture: "O God who. . . . . etc. etc. etc." There
is a new (or rather, rediscovered) emphasis on the theology
of Baptism, whereby prayer is not to stop short with en-
counter with the living Lord, but to proceed to incorporation, a sharing, in the Sacred Humanity. We live not only
with Jesus, but *in* him.

However theological fashion changes, there is always reaction. My *Spiritual Direction* is something of a swing of
the pendulum, insisting that all analysis cannot be entirely
abandoned, history still has its lessons for this and every
age. The historic schools of prayer are still important for
the glorious reason that God's creativity insists that everyone is different, and that rigorous analysis is necessary in
order to discover how unique individuality is best to be
nurtured and guided aright. The alternative is a series of
pious little conversations that comfortably get nobody
anywhere. While we can rejoice in contemporary theological
expression as a creative basis for simple contemplative
prayer, the old patristic and scholastic categories, now so
unpopular, still have their essential place in spiritual direction. Modern spirituality demands this past wisdom—not to
employ it directly, but to use it as applicable foundation.

Perhaps the most significant of the new factors that have
arisen since 1963 is an increased focus upon psychological
factors as these can be brought to bear on the study of
ascetical theology. The interrelation between theology and
psychology as it affects spirituality is in itself nothing new.
All the great teachers of prayer—SS. Paul, Augustine, Benedict, Anselm, Aquinas—were profound psychologists, but
today's new insights, coupled with recent studies of eastern
religion, have placed greater emphasis upon this side of
things, especially in America. In fact there has arisen a clear

difference of approach, even a conflict, on either side of the
Atlantic.

American asceticists have become more and more concerned with psychology—one thinks of such writers as
Merton, Kelsey, Holmes, Greeley and Watts—almost to the
detriment of traditional theological insight. European writers,
on the other hand, are more inclined to stick with the spiritual wisdom of the past, although without entirely neglecting
the insights of such thinkers as Freud and Jung. No doubt
there is imbalance on both sides and it is to be admitted,
whether with pride or apology, that by this criterion the
present book is very European indeed. This is hardly surprising if we are dealing with spirituality which is both
English and Anglican, a strong characteristic of which is
insistence upon biblical and patristic roots as foundation to a
living tradition. In fine, the American is tempted to look on
Europe as archaic, antiquated and reactionary, while Europe
might accuse America of having slipped its theological
moorings in favour of psychology. The future health of
spirituality could depend on a greater trans-Atlantic co-operation and dialogue. I gladly acknowledge my debt to the
work of Morton Kelsey, while at the same time worrying a
little about his fleeting or nonexistent references to Anselm,
Benedict, Bernard and Aquinas; it might not be too much
to hope that *English Spirituality* and *Companions on the
Inner Way* could enlighten and compliment each other.

I do not think that anyone has managed to produce or
edit a reasonably comprehensive study of Christian spirituality in less than three fat volumes, say, a minimum of a
half-million words. It is inevitable that the following account,
restricted to a single tradition, still contains glaring omissions,
of which the most obvious, and also the most topical, is its
neglect of the spirituality of Eastern Orthodoxy. This spirituality points up a most remarkable development, especially
in Western Europe and perhaps more especially in the United
Kingdom, since the 1960's.

For a long time Orthodoxy has had its significant place in

American Christianity, but if I am not wholly misinformed this has been largely confined to America's large population of Eastern European immigrants. In England such immigration is a comparatively recent phenomenon,. much accelerated since the end of the second world war. For some time there has been a significant Greek Orthodox presence in the larger English cities, which is now supported by Russian, Serbian and Polish communities up and down the country, while more serious Anglicans have long been inspired and fascinated by the writings of Bishop Anthony Bloom and Archimandrite Kallistos Ware, by the Holy Liturgy, and by the Jesus Prayer. But until recently I have regarded Orthodoxy's ascetical system as somewhat alien to the English tradition and temperament. Recent developments have proved me totally and excitingly wrong; Anglicans are entering Orthodox congregations in considerable numbers and English-Orthodox congregations are being established.

It would be interesting, if a little outside our present scope, to speculate as to why. Suffice it to note that in the past, disenchanted Anglicans have tended to look to Rome as the only alternative, yet since Vatican II a general pastoral and spiritual convergence has made great strides. Both have an almost identical vernacular liturgy, a common Eucharistic lectionary, and indeed common problems with theological rebels.

More important is to look for some common spiritual strands within Anglican-Orthodoxy, despite initial appearances to the contrary, and to discover whether an Anglican-Orthodox marriage could breed its own characteristic school. What facets of Orthodoxy are Anglicans now finding attractive? Dogmatic certainty, sane discipline, deep anti-Pelagian spirituality and a sense of mystery obviously counteract the traditional weaknesses of English religion. On the positive side, a weekly liturgy followed by a gentle but firm domesticity, a family emphasis, and great stress on the doctrine of creation are all attributes of the best of Anglicanism. A school of prayer is not an insular autonomous organism, as I hope this book makes clear, but a gradual emergence of a pure tradition made up of a composite spiritual ancestry. And it must frequently be revitalised by an ordered transfusion of new blood, all of which makes an Anglican-Orthodox synthesis an exciting possibility. Such a synthesis would not be entirely novel and would certainly not be without precedent, since the seventeenth century Anglican divines who consolidated (but did not invent) our tradition were all thoroughly immersed in the spiritual theology of the Eastern patristic tradition. Having offered friendly criticism to some American writers for making so little of Anselm, Benedict, Bernard and Aquinas, I must confess my own criminally scant treatment here of Orthodoxy from the Cappadocians and Chrysostom to St Seraphim of Serov. I can only suggest and hope, at this late stage, that readers of the present volume will fill in the gap by reference to those better qualified to help; more particularly, to Orthodox asceticists themselves.

Speculation on the future is a dangerous game, and with a vast quantity of new and exciting ascetical thought pouring from the presses, might it not be a little foolhardy to bother with a book over twenty years old? Or, as some might naturally assume, over twenty years out-of-date? What is the point of such a risk? Implications behind two more recent quotations hint at an answer. In *The Man from the Plains*, David Kucharsky's study of President Carter, comes the succinct statement: "A plant severed from its roots is more likely to attract parasites than to bear fruit. There is no substitute for direct connections with the past." (p. 116) The ecumenical scene is subtly changing, the familiar parrot cry "Unity without uniformity" is deepening into positive objection to syncretism. The idea and ideal of the schools of prayer is returning to favour, which means that their health is expressed by evolution, not stagnation, by development through cross-fertilisation, not by conservative insularity. This principle was vividly brought home to me by my liturgical experiences in Transkei. My first such experience was in the cathedral at Umtata: Book of Common Prayer in English, Victorian hymns, Merbecke, and so on. It was supremely dreadful. Then came the liturgy at St Cuthbert's mission: every word in Xhosa, tribal folk music, all of it as exhilarating as the Orthodox liturgy, to which it bore obvious resemblance—including its length. Following this there were seminars centred upon patristic theology: their (my host's) choice, not mine. So the question arises: which was Anglican? Assuredly the latter, for "there is no substitute for direct connections with the past."

Barry and Connolly's *The Practice of Spiritual Direction* prophesies that "a new age of mutual collaboration which will heal the rift between dogmatic or school theology and spirituality may well be upon us." (p. 21) Incidentally this new book also goes a long way to heal the Europe-American, theology-psychology rift, a healing which I previously mentioned as a vital future need. Serious and enthusiastic concern for living prayer, vital experience of God manifested in the risen and glorified Christ, continues to grow. There is a new sense of freedom and a new quest for spiritual adventure; there is a new simplicity in the deep sense of contemplative harmony. But it still needs a theological foundation: "A plant severed from its roots. . . . ." You cannot worship chunks of school theology and you cannot adore the Chalcedonian Definition, but neither can you worship and adore Jesus Christ without something like it. The more honest, "simple", and adventurous we become, the more that the inherited wisdom of the past, the historical roots, grow in importance as ultimate foundation.

That is perhaps the operative point in the republication of *English Spirituality*. The exciting new flowers are lovely, but they will die without roots. Transkei has got it right: Anglican-based spirituality, flowing from the early Church but with little resemblance to Victorian England. Let us not be ashamed or embarrassed of the English-Anglican roots. If our tradition is to continue to grow, to become more exciting, proficient, and liberated from some of the old traditional restrictions, then something like *English Spirituality*, a book covering the same ground, is absolutely essential background. If there is one incontrovertible fact, it is that the book could be much better than it is and produced by a far more competent writer. The thinking behind the decision of the present publishers is that, in the present climate, such a better book by a more competent writer is pretty unlikely to appear. I can only hope that this reissue of *English Spirituality* fulfils its supportive role in supplementing newer insights.

Martin Thornton
Autumn 1985

PART ONE

Preliminary Surveys:
Pastoral
Theological
Biblical

1

THE PASTORAL SITUATION TO-DAY

I. THE DEMAND FOR SPIRITUAL GUIDANCE

In 1935 William Temple wrote to the present Dean of Westminster, who had been appointed Warden of The Bishop's Hostel, Lincoln: "You will use it as a basis for what we need more than all else—to teach the clergy to be teachers of prayer."[1] In any pastoral context, this nurture of the manifold gifts and graces which God so profusely pours upon his disciples must be central, for it is by this means that God performs his miracles of redemption. But if William Temple were alive to-day I believe that he would repeat his injunction with even greater emphasis: the pastoral situation demands it.

The signs portend the beginning of a religious revival of a deep and subtle type. It is not "revivalism" as that word is generally understood, but a profound and secret groping after real religion among the faithful, and a more thoughtful attitude towards the Christian Faith by a significant minority outside, or on the fringe of, the Church. Various factors support this assessment.

Ten years after the letter referred to, Dean Abbott was telling his students (of whom I was privileged to be one) that if they took moral and ascetical theology seriously, and continued their own spiritual struggle, then he could promise that their ministry would be sought and used. That promise appears to have been honoured. In any group of clergy to-day, the evangelists, youth experts, preachers, and organizers only retain their zeal amid a good deal of frustration and pessimism. Those called to spiritual guidance suffer vicarious agonies of responsibility and intercession for their children in God, for that is part of the job, but there is no frustration and no pessimism. The former group are concerned with how a demand for their ministrations can be created; the latter with how the growing demand for guidance can be met. Correspondence arrives with frightening regularity from laypeople seeking serious personal

[1] F. A. Iremonger, *William Temple* (1948), p. 513.

guidance: with disarming loyalty it is explained that their parish priest is an excellent and dedicated man, but that he is uninterested, or frankly incompetent, in this kind of work. I have no doubt than in many cases this judgement is wrong, but it remains a serious indictment of our pastoral practice.

Another factor is the remarkable increase, over the last twenty years, of adult converts presenting themselves for Confirmation. This is a national phenomenon offering an uncomfortable challenge. Mature men and women, some in responsible positions of considerable civic and social standing, do not take such a step lightheartedly. The Church is not fashionable, and for the artisan and factory hand the decision to seek Confirmation is even more difficult, often demanding renunciation and courage. This army of new blood entering the Church will not be satisfied with conventions and platitudes with which older Church people have become far too content. They will demand the real thing.

A corollary to this deepening movement is the growing number of older men offering themselves for Ordination. This group is of so variable a nature as to be impossible to classify, yet one or two pertinent points suggest themselves. There is a considerable number of ex-Nonconformist ministers, who for various reasons have grown worried and dissatisfied with their denomination. Spiritually and pastorally, however, the central attraction of Anglicanism is undoubtedly the Book of Common Prayer seen as a system of Christian life.[1] These men have become dissatisfied with the piecemeal character of Free Church devotion, however excellent some of the pieces may be. It is chastening to realize that, in seeing the Prayer Book primarily as an ascetical system, this band of converts have discovered a fundamental Anglican truth which some of our senior priests seem to have forgotten. The latter think of *regularity* of Church attendance, the former of the *continuity* of Christian living based on the Prayer Book pattern. In terms of English spirituality, we shall discover that the latter interpretation is certainly the traditional one.

Many more of these older ordinands are not so much "late vocations" as vocations hitherto frustrated by circumstances; the renunciation and integrity involved is parallel with that of the older Confirmation candidate. Many feel genuinely called to serve an understaffed parish in their later years, but there is also a more

[1] See Dewi Morgan (ed.), *They Became Anglicans* (1959).

ominous and almost subconscious motive. It is that older men, having served the Church loyally but conventionally for a lifetime, see Holy Orders as the only hope of real growth under guidance. They are doubtful whether, as laymen, they will be taken seriously and guided competently. That is another serious indictment of the present position, and one which conflicts with well over a thousand years of English spiritual tradition.

This total situation is again illustrated by the almost incredible growth of the Retreat Movement. There are multifarious motives for "going to church", but lay-people—at the rate of some 40,000 a year [1]—do not undertake a disciplined three-day search for God unless they seriously hope to find him.

II. SOCIAL FACTORS IN MODERN RELIGION

What are the reasons behind this revival? God works in mysterious ways but it is conceivable that he also works according to some kind of logic. The Holy Ghost is not unconcerned with human situations; thus the study of social environment becomes part of pastoral theology, and the adaptation of Christian truth to that environment has always been a prominent aspect of ascetical thought. In the present revival, the growing efficiency and discipline within English parishes is obviously a large factor: more frequent celebrations of the Eucharist, stricter recitation of the Office, more disciplined prayer, all have their inevitable effect. The zeal of the new converts and spiritual deepening of the faithful must carry subtle power into the world. But why the converts and why the deepening just at this time?

A common suggestion is that there is a reaction amongst the middle-aged against the spiritual emptiness of their formative years. For whatever the shortcomings of the present age it is not so disastrously shallow as the between-the-wars period. Compared with the smart set of those days, the modern "beatnik" and "angry young man" are intensely serious people. The former reaction was no doubt against conventional religion, but it was also against all "seriousness". In the 1920s and 30s, philosophy, the arts, music and literature were all as unpopular as religion: then the "war to end war" had ended; to-day we face the threat of a war to end everything. That is a situation which only religion can face squarely.

We may also be at the beginning of a general reaction against two

[1] Figure supplied in consultation with the Association for Promoting Retreats.

centuries of rationalistic materialism. The Church has been hoping
for such a movement for a long time, but it is surprising how
frequently this view is now assumed, not by religious writers but
by political and economic journalists. Mr Edward Crankshaw,
an acknowledged expert on Russian affairs, recently predicted
the failure of the Soviet twenty-year plan because it was *too
materialistic*:

> The young are already asking questions. They have never suffered
> as their parents suffered. They earn enough, have enough to eat,
> can clothe themselves sufficiently. They take all this for granted.
> Why go on about it? Why talk as though food and drink and shoes
> and washing machines are the end-all and be-all of existence?
>
> This mood was strong three or four years ago; it has grown
> since then. Now the questioners are told in effect that for the next
> twenty years they must think of nothing at all but material
> betterment and increased production—and this at a time when
> the more advanced nations of the West are disillusioned by the
> failure of material betterment as a panacea and are plunging
> wildly in search of new ideas.[1]

That is an especially significant passage to us in our search for a
pastoral approach to what has come to be called an "affluent
society", and in the second sentence Mr Crankshaw lights upon a
theological truth so often missed. It is *because* the Russian youth
have not suffered the poverty of their parents that they are *less*
materialistic. Holy poverty is one of the most misunderstood of all
ascetical themes. The ambiguous adjective is the operative word:
no serious Christian writer imputes virtue to poverty as such. A
tiny minority of heroic saints embraced poverty having known
nothing else; no doubt peasants, paupers, and slaves have sometimes
found religious faith an alleviation to their misery; but "holy
poverty", in its real sense, invariably grows by reaction against
wealth. It is sometimes forgotten that St Francis of Assisi spent his
early youth in the most exotic luxury. There is no doubt that affluence
too will soon pall, here as in Russia; material value will be found
wanting. It is hardly surprising that some mature people, "plunging
wildly in search of new ideas", have found themselves confronting
the Holy Ghost. Again they demand the real thing and it will be a
monstrous tragedy if the Church does not supply it. The Church

[1] From *The Observer*, 22 October 1961.

concerning itself primarily with cultural and social activities must fail, for it is but substituting one kind of materialism for another. It is significant that the American Church, with all the money and practical appurtenances it needs, is now worried by its own "activism" which is but an American term for Pelagianism.

Dr H. R. McAdoo describes the Caroline Age as one when "theology was as common a topic of conversation as association football is today. . . . Particular events evoked different treatises and theologians wrote to supply the present demand or because events required theological explanations."[1] The science–religion relation may be turning full circle and the modern world returning to that position. Theology looks like becoming the only frame into which current questions can be fitted. If we are bold enough to face the implications of nuclear warfare, the old martial ideas of courage, strategy, and resistance to a conquering tyrant have no more meaning; we can only think in terms of the mystery of the resurrection of the body which embraces the final consummation in glory of God's creation. The Industrial Revolution led to scientific materialism, and then to the social problems it had created; the exploration of space is different, it is not sociological, and we are left with the strictly theological concept of wonder. Even the jet airliner is different from the steam engine; there is again wonder, but also the impression that the world is very small and, in itself, insignificant. But is the world anything "in itself"? That is another theological question.

On the other side of the coin are problems of over-population, starvation, and famine. But these questions have ceased to be entirely agricultural and economic ones; we must face anew the whole question of what the human soul *is*. The time was when evil was what a man and his friends did wrong: now tyranny, nuclear bombs, concentration camps, place the whole concept in a cosmic setting in which all must share. The doctrine of original sin has become current news.

On the optimistic assumption that the bomb will not go off we are left with what journalism calls the "ideological" war between East and West, but ideology is clearly no more satisfactory than materialism itself: the frame is still too small to contain current events. The single hope and need is in the Body of Christ fulfilling its

[1] *The Structure of Caroline Moral Theology* (1949), p. 8.

redemptive function, that is its supernatural function, through the unique contribution of each of its members. That implies serious, personal, spiritual guidance.

III. THE SPIRITUAL TEMPER OF THE AGE

In this book I have no wish either to assume or to defend any particular pastoral system. Readers are free to place spiritual guidance in their own lists of priorities, and I would only maintain that, especially when interpreted in the wide English sense, it cannot be left out altogether. I hope that it is clear that such guidance is a total pastoral activity which is by no means confined to the very faithful or "advanced", but if we are to discover the most creative approach to the question it is to the progressive minority of the faithful that we must look.

The Church of England presents a complex pattern; it contains laity of greater devotion, discipline, and integrity than any other communion or denomination, and at the other end of the scale it allows a laxity which no other society would tolerate for a moment. But that is the price any society must pay for being adult: "Very few of the denominations are willing to take a chance on man living up to his responsibilities. The Anglican Church is willing. Often people fail, but when they do live up to their full Christian responsibility how much stronger they are. This, to me, is one of the great strengths of the Anglican Church."[1]

The Church is one and pastoral theology must embrace the whole, but if we are truly to discern present trends, if we seek to guide the whole Church into a revivified spirituality consonant with our heritage, then we must look to the progressive rather than to the irresponsible. In any context, the progress of a body depends on the progress of its leaders.

We must also begin with the first rule of all pastoral theology, which is to accept the situation as it is; neither inventing some hypothetical set of circumstances that we would prefer, nor accepting the doubtful assumptions of popular opinion. It is frequently implied, for example, that the "average congregation" consists of a church full of imbeciles, all of whom have suddenly decided to go to church for the first time in twelve months. Far from being average, such an assembly would be very remarkable indeed. If the phrase has any meaning at all, the "average congregation" is far more likely

[1] J. W. Reinhardt, in *They Became Anglicans* (1959), p. 127.

to be a small group of very faithful people, thirsting for real progress and guidance.

From this viewpoint, which I regard as a realistic one, there are six discernible trends in the religious outlook of to-day. They are:

1. The "revival" itself, moving away from convention towards a deeper faith and devotion. This creates a new demand for spiritual direction, but it is not a return to authoritarianism, still less to clericalism. It demands a priesthood which is friendly, honest, and competent; which does a job rather than plays a part. That, we shall see, is fully in line with the English pastoral tradition.

2. There is a trend towards system and away from piecemeal devotions; towards Christian living and away from a mere series of religious exercises. This, too, is a return to traditional English spirituality, with its strong emphasis on habitual recollection. To-day none can escape from "planning", which, in ascetical terms, means integrated Rule rather than a fussy list of "rules". Pastorally it leads to a reaction against some of the more exotic experiments in "Catholic" devotion popular thirty or forty years ago; a reaction not aimed at the devotions themselves, still less against "Catholicism", but against ascetical disorder. The modern faithful go to confession and say the Office, not because they are "Catholic" but because they are necessary parts of a system of living.

3. There is a revolt against barren theological scholarship which is ascetical rather than obscurantist. There was a time when it was considered important whether a Christian accepted 4004 B.C. as the date of creation or whether he believed in an evolutionary process. Now the faithful are more concerned with what the doctrine of creation means to their daily attitude to created things. The burning question used to be, Is the Bible true and what does it mean? The current question is, How should it be used? Serious Christians to-day would have their faith prove effective, not merely proved right.

4. This trend against barren theory is also anti-sentimental. Affective devotion has its place in all Christian spirituality, not least in our native school, but there is a clear swing towards loyal duty of a common-sense kind and away from forced affectiveness. Some of the "devotional" writings of the last forty years are quite out of harmony with the prevailing temper: the Rule of St Benedict is curiously topical.

5. Christianity always maintains a certain tension between the corporate Church and its demands, and the individual soul with its unique needs. The present social emphasis is on "community", which is carried over into the Liturgical Movement, Parish Communion, and the rediscovery of the value of the common Office.

6. Lastly, and as something of a summary of the foregoing, is a growth towards balance and religious maturity. This is perhaps best expressed by E. J. Tinsley's important theory that the proper Christian approach to life and religion is "ironical".[1] In its original sense, this ambiguous word means contradictory or paradoxical; in its religious context it implies both reason and wonder in man's approach to the transcendent. According to Tinsley, many of our Lord's sayings are, in this sense, "irony": mysterious, paradoxical, offering simple teaching which contains inexhaustible profundity as well. To find life we are to lose it; to love God we must hate parents and friends; to be rich we need to become poor; to reach maturity means to become as little children. Such an approach implies, as G. K. Chesterton teaches so vividly, that a sense of humour is not barely permissible to religion but a profound religious quality: pride is the worst of the sins and the worst form of pride is to take oneself too seriously. This approach is ultimately a pastoral application of the Thomist doctrine of analogy: the mind of God is both revealed in Christ and yet never directly accessible to men. We must strive to know God, love God, and trust in God, while never forgetting our creaturely limitations.

In practice we must make a complete oblation of ourselves to God, our worship must be as perfect as we can make it, ritual, music, ornaments, and ceremonial must be the very best we can offer: then we must seriously wonder whether God sees our perfect High Mass as something acceptable but comic. We should take our ascetical disciplines very seriously, we must honour the details of the Church's tradition, since the Divine Compassion forbids laxity: yet we must try to see that beefsteak on Friday is unlikely to reduce God Almighty to tears, and to think that it might is a very long way from Christian penitence.

This is the principle behind the discipline of the daily Office, of not being too disturbed by the curious and cursing parts of the

[1] In an unpublished lecture at Durham, July 1961.

psalms, of refusing to be worried by occasional absence of devotion, or even absence of mind.

IV. SPIRITUAL THEOLOGY IN THE CHURCH TO-DAY

The key question arises: what is the state of Anglican ascetical thought to-day, and to what extent can it meet the needs of modern people? As I have briefly discussed elsewhere, the answer forms another paradox.[1]

The Fathers and Doctors of the Church, as well as the Caroline divines, wrote "occasional" theology because it was necessary to Christian life. They refuted heresies as they arose, and offered guidance to the faithful in particular situations. Modern theology appears to be returning to this position and away from the ideal of "pure" or "academic" scholarship. But in ascetical theology, as such, we have to look back a good thirty years before finding anything that can remotely be seen as a "school of thought". There is no group of modern writers comparable to Oscar Hardman, Bede Frost, Evelyn Underhill, F. P. Harton, C. F. Rogers, H. S. Box, and F. G. Belton. This period still supplies the current textbooks in spiritual theology, which, whatever their intrinsic value, are the products of a dying theological outlook. The paradox is that we now find scholarship with an intensely pastoral and spiritual emphasis while spiritual and pastoral theology remains thoroughly academic.

This group of writings, thirty years old yet still in current use, must not be underrated. It gave a new impetus to Anglican spirituality and laid a foundation upon which we can continue to build. That it is outdated and incompatible with present trends is a compliment to it; for it must have sparked off the advances in pastoral religion which have now outrun it: pastoral religion amongst the faithful is in advance of pastoral thought. But it is important to see how obsolete this group of writings is, and how it runs counter to the conclusions reached in the previous section.

Where spiritual guidance is directly dealt with there is a strong authoritarian flavour. The priest-director is very much the master of a pupil, or, significantly, a "penitent". There is little of that empirical relationship which, we shall see, is not only at the heart of English ascetical theology, but has also largely created it.

This teaching is also unsatisfactory because it assumes a uniform

[1] In *Theology*, August 1960, pp. 313–9.

"Catholic spirituality" of which the Counter-Reformation is the only culmination, whereas, in fact, Catholicity involves a glorious complex of schools, emphases, and techniques, all founded upon the Creeds yet catering for different conditions and temperaments. There is no one way of Christian Prayer, no stereotyped Christian life, and until this is understood ascetical teaching remains mere theory.

This school of the 1930s is "academic", mainly because it deals with the terms of ascetical theology by intellectual definition. It explains the meaning of the virtues, the capital sins, the Three Ways, and so on, with little direct application. That indeed is necessary: before any subject can be understood its terminology must be explained, but terminology is not the subject. The rules and terms of tennis do not teach the skills of the game. This teaching of terminology is, nevertheless, of much value, especially in the most maligned of all the books of this age, F. P. Harton's *The Elements of the Spiritual Life*. For twenty years Anglicans have been saying that this book needs to be replaced, but although it could undoubtedly be improved it still supplies the student with the bare bones of ascetical doctrine. It is not the author's fault if it is in the nature of bare bones to be a little on the dry side. The need is not so much to rearrange the bare bones as to clothe them with flesh and blood, which analogy underlines the error of seeing "Catholic spirituality" as a solid uniformity. One skeleton is very like another: so soon as it supports living flesh and blood it becomes a unique person within a particular society with definite characteristics.

My hope is that this present book will in some measure complement Harton; will add a little life to his bare bones; conversely that *The Elements of the Spiritual Life* may be a useful reference book, even a glossary, to support this study.

I have mentioned that these older writers deal with affective devotion quite separately—which is un-English—and in an idiom that is out of tune with the modern temper. These writers were not sentimentalists; their devotion was deep, honest, and real: the fact remains that their particular expression has lost its appeal. Most of this teaching on private prayer also runs counter to current trends in being intensely individualistic. In the face of one of the most fundamental of all ascetical principles, corporate worship and private devotion are treated as two isolated things: daily Mattins and Evensong being invariably known as the "priest's Office".

It is significant that this era gave rise to an almost puerile enthusiasm for the more obscure and exotic forms of "mysticism", usually undefined and often misunderstood. Some writers—a few very well known—reached the stage when practically any Christian who said his prayers affectively was a "mystic". Pastorally the whole thing became very unhealthy indeed.[1]

Lastly, these scholars were neither prudes nor fanatics, yet their books read as if they would be terribly shocked by Mr Tinsley and perhaps even more by me: 400 pages without the semblance of a smile, life is very grim and very earnest, and Christian life a good deal grimmer than any other. Meditations for Easter Day sometimes read as if the Resurrection was some intolerable tragedy; Christian joy is to be embraced as a somewhat unpleasant duty. That is not the outlook of English Christianity—ancient or modern.

It is intrinsic to ascetical theology to adapt itself to the contemporary situation, yet it can only evolve out of a living tradition with roots in the past. We have now discovered, rather painfully, that a scholar cannot just sit down and compose a new liturgy; nor can another scholar sit down and write a modern spirituality. Both depend upon the worshipping community developing a tradition. That, by the grace of God, seems to be happening, but it needs a compatible ascetical theology to support, guide, and nurture it, and the only source of such a theology is the tradition itself: it is sometimes more progressive to look back a thousand years than to look forward three weeks.

Our liturgists have also discovered, again with some pain, that anyone unfortunate enough to have to compose a "special service" cannot do worse than pick prayers and hymns from here, there, and everywhere, and stir the mixture. English spirituality continues to suffer from just that. A recently published symposium—*Christian Spirituality To-day*—contains excellent essays on Ignatian, Benedictine, and Eastern Orthodox spirituality in an inexpensive paperback series. But what is the ordinary English reader supposed to make of it? He is hardly expected to make his choice and turn Orthodox or Jesuit, nor can he extract a little from each and mix it with the Book of Common Prayer. If we add a little Carmelite mysticism, Oratorian priesthood, Franciscan popular devotion, meditations from the German Dominicans, and moral theology from the Council of Trent, we have no great exaggeration of Anglican ascetical studies, and indeed, pastoral practice.

[1] See Valerie Pitt, "Clouds of Unknowing", in *Prism* (June 1959), pp. 7–12.

Well in the background remains the English School of Spirituality: sane, wise, ancient, modern, sound, and simple; with roots in the New Testament and the Fathers, and of noble pedigree; with its golden periods and its full quota of saints and doctors; never obtrusive, seldom in serious error, ever holding its essential place within the glorious diversity of Catholic Christendom. Our most pressing task is to rediscover it.

V. THE ECUMENICAL MOVEMENT

In these days of ecumenical thinking it is important that unity is not confused with uniformity, which is quite contrary to the Catholic tradition: "diversity in unity is the principle of Christendom". Rightly rejoicing in present trends towards a better understanding between Christians, and eventually we hope towards reunion, we should nevertheless beware of certain dangers inherent in unguarded ecumenical zeal.

1. The first of these dangers is the failure to understand the great principle of St Peter of Cluny just quoted: theological agreement does not mean ascetical uniformity. In the Middle Ages, Benedictines and Franciscans were united in one Church bound by one dogmatic theology, yet their expressions of it were more different than those between most of the warring factions of the modern Church. The oblation of the Church to God should be as rich and varied as God's own creation: the analogy of the Good Shepherd and his *sheep* is open to at least one unfortunate interpretation.

2. It follows that if Anglicanism is to play its part in the ecumenical movement it must be true to itself. Like the *via media* concept, the "bridge Church" idea must be seen in terms of synthesis and not of heterogeneity. The supplanting of Mattins by the "Jesus Prayer" and Evensong by the Rosary is unlikely to further the cause of reunion with Eastern Orthodoxy and Rome!

3. Ecumenicity may incite morbid fears of "insularity" or "parochialism". It is necessary to recognize that the Church of England is only a tiny part of the Anglican Communion, which, in turn, is a small part of the Church Militant. But it is a terrible mistake to deduce from this that the ordinary English parish is of no importance. Some of the newer Anglican churches set examples of integrity, discipline, and heroism which must make us at home deeply

penitent, yet the concept of the "Mother Church" has not lost all of its meaning; inspiration of world significance could still come from Canterbury and York. It is admirable that Anglican arch-bishops should meet with Orthodox patriarchs and Roman prelates, but that many an English village parish is grinding to a standstill is no help to the success of such meetings.

The rediscovery of our native spiritual genius, and the guidance of individual people by it, is neither narrow nor "parochial": it is the traditional Catholic way.

2

THE MEANING AND PURPOSE
OF ASCETICAL THEOLOGY

I. TERMINOLOGY

"Academic" theology is a comparatively recent innovation which
has given rise to the departmental divisions, employing a host of new
adjectives, with which we are now familiar. The Fathers and
Medievals thought and wrote theology without qualifying any
particular work as "biblical", "dogmatic", "historical", "sacramental", "liturgical", and so on: it was a composite subject embracing all these aspects. If these adjectives were used at all they
were confined to an immediate context, and did not indicate a
specific "subject". The modern use of these terms, therefore,
especially as they affect "pastoral" theology, is very ambiguous, and
recent studies have done little to clarify the position. Words like
"contemplative", "mystical", "spirituality" and "ascetical" still
mean very much what each individual writer wants them to mean.
Every new book begins with a chapter of definitions, each slightly
different from the others: in short, the terminology of the spiritual
life is completely out of hand. I have no choice but to follow the
pattern, and to explain my terms as simply and briefly as possible.

There are aspects of the terminological problem, however, which
have interesting implications for this study as a whole. Modern
scholarship is reacting against excessive "departmentalism", and
against "pure scholarship" divorced from pastoral practice. In the
nature of the case, "spiritual theology" itself forms part of this
trend towards integration. Its terms are synthetic not analytic:
"spirituality" is not pietism but the total practice of every aspect
of Christian living. A "spiritual" life is one in which the spirit of
God, sought and nurtured in prayer, controls its every minute and
every aspect. Similarly, ascetical theology is primarily a practical
approach to all other branches of theology, a catalyst or synthesizing
agent which welds all the departments into a creative whole. Only

in a secondary sense can it be regarded as another "subject". To this we must return; but first an attempt must be made to iron out some of the ambiguities of modern spiritual writing.

According to Pourrat: "Spiritual theology . . . is divided into *Ascetic Theology* and *Mystical Theology*".

The former treats of the exercises required of aspirants to perfection. Ordinarily the soul rises to perfection by passing through three stages. First of all, it gets free from sin by penance and mortification; then it forms inner virtues by prayer and the imitation of Christ; and, lastly, it advances in the love of God till it reaches habitual union with Him.[1] It is for us to enter the path of perfection and to traverse its stages more or less quickly. God calls us to do this, and gives us the graces needed for corresponding with His call.

It is otherwise with the extraordinary states dealt with in mystical theology—states such as mystical union with its concomitant manifestations—i.e., ecstasy, visions, and revelations. The mark of these states is their independence of those who experience them. They are the privilege of the few to whom God unites Himself ineffably by flooding them with light and love. No one can effect these mystical phenomena within himself by any efforts or merits of his own. The soul of the ascetic with the help of grace makes an effort to rise towards God; but the soul of the mystic is suddenly and impetuously visited by God without exerting any activity beyond that of receiving and enjoying the Divine gift.[2]

That passage has the advantage of great clarity, but—as Pourrat himself admits in a footnote—it is open to two objections. First, it is a little too clear-cut; both the stages of the Three Ways scheme and the ascetic-mystic distinctions tend to become blurred in experience. As Goodier writes: "There is no true mysticism, whatever may be accepted as its definition, without asceticism; and there is no true asceticism, taken in the Christian sense, without at least some deep insight into the vision of God."[3] The second objection is that many scholars would protest at the restriction of mystical experience to "extraordinary states . . . ecstasy, visions, and revelations". Nevertheless it is in this sense—right or wrong—that I think most

[1] i.e. the classical "Three Ways". [2] *Christian Spirituality* (1922), Preface, p. v.
[3] *Ascetical and Mystical Theology* (1925), p. 4.

students of spirituality would normally interpret the word, and it is certainly in this sense that the subject gained an unhealthy vogue in the 1930s.

The greatest confusion arises with the ambiguous use of the terms "mysticism" and "contemplation"; the first closely associated with the teaching of Dionysius, the pseudo-Areopagite, and the second being the normal—and I would say the correct—word for non-discursive prayer and experience: "the dim yet direct perception of God". But throughout the ages, Christian writers have inclined to use one word or the other to denote much the same thing. To-day they are treated as synonyms. This may be justified when the "higher" experiences of the unitive way are under discussion, but the important distinction—to my mind—is that contemplation covers a much wider range of experience, reaching down to comparatively elementary aspects of Christian life. In other words, modern writers on mysticism tend to the departmental attitude, isolating particular persons and phenomena from everything else. Ancient authors treat contemplation in relation to the whole Christian life.

For example, I have tried to explain elsewhere[1] that a saint habitually living in a state of union with God may properly be called either a Contemplative or a Mystic. On the other hand, one of the most elementary spiritual experiences is a sense of union or harmony with creation, which is correctly known as the "first form of contemplation".[2] Similarly, such "ordinary" experiences as the "absorbed faith" of William of St Thierry,[3] the unitive love for creatures associated with St Francis,[4] and simple, wordless prayers of "simplicity" and "loving regard", are contemplative since they imply a direct, intuitive awareness of God rather than discursive mental activity. It follows that virtues like penitence and recollection usually contain a contemplative element whenever they are qualified by the term "habitual" as distinct from "actual". The latter adjective means a single, isolated, *act* of prayer; the former infers a deep, intuitive *state*. Grace before meals is an *act* of recollection, we suddenly think of God and offer a short vocal prayer; *habitual* recollection is a continuous, even subconscious, awareness of the divine presence everywhere. The terminological point is that, if comparatively common experiences of this kind are rightly called

[1] *Pastoral Theology: a Reorientation*, p. 97, n. 1.   [2] *Ibid.*, pp. 152–76.
[3] See Ch. 8 below.   [4] See Ch. 10 below.

"contemplative", they would not normally be described as "mystical".

In an attempt to grapple with the ascetical–mystical muddle, some modern writers make much use of the terms "acquired" and "infused": Pourrat hints at the distinction in the passage already quoted. It is argued that ascetical theology is mainly concerned with acquired prayer and virtue, since it deals with our volitional response to the love of God by training, effort and discipline, freely undertaken. Mysticism is largely infused since it is the direct gift of God: "No one can effect these mystical phenomena within himself by any efforts or merits of his own." This distinction is also clear and useful so long as it is not interpreted too rigidly: although many common Christian duties largely depend on our free-will, ascetical theology is grounded on the doctrine of prevenient grace. God always acts first, so there is a sense in which everything is his direct gift. Moreover, the very first step in the Christian pilgrimage, the experience of conversion, cannot be described as "acquired" since no effort or discipline on the subject's part could be involved. Conversion must be "infused", but it is not necessarily "mystical".

It is this wretched word "mystical" that is really the cause of all the trouble, and I would much prefer to eliminate it altogether. But it is now so firmly entrenched in the vocabulary of spiritual writing that this simple and attractive solution would be a little irresponsible. I hope at least some of my readers will move through this introductory volume to a deeper study of English spiritual theology, and they will certainly come across "mysticism" in other books whether or not the word is expurgated from this one.

From all this confusion, however, some order emerges, at least in so far as the present book is concerned. I do not claim that my use of terms is irrefragably right and all others wrong, but for immediate purposes the position may be summarized thus:

1. The main subject of the book is ascetical theology, dealing with the fundamental duties and disciplines of the Christian life, which nurture the ordinary ways of prayer, and which discover and foster those spiritual gifts and graces constantly found in ordinary people. It is essentially a *pastoral* book, aiming only at the needs of parish priests in their central responsibility of guiding the faithful towards deepening faith and love. It is, therefore, mainly, if not entirely,

concerned with prayer, virtues, gifts and graces, usually described as "acquired"; including of course, acquired contemplation.

2. The word "contemplation" is preferred to "mysticism", and on the rare occasions when the latter term is used, it means—right or wrong—only the "extraordinary" states usually associated with the teaching of the pseudo-Dionysius.

3. "Contemplation" is used in its traditional width of meaning and subject to the usual qualifying terms. When applied to prayer and recollection, without qualification, it usually means a direct, if dim perception of God as distinct from the discursive, imaginative, and intellectual processes of "meditation", vocal prayer, and liturgical worship. This does not mean that the Office and Eucharist are inconsonant with contemplative experience, but that we normally approach them in a thoughtful, discursive way. Neither does it mean that the imaginative, intellectual, and volitional aspects of meditation never fuse into a simple contemplative love, for that, indeed, is one of the principal ends of mental prayer.

4. The terms "actual" and "acquired", "habitual" and "infused" are generally used in the ordinary way: the former pair usually, but not always, linked with an ascetical, discursive, and volitional effort; the latter pair tending towards contemplation. In English spirituality, the word "habitual" takes on a special, richer meaning when the characteristic word "homely" is introduced in the fourteenth century.[1]

II. ASCETICAL THEOLOGY

I have said that ascetical theology is *primarily* a practical and synthetic approach to all other branches of theology, and only in a *secondary* sense is it a "subject" within theology. It may be convenient to think of the first as "*ascetical* theology", an approach or process of theological thinking, and the secondary subject as "ascetical-theology": In the first phrase "*ascetical*" is an adjective, the second phrase is a compound noun. The second derives from the first; the *subject* grows out of the *process*. Let us look at each in turn and then see their connection, and its implication to practical guidance.

[1] See Ch. 17, VII, below.

1. *Ascetical* theology makes the bold and exciting assumption that every truth flowing from the Incarnation, from the entrance of God into the human world as man, must have its practical lesson. If theology is incarnational, then it must be pastoral.

It is a common dilemma of theological students, absorbed, or otherwise, in a lecture on Old Testament sources, the synoptic problem, or some intricate piece of Scholastic philosophy, to sit back and ask themselves "if I am training to be a parish priest, what has all this to do with it?" Ascetical theology asks the same question but in a way which excludes the answer "nothing at all". The question becomes honest and exciting instead of frustrating; one of the lesser values of ascetical study is to colour and bring alive some aspects of theology which, to the average student, would otherwise be academic and dull. The process should become clearer as we proceed.

2. Ascetical-theology as by-product of *ascetical* theology deals with the subject matter to be found in a book like *The Elements of the Spiritual Life*: the cardinal and theological virtues, the gifts of the Spirit, sin and its divisions, methods of prayer, the Three Ways, and so on. It is to be noted that, if our definition is acceptable, all this is no medieval invention but is rooted in the faith once delivered to the saints and is all ultimately biblical.

Apart from this subject-matter, ascetical-theology is generally held to have three over-all qualities:

a. It is *elementary*, dealing with the ordinary, "lower", mainly acquired ways of prayer, and with the active virtues of Christian life. As always, we must take care not to make our distinctions too rigid, there is a certain overlapping; just when contemplation, for example, ceases to be acquired and becomes infused will always be an insoluble puzzle. Everything depends upon God, all Christian life begins with grace, all prayer is inspired by the Holy Ghost, but we can learn to respond to, or co-operate with, this divine action upon us. The experience of the Church throughout the ages guides us as to how this response or co-operation can best be achieved. Ascetical-theology is the codification of this experience into methods, techniques, ways and means. In this elementary sense, the term is applicable to all stages of Christian life from Sunday school to the discovery and development of special graces in gifted people.

b. Ascetical-theology is concerned with Christian *progress*, which does not necessarily mean climbing the spiritual hierarchy from "lower" to "higher" forms of prayer, but rather with praying better in whatever way or state we happen to be. It is axiomatic to spiritual theology that progress is tested not by experience or feeling but by moral theology. Whatever our prayer, in whatever elementary stage it remains, we are making progress if we commit fewer sins. The spiritual guide has to try to improve prayer and life as it is, rather than push it up some progressive scheme, while introducing the "higher" forms as and when they are plainly called for.

A good deal of ascetical-theology, therefore, comes down to us in the form of "progressions" and hierarchies: the Three Ways of Purgation, Illumination, and Union are fundamental to Catholic spirituality; St Thomas makes them personal with the classification Beginners, Proficients and Perfect. There is St Benedict's twelve degrees of humility in ch. 7 of the *Regula*, Hugh of St Victor's five-fold ladder, and so on. It is not surprising that so many of the spiritual classics include in their titles words like "scale", "ladder", "ascent", and the "mountain" up which the Christian is to climb. Such schemes are, in the best sense, *theoretical*. That does not mean useless, unpractical, or "academic", but that they must be properly interpreted and used. I will return to this point in the next section. Meanwhile the whole idea of progress suggests two points of general interest.

It is a common complaint that so much pastoral religion is static and conventional: people, parishes, and congregations, are apt to get into a rut. This is a danger inherent in a religion which is so largely institutional and historical. We rightly continue to seek inspiration from the past, from the great historical facts of the faith, we rejoice in the comfort of unchangeable dogma, and we acknowledge the value of ancient liturgy. The danger is plain; it is equally plain that ascetical-theology and ascetical thinking, with this characteristic emphasis on progress, is a safeguard against it.

Ascetical-theology, with its emphasis on techniques and disciplines proper to the earlier stages of Christian life, on active life in the world, is ever in danger of confusing the means with the end. The Christian goal is the Vision of God and nothing less will ever do: however long the journey, however remote the end may seem, our eyes must be constantly fixed upon it. We must take comfort in the fact that so long as we progress, however slowly, all is well, but progress is meaningless without a destination. All our methods, disciplines, Rules, fasts, mortifications, etc. are pointless unless we move towards our final glory in heaven, where, as St Augustine teaches, we shall see God and love God and praise God and rest in God. However obscure and difficult to us, it is here that the mystics can help us towards some understanding of what that means.

c. Ascetical-theology deals with Christian *perfection*, which forms a summary of the two preceding points. It will suffice to note that this is another technical word slightly different in meaning from common use. Christian perfection admits of degrees and types, it is applicable to any Christian in any of the Ways or other classification. One may attain perfection as a mystic or as an ascetic, in the world or in the cloister, married or single, priest or layman. To be perfect, according to St Thomas, means to fulfil the function for which one was created, and the Church embraces a diversity of function. Hence the need for care in the interpretation of hierarchies and progressions, and the need for recognizing the eternal adoration of God in glory as the only purpose for which mankind was made.[1]

3. Ascetical theology in its fullness is a combination of both these aspects: the wider *ascetical* theology (1 above) and its product, ascetical-theology (2 above). An illustration should serve to show how the connection arises.

If a modern student were to read Gregory of Nazianzus' treatise against Apollinarius, he would have no doubt that he was studying "patristics" or "dogmatic theology", and he might be excused, here and there, for wondering what it all had to do with pastoral work in the twentieth century. Being a good student he would conclude his studies in order to say his prayers and he would use a "devotional" book—as a change from "dogmatics"—to help with his meditation. Looking for something as different as possible from Gregory of Nazianzus, he might choose some of the sermons of St Bernard of Clairvaux.

The point, of course, is that these two Fathers are only different in approach: they are both teaching exactly the same thing, they are both using the same piece of Christian doctrine, they are both concerned with the full and perfect human nature in the Person of Christ. To introduce the terms which make the most fundamental of all ascetical classifications, St Gregory of Nazianzus is "speculative", St Bernard is "affective". The first is intellectual and doctrinal; the second is tenderly emotional, loving God with "sensible devotion".

[1] See further my *Pastoral Theology: a Reorientation*, ch. 13.

Ascetical theology is concerned with maintaining a proper balance, ideally a synthesis, of these two attitudes. The affective emotions have an important place in Christian life but they must not be allowed to break loose from doctrine. Doctrine, on the other hand, should have a devotional element; theological study can, and should, be prayerful. All Catholic schools of prayer contain both elements in varying proportions but most of them have sufficient bias to one side or the other to be easily classified: the Cistercians produced great scholars but they are clearly affective, the Dominicans produced devout saints yet their emphasis is plainly speculative. The central characteristic of the English school is that it cannot be classified in this way; with remarkable constancy it maintains an almost perfect synthesis.

This is why ascetical theology, especially within the English school, must oppose and break down the departmental divisions of modern theology. It liberates Gregory of Nazianzus from a prison called "dogmatics" and St Bernard from another prison marked "devotion". It brings them together into a creative union: Gregory's doctrine is enriched by Bernard's devotion, Cistercian affectiveness for the Sacred Humanity is kept healthy by orthodox Christology.

All this is *ascetical* theology in the wide sense. To go a stage further, St Bernard's affective devotion to the humanity of Christ is only made possible by the Christology of former scholars; the intellectual labours which led to the Chalcedonian Definition form the basis of Cistercian prayer. But St Bernard, having taken over this doctrine and interpreted it in his own way, thinks out its meaning for the direction of souls. The result of this reflection is the *De Diligendo Deo* with its four degrees of the love of God. We have reached a *progression*, a plan or system of spirituality, we have arrived at "ascetical-theology" in the secondary sense. All other progressions and schemes, from St Benedict's *Regula* to the elaborate systems of St Ignatius and the Spanish Carmelites, proceed from the same kind of ascetical process; they grow from dogma.

Following William Temple, we can summarize thus: ascetical theology is Christian doctrine interpreted and applied by a teacher of prayer together with the mental and physical disciplines which nurture and support it. The experience of the Church, codified by her saints and doctors, assures us that this total discipline is necessary as means to an end. Fasting, mortification, and so on are needed, but they do not constitute ascetical theology, they are subsidiary parts of it. Or we can say with St John of the Cross that ascetical theology consists in those methods and disciplines which dispose the soul to receive the motions of the Holy Ghost: it is the art of co-operating with grace.[1]

Needless to say, when we speak of teaching *prayer*, we mean that total spirituality which controls the whole of human life, that which includes not only liturgical and formal private prayer but also habitual recollection colouring and inspiring every minute and every action of a lifetime. To the Christian, then, ascetical theology is the key to the art of living as fully, creatively, and indeed joyfully, as mankind is capable.

III. THE USE OF ASCETICAL THEOLOGY

Exactly how is all this to be learned and applied in spiritual guidance? My hypothetical student, having by now returned to Gregory of Nazianzus, has received but a partial and indirect answer to his question, "What has all this to do with my practical work in the parish?" The full answer depends upon whether his Christology is dogmatic or ascetical theology, and in this instance on whether Apollinarianism is a musty old fourth-century heresy or a living issue for modern people. I have no doubt at all that in both cases, the latter answer is the right one. Nine out of ten devout people to-day make an imaginative picture of Jesus Christ in mental prayer, in acts of recollection, and as they adore the Real Presence at the altar: but these images contain little humanity. False devotion continues to shrink from attributing real human qualities to the Son of God, whose presence is degraded to a hazy holy idea. The error gives rise to restrictive tension and ultimately to some form of Manichaeism. The proper spiritual guidance in this case is the application of anti-Apollinarian doctrine, and the more we read Gregory of Nazianzus the more competent we shall be. But we also need the example of St Bernard to shew us how to apply it.

The general teaching derived from this example is that the essential content of ascetical theology, the knowledge needed to be a teacher of prayer, is not so much methods, techniques, and practical hints, but dogmatic theology. The spiritual director's main and constant source of study is not Ignatian categories but the Creeds and the Bible. It is useless to begin a meditation with "composition of place" until we realize the significance of places according to the

[1] See K. E. Kirk, *Some Principles of Moral Theology* (1920), pp. 18–19.

doctrine of creation; the presence of Jesus is meaningless without Christology; and without the doctrines derived from the resurrection and ascension, even the "resolution" will probably be false without moral theology. And here is an example of how spiritual direction overflows into the whole of pastoral work: sermons, classes, discussion groups and everything connected with teaching the faith are concerned with prayer which overflows into life.

The basis of spiritual guidance is this *ascetical* theology, but it still issues in ascetical-theology: in the methods and techniques, the progressions, patterns and plans. What is all this for and how is it to be used? Coupled with dogmatic theology, methods of prayer and techniques relating to recollection and meditation can be useful if carefully applied to the needs and capacities of individual people. "Intellectual meditation" may teach and clarify doctrine itself.

The bulk of ascetical-theology is always to be seen in the light of two inviolable facts: the first is that it is *theoretical*, the second is that we cannot do without such theory. Let us reject once and for all the nonsense about "practical" clergy who have "no use for theory"; it is as sensible to speak of practical accountants who have no use for mathematics. But it is necessary to insist that one does not literally work through the four degrees of the love of God or climb the twelve steps of humility one by one. The key to the matter is to see any particular progression or scheme as a map rather than a programme; as a kind of backcloth against which the position, needs, and capacity of a particular spiritual life can be calculated. Half an hour's conversation about spiritual things produces a jumble of facts, difficulties, ideas and feelings, which, in themselves, mean little. Once these are looked at in the light of the relationship between the theological and cardinal virtues and the gifts of the Spirit, the jumble becomes a pattern. If it does not, then we must try another map or backcloth. Later we will discover a good deal of criticism against the distinction between "mortal" and "venial" sin. Moral theologians are not wholly satisfied with the list of seven capital sins, but without some such plan and distinction it is almost impossible to distinguish one confession from another. We must not try to guide people "by the book" but we certainly cannot do without the book, and it is only from ascetical theory that guidance can become clear and simple.

IV. THE READING AND WRITING
OF ASCETICAL THEOLOGY

Ascetical theology usually comes to us in one of three forms. They
are:

1. As definition and exposition of its fundamental terms; the
method employed by F. P. Harton and nearly all the Anglican
writers of the 1930 era. These books give essential information, for a
certain amount of spadework is required by any subject. We must
know the terms and categories, although I am doubtful if "learning"
them, like Latin declensions, is the only way or even the best way.
The objection to this method is that it is so dull, and in ascetical
theology, purporting to deal with living religion, that is a serious
fault. Apart from the boredom of students, such a presentation seems
remote from experience: to be theoretical is not the same as to be
academic.

2. There is moral and ascetical casuistry, or the "case" method,
consisting in a series of practical examples, of which great use is
made by Scaramelli and by Jeremy Taylor in the *Ductor Dubitantium*.
Hypothetical people are described in various states and conditions,
which are analysed, commented upon, and counsel suggested. This
has the advantage of bringing the subject to life and of being very
practical, but two objections can be brought against it. First, it is a
little *too* practical, and is liable to degenerate into formal rule of
thumb. It is the system of the medieval *Penitential*, wherein comparatively unlearned priests were simply to look up the appropriate
example and prescribe the given penance. It is also the criticism
brought against the minute classifications of some modern Roman
moral theology. It is direction "by the book" rather than applied
from the book.

The second objection is that the human soul, and each human
situation, is unique, and no amount of "cases" can cover every
problem. In the *Directorium Asceticum*, Scaramelli devotes 300
pages—a quarter of the work—to "practical suggestions"; Taylor's
proportion is larger; yet it is not always easy to find an example
which *exactly* fits the "cases" with which one has to deal. The
human leg may be broken in an infinity of ways and places, no two
fractures are exactly alike. The study of "cases" both in theory and
practice, helps a surgeon to gain competence in setting broken legs,
but no amount of such experience is sufficient in itself. The first

need is for a "theoretical" knowledge of anatomy which can be applied to all fractures as they come along.

3. The third method is that used by Père Pourrat in his forty-years-old but still indispensable *Christian Spirituality*. This is something of a composite method: it contains some reference to terms and fundamental categories, and there is an occasional illustration or "case", but the main emphasis is upon the living experience of the Church as taught by saints and doctors and interpreted by various schools. This is the method I have tried to follow in the present book, and it is in the spirit of Pourrat that I should prefer it to be read. This approach, presupposes four things:

a. That the reader either knows the fundamental terms and categories—which Anglicans can get from Harton—or that he will take care to discover their meaning as he goes along.

b. That we are dealing with the *real* experience of the living Church, not with imaginary "cases" but with saints and doctors who are our contemporaries in the threefold Church, and with whom we are in communion through prayer: the doctrine of the communion of saints is ascetical not academic!

c. Books of this type can never be more than introductory; they presuppose continuous, unhurried, lifelong reference to the works of the saints themselves in both study and prayer.

d. Practical students of spirituality, particularly Anglicans, must not expect the glib answers of the "case" method. The aim is rather to gain a background knowledge by means of which one can look at human beings in theological terms (*ascetical* theology) and see their needs in the light of the Church's total experience (ascetical-theology). To use Fr Patrick Thompson's terms, spiritual guidance is both art and science: science, theory, theology, is the first need, but personal guidance always demands personal skill, interpretation, or art.[1]

Let us illustrate the whole position with a simple example: suppose someone claims an unusual spiritual experience, say a corporeal vision of the Holy Family. What does it mean? What should be done? Without ascetical theology at all, the consultant would assume either that he was dealing with a saint of unparalleled holiness or with a lunatic suffering from hallucination. Both would almost certainly be wrong and quite certainly useless.

[1] H. S. Box (ed.), *Priesthood* (1937), pp. 267ff

Or the question could be approached by taking down Scaramelli or Poulain and looking up "Holy Family, vision of". This information could be useful, there might be a "case" bearing some resemblance to the one in hand; or there might not. It is all a little uncertain.

Another method, not unknown to English clergy, is to pop the person on the first train to Nashdom or Mirfield to consult a specialist.

The fourth, and I think proper, approach is this: there could be some preliminary conversation about the theology implied by the Holy Family—the Incarnation; the relation between Christ, his Mother, St Joseph, and the Church; the relation between community and individual. That would give a reasonable foundation to the subject of spiritual experience as such, and would lead an obviously affective soul towards the speculative side. It would clear the air and could not possibly be wrong.

This person could then be placed on the "map", or against a backcloth. Let us try the Three Ways as expounded by our own Walter Hilton. Here we learn that this sort of experience more often occurs at one of two stages in the spiritual pilgrimage, or, to use Hilton's title, at two points in *The Scale of Perfection*: either early in the Purgative Way (in Hilton, "reformation in faith") or towards the end of the Illuminative Way ("reformation in feeling"). If this man is but recently absolved, confirmed, and communicated, perhaps after sudden conversion, if he is struggling against habitual sin and is a little erratic in ordinary discipline, then he most likely comes into the first group. Counsel is straightforward: he should be encouraged in the basic duties of loyal Churchmanship, guided in private devotion, warned about doubts and aridities to come, and persuaded to think about doctrine. The ascetical keys to this situation which come to my mind are the cardinal virtues of Prudence and Fortitude.

In this case the "vision" need not be dismissed as false or unimportant, but it is irrelevant. If it is "genuine" it is probably the encouragement of God to a beginner, if a diabolical hallucination then we are beating the devil at his own game: for in either case, Prudence, Fortitude, loyalty, discipline, and such counsel proper to a beginner, cannot be wrong.

Suppose, on the other hand, that the man has been devoutly loyal to Christian demands for thirty years, that he has conquered gross sin, and that the Gifts of the Spirit are plainly manifested in his life. This looks like Hilton's second, very different, position. Here "discernment of spirits" applied to the vision is of the first importance. The experience could portend the approach of a new contemplative state; if in any way "false" we are faced with an extremely serious thing: in this instance the train to Nashdom might not be a bad idea. The pastoral need is to be able to make the distinction. It would be intolerable if a spiritual guide did *not* feel inadequate, but we must not confuse humility with incompetence.

This simple example is, of course, *too* simple: that is always the trouble with "cases". There will be many subsidiary factors to be examined by other maps and plans, counsel will seldom be quite so cut and dried, a few weeks of devout experiment might precede definite conclusions: the Holy Ghost will not be hurried. All the example is meant to illustrate is the basic purpose of ascetical-theology, how it should be used and how it can be misused: here our hypothetical guide has, I think, been of some use. He has relied on the experience of the Church, on orthodoxy, but he has not reduced a human soul to a mathematical equation; he has been responsible enough as an ordinary practitioner yet competent enough to know his limitations; and he has neither misused ascetical theology nor usurped God's prerogative by trying to push a Christian up a ladder or scale or Way.

3

SPIRITUALITY
AND THE NEW TESTAMENT

I. THE OPEN BIBLE

A comprehensive study of the ascetical theology of the New
Testament is urgently needed, and present trends in biblical
scholarship raise some hope that this need may soon be met. The
more recent work of Professor Alan Richardson and Dr J. A. T.
Robinson marks a drawing away from the "academic" approach
towards something more synthetic and pastoral. G. B. Verity's *Life
in Christ* carries the process several stages further, while E. J.
Tinsley's *The Imitation of God in Christ*, aptly sub-titled *An Essay
on the Biblical basis of Christian Spirituality*, points to an altogether
new stage the significance of which it is difficult to exaggerate. It is
to be hoped that these scholars, and others, will work towards a
further narrowing of the gap.

That the gap exists is obvious, but not, I think, obvious enough.
The critical upheaval of the last century has convinced the layman
that the Bible is a subtle and difficult book, put together piecemeal,
out of all chronological order, repetitive, contradictory, and translated through two or three languages at least. Yet he is still glibly
exhorted "to read it", just like that. He is still offered the delusion
that there is a kind of devotional magic about "Bible reading" and
that to read it through from Genesis to Revelation "once in the
year" is a sure passport to heaven. When the "Word of God" was
unfamiliar to the English laity, when vernacular Scriptures were
new, and when they were supposed to consist of simple propositional truths about daily conduct, then "reading the Bible" was the
logical thing to do. But if the Bible is an immensely complex record
of God's revelation of himself to mankind, then just "reading" is
surely inadequate. *How* is it to be read, studied, approached, or
used, for lay devotion?

Under the inspiration of William Temple's *Readings in St John's*

Gospel,[1] I have expressed the view that imaginative meditation, controlled by doctrine, is the more constructive approach for ordinary people than "Bible Study".[2] That is the method sublimely employed by Julian of Norwich and Margery Kempe: our scholars live very much in the twentieth century while pastoral practice remains embedded in the seventeenth century, having failed to catch up with the fourteenth.

I have suggested that if "Bible reading" is insufficient to-day, "Bible study" is no more than a watered down version of biblical scholarship, which, without long training in the disciplines of the craft, is not going to get the laity very far. Imaginative meditation, discarding the search for propositional truths—what does the Bible "mean"?—seeks a deeper knowledge of God as revealed in the life and Person of Jesus Christ. It is a simple entering into the mind of our Lord, a loving approach to himself.

In general, I adhere to that viewpoint, but I can now see a serious objection. Our faithful laity, sound and mature as they are, are unlikely to reach the sublime synthesis of devotion and doctrine achieved by Julian of Norwich. Their meditations will be almost entirely affective. There is nothing intrinsically wrong with that except that, if we are true to English spirituality, this speculative-affective synthesis must never consciously be rejected. The intellect has its place even in affective prayer; if we have relegated "What does the Bible mean?" to second or third place, it is still an important question.

The modern Christian is no fool. He knows that the Bible is a subtle volume which demands a modicum of care if it is to be used constructively, but he has a reasonable case when he accuses the scholar of turning it into an insoluble puzzle. If the English Bible is to remain "open", the layman must be able to retain a certain confidence in it. If the exact words of Jesus were imperfectly recorded, if they lost something in translation from Aramaic to Greek, and a little more as they were put into English, we must not assume that when Jesus said "white" the Authorized Version says "black". Were that the case, the open Bible must be shut.

Our pastoral need is for some simple key, some clear approach, which ordinary Christians can use with confidence. Can ascetical theology supply it? It can at least make two suggestions.

---

[1] See especially *Introduction* (1939) p. ix.
[2] *Essays in Pastoral Reconstruction*, ch. 11.

1. In affective meditation, which includes consideration of our Lord's sayings; these can always safely be regarded as "irony". They must mean far more than is immediately apparent, not because scholars have played games with the text but because they are spoken by the Son of God. In other words we reject the search for direct tenets in favour of an empathetic union with Christ himself. "Whosoever will lose his life for my sake shall find it" is either an exhortation to suicide or it is "irony". This approach, within meditation, encourages rather than detracts from intellectual endeavour: it brings in the speculative side.

2. More generally, we can look at the Bible *ascetically*: confronted with a saying or passage, we can ask the ascetical rather than the propositional or moral question. Not "What does this mean?", or "How does it teach me to behave?", but "How does it impinge on my total Christian life which is grounded on my prayer?". As a divine proposition, "take no thought for the morrow" suggests a reasonable possibility that this world is not going to last much longer. As a moral exhortation, we must be obliged to burn all our insurance policies. As ascetic, it leads to common-sense teaching on "surrender", "abandonment to divine Providence", habitual recollection, the sinfulness of anxiety, temporal–eternal relations in the sacraments of the threefold Church, and so on. This chapter forms a preliminary skirmish in this approach.

II. THE BIBLICAL BASIS OF
THE ASCETICAL CATEGORIES

Anglicanism is rooted in the Bible, and any attempt to recreate an English spirituality must take the 6th Article seriously: it should not insist on "whatsoever is not read therein, nor may be proved thereby". The Article presents its problems, especially when we are dealing with creative progress rather than bare "necessities to salvation"; nevertheless it is important to refute the common idea that medieval and modern ascetical doctrine, with its methods, progressions, and categories, is artificial and unbiblical. Living religion, expressed in prayer and pastoral practice, must rightly develop with the experience of the Church: as a development from the Last Supper, High Mass is not unbiblical; the Mothers' Union is not condemnable because its New Testament authority is a little obscure. But, especially to Anglicans, the *roots* must be there, and it is for these that we must look.

1. *The Three Ways* are fundamental to all Catholic ascetic. They bear a clear relation to the three qualities of ascetical-theology with which we began: it is *elementary*—the *purgative* way, it is concerned with *progress—illumination* by the Holy Spirit, and *perfection*—the *unitive* way. Although fundamental, the saints vary this terminology a good deal, but at present it is necessary to remember only St Thomas's rendering of it into personal terms: Beginners, Proficients, Perfect.

It may be remarked at the outset that the Bible itself is the record of God's *progressive* revelation to the world, and that the progression follows the pattern. At least up to the Exile, Israel is shown in the purgative state, during which sin–repentance–struggle–sin is the typical pattern. The Prophets, by definition, are illumined, and the Incarnation consummates the union between God and man.

In personal terms, this biblical progression is often recapitulated in the growth of any religious life. The first stirrings of a supernatural awareness in children, whether expressed in gods, ghosts, or fairies, is not so different from the religion of Mosaic times. Every parish priest knows that the idea of a God who wins battles and sends rewards to the righteous and directly punishes disobedience is not confined to Kings and Chronicles. The cult of ancestors is all too apparent to anyone who walks through an English churchyard on Saturday afternoon. Then, in most Christian lives, comes both a Sadducaic enthusiasm for ceremonial and an absorption in social and moral questions reminiscent of Hosea and Amos. The transcendent God of Deutero-Isaiah, often seen in intellectual terms, paved the way for the fullness of incarnational religion. Dr Vidler has shown an all-important ascetical progression in the world-affirmation of David—the right use of creatures or the ascetic of creation; the renunciation of St John Baptist—mortification; and the perfect sacramental synthesis in the life of Christ.[1]

New Testament religion starts with the most elementary of spiritual needs: the Baptist's rallying cry, "repent", an invitation to embrace the purgative way. St Paul goes on to the next stage in progression; from "carnal" to "spiritual", from "babes in Christ" to "strong men", each requiring the appropriate food:[2] here is the source of St Thomas' Beginners and Proficients. In Hebrews, especially, progress towards perfection is the constant theme. Our Lord constantly preaches progress against the idea of salvation as a

[1] *Essays in Liberality* (1957), V.   [2] 1 Cor. 3.1,2.

static fact: "no man, having put his hand to the plough, and looking back, is fit for the kingdom of God."[1] "And because iniquity shall abound, the love of many shall wax cold. But he that shall endure unto the end, the same shall be saved."[2] Circumstances and sin shall create aridity, lukewarmness which calls for endurance, fortitude, spiritual stamina, the daily plod of obedience. He is the way (along which one moves), the truth (in which one lives), and the life (the character of which is movement).[3]

In a letter to Timothy (2.4,7) St Paul joyfully proclaims that he has "finished his course", and from 1 Cor. 9.24–6 comes the original *askesis* analogy; the spiritual athlete in training for the race, the boxer acquiring his technique.

Finally there is the frighteningly blunt command: "be ye therefore perfect".[4] "If thou wilt be perfect, go . . .".[5] St Paul introduces the technical or "Thomist" sense in pastoral context: "we speak wisdom among them that are perfect".[6] The same sense is in James: "the same is a perfect man".[7] And Hebrews: "make you perfect in every good work to do his will".[8] Many more texts could be quoted, some obvious, others less so, but all dealing with the Christian life as one of progress from an elementary beginning to a perfect end. The one point I wish to make here is that if "not to long for progress is to fail in prayer" is a "Cistercian" motto, it was not an original invention of St Bernard, nor were the Three Ways invented by St Bonaventure. I submit the hypothesis that most of the "medieval" ascetical and spiritual theology was a natural development from the teaching of Jesus Christ.

2. The Catholic *Threefold Rule* follows the same pattern: it was not invented by St Benedict. Fundamental to the Biblical doctrine of man is the principle of total integration. Human beings cannot be split up into parts and "faculties"; body and spirit form an indissoluble unity. Nor can Christian life be split into departments, sacred and secular, religious and social; the Bible will have nothing to do with religiosity, "spirituality" in its modern degraded sense. Christian prayer, therefore, is one integrated thing, a total life.

It is unnecessary to quote texts in support of our Lord's institution of the Holy Eucharist, or in support of his exhortation to personal

[1] Luke 9.62. [2] Matt. 24.12,13. [3] John 14.6.
[4] Matt. 5.48. [5] Matt. 19.21. [6] 1 Cor. 2.6.
[7] Jas. 3.2. [8] Heb. 13.21.

devotion given to people as different as Martha from Mary, Paul
from James, and Peter from John. Yet to the direct question, "teach
us to pray", Christ's answer was to compose an Office, the "set
prayer" so much despised by English Puritans. Is there any significance in the Lucan version (11.1) where the disciples refer to the
Baptist? May we guess that the spiritual teaching of this inspired
solitary, this "professional" ascetic, would be very personal and
interior? If so it is still more significant that Jesus should come back
with a simple, objective, "set form" of corporate emphasis. Nevertheless, Matt. 6.9–13 is completed, not contradicted by, Matt. 6.6.

   The Lord's Prayer, of course, is the pattern prayer containing in
embryo the whole of Catholic ascetical doctrine; an inexhaustible
mine of spirituality. All we are concerned with here is that the New
Testament gives the threefold pattern which is at the heart of all
Catholic practice: Eucharist–Office–personal devotion. And that the
Church never doubted its importance: "And they continued stead-
fastly in the apostles' doctrine and fellowship, and in breaking of
bread, and in the prayers."[1] The *Opus Dei* was Christian long before
it was Benedictine.

3. *Ascetical syntheses.* It is commonly taught that our Lord's
teaching is divisible into dogmatic and practical ("ascetical")
doctrine; that he proclaims facts about God, his kingdom, his
Fatherhood, about sin and redemption, and follows this doctrine
with its practical and moral implications for human life. He emphasizes the transcendent majesty of God as well as his comforting
presence, the other-worldliness of his kingdom is coupled with the
symbolism of creation as manifestation of the Creator's love. His
practical example follows the same pattern; he gently leads
the disciples to the facts about himself, proclaimed by St Peter at
Caesarea Philippi, before introducing the more affective note of
loving discipleship: love depends on knowledge. St Paul follows his
Master's message in most of the Epistles: the proclamation of facts
followed by their pastoral application.

   Pervading the New Testament, therefore, are these doctrinal–
practical, knowledge–love combinations all leading to what we now
call the speculative–affective synthesis at the heart of Christian
spirituality: "I will pray with the spirit, and I will pray with the
understanding also".[2]

---

[1] Acts 2.42.   [2] 1 Cor. 14.15.

There follows a secondary series of syntheses. By both teaching and example, our Lord perfectly combines what theology now calls rigorism and humanism (cf. Matt. 10.37-40 with 11.28-30). He never makes the recurrent error of dividing ethic from ascetic, of splitting behaviour from prayer. Discipline and mortification are ever subservient to prayer; circumstances and needs dictate practice. He who refused to turn stones into bread when he was fasting for a purpose, happily turned water into wine—120 gallons of it—when everyone had had enough already, and even then the true Bridegroom of Israel was not recognized!—the bridegroom of the Cana wedding was not the *real* bridegroom at all: "irony" at its most sublime. And we have mentioned how our Lord is neither worldly nor other-worldly, but sacramental, using creatures for spiritual purposes, neither despising nor abusing them. Here he is Victorine, there he is Franciscan, sometimes he is Benedictine and sometimes Cistercian, and sometimes, as in the speculative-affective synthesis, he is very English. To be rid of these anachronisms and return to the single point: all these modern and medieval schools are developments from the Gospel.

III. MINOR ASCETICAL CLASSIFICATIONS

We must not lose sight of the prior fact that Anglican doctrine is grounded on the Scriptures and that the first need in spiritual guidance is the application of this dogma: the primary ascetical doctrines are the Trinity, the Incarnation, and the Atonement. We can, however, go a good deal further in seeking a biblical basis for orthodox spirituality.

F. P. Harton makes the impressive claim that not only a general doctrine of grace but the later practical distinctions—habitual, actual, sanctifying, sacramental, prevenient, concomitant, sufficient, efficacious—are all traceable to a biblical source. With grace as the first Christian need, the thirteen texts [1] given by Harton in support of his theory would make a good start to any study of biblical ascetic.

The theological virtues are plainly set out in 1 Corinthians 13. The cardinal virtues are the "natural" virtues put into Christian form in various places in the Gospel. [2] The accepted *locus classicus* for the Gifts of the Spirit is Isaiah 11. 2-3, again carried over into Catholic ascetic *via* Galatians 5. 22-3, 2 Timothy 1. 7, and

[1] *The Elements of the Spiritual Life* (1932), pp. 13-21.   [2] See K. E. Kirk, *Some Principles of Mora Theology* (1920), pp. 33ff; cf. Harton op. cit., pp. 62-70.

1 Cor. 12. 4–11.[1] The capital sins arise out of our Lord's own exposition of the Mosaic decalogue in Exodus 20, while their three-fold grouping, so beloved of the compilers of self-examination manuals, is set out in 1 John 2. 16. As with the later distinctions qualifying grace, so all the modern ascetical and pastoral distinctions of sin are traceable to biblical bases.[2] That there is biblical teaching on fasting and mortification (Matt. 9.14–21; 12. 1–11; etc.), on formalism and legalism, temptation and repentance, in fact on all the common chapter headings in ascetical text-books, is obvious enough.

A good deal of New Testament ascetical teaching, however, is less obvious. We are forced to conclude—often rather half-heartedly—that the story of Martha and Mary must mean that contemplation is superior to active works of charity; we do not usually look at it as both a progression and a relation between "mixed" and contemplative life within the one Church. We read the meaning of the Transfiguration as doctrine, as the manifestation of Christ's divinity, of the fulfilment of his Messianic claim, thence in terms of Christology; but we invariably miss its incalculable importance to recollection and mental prayer.[3] Jesus exhorts: "watch! for ye know not the hour . . .",[4] and everyone studies eschatology. No one bothers with the practical business of actual and habitual recollection. "The Jews require a sign, and the Greeks seek after wisdom . . ."[5] certainly teaches about faith and fortitude, but what about the "discernment of spirits"? (Compare 1 John 4.1–3.) Compare further the doubts of St Thomas: "because thou hast seen me, thou hast believed: blessed are they that have not seen, and yet have believed".[6] Again faith, of course, but what of the importance of sensible devotion, consolations, aridity? Or are these the inventions of seventeenth-century asceticists and spiritual directors? My guess —I call it no more—is that all the "modern and artificial" spiritual categories of writers like Scaramelli, de Guibert, or Poulain are to be found somewhere in the Bible, and in using orthodox ascetical doctrine, Anglicans need have no fear of departing from their sane biblical tradition. But I shall strongly advise them to stick to the particular interpretation of the English school.

---

[1] J. de Guibert, *The Theology of the Spiritual Life* (1954), pp. 121ff.

[2] Kirk, op. cit., pp. 229–32.

[3] See R. E. Cant, *Christian Prayer* (1961), pp. 42–8; cf. *Christian Proficiency*, pp. 78–80.

[4] Matt. 24.42.   [5] 1 Cor. 1.22.   [6] John 20.29.

IV. THE SERMON ON THE MOUNT:
AN EXPERIMENT IN "ASCETICAL THINKING"

I have suggested that the faithful Christian, reading his Bible, should ask: "What does this tell me about my prayer, which is the basis of my life?" What happens if we approach the Matthean account of the Sermon on the Mount in this way?

Two preliminary points stand out immediately. First, that these chapters form a curiously disjointed sort of sermon; guided here by the experts we see that it is really a collection of instructions given at various times to the disciples in private. It is, in fact, what we assume it to be; not a sermon but spiritual direction. Secondly, as is to be expected, it contains a good deal of quite blunt teaching about prayer, as well as more subtle instruction we hope to discover.

Let us then attempt a kind of cursory ascetical-commentary, seeking a little help from the scholars here and there, but retaining some confidence in the English texts as they stand.

St Matt. 5.1–20: Blessedness belongs to people who are: (*a*) poor in spirit, (*b*) that mourn, (*c*) are meek, (*d*) who hunger and thirst after righteousness, (*e*) are merciful, (*f*) are pure in heart, (*g*) are peacemakers, (*h*) are persecuted for righteousness' sake.

Now we are told that the teaching of Jesus was revolutionary, and that the conservative Pharisee could hardly be blamed for being a little shocked by it. Yet our familiarity with the Beatitudes still prevents us from seeing what an extraordinary list it is. From the point of view of ordinary human experience it makes very little sense. If we ask help, or play a very elementary game with an armful of text-books, we find that the Greek reads something like this: "how blessed are those who: (*a*) are humble, detached, and sensitive to spiritual things, (*b*) are sympathetic and penitent, the deep-feeling intercessors, (*c*) understand the joy of humility, (*d*) crave to progress towards union with God, (*e*) are compassionate, (*f*) are constant in religion, (*g*) are prudent in search for harmony with men, (*h*) have fortitude under creative suffering. The list now emerges with something of a familiar ring: detachment, penitence, inter-cession, humility, progress, union, mercy, fortitude, simplicity, harmony, cross-bearing. These still make something of a jumble as an ethical system, but they are precisely the headings we would expect to find in books on prayer. This is the way to the Vision of

God, to Christian Perfection, and it cannot be made to lead anywhere else.

But if it is not ethics, neither is it pietism; there is an underlying
worldly strain: verses 13–16 offer a paradox. Are we to pervade the
world with subtle spiritual power, the salt in the stew? *or* are we to
defy the world more courageously, the light stuck arrogantly on its
candlestick? The faithful Remnant or mass evangelism? The
paradox seems to need ascetical theology for its resolution: both
ways are right according to circumstances and spirituality. The first
is Benedictine, the second Franciscan; we are concerned with schools
of spirituality.

Matt. 5.21–48: Read simply, in terms of proposition or ethics, this
passage starts with moral sense, becomes a little difficult and ends
with nonsense. The passage is frequently called the "revision of the
old law", the difficult and nonsensical parts are interpreted as
eschatology, *interimsethik*, and in other ways. Sometimes it is seen as
a call to Christian heroism. I have no qualification to expound these
theories: the pastoral point remains that to the layman they seem
mere evasions or his Bible has become an enigma. He had better
stick to affective meditation or the open Bible should be shut. Or
could it be ascetical teaching?

Verses 21–6 offer reasonable moral guidance: anger is sinful as
well as murder. It is also ascetical: anger is a distraction, you are not
going to communicate very worthily if you are in a seething rage;
recollection insists that you make up the quarrel first; it is so practical.
Verses 27–48 do not make moral sense: impurity of thought is sinful
and so is adultery, but they are just not the same thing. Are we
really to reward theft by giving presents to the thief? Is self-
mutilation virtuous? What does it all mean? First, of course,
"irony"; secondly ascetical doctrine. In terms of progress towards
perfection, a habitual state of imaginative lust may well be more
serious than an isolated act of passion, so "custody of the eyes",
pluck it out—irony—take it away, look somewhere else. The danger
of possessions is covetousness. Distraction arises through too much
worry over the safety of one's goods, but that hinders habitual
recollection; do not worry, let the thief have your cloak, get things
in perspective. Do not quarrel, do not have enemies, it hinders
spiritual progress, so turn enmity into intercession. An impossible
ethic has turned into orthodox ascetic: custody of the senses,

mortification, renunciation of all that impedes spiritual progress, habitual recollection, intercession, bearing one's cross, keeping the true end in sight, interior disposition and outward act, perfection.

Matt. 6.1–18. Verses 1–4 teach that almsgiving is not philanthropy to men so much as devotion to God: a point that a purely moral interpretation would miss. Verses 16–18 teach that fasting is creative and joyful: how Franciscan! Again, fasting as mere moral duty, divorced from ascetical theology, misses the point.

Verses 5–13 are either a blatant contradiction or they teach a necessary relation between private devotion "in secret" and the formal Office, our Lord's "set form". The Lord's Prayer itself, we have seen, contains an inexhaustible mine of spiritual teaching. The corporate–individual relation, objective and subjective elements, the Eucharist–Office–devotion–recollection pattern, adoration–confession–thanksgiving–supplication as a linked progression: all that is deducible from it.[1]

Matt. 6.19–34. These verses continue personal ascetical instruction: think in terms of spiritual values (19–23), but there is a proper use for creation (28–32), no doubt the source of a good deal of the teaching of both St Francis and the school of St Victor. "Abandonment to the Divine Providence" was not a brand-new technique invented by Caussade!

Matt. 7. This chapter underlines and elaborates a good deal of what has gone before. Verses 7–12 speak plainly of petition and expand the teaching of the Lord's Prayer. The new point, so much needed to-day, is that petition should be *honest* and faithful, not merely "devout".[2] Verses 13–14 have very clear ascetical implications: a vague conglomeration of devotions will not do; there must be a *system*. Verses 15–20 deal with the discernment of spirits, and give the very important axiom that only moral theology provides a certain test for spiritual progress. And is it straining the text too far to see orthodox ascetical discipline, the basic Christian system of prayer, developing out of the Bible and the Creeds, as the rock upon which life is to be built?

That, I think, is the sort of interpretation a non-technical but faithful layman would arrive at if he approached his Bible in this way. How far is he wrong? I would answer that he is certainly less

[1] See *Christian Proficiency*, pp. 22ff.   [2] Cf. Matt. 6.4,6,18.

wrong than he would be if he used either the propositional or moral approach. Would it not be worthwhile for serious scholarship to take up the approach in searching for an authoritative New Testament ascetical theology?

V. THE FOURTH GOSPEL:
AN EXPERIMENT IN ASCETICAL-THEOLOGY

Let us search for practical teaching on prayer in three passages: John 11.33–42, the raising of Lazarus; 12.27, the summary of the agony in Gethsemane; and 13.21–30, the expulsion of Judas Iscariot from the Upper Room. All these stories show our Lord in prayer; they have obvious similarities and subtle differences. They all begin by Jesus being "troubled in spirit", but for three different reasons. First out of human compassion for the sisters at Bethany, possibly for their doubts and perhaps for the silly hypocrisy of the wailing Jews. In Gethsemane it is because of his own natural reaction to the approaching Passion. In the Upper Room it is sorrow caused by the betrayal of a disciple. Then comes colloquy with the Father; long, honest, painful and patient. Then comes the "answer" to his petition: in the first case it is "yes", Lazarus will be raised from the dead. In the second it is "no", the cup cannot be taken from him, for this cause came he to this hour. In the third case, the answer is the pronouncement of a fact, the treachery of Judas, followed by action, his expulsion.

Then comes "surrender" to the divine will, the bringing of his own will into conformity with that of his Father. Finally, in all three cases, comes adoration: "Father, glorify thy name".

The three prayers follow a pattern, they form a single method, progression, or technique: they make ascetical theology. Each prayer develops through four stages: being "troubled in spirit–petition and colloquy–surrender–adoration. From this at least six points of practical value emerge:

1. "Spirituality" is not departmental religiousness; prayer begins in the world and grows out of human situations. The Tractarians said the proper preparation for prayer is a holy life; St Ignatius Loyola called it remote and immediate preparation; St François de Sales and Brother Lawrence spoke of the practice of the presence of God, and general orthodoxy calls it habitual recollection. But it all comes to much the same thing, and it is all "in the Bible"!

2. Petition and colloquy must be honest and hard; even the Son of God found prayer difficult.

3. Whatever the "answer"—which may well be "no"—the proper end of colloquy is surrender: the abandonment of the will to God. But this is shown to be very different from stoicism or fatalism; it is not passive yielding but something actively acquired. The seventeenth-century Quietist controversy—Bossuet, de Caussade, Mme Guyon, Fénelon, Molinos—is "in the Bible" too.

4. Our Lord knew consolation in the first story and desolation in the second; neither was very important to the prayer. The selfish quest for feeling has no part in Christian ascetical theory.

5. Anxiety is sinful. To the Christian, sensitivity and compassion find their natural outlet in intercession, and daily life provides its raw material.

6. The proper conclusion of all prayer, and all life, is the adoration of God: "Father, glorify thy name".

So far as this book is concerned, that is as far as I can go, and this chapter remains the most tentative start, the lightest scratch on the surface of the subject. A comprehensive biblical ascetic would have to move on to the New Testament doctrine of redemption through the Person of Christ; to the doctrine of the Holy Spirit, the Church, and the sacraments. It must be hoped that biblical scholarship will continue to interest itself in this pastoral need.

4

THE ENGLISH SCHOOL:
ITS DEVELOPMENT AND CHARACTER

There is much to be said for the detective story in which the solution is carefully obscured until the last page; the greater the jumble of possibilities in the middle, the more exciting it is. But I doubt if that is the easiest way to arrange a book on ascetical theology. It will be found more convenient to start with a brief synopsis of the studies we are to pursue, and plainly to state the main conclusions at which we shall arrive.

I. THE CATHOLIC SCHOOLS OF SPIRITUALITY

Christian life combines corporateness with individuality. The Church demands a common discipline, and a large part of Christian spirituality consists in common worship. Yet Christianity insists equally strongly on the uniqueness of every individual. But this does not make practical sense unless we introduce a middle or social term. The doctrine can only be expressed when we consider our membership not only of the "Church" or of "humanity", but of a group, parish, or race. It is this local or social manifestation of the Faith that gives rise to the various schools of spirituality within it.

"Because Christianity is universal, it is in every country, but because it is sacramental it is intensely local, found in each country in a special and unique fashion, not a spirit only but a spirit clothed in material form."[1]

As I wrote in my little study of Margery Kempe: "A school of spirituality is the local and corporate expression of the great Pauline doctrine of diverse gifts within the unity of the Mystical Body; and it is the logical consequence of the Incarnation itself. In one sense, Jesus Christ, the second Adam, recapitulates the whole of humanity within himself, and the doctrine issuing from this fact is dogmatic, changeless and Catholic. On the other hand, Jesus is a

[1] Maisie Ward (ed.), *The English Way* (1934), p. 7.

man, with a particular personality and temperament, and of a particular race. His own spiritual life, and his death, redeemed the whole world, yet he lived within the pattern of a particular strain of first-century Judaism. The prayer of Christ is the prayer of humanity, because all true prayer is the prayer of Christ. But Christ's prayer was also specialized; it was a synthesis of the priestly and prophetic strands of the Jewish tradition: Christ belonged to a "school".[1]

"From this balance between the total Body and the unique characteristics of every human soul, there arise the great Catholic Schools of Spirituality, all differing according to temperamental and racial traits yet all in harmony with the dogmatic facts of the one Faith. As twelve musical notes are arranged and woven into an infinity of harmonies, so the clauses of the Creeds, by emphasis and arrangement but without omission, are woven into the rich diversity of Catholic Spirituality."[2]

To carry the analogy a stage further, it needs little musical knowledge to see a stream of development from Mozart to Beethoven to Brahms; later works of Mozart resemble early Beethoven, and Brahms's first symphony has been called the "Beethoven tenth". These composers form a continuous German tradition yet each has a markedly individual style. So with spirituality. A significant aspect of ascetical theology is that it takes account of temperament, racial characteristics, historical situations, environment, and even climate. But a school of spirituality, particularly the English school, means neither uniformity nor insularity. A school is not a sect but a living tradition which develops as it borrows and adapts from other traditions. In spiritual guidance, we must avoid the extremes of narrowness and eclecticism; borrowing from foreign traditions what may usefully be absorbed into our own, yet not swamping it with a jumble of forms and methods from here, there, and everywhere.

II. THE DEVELOPMENT OF THE ENGLISH SCHOOL

I have done my best to show that Christian spirituality is rooted in the New Testament. Then follow the experiments, often wildly empirical, of the Desert Fathers, coupled with an equally erratic attempt at an intellectual basis for spirituality by the school of Alexandria. From this period many names are put forward as the

[1] See J. W. Bowman, *The Intention of Jesus* (1945), ch. 2.
[2] *Margery Kempe*, pp. 9f.

founders of ascetical theology: Pachomius, Evagrius, Cassian, Clement, Origen, Athanasius. But these claims depend on the narrowing of the subject to the immediate, practical disciplines and methods of prayer: to ascetical-theology. If we widen the term to *ascetical* theology, the general approach to all Christian doctrine which carries it over into prayer as the basis of life, then the founders must be St Augustine and St Benedict. The doctrines of these two saints form a marriage from which all Catholic schools are to be born. Some of the offspring are to depart radically from their parents, while the English school remains extraordinarily loyal to them. Anglican theology retains a strong Augustinian stamp, while in some aspects of spiritual theology the modern English Church is still thoroughly Benedictine.

The Augustinian line which most deeply influences our tradition continues through St Anselm, the Austin canons regular, and especially the school of St Victor; the ascetical theology of Hugh making a deeper impression than the better known writings of Richard. This more speculative side leads on to St Thomas and the Dominicans; St Thomas himself providing a prime source of Caroline theology and the preaching friars exerting their influence in English parishes. All these sources are clearly apparent in the fourteenth-century consummation of English religion.

The Benedictine line follows into the Cistercian reform, of which the influence on England is apparent to anyone who has looked at our monastic history. This is the affective side, but English spirituality follows the Cistercianism of the more thoughtful William of St Thierry and the less austere Aelred of Rievaulx, rather than that of St Bernard. In the story of English religion, William of St Thierry plays the part of a kind of Jack-in-the-box: always popping up in unexpected places. Franciscan influence carries on the affective strain, but for ascetical doctrine it is to St Bonaventure, rather than to St Francis himself, that we must look. This line, too, leads directly into the formulated English school of the fourteenth century.

It is interesting to note a subsidiary strain of English monasticism. Before the conquest England was known as "the land of the Benedictines" (in spiritual theology rather than monastic order I think it still is), and in the middle ages it could almost have been called the land of the Cistercians. But as a purely English offshoot comes St Gilbert of Sempringham, then Nicholas Ferrar and Little

Gidding, then the revived communities at Nashdom, Cowley, and Mirfield; all of which may be seen to have a decided family resemblance.

If St Augustine and St Benedict are the founders of Catholic spirituality, and if we have briefly traced the more remote ancestry of English spirituality from them, we must now look more closely at the English school in its final form. There is a certain interest in the Celtic Church, especially in its penitential system, and in pre-Conquest Benedictinism. But our own father-founder, in whom English spirituality is first plainly embodied, the first of the pure breed as it were, appears in the person of St Anselm.

Our first golden age—with the English School fully formed as a recognizable entity—comes in the fourteenth century, and our second in the seventeenth. The Reformation which divides them has ascetical implications which are apt to be buried beneath the doctrinal and political events of the period. But I believe it to be this deep religious undercurrent that forges the link between our great medieval and Caroline ages. It is plainly important to Anglicanism that its spirituality, no less than its liturgy and theology, should be directly traceable to apostolic origins. I shall argue that vernacular Scripture, emphasis on recollection rather than formal private prayer, and meditation rather than extra-liturgical devotions, are direct developments from fourteenth-century practice. I shall also maintain that the Book of Common Prayer, as a system, is one of the most brilliant pieces of ascetical construction there has ever been, that it is the consummation of centuries of spiritual development, and that, regarded as ascetical theology, it is almost as Benedictine as the *Regula* itself.

The rest of the story is one of disintegration interspersed with haphazard attempts at revival. If we are to regain the genius of English spirituality and develop it in twentieth-century idiom, I see no alternative but to pay some attention to its patristic roots and then continue a most careful study of both fourteenth-and seventeenth-century writings.

III. THE ENGLISH SCHOOL AND THE CREED

By the analogy of music, it was suggested that as the basic notes form an infinity of harmonies, so the clauses of the Creed are variously arranged to form specific spiritual traditions. It is interesting to notice that with our patristic ancestry this is precisely what we have.

There is a sense in which the whole Creed is covered by the "occasional" theology of St Augustine; more especially he gives us the doctrine of the Trinity interpreted also in terms of the creation of man, thence a religious psychology. The Manichaean controversy supplies a more general doctrine of creation, the Pelagian battle leads to grace and the sacraments, while the *De Civitate Dei* and the anti-Donatist writings treat of the doctrine of the Church. St Benedict, supported later by English Cistercianism, St Gilbert, and the Austin Canons, gives a characteristic stamp to the doctrine of the Church as it appears in our unique pastoral tradition.

Devotion flowing from the Incarnation, necessarily coupled with the Blessed Virgin, is also Cistercian, while devotion to the Passion stems from the Franciscans. But coupled with this is an Atonement doctrine, thence a penitential and moral system, which is traceable to the Celtic Church and which later bears the pastoral stamp of Aelred of Rievaulx and William of St Thierry.

The doctrine of creation, so neglected and yet so vital to a balanced ascetic, comes down to us in a progressive line of development from Augustine, through the Victorines and St Francis, to Aquinas.

The doctrines of death and resurrection flowing from Franciscan penitence through St Bonaventure, are taken up by the Caroline divines in a special way, and, in ascetical terms, all owe something to the concluding chapters of the *De Civitate Dei*. And if the whole Creed is initially covered by St Augustine, it is all fully consolidated as English spirituality by St Anselm. If the Creed is read through side by side with these names and emphases, I do not think anything is left out.

What are the particular characteristics of the English school of spirituality which emerge from this dogmatic–ascetical synthesis?

IV. THE CHARACTER OF THE ENGLISH SCHOOL

If we look at St Anselm, the fourteenth-century writers, and the Caroline Church, it is not difficult to discern six common characteristics. All are found throughout Christendom, but together they set the English school apart from all others. They are:

1. An extraordinary consistency in maintaining *the speculative-affective synthesis*; the theological and the emotional, doctrine and devotion, fact and feeling. This, I suggest, is the deepest meaning of

the Anglican *via media*; it is the insistence that prayer, worship, and life itself, are grounded upon dogmatic fact, that in everyday religious experience head and heart are wedded. English Christianity has constantly rejected the ecstatic, spectacular, and baroque, not because they are "Roman", or because of "superstition" and "enthusiasm", or even because "one should not go too far"—they are but passing manifestations—but because of this deep-rooted ascetical principle, of which our saints and teachers will never let go. On the other hand (one obvious exception notwithstanding) we have never been happy with the cold rationalism of an Abelard.

The supreme exponent of this spiritual harmony is St Anselm. Our greatest single work, illustrative of it, is probably the *Revelations of Divine Love*, in which Julian of Norwich combines the most vivid, most disturbingly affective meditation on every distressing detail of the Passion with almost a treatise on the doctrine of the Atonement. The strain continues with what the Prayer Book so simply calls "true piety and sound learning", but we must be careful to interpret "and" as a conjunction of synthesis, not of duality: to be a trifle pedantic, true piety "with", "from", or "based upon" sound learning would be more accurate.

2. There is a strong pastoral insistence on *the unity of the Church Militant*, wherein a deep family relationship exists between priest and layman, monk and secular; hence the Englishness of the Gilbertines and Margery Kempe's Norfolk. Our distrust of clericalism and authoritarianism is no shallow—or modern—trait, but the result of a long pastoral heritage, based on the doctrine of the Body of Christ. When the squire objects to the parson's biretta and lace cotta, or the Churchwarden rejects the advice of the vicar, we are inclined to say that they do not understand the Catholic faith and have no respect for its priesthood. That may be true, but their attitude is not wholly inconsistent with a truly theological tradition: Margery Kempe would agree with them, so would Richard Rolle, and possibly Aelred of Rievaulx as well.

The principle underlies the ascetical structure of the Book of Common Prayer. Seen as a system, not a series of services, it is the common basis for the Christian lives of the Archbishop of Canterbury, the Superior of Mirfield, and all the schoolgirls who were confirmed yesterday. It embodies the pastoral spirit and domestic emphasis of the Benedictine Rule.

5—E.S.

It follows, logically and inevitably, that Anglican spiritual direction must be empirical, not dogmatic; not as something amateur or watered down, still less because it is rather nice that way, but because our spirituality demands it.

3. Flowing from these two characteristics, comes *a unique humanism and a unique optimism*. The harsher elements of St Augustine (regrettably the better known part of his ascetic), or of Carmelite and Carthusian religion find little place in English spiritual writing. Yet it is neither sentimental nor lax. The agonizing penitence of Margery Kempe and Julian of Norwich is as plain as can be, but so is the tremendous virtue of unquenchable hope: "all shall be well, and all shall be well, and all manner of thing shall be well". The Caroline moralists must be technically grouped as "rigorists"; like their fourteenth-century ancestors they make no bones about the hardship along the narrow way, but a calm optimism still reigns. The Middle English writings in particular, give rise to a whole new spiritual vocabulary of a pronounced "domestic" flavour, while the satanic sulphur and fiery brimstone analogies, or the Christian militarism so loved by St Ignatius Loyola, are very rarely found. St Benedict's family theme remains constant: it may be a hard home but it is not a barracks.

Two more Benedictine emphases follow:

4. The foundation of Christian life is the *liturgy*, seen as both Mass and Office, from which flows personal devotion based on the *Bible*. Neither the *Regula* nor the Prayer Book have much to say about private prayer except to assume and encourage it: there are no "methods". That the Carolines returned to the principle of liturgy directly inspiring devotion, and strongly insisted on the private use of the Bible, is common knowledge. It is not such common knowledge that "meditation" on the Gospel narrative played an equally large part in the spirituality of Margery Kempe and Julian. On the seventeenth century, C. J. Stranks writes: "Thus the idea of God in the worshipper's mind, when he addressed himself to prayer, was that which he had learned from the Bible. The rare use of a crucifix, or sacred pictures, compelled him to make his own mental image."[1] Whether or not Margery and Julian were thus compelled, they certainly made their own mental images! They had to learn what they could of the Bible from the Dominican and Franciscan

[1] *Anglican Devotion* (1961), p. 274.

preachers (Margery found a priest friend to read it to her) while their religion remained centred on the Mass and the lay Office of Our Lady. Fourteenth-century England plainly needed, and must eventually have demanded, both a common Office and a vernacular Bible: Reformation or not, it is but the logical development of their spirituality.

5. But here and throughout, formal private prayer, at set periods and according to some plan, remains subservient to *habitual recollection*. It is in the streets of King's Lynn and Norwich, on roads and ships and pilgrimage, that Margery's vivid meditations and colloquies take place. Even with the English anchoress, like the Benedictine monk, it is the constant recollection of Christ's presence, rather than formal meditation, that links up the Offices and liturgy.

The Caroline emphasis is also on a total Christian life in the world supported by the liturgy, especially by the morning and evening Offices, but here the moral element, the practical doing of God's will, is much more pronounced than the affective. We shall see that neither recollective technique is wholly satisfactory, and that if modern Christians are to live continually in their faith they must be guided to a combination of both fourteenth- and seventeenth-century practice: the one supplies what the other lacks.

It is here and in the preceding characteristic that the meditative methods and techniques of Counter-Reformation spirituality can be either a blessing or a curse. Sensibly used, they can help us to a more vivid sense of the presence of Christ and to a more intimate understanding of his mind, to be carried over into habitual recollection. An undisciplined enthusiasm for these methods which detracts from recollection, or worse still supplants the daily Office, ends in chaos. Parts of the teaching of St Ignatius Loyola supply something useful which the English tradition lacks, while the complete *Exercises* form an ascetical system incompatible with our own.

6. *Spiritual direction* is itself central to English spirituality, not only as pastoral practice but also as the source and inspiration of ascetical theology. The English system has developed through the centuries, not out of monastic order but from empirical guidance of individual people. The Celtic penitential discipline was intensely personal and strictly private; St Anselm was a renowned spiritual guide; all the fourteenth-century writings were addressed to, or compiled by, anchorites or anchoresses; they are personal instructions, not

monastic rules. Caroline ascetical and moral theology largely arose through the guidance of individuals, or through the private discussion of sermons by small groups.

If the phrase "spiritual direction" has come to acquire an authoritarian, Counter-Reformation taint, it is due to the confusion between their dogmatic and juridical, and our empirical, methods.

These six characteristics, and their numerous corollaries, combine to form an English school of spirituality of incalculable worth to Christendom. But all good things have their weaknesses and dangers; it is as well to find out what they are.

V. DANGERS IN THE ENGLISH SCHOOL

1. The danger inherent in any doctrine of *via media* is not so much over-emphasis on one side against the other as under-emphasis on both. The speculative-affective synthesis, supported by optimism in a domestic setting (the first three points in the last section) produces sublimity in our saints. Our native saints have not lacked courage, we have our martyrs, but most of them have still displayed Benedictine rather than a Franciscan type of sanctity: the no less heroic but hidden and domestic virtues rather than the more spectacular ones. But when most of us are not saints the *via media* too easily becomes merely tame; it degenerates into "not going too far". I do not believe that the ordinary English Churchman is in much danger of allowing affectiveness to run into uncurbed emotionalism, or of embracing a thorough-going rationalism. He is in danger of being content with a "little of each". "Balance" is achieved when both sides carry equal weights, not only when they carry small weights, and we completely misunderstand Julian of Norwich if we regard her as "not too speculative and not too affective". She was wholly affective, as full-blooded in her devotion to Christ's humanity as St Bernard himself, but at the same time she was as coolly logical as the Schoolmen. Her ascetical scale is "balanced" by an equal distribution of tons, our danger is to be content with grams; the miserable heresy of "moderation in all things".

The English Church, of course, has had its outbreaks of rationalism, superstition, and quietism ("enthusiasm"), but, spread over fifteen centuries, they have been remarkably few. Isolated cases do not make an epidemic, and to concentrate our forces against these errors is to risk the far greater dangers of apathy, spiritual cowardice, and "moderation". English iconoclasm, anti-ritualism, and the suppression of devotion to the Blessed Sacrament are like an intensive campaign against a disease that no one is very likely to catch.

2. Emphasis on liturgy and habitual recollection rather than formal private prayer creates the dangers of both legalism and laxity. The former error may not be very apparent in English Church life—in general we need more law not less—but among the faithful it commonly occurs in two subsidiary ways. There is a pronounced legalist attitude to the principle of "Rule",[1] and there is still something a little magical about "going to church".

Emphasis on habitual recollection, whether fourteenth-century affective or seventeenth-century moral, leads all too easily into Pelagianism, thence laxity. The sterner duties of Christian discipleship are apt to be overlooked in favour of a vague "good life", and religion becomes earth-bound. The comparatively greater stress that other Schools place on formal periods of prayer, has the advantage of making laxity much more apparent: one is not always aware of a state of distraction or of the "goodness" of life, but one does know whether formal prayers have been said or not!

3. The English Church presupposes *adult* membership. In true context, our notorious "individualism" is no bad thing, in fact it is a very good thing, for our whole system is dependent upon it. Whether St Anselm's disciples, the fourteenth-century anchoress, or the Caroline Churchman with his well-trained conscience, it is the development of the individual person from which our spirituality has sprung. But the dangers are constant and obvious. The speculative Orders, like the Dominicans, have a safeguard against error in their deep and disciplined learning. The strongly affective schools are rightly disciplined by a strongly authoritarian priesthood. The English Churchman has neither safeguard unless he purposely seeks it, while his traditional support remains spiritual guidance itself, but of our own empirical type which still preserves his adult responsibility.

VI. OMISSIONS FROM CATHOLIC SPIRITUALITY

If I have managed to give some idea of what the English school is, and how it fits into the total spirituality of the Church, it might bring things into sharper relief if we note a few of the more important omissions.

[1] See *Christian Proficiency*, ch. 5.

1. I have said little about Eastern Orthodox spirituality; mainly because it would stretch the early part of the book out of all proportion, and because I am incompetent to give the subject the treatment it deserves. But I also think the omission is a proper one. It is plain that any school of prayer with roots in the New Testament must be influenced by this mighty eastern source; St Basil is parent to St Benedict, Anglican theology owes much to the Greek fathers, and it is impossible to assess the influence of Eastern monasticism. But I incline to the view—even against some very learned friends— that when Cassian and St Martin of Tours adapted Eastern monachism and Eastern spirituality to the needs and temper of Gaul, they made a thorough job of it: not only in miles are Egypt and France a long way apart.

At the modern end of the story, we still sing *Kyrie eleison* and speak of the "Eucharist", devotions like the "Jesus prayer" (a method of recollection) retain their popularity, and we rejoice in amicable relations with the Orthodox Church. It can teach us a great deal, and the more study—and perhaps experiment—we give to Orthodox spirituality the better we will be. But I prefer to think of such study and experiment as a courtship between two noble lines rather than—as some would suggest—a marriage between second cousins of the same family. In the context of pastoral guidance of modern English people I must regard this omission as justified.

2. The affective prayer of St Bernard gave rise to many distinct traditions in Medieval Catholicism, which, on the Continent of Europe, became grouped as "Cistercian" or "late Benedictine". The vast movement includes some of the greatest and most familiar saints of the Christian Church. I have omitted much of this because, again in our special and practical context, I think English Cistercianism is distinctly that of William of St Thierry and Aelred of Rievaulx.

3. Following a similar pattern, the Dominicans had much to do with the development of our tradition. St Thomas himself is source and inspiration of many Caroline writers. But it is doubtful if we owe very much to the Dominicans of the Rhineland who departed a great deal from the spirituality of Aquinas. Eckhart, Suso, and Tauler were much read in seventeenth-century England (as indeed was Greek theology) but their affective and mystical works play little part in our formulated tradition.

4. The most glaring omission of all is the spiritual theology of the Counter-Reformation. The monumental systems of St Ignatius Loyola, St John of the Cross, and St Teresa of Avila are comparable to the theology of Aquinas; they make up the most comprehensive system that the Church has ever produced, and very probably ever will produce. No student or spiritual guide can afford to neglect it, but here more than anywhere adaptation to our own tradition and incorporation into it is of the first importance. The spirit and outlook of the two systems is radically different, and much harm has been done by failure to recognize this fact. This spirituality, like that of the German Dominicans, was widely read by Caroline scholars. There is no reason why it should not be read to-day, but in proportion and as little more than an appendage to our own system.

A further reason for my omission is that this school has already received very thorough examination; for every word on Walter Hilton, millions have been expended on St John of the Cross.

5. Like the theology of the Greek Church, the influence of Protestant spirituality is considerable but indirect. Calvin and Luther leave their stamp on the Book of Common Prayer, their doctrines have sometimes inveigled themselves into English religion, but it is difficult to impute any definite characteristic to them. Puritanism is a strong subsidiary characteristic to our tradition, but it is the puritanism of St Bernard—who could be as puritanical as anyone when he wished—rather than that of Calvin. A certain austerity, a Cistercian simplicity, is to be found in St Anselm, Hilton, Rolle, and the Caroline divines, while the full Calvinist system survived in England for only eight years out of fifteen hundred. In the Cistercian sense we have a puritan tradition, in another, English Puritanism can easily be exaggerated.

VII. "THE ENGLISH TEMPERAMENT"

A large part of ascetical theology consists in adapting dogmatic truth to the needs of different temperaments. That is how the great Catholic Schools of spirituality have arisen. "The English Temperament" obviously embraces enormous diversity and discussions about it tend to become unreal, or to degenerate into jokes and aphorisms, fondly held to typify our racial traits. Yet the English temperament remains a recognizable entity, bearing on the development of our spirituality. In section II of this chapter, the main sources which make up the English School were traced; in section VI the omissions from Catholic Christendom were pointed out. This selection could not have been fortuitous; there must be some racial instinct which naturally inclines to some saints and teachers and which intuitively rejects others. There must be some deep-seated reason why Benedictines, Cistercians, Franciscans, and Austin Canons flourished in England—which means that Englishmen were attracted to these orders—while Cluniacs, Carmelites, and Carthusians did not.

In an attempt to describe the character of English spirituality, and the dangers inherent in it (sections IV and V *supra*), hints of the popular idea of the English temperament constantly peep out. Many of the essential elements and characteristics of the English School can be paralleled by these popular ideas: even the jokes and aphorisms contain a kernel of truth.

The central speculative–affective synthesis of ascetical theology could easily arise from "English reserve"; from control of the emotions, which is not the same as their suppression. "British phlegm" could lead either to apathy or simplicity. At its best it suggests spiritual sanity, purity in liturgical expression, and an abhorrence of fussiness and ostentation. Such ascetical simplicity is expressed in Norman and Perpendicular churches and in the "English" sanctuary, not in the Romanesque or the baroque. It is the character of the Benedictine Rule and the Book of Common Prayer, and perhaps it is not too far-fetched to see this practical outlook and absence of ostentation manifested in an emphasis on habitual recollection rather than on intricate methods and techniques of devotion.

"Rugged individualism" could be at the bottom of our empirical direction and pastoral relationships. Some such ingrained characteristic must be responsible for our lack of clericalism, and for the centrality of the anchorite movement in the development of English ascetical theology. On the other side it strongly suggests that Pelagius had to be an Englishman. Then there is domesticity: that "the Englishman's home is his castle", and that we are "a nation of shopkeepers", are propositions which could almost be proved not only by social history but from the writings of Walter Hilton and Julian of Norwich. Military history may mock at Napoleon's gibe, yet in spirituality he was surely right; the military analogy, freely employed by St Ignatius Loyola—and by St Paul—is very seldom found in English spiritual writing. Our ascetical ethos is better expressed by "Lead kindly Light" than by "Onward Christian Soldiers". The English Church consists of God's servants, God's children, God's handmaidens, not of God's militia.

PART TWO

The English School:
Patristic and Medieval
Development

5

CATHOLIC ASCETIC:
ST AUGUSTINE

I. THE ORIGINS OF CATHOLIC ASCETIC

One of the functions of ascetical theology is to adapt doctrine and discipline to particular circumstances. The first centuries of ascetical experiment were overshadowed by two things: first, the idea of an imminent *parousia*, and secondly, the fact of persecution. It is only to be expected that the spiritual teaching of this age was grim and austere. If Christ is returning next week to consummate all things in glory, there is no place for marriage, family life, and the domestic virtues; if martyrdom is certain there is no use for slow, progressive schemes, scales, and methods of prayer. Rigorous mortification, celibacy, and fasting were seen as training for martyrdom; which, under the circumstances, was very sound ascetic. But it does not mean that these things are essential parts of the Christian *askesis*, nor that gentle, patient effort is of no importance. Situations change and it is part of ascetical theology to change with them.

After persecution came popularity. At the conversion of Constantine the Church was faced with the alternatives which still confront us: either we defy laxity and luxury so that the Christian light shines against the surrounding darkness, the candle firmly aloft on its candlestick, or we try to exert a more subtle influence upon the world, serving it, loving it, salting the stew, leavening the lump. Should we follow St Francis or St Benedict?

The ascetical experiments of the Desert Fathers were of the former kind; they defied the world by heroic flight. They fled for various reasons: to find God in silence and solitude, to conquer Satan, whom they thought—a trifle optimistically—had been driven from the cities, to experiment in *askesis*, or simply to get away from temptation. They made mistakes, but their intentions were right.

Their errors were brought to light, and even consolidated, by the school of Alexandria. Encratism, or austerity for its own sake, a constant ascetical danger; the quasi-Gnosticism of Origen; the attempt to synthesize Judaism and Hellenism by St Clement (a happily unsuccessful attempt to "present the faith in modern thought"), the quest for *apatheia* by Evagrius and Cassian; *anaesthesia* and "negative mysticism": all that is matter for ecclesiastical history.[1] But out of this melting-pot came problems which are fundamental to spiritual theology: How does one find God? By self-discipline or through grace; alone or in community; by suppression of the flesh or by harmonizing the personality? Whatever value and inspiration we find in the empiricism of the Desert, the solution of these problems is the work of St Augustine.

II. ST AUGUSTINE'S "OCCASIONAL" THEOLOGY

In modern spiritual writing "Augustinian" has become almost a term of abuse. It is associated with a thorough-going pessimism about human nature, a doctrine of the Church which blithely condemns unbaptized babies to hell, and a double predestinarian doctrine which properly belongs to Calvin. His "devotional" writing is seen to consist only in the *Confessions*, with sometimes the *Enchiridion* and a sermon or two thrown in. That Augustine was responsible for some serious errors is freely acknowledged, while the best of his teaching needed almost a thousand years fully to develop; but this popular idea remains a travesty of his value to English spirituality.

1. Amongst his vast literary output, it is difficult to find anything that is not "occasional". The work which most concerns us here consists in a bishop's refutation of heresy within his diocese, the writings against the Donatists, Manichaeism, and Pelagius: pastoral theology if ever there were any. The *City of God* was "occasioned" by the fall of Rome to Alaric in 410: scarcely an "academic" matter. The *Enchiridion* is a personal manual of faith and practice written for the layman Laurentius, and even the *De Trinitate*—dispatched without hesitation to the "dogmatics" section of the library—contains the psychological analogy wherein trinitarian man is made in the image of a trinitarian God: a doctrine of inexhaustible pastoral interest. It is ironical that if "academic" theology is that written for no immediate purpose or specific practical need, then the *Confessions* is the most academic book of all.

[1] See especially W. O. Chadwick, *John Cassian* (1950).

St Augustine is "occasional", or in the wide sense ascetical, by nature, and it is doubtful if he could have approached theology in any other way.

"The difference between Augustine and his predecessors lies neither in the problem he raised nor in the solution he provided, but in the intensity with which he lived his problem."[1] "A . . . trait which distinguishes the spirit of Augustinian philosophy from that of any other is its continual refusal to separate speculation from action. . . . Augustinism recognizes as true only that philosophy which is not satisfied to point out the end but provides the means of reaching it."[2] "He wants to find a rule of life rather than the solution to a problem."[3]

2. Central to St Augustine's theology is the relation between knowledge and love, or if it is preferred, between reason and revelation. That is a truism, yet it is less obvious that this is the first expression of the speculative–affective synthesis of English ascetical doctrine: it is the inspiration of St Anselm.

One of the strange contrasts of his richly-dowered mind consists in having given expression with inexorable rigour to the rights of divine justice, while at the same time he succeeds in describing in touching terms the delights of the love of God. . . . To study him makes us better, for nowhere else do we find knowledge so completely transformed into love.[4]

In the face of St Anselm and Julian I am tempted to challenge the latter statement. But the point is well made: here is the core of our ascetical theology.

III. BASIC PRINCIPLES

St Augustine is a thinker who cannot possibly be confined to one short chapter, yet his fundamental teaching cannot be altogether omitted from any study of English spirituality, nor can he be neglected by a serious spiritual director. I can only hope to indicate these basic principles.

1. *Religious psychology.* Man is made in the image of God because God is Trinity-in-unity and man is trinity-in-unity, or rather a

[1] Etienne Gilson, *The Christian Philosophy of Saint Augustine*, Eng. tr. (1961), p. 234.   [2] Ibid., pp. 242-3f.   [3] Ibid., p. 235.
[4] P. Pourrat, *Christian Spirituality* (1922), Vol. I, p. 185.

series of trinities. This, of course, is analogy: "there is nothing in nature that does not bear some resemblance to the Trinity and that may not, as a result, help us to get some idea of it. In its proper sense, however, the distinction of being an image belongs only to man, and in man it belongs by right only to the mind (*mens*), for this is his highest part and the one nearest to God."[1]

Augustine thinks sometimes of mind, knowledge, and love; sometimes of memory, intellect, and will (the later "three point" meditation), sometimes of the perception of God, knowledge of God, love of God. All have their ascetical value, for all constitute, in some way, "progressions". But the simplest and most immediately important is the unity of body–mind–spirit, arranged in a hierarchy in which spirit, or the indwelling of God in the soul, controls and inspires reason, which in turn rules the carnal appetites:

> peace is established in the will through the mind's control over the senses, and order established in the mind through a system of truths which is secure against relapse into doubt.... true philosophy implies an act of adherence to the supernatural order which frees the will from the flesh through grace and the mind from scepticism through revelation.[2]

2. *Creation and the Fall.* Creation is continually caused by the love of God and all things are good in so far as they exist. There can be nothing intrinsically evil in the flesh or its appetites, but original sin, brought about by Adam's fall, reduces man to "infirmity, corruption, and misery". This sounds contradictory until we see that these are negative terms; they imply the absence of health and happiness. Sin, therefore, is but a deprivation of good, a wrong choice in the human search for happiness. Original sin becomes a disease affecting the entire human race, it is a congenital infirmity, but this again is a negative idea. The total man, as he exists in body, mind, and spirit, is still good; what he has lost is both clearsightedness and harmony. The carnal desires overthrow the reason because the mind has lost its ability to see its true happiness. This disharmony, and consequent weakening of reason and will, is *concupiscence*.

But man retains free-will. He has lost the power to follow a right choice alone but he still has the power of discernment between good and evil. Further he has the free-will to use the power which God supplies to overcome his infirmity: grace. "He who wills to do the

[1] E. Gilson, op. cit., p. 219.   [2] Ibid., p. 235.

will of God obtains through prayer the grace with which he can do all things. For he has always the power to pray, and prayer wins for him the power to act. It is chiefly in having recourse to prayer to get grace that man's free will is exercised."[1]

3. *Perfection.* "Christian perfection is perfect justice, and perfect justice is perfect charity. . . . Perfect justice consists in the keeping of God's commandments so strictly that all sin, even the least, is avoided. But it is charity that makes us respect God's commandments."[2] But such perfection is not possible in this life, it is the final goal towards which we strive, and such habitual striving, pastorally speaking, is to be in the "way of perfection". This is "a constant endeavour towards that which is best, towards that fullness of charity when sin is no longer committed: it is a voyage, so to speak, in which we sail onwards to our fatherland, which is heaven: it is a forward march without a halt; a race towards the most perfect, a mounting upwards to God. These Augustinian expressions hereafter became classical in spirituality.

"If the perfecting of our spiritual life be nothing else than growth in justice and charity, then its essential law will be progress."[3]

So we have sin opposed by grace, progress, perfection; the Three Ways at the centre of St Augustine's thought, proving him to be—if such proof were required—an *ascetical* theologian.[4]

The pastoral teaching which follows from this is of the first importance, and it goes some way to clear up the popular misunderstanding of St Augustine's so-called "pessimism". Concupiscence is the disharmony of human personality caused by sin, original and actual. The psychological, or subjective, aim is towards—to introduce a typical Augustinian term—*tranquillitas*; harmony rather than tranquillity because, although it may suggest an element of the "peace of God", it is an active not a passive state. *Tranquillitas* is the end of the purgative way and therefore the beginning of real progress. The quest for happiness is a proper human aim, all desire is essentially right until concupiscence causes it to be erroneous. The soul in *tranquillitas* desires happiness in God, it desires progress towards perfection, but this is never fully attainable in this life. Christian life, therefore, is always a quest, a longing, for God. The

---

[1] Pourrat, op. cit., p. 176.   [2] Ibid., p. 185.   [3] Ibid., p. 187.
[4] Cf. *Enchiridion*, ch. 118.

subjective *tranquillitas* is completed by the objective going out to God, psychology is completed by ontology.[1]

In pastoral guidance, therefore, we may say that the quest for happiness is a worthy reason for embracing the Faith, but we must be careful, and honest, before we make extravagant claims for the "satisfaction" of being a Christian. We must avoid presenting the Faith as a panacea for all problems and troubles; it remains a *longing*, a desire never fulfilled on earth. On the other hand we must beware of undervaluing the affective state, and of exaggerating the burden of duty and discipline, for there is always a delight in the service of the beloved. "*Amor*: love, is both quest and enjoyment; feeling is an indispensable pre-supposition of conation."[2]

In another classic analogy, Christian life is a courtship with God, with all its joys and hopes as well as its frustrations and difficulties; only to be consummated in heaven. Perhaps more than anyone, St Augustine warns us of the ascetical danger of confusing the end with the means; we must ever keep our eyes on heaven, on the Beatific Vision, described so sublimely in the concluding chapters of the City of God.[3]

4. *Temptation and self-examination.* St Augustine's pastoral teaching here is still valid and applicable. Self-examination is a prior Christian duty; we must look into the very depths of the soul, for unless we face the truth about ourselves we cannot achieve any proper relation with God. In ourselves we find concupiscence, a disharmony between the carnal desires, reason, will, and spirit, a blindness towards the true good: "men *will* not what is right, either because the right is hidden from them, or because they take no delight in it, for the strength of our will to anything is proportionate to the certainty of our knowledge of its goodness, and the ardour of our delight in it."[4] "Ignorance and infirmity are the two causes of sin, against which we must pray for the grace which illuminates as well as confers the 'delight in righteousness'."[5]

Because of original sin, concupiscence is our state. Baptism destroys original sin and the culpableness of concupiscence, but not the innate weakness itself. Discounting grace, certain psychologists teach that the results of this state cannot be helped and therefore—

---

[1] See J. Burnaby, *Amor Dei* (1944), pp. 45 foll.   [2] Ibid., p. 222.
[3] For a concise commentary, see E. L. Mascall, *Grace and Glory* (1961).
[4] *De Pecc. Merit.* 2. 26.   [5] *Enchiridion*, 22.

blatant *non sequitur*—cannot be called sinful. St Augustine agrees that the state is unavoidable, but his whole point is that its results *are* sinful: we are "born in sin" and might as well face facts. This is "pessimistic" only so long as we leave out grace, and to leave out grace is to leave out Augustine.

Self-examination, then, leading to the fight against sin by grace, aims at *tranquillitas*; not the suppression of desire, not *apatheia*, but harmony between the elements of personality.

Temptation arises in this way: first, evil insinuates itself into the imaginative mind, then the concupiscent soul (body–mind–spirit in its entirety) instinctively takes pleasure in the evil thought, suggesting acquiescence to the will. Finally comes the temptation proper in which the soul conquers or submits. Neither the initial thought, nor its pleasurable entertainment, constitutes sin, but only the final submission. St Augustine, as is to be expected, deduces this doctrine from Genesis: the Fall is not brought about either by the suggestion of the serpent or by the pleasurable anticipation of Eve, but solely by Adam's consent. The music-hall joke that all our troubles are due to the ladies is wrong in fact; the culprit is Adam.

The pastoral value of this doctrine lies in its clear distinction between temptation and sin, more subtly between temptation and "sins of thought", which is always disturbing faithful people. But it should also be noticed that, however Augustine may have exaggerated the sins of the flesh and however rigorous his discipline in this direction, he is quite clear that temptation begins in the *mind*. It is the mind, not the instincts and appetites, which needs the greater discipline. St Augustine, nevertheless, will have no "faculty psychology": man is a unity, the whole man is tempted, the whole man sins, the whole man is assisted by grace.

Slight as it is, I hope that this discussion of the basic principles of St Augustine's ascetical teaching will enable us to see more clearly into the significance of the great "pastoral" controversies.

IV. MANICHAEISM

Dualism is a constant ascetical danger. It crept into the Egyptian Desert, it more than crept into the Greek-conscious school of Alexandria: had not St Paul said "the flesh lusteth against the spirit and the spirit against the flesh"? Is not to walk after the spirit to free oneself from the senses by every effort of mortification? Is it not common Christian knowledge that the spirit is willing but the flesh is weak?

Manichaeism is a thoroughgoing form of this dualism: it assumes two conflicting principles, good and evil or light and darkness, borrowed from Persian philosophy. Good is pure spirit, matter is evil; and here is the root of that vast group of heresies which come under the general heading of Puritanism—strictly speaking, the quest for pure spirit, and only secondarily the distrust and suppression of creatures and the bodily appetites.

The Oxford Dictionary of the Christian Church states, a little optimistically, that of the three "pastoral" heresies that faced Augustine. "The least dangerous was Manichaeism, for its doctrines were too obviously remote from historic Christianity to have any real hope of success at that late date".[1] It is "a hotch-potch of many long dead heresies".[2] That may be true, but dualism, albeit in subtler forms, is to be found in most modern parishes, and is not unknown in current textbooks on moral and ascetical theology. It is still frequently taught that, in terms of Christian living, creatures are divisible into necessities, the useful, and luxuries: the very plain implication, even if not tacitly stated, is that the first are good, the second tolerable, and the third evil. Spiritual directors should be clear that, although a good deal of danger and nonsense may surround them, oysters, mink, and diamonds are very good creatures of a very good God.

Temptation is often countered with the advice to reject the thought from the mind; that is sometimes wise and sometimes impossible. But impurity of thought means the mental image of a creature, and the implication, again not tacitly stated, is that this creature is evil: "stop thinking of *that* and think about something *good*". But *that*, dancing-girl, bottle of beer, hot favourite for the two-thirty, or whatever it may be, *is* a good thing. It is sometimes more effective to retain the image and look at it from God's point of view than to reject it, or try to. St Augustine is quite clear that drunkenness not drink is the evil, covetousness is sinful not the creatures coveted.

No one to-day would hold that St Augustine's answer to Manichaeism is entirely satisfactory, but his basic conclusions remain pastorally valid and useful: that God is the sole creator and sustainer of all things; that sin arises from concupiscence, not directly from the appetites and passions; that man is an integrated unity, fallen

[1] P. 107.   [2] Ibid., p. 848.

through sin, restored by grace and made for the enjoyment of God.

It is part of the greatness of Augustine that these principles *are* basic, hence his influence on Christian thought through the centuries. But such first principles need development; they are the foundation of ascetic, not the superstructure. His doctrine of creation especially needs to be supplemented by the ascetical treatment of the School of St Victor, and then of Aquinas.

V. DONATISM

With the possible exception of the state of affairs described in 1 Cor. 1—3, Donatism was the precursor of everything we would now call "sectarianism". The Donatists were a schismatic sect who taught that, to maintain the purity of the Church, sinners, especially apostates, were to be rigorously excluded, unworthy priests deposed, and a fanatical discipline imposed on the holy few who remained. Like Manichaeism, it sounds too silly to be taken seriously to-day, and yet, also like Manichaeism, it cannot be regarded as dead. The importance lies in St Augustine's refutation, in which, as is to be expected, pastoral teaching abounds.

Out of this controversy three doctrines emerge, which are of fundamental importance to all sound pastoral theology.

1. The very first rung on the spiritual ladder is not holiness but penitence; thereafter, that no sin can be so great as to be excluded from the redemption of Christ's Cross. To Augustine, the Church might be the "ark of salvation", but it is also a hard school for sinners, never an exclusive club for the "elect" in the Donatist sense. Whatever Augustine's predestinarianism really was, it certainly included penitent sinners because it included himself. Good men may exist outside it, but bad certainly were to be found within it: the parables of the Tares and the Drag-Net made that clear enough.

2. In the words of our 26th Article, "the unworthiness of the ministers hinders not the effect of the Sacrament". For centuries the Church has so taken this for granted that we overlook its tremendous importance. What the Church has sometimes forgotten, and it has been disastrous, is St Augustine's reason for the doctrine, which is also plainly stated in Article 26: "forasmuch as they do not the same in their own name, but in Christ's, and do minister by his commission and authority". If certain schools of the thirteenth

century, notably those misinterpreting St Bernard, had remembered that it was Christ, not the priest, who ministered the sacraments, the Church might have been saved from the sillier sort of sacerdotalism. This is the beginning of the notorious priest–lay rift, of clericalism, to which the English Church has always objected. True to St Augustine, as the Article itself bears witness, the English tradition insists that every kind, not only good and bad, but priest and layman, monk and prelate, are united in the one Church Militant.

3. Most important of all, the Donatist controversy forced Augustine to give more attention to the doctrine of sacramental grace than he might otherwise have done. This has far-reaching effects on the pastoral and ascetical implications of Pelagianism.

Ascetical theology, essentially a synthetic study, always tries to see Christian spirituality, and its development, as a whole. Yet so many modern writers, even in this case Pourrat, create confusion and ambiguity by a semi-departmental approach. In his otherwise illuminating treatment of Pelagianism, Pourrat constantly says that, to St Augustine, grace is won by "prayer". But what does Augustine mean by "prayer"? Without disparaging the efficacy of simple petition, he surely means more than that. If we remember his insistence on the unity of personality, on the Christian life as a total progress, on piety as "the sum of religious duties", and on his teaching about eucharistic grace, he can mean no less than composite Rule. Anti-Pelagian teaching cannot be isolated from anti-Donatist doctrine, while the ascetical implications of both are only complete when worked out by St Benedict.

VI. PELAGIANISM

Pelagius taught that the sin of Adam left the human race unaffected, that human nature remains all-powerful in the moral sphere, and that men were capable of achieving salvation by their own efforts, apart from the assistance of divine grace. He did not, of course, deny either the reality or worth of divine grace, but reduced it to a kind of subsidiary help towards moral perfection which men could use or not, as they wished. Very glibly, it is a doctrine of justification by works.

St Augustine attacked this teaching on the grounds that, because of the infection of the whole race by original sin, man was utterly incapable of any good action without the help of grace. From this initial position, he was forced to formulate the doctrines of grace as "prevenient" and "irresistible". God always acted first, grace was prevenient whether conferred by Baptism or directly infused by God into the predestined. Pelagius claimed free-will unimpaired by any weakness, Augustine did not deny free-will as the power of discernment between good and evil, but man was incapable of following the good discerned except by the help of grace.

Questions arise out of this conflict, the answers to which are of the first pastoral importance.

1. If grace is prevenient and irresistible, can there be free-will? The short answer is "yes", because free-will is that which seeks and co-operates with grace, but that is no satisfactory answer unless we understand what is meant by grace. To Pelagius it is merely a help, offered by God in the moral struggle, a kind of strengthening pill, a moral tonic, which, having been taken, must have its irresistible effect. Grace to Augustine is that love which lies at the heart of his spirituality: it is that which, by its very nature, confers independence on the object of its love. It gives, compelling no return, it is the one force that cannot bargain, it is the opposite of irresistible passion, for it liberates rather than enslaves, creates not destroys, strengthens rather than weakens free volition: in more familiar language, "the service of God is perfect freedom". What Augustine is insisting upon is the first principle of all sound theology, that God acts first in both creation and redemption, and that his love is the force behind both. We are called to respond to that love, but because of frailty response is difficult, because of concupiscence we are drawn to other, unworthy objects of love. Therefore we need discipline, especially the disciplines of prayer: ascetical theology is the technique of loving God.

St Augustine makes sense of common experience. Whatever the psychological interest in theories like behaviourism or determinism, every Christian is quite sure of two things: that whether he gets drunk or stays sober is, at least to some extent, his own choice, but that the conquest of his besetting sins is quite beyond his own unaided power. A great deal of trouble and difficulty arises, however, because many devout people, who would be horrified to be called Pelagians, subconsciously assume something like the Pelagian idea of grace. They come away from Holy Communion with the idea of having been *strengthened*, not with the idea of having been *loved*.

2. If prevenient and irresistible grace implies predestination, is there any point in the moral struggle: why not sit back and let grace do its inevitable work? The conclusion of the previous point answers the first part of the question, experience answers the second, in that sitting back passively invariably leads to temptation: response to grace can only be active.

But the predestinarian difficulty remains a real one which St Augustine left unsolved. Two points of criticism arise. First, in spite of his doctrine of creation in which existence itself implies goodness, St Augustine seems not to have examined the *pastoral* distinction between *gratia Dei* and *gratia Christi*. In a sense the Incarnation itself embraces all men, baptized or not, since Christ is verily the Second Adam, the creator of a new race. And the grace of God is not confined to his ordinances for us. Secondly, it follows that, in spite of the Donatist controversy and its solution, St Augustine failed to see the Church as the channel of redemptive grace, of vicarious efficacy to the world outside it. He allowed the sinner to seek salvation within the Church, he allowed that there were good men outside it, but there was no connection: the Church was still the ark of salvation, not the redemptive agent. The error is in the "transmission" theory of original sin.

Experience insists on some kind of predestinarianism: some are Christians, some are not, and no Christian can take credit for his own conversion. But we may think of being "elected", not to inevitable salvation, but to the Christian struggle on behalf of others. St Augustine did insist that love of God and love of neighbour were indistinguishable, service is a part of *askesis*, prayer in the Church is of vicarious efficacy. We shall see that it is St Benedict who supplies what St Augustine omits.

3. We now come to a most intriguing question: as the practical basis for Christian living, is not ascetical theology itself Pelagian? Are not fasts, methods, physical disciplines, even, as Barth would have it, Offices and prayers, nothing but a system of justification by works? The answer is "no", because grace is love and the quest for love is not a justifying work but an ultimate end. We arrive at the conclusion that ascetic starts with the assumption of prevenient grace, that it assumes not only that good works do not justify but that, without grace, they are impossible. The whole of ascetical theology consists in the quest for, and response to, grace which is the

love of God. If the key text for the unitive way is "be ye therefore perfect", and for the illuminative way "take up thy cross and follow me", the Christian life begins with the purgative way based on "without me ye can do nothing". Here St Augustine lays the foundation of ascetical theology as the response to love. At best Pelagius, despite the austerity of his life, can produce no more than a deistic moral code. Three practical conclusions follow.

a. The fundamental ascetical disciplines consist in a positive response to grace offered, and grace, love, the fruits of the Cross and Passion, are most plainly offered in the sacraments of Holy Communion and Confession. The Eucharist is the centre of Christian life, supported by the Office and private devotion: "prayer". The prior Christian asceticism, therefore, is not fasting, mortification, bare boards and hair shirts, but getting up on cold mornings to go to Mass, rising earlier to recite the Office, and forgoing the exciting television programme to give time to prayer. Daily mortifications in the usual sense *must* come second, and *must* be directly linked with spiritual progress; otherwise ascetic has degenerated into justification by works.[1]

b. The battle with sin involves free-will, but only after it has been strengthened by grace; success in the moral struggle depends on spiritual growth in response to the love of God. The confessions of the faithful are apt to have a depressing sameness about them, the same old sins continually recur, the struggle is long and slow. Confessors sometimes have to attempt an objective judgement as to whether a penitent is really struggling against temptation, or whether he has sunk into a rather half-hearted rut. It is a very difficult matter with no cut and dried test, but it can be forgotten that the actual quest for grace in the sacraments still comes first. Recurrence of the same sins need not imply laxity, failure to use the sacraments most certainly does: "sloth in prayer" is likely to be pushed in at the end of a Confession, but if Pelagius was wrong it must come first, as the cause of all the rest.

c. The Pelagian controversy was essentially one of prevenience. Pastorally, we are not concerned with grace *versus* free-will but with which comes first. How does one guide the habitual sinner? By an appeal to resist temptation, aided by hints from psychiatry, or by a prior stress on sacramental grace and co-operating prayer? What is our approach to one who has lost his faith? Is it in terms of rational

[1] See K. E. Kirk, *Some Principles of Moral Theology* (1920), pp. 18f.

argument or emotional appeal, or in terms of ontology, of the doctrine of Baptism, of the vicarious nature of the Church through which grace flows? What is the doctrine behind evangelistic preaching? Are we to stir up our hearers to make strong decisions or to respond to grace already given? Some of these questions are very difficult, but they cannot be answered in terms of expediency: they are questions of orthodoxy or heresy.

VII. CURIOSITIES AND CONCLUSIONS

Nobody to-day could give unqualified support to everything St Augustine taught; the English in particular retain a misguided affection for their arch-heretic! I have tried to explain that Augustine's great importance is to lay the foundation of Christian spirituality, not to complete its superstructure. The position is complex, but there remain certain fundamental curiosities, or ironies, which pastors—especially Augustine's detractors—should consider.

1. In the "semi-Pelagian" controversy, Cassian rejected—and many say rightly—the extreme implications of irresistible grace and its predestinarian consequences. He was not prepared, rightly, to give up the positive moral struggle, he wanted, wrongly, just a tiny element of free-will acting independently of grace. Dr W. O. Chadwick writes:

> Cassian was certainly in error. Christianity demands that the human personality shall be wholly surrendered into the hands of God, that there be no reserve. Not the least of Augustine's services to the Church is the framing of this truth. Even if a tiny portion, an *ortus bonae voluntatis*, is kept out of the sphere of God, men may be encouraged to place ultimate reliance upon human nature instead of God.[1]

On the question of prevenient grace, Cassian tried to meet Augustine half-way; he would have fallen human nature to be very sick but not dead. It is possible for the sick to recover, but only God can raise the dead.

The irony of the position is twofold. First, the firmest foundation to Christian spirituality is laid because Cassian, the ascetical-theologian, was wrong, and Augustine, the *ascetical* theologian, was right. Cassian was wrong because his thinking, generally, was of the

[1] *John Cassian* (1950), p. 137.

narrower, practical kind, with prior concern for methods and techniques of prayer. Augustine was right because he saw the whole spiritual life in terms of dogmatic theology. Secondly, Cassian's error was the quest for "moderation", without concern for truth or synthesis: the *via media* is not compromise.

2. It is ironical that the Pelagian "optimism" about human nature manifests itself in the most extreme rigorism and ends in despair. If we can save ourselves from sin by our own powers there is neither excuse nor remedy for the slightest fall. St Augustine's "pessimism", insisting on prevenient grace, on total reliance on God, on redemption won only by the Cross of Christ, leads first to penitential joy and finally to perfect love.

3. The Pelagian emphasis on austerity and rigour makes creative ascetical progress quite impossible. St Augustine's doctrine of prevenient grace creates it.

4. Perhaps the greatest irony of all is that Calvin, regarded so often as a kind of super-Augustinian, ends with precisely the same pastoral manifestations as Pelagius: grim, unremitting austerity, doubts about election and therefore despair of forgiveness.

St Augustine, we may conclude, was anything but an "academic" thinker, and I hope this cursory treatment is enough to present him as an asceticist still worthy of notice, and to give meaning to the many references to him which follow. But he was a thinker rather than an organizer. His spiritual doctrine is to be supplemented and demonstrated by St Benedict.

ST BENEDICT

Like many another of his Order, Dom Cuthbert Butler denies any such thing as "Benedictine spirituality"; it is simply Catholicism, simply Christianity. All the later medieval schools of spirituality have their roots in Benedictinism, even if, as Dom Cuthbert is first to admit, some of them departed a good way from the parent tradition. But there is another sense in which this claim is true: it is that the genius of St Benedict cannot be confined within the walls of Monte Cassino or any other monastery. The *Regula* is not only a system of monastic order, it is a system of ascetical theology, the basis of which is as applicable to modern England as it was to sixth-century Italy. Our task is to abstract these practical principles from their necessarily "occasional" setting.

I. THE CATHOLIC RULE

The greatest Benedictine achievement (from this point of view) is the final consolidation of the threefold Rule of prayer which is absolutely fundamental to all Catholic spirituality: the common Office (*opus Dei*) supporting private prayer (*orationes peculiares*) both of which are allied to, and consummated by, the Mass. To call this the greatest Benedictine achievement is not to exaggerate, for here Dom Cuthbert is unquestionably right. Here is the basic Rule of the Church which, varying in detail, is common to East and West, monastic and secular, to all the individual schools without exception, and which forms the over-all structure of the Book of Common Prayer. Amongst all the tests of Catholicity or orthodoxy, it is curious that this infallible and living test, is so seldom applied. We write and argue endlessly about the apostolic tradition, about episcopacy, sacramentalism, creeds, doctrine, the Bible—all very important things—yet we fail to see that no group of Christians is true to orthodoxy if it fails to *live* by this Rule of trinity-in-unity: Mass–Office–devotion.

Whenever this has become unbalanced, error has arisen. Later

Benedictinism, as at Cluny, so elaborated the Office as to squeeze out devotion and recollected work; this was one of the major factors behind the Cistercian reform. The Franciscans, in an over-zealous thirst for evangelism, began by minimizing the Office and ended by creating the modern Breviary! In spite of such ups and downs, the Catholic Church has always reformed itself back to St Benedict. Protestantism tends to distrust the common Office in favour of personal religion; the result is subjectivism or moralism. Some schools have reversed the emphasis and ended with formalism. And it is ironical that some of our Tractarians, isolating the Mass and deriding Morning and Evening Prayer, even replacing these by more "Catholic" devotions, were in fact overthrowing the first principle of Catholicism. To-day irony becomes ridicule when the Office is either turned into a subjective devotion, or omitted in favour of intricate methods of private meditation, for which St Benedict, the Prayer Book, and the English tradition have never had much use.

In the *Regula*, thirteen chapters of minute regulation are devoted to the *opus Dei*, and all is centred upon it. It is not always realized that a good two-thirds of the Prayer Book are concerned directly with the Mass and Office. Both exhort to private devotion, both insist on habitual recollection, neither teach any methods. The principle maintained, so obvious yet so forgotten, is that you cannot classify the unique. Private devotion can be guided by competent direction but it cannot be regimented: the Salesian method may be useful but it cannot be imposed even on all Salesians.

Why is this simple threefold scheme so important? The short answer is: because it effects everything that ascetical theology is supposed to effect; it provides a system of prayer which translates all the clauses of the Creed into practical terms and manifests a living faith in them. The Benedictine threefold Rule expresses faith in the Holy Trinity, in the Incarnation and Atonement, in the three-fold Church and the Communion of Saints. Loyalty to this Rule also guards us from error and forms the basis of a continuous, and progressive, Christian life. A more detailed examination of these claims will be made when we study the Benedictine influence on the Book of Common Prayer.[1]

---

[1] Ch. 20, section VI, below.

II. THE DOCTRINE OF THE CHURCH MILITANT

The threefold Rule ensures the most perfect possible balance between the corporate and individual aspects of Christian life. It manifests both the corporate nature of the Body of Christ into which we are incorporated by Baptism, and the unique value and glory of every individual soul created in the image of God. That is why the common Office must *be* common, without deviation by a syllable, and private prayer must be private, not regimented by method but unique to each person. With the use of both Office and private devotion, the Christian brings to our Lord in the Eucharist both selfless loyalty and his own unique gifts of oblation.

It is a mistake to think that St Benedict detracts from either individuality or personal devotion—he strongly insists on habitual recollection—but he reverses the Cassianic preference for the eremitical against the cenobite ideal. To Cassian, life in community was a preparation for solitude; to St Benedict, the common life is an essential element in Christianity itself. It is here that St Benedict supplements a deficiency in the ascetical teaching of St Augustine. Augustine taught a full doctrine of the threefold Church: in the Donatist controversy he defended a comprehensive Church embracing all kinds of people in all kinds of spiritual states, and at Hippo he surrounded himself with a group of priests under common Rule, but his teaching remained largely individualistic. The Church was still the "ark of salvation" for individual souls; there was little sense of vicarious responsibility either within it or towards the world around it. Had it been otherwise, the problems of personal predestination, and of prevenient and irresistible grace personally received, could have been alleviated.[1]

To St Benedict the emphasis is domestic, the Church—whether at Monte Cassino or outside—is a united family of God; self-contained in a complete life covering every aspect from making shoes to the *opus Dei*. But if Monte Cassino was complete and self-contained it was not the insular "ark of salvation". St Basil had formulated a monachism which was to serve the world in good works; in visiting the sick and succouring the poor. St Benedict followed him in the strong insistence on hospitality and on education. It is doubtful if

---

[1] St Augustine's individualist bias in the anti-Pelagian writings is to some extent countered by his teaching on the Mystical Body, especially in the *Enarrations on the Psalms*. But this is still some way from the Benedictine "family" concept.

either developed a doctrine of the full vicariousness of the Church; of the Body of Christ as the redemptive channel through which the love of God flowed on to the world. But the idea of monks as the world's intercessors is a short step from his corporate ideal and this was St Augustine of Canterbury's method in the mission to England. No doubt he and his forty companions preached and taught, but the converting power of the mission was plainly in the stable Canterbury community life.[1] And at the centre of that was the three-fold Rule.

These first two points together form St Benedict's most vital message to the Church to-day: *that loyalty to this basic threefold Rule—Mass, Office, devotion—is always the prior ascetical discipline.* It is the foundation of all Christian life, the essential work of the Church, the supreme intercession, the power of evangelism. It is of incalculably greater importance than all fasts, mortifications, and works whatsoever; the only function of which is to support it, without it all is a sham. As spiritual guides we must insist upon it; if we are true to the primitive Church, we must insist upon it; if we are true to our medieval heritage, we must insist upon it. If we think of Anglicanism in a narrower sense, let it be remembered that the seventeenth-century battles between Puritan and Caroline churchman were fought over the Prayer Book, especially over "set prayers". They were battles for and against Benedictine principles.

III. THE COUNSELS

As St Basil had taught a century earlier (and no doubt this was the source of St Benedict's teaching) obedience, poverty, and chastity are not monastic but Christian virtues. According to most Bene-dictine commentators, including St Bernard, obedience is to be "according to the Rule"; what we might call canonical obedience, holy obedience, or even loyalty, but certainly not servile submission.[2] This is to become even more pastoral with the interpretation of William of St Thierry, and is plainly needful in any creative Christian life.

Poverty may similarly be seen either as a part of monastic organiza-tion or as an ascetical principle, or both. It is the latter in which St Benedict is most interested: it is, in Bishop Augustine O'Neill's striking illustration, "the poverty of a workman's home,—who is

[1] Cardinal Gasquet, *Rule of St Benedict* (1925), introd., pp. xi–xii.
[2] Dom Cuthbert Butler, *Benedictine Monachism* (1919), pp. 141 foll.

earning good wages".[1] "For Benedictines to emulate the poverty
and nakedness so admirable in Franciscans would not be admirable
but fanatical. Benedictine virtue in this, as in most other things,
consists in keeping a happy mean between rigorism and laxity that is
the perennial problem of Black Benedictinism."[2] How very
Anglican!

Again following St Basil, chastity is both a practical monastic
rule and a general Christian virtue, applicable to both married and
single alike. The evangelical counsels have properly acquired a
monastic stamp, but in Benedictinism they are never isolated
virtues. They are always part of a composite ascetic–moral system,
and their absence, in any context, invariably means the presence of
all the capital sins. And that means the end of spiritual progress
towards the love of God.

IV. THE DAILY MINUTIAE

St Benedict's aim was to create the best possible conditions wherein,
as St John of the Cross was to say, "souls could best be placed so as
to receive the motions of the Holy Ghost". In Augustinian terms,
it was the kind of life which gave the greatest response to prevenient
grace. It was a lay movement, "a little Rule for beginners", comprising "a regime which was no more than was often imposed on
Christians living in the world".[3] "It is worthy of note that in St
Benedict's Instruments (*Regula*, 4; a list of moral and spiritual
precepts for daily use) there is nothing monastic or 'religious' in the
technical sense: they are all mere Christianity, elementary morality,
fundamental religion."[4] It is the core of practical teaching for all
time, applicable in detail to the ethos of succeeding ages and conditions. Yet at first sight, the minute regulations about food,
clothing, hours of sleep, and so on, seem fussy and unreal; but, like
the counsels, all these minutiae contain spiritual lessons which never
change. The good life is completely God-centred; St Benedict calls
the *opus Dei* "the praises of the Creator"; the Church is no longer
the ark of salvation, the society of saints, or the school for sinners,
but "the society of Divine praise".[5] The *orationes peculiares* should
be "short and frequent"—habitual recollection—and all is ordered
to achieve that end. The continual need to choose food and clothing

[1] Ibid., pp. 148ff.   [2] Ibid., p. 152.
[3] G. Morin, *The Monastic Ideal* (1908), p. iii.   [4] Butler, op. cit., p. 51.
[5] Cuthbert Butler, *Ways of Christian Life* (1932), pp. 188f.

is a distraction, so let all be regulated in the first place; both hunger and gluttony impair spiritual health, so let quantities be decided once and for all. It is not so much a matter of "moderation" as of getting things exactly *right*. What St Benedict is saying to us to-day is that regularity over the ordinary details of daily life helps towards continual recollective praise. If we do not have regular meals and sleep it is unlikely that we shall achieve orderly prayer. As V. A. Demant has pointed out, modern ascetical discipline might well consist in such things as regular solitude, resistance to "insidious commercial propaganda to increase our wants", and discipline over unceasing flippancies and amusements.[1] A solid habit of the evening Office at 7.10 followed by a family meal at 7.30, overriding all demands of radio and television, could constitute a creative *askesis*; Christian and Benedictine. If we look at modern life in logical ascetical terms, we must conclude that the coffee bar, self-service canteen, sandwiches between radio programmes, and the inability to stay in the same place for more than half a day, are far more spiritually destructive than a regular pint of beer or a flutter on the Derby.

V. THE BENEDICTINE SPIRIT

It is always difficult to describe the "spirit" of anything, but I hope I have already given some idea of how Benedictinism and Anglicanism have affinities in outlook and temperament. Two further aspects of the Benedictine ideal are relevant.

1. The "family" ideal is bluntly interpreted as of both supernatural and *natural* ties: "We find, as in St Thomas later, a religion rooted in Nature, an intimate relation between Nature and Grace, natural and supernatural."[2] The theme is beautifully treated by Dom Cuthbert Butler,[3] who sees here the ideal behind the "fourth counsel" of stability. In monasticism in general, the postulant seeks admission to an Order,[4] an ethos or way of life, while the Benedictine is stabilized in a single community, a family of such importance that numbers in any one house are rigidly limited. It is to be noted that the quarrel between the Cistercians and Cluniacs was not simply because Cluny was too rich and comfortable but because it was too

---

[1] *Christian Spirituality To-day* (1961), pp. 52–5.
[2] Butler, *Ways of Christian life*, pp. 5ff. [3] *Benedictine Monachism*, ch. 13.
[4] Ibid., p. 258: "there is no such thing as a Benedictine Order".

7—E.S.

big.[1] The pastoral implications are far-reaching, and it is beyond our scope to discuss questions of pastoral organization, but it might be mentioned that a faithful village community could be more spiritually creative than a parish of 20,000, and constitute "more important" work for a single priest. It might also be noted that, however you arrange churches, altars, and celebrants, a congregation of 500 can never be a Benedictine "family" with all that it stands for: how the faithful, and their priest, secretly long for the Mass on Monday morning!

"It may all be summed up in saying that, while for the friar or regular clerk *detachment* from any particular place is the ideal, in the monk *attachment* to his own one monastery is a virtue."[2] Here is an expression and elaboration of St Augustine's doctrine of creation, and a movement towards "the first form of contemplation" in the sense of harmony with environment.[3] It is not far-fetched to see here a fundamental *parochial* ascetic: "The life established by the Rule is nothing else than one that aims at carrying out to the full the Gospel precepts and Gospel counsels by a body of men living together under rule and discipline. These are the common sort of conditions under which men have to live and work out their salvation, as members of societies of various kinds, the family, the parish, the village."[4] Ch. 72 of the *Regula* is similarly described as "formal precepts for the community life, which indeed are golden rules for regulating the life of any family, natural no less than monastic."[5]

Although I felt obliged to coin the phrase "parochial theology" to describe corporate ascetical principle, it is hardly a new idea!

2. Following on the first point is the problem of personal relationships, especially as they affect spiritual guidance. Here, too, the "detachment" of Counter-Reformation teachers, the clerical frigidity of the French Oratorian ideal, is repellent rather than admirable to the Benedictine spirit. It is destructive of the family ideal and incompatible with empirical guidance. With a sly little dig at the seventeenth-century teachers, Dom Cuthbert hints that they must find the friendship between SS. Benedict and Scholastica, Bernard and Gerard, most unpalatable. "St Bernard clearly does

---

[1] Ibid., p. 210.   [2] Ibid., p. 201.
[3] See my *Pastoral Theology: a Re-orientation*, pp. 152–78, 263–6.
[4] Butler, *Benedictine Monachism*, p. 202.   [5] Ibid., p. 204; cf. *Regula*, ch. 63.

not come up to the standard of detachment required by St John of
the Cross and Fr Baker."[1] Presumably St Aelred of Rievaulx is
quite beyond the pale and Margery Kempe's Master Aleyne past
praying for. But "This is no Platonic or even merely spiritual
affection, but something very real and natural, in the good sense."[2]

> In all these things here enumerated—private prayer, devotions,
> austerities—Benedictines are free to follow their personal
> attractions, the only principle of choice being that which they
> find suits their spirit best and brings them nearer to God. . . .
> This is part of what is meant by "Benedictine liberty of
> Spirit"[3]. . . . His discipline is not military discipline, but the
> freer discipline of a well regulated family life. . . . The expression
> "well drilled" is sometimes applied to a community[4] as high
> praise; but a regiment is drilled, a family is not.[5]

It is plain that the freedom inherent in the English domestic
ethos, the "homeliness" of Julian and Margery, the pastoral
warmth of George Herbert, John Donne, and Nicholas Ferrar: all
this is no watered-down mediocrity, no pastoral amateurishness, but
a deep-rooted characteristic of Benedictine orthodoxy, springing
from the doctrine of the Church. This characteristic strain of
thought, beginning with the *Regula*, is still worthy of our serious
study. We neglect it at our peril.

Consider, as but one example, current thought on the remarkable
revival of the retreat movement. Book after book, conference after
conference, presents us with the advantages of both Benedictine and
Ignatian methods. Each is admirably presented by experts, and the
methods are analysed and compared. No one, so far as I know, has
ever bothered to mention that, whatever the intrinsic qualities of the
methods, it is the "older spirituality" of Benedictinism which alone
corresponds with English religion: it fits easily and naturally into a
retreat based on the Mass and twofold Office; the Ignatian method
does not.

[1] Ibid., p. 56.   [2] Ibid., p. 203.   [3] Ibid., p. 306.
[4] and congregation!   [5] Ibid., p. 206.

7

THE CISTERCIAN REFORM:
ST BERNARD

I. AFFECTIVE CHRISTOLOGY:
DE DILIGENDO DEO

St Augustine was perfectly clear about the Incarnation, and St Benedict's theocentricity based itself on the revelation of God in Christ. Developed further by St Gregory the Great, all this amounted to a restrained, orderly expression of praise to God centred on the Office and liturgy. It was the speculative and administrative side of ascetical theology, dealing mainly with that aspect of Christian life which, following St Thomas, we now call "proficiency". Now, with St Bernard, Christology is set on fire.

The debate continues as to what extent St Bernard is a speculative theologian whose teaching is reducible to some sort of order. The older view, held by Pourrat, that he is inspiring but hopelessly unsystematic, is countered by M. Etienne Gilson's brave attempt at classification.[1] We can compromise by regarding him as a thoughtful spiritual guide who is forced, perhaps against his inclination, to make some attempt at progressive schemes.

He hints at this in the *De Diligendo Deo*, introducing, at the same time, his psychological affinity with St Augustine: "Because we are flesh and were born of the desire of the flesh, our desire and our love necessarily take their beginning from the flesh, which, if directed aright, proceeding by certain stages of its own under the leadership of grace, will be at length perfected spiritually." The four "certain stages" of the *De Diligendo Deo* are: (1) "Man first loves himself for his own sake; he is flesh, and so incapable of knowing anything apart from himself."[2] Next comes the sense of dependence, thence

---

[1] *The Mystical Theology of St Bernard* (1940), see p. viii.

[2] All quotations are from Watkin Williams, *St Bernard of Clairvaux: De. Dil. Deo* (Cambridge Patristic Texts, 1926).

the idea of God and the second degree: (2) "he loves God, but for his own sake not for God's sake". (3) The third stage is the result of co-operation with grace by ascetical exercise: "when he has begun, prompted by his own needs, to worship God and frequently to seek his presence by meditation, by reading, by prayer, by obedience, from a certain familiarity in so doing little by little and sensibly God becomes known to him and in due course also sweet to him; and thus having tasted how sweet the Lord is (Psalm 33,9), he passes to the third degree and loves God no longer for his own sake but for God's sake. Verily in this degree he long remains". (4) For the fourth degree is perfection when "he loves himself solely for the sake of God".

It is illuminating to see how the cold, factual statements in the fourfold progression of St Augustine (*Enchiridion*, ch. 118) have here been made personal and affective. St Augustine had written: "man's first estate is to live according to the flesh in the profound darkness of ignorance, and without any opposition from reason. Next . . . with a knowledge of sin, while desiring to live according to law, he finds himself overcome: he sins with full knowledge, and becomes the subject and servant of sin."[1] There follows the conflict against concupiscence, aided by grace, and finally perfection when the full harmony is restored.

St Augustine and St Bernard are clearly saying the same thing, yet the former almost asks for long technical commentary while the latter is simple, pastoral, down-to-earth, and so deeply affective as immediately to inspire. The first is for a well-educated Roman, the second for illiterate peasant-monks. And it is the heart of Cistercian spirituality.

"Carnal love", in the first degree of Bernard, means not only selfishness but also that which is only perceptible to the senses. How, then, can God, who is Spirit, be loved "carnally"? How can stages 2 and 3 ever be reached? Only through the Incarnation; by "carnal" love towards the Sacred Humanity of Jesus Christ, which is the first step towards love for the divinity which it veils. "Here, then, is the place occupied in Cistercian mysticism by the meditation on the visible Humanity of Christ. It is but a beginning, but an absolutely necessary beginning."[2]

---

[1] Translated from Benedictine text by Ernest Evans (1953).

[2] Gilson *The Mystical Theology of St Bernard*, p. 79; cf. Louis Bouyer, *The Cistercian Heritage* (1958), pp. 46ff.

Bernard brought emotion into Christian Spirituality. He gave a place, and a fundamental place, to the "carnal love" of Jesus in the mysticism of the Word. He introduced a completely subjective psychology into spiritual teaching, which until then had been almost entirely absorbed with objective contemplation of the truths of the faith.[1]

That is how St Bernard and the Cistercian school form the affective complement to the doctrine of St Gregory Nazianzus and the anti-Apollinarian Fathers. St Bernard is careful to insist that the Sacred Humanity is indissociable from the Divinity in Christ; we may *begin* with the first only in order to *perceive* the second, yet the total process demands, again *first*, "carnal love".

It is by boldly facing the spiritual implications of the Sacred Humanity that led St Bernard to interpret the love of God in terms of *eros* and *philia* against the Augustinian *eros* and *agape*.

For it broke through the traditional "*reverentia*", the over-emphasis of the divine "self-sufficiency", which stood in the way of recognition and acceptance of a real mutuality in love between God and Man. The Bridegroom *delights* in the bride as she in Him.[2]

The bold carrying out of this doctrine makes Margery Kempe, in fourteenth-century England, the true spiritual daughter of Bernard. It is why she can love Christ in the *philia* sense while retaining St Bernard's own sense of humility: "the virtue by which man, knowing himself most intimately, is despicable in his own sight".[3] It is a development of St Augustine's stress on self-knowledge (not self-analysis) as the first rung of the spiritual ladder. The *De Gradibus Humilitatis* is an elaboration of the seventh chapter of the Benedictine Rule. It is with sublime simplicity and immaculate orthodoxy that Margery calls herself *both* "this creature" *and* the Lord's "dearworthy darling". Some of her penitential professions may sound a little strained, her physical expressions and crude endearments may shock us, yet she remains truly Cistercian and orthodox while so much modern devotion, nice as it sounds, is condemnable as Apollinarian pietism.

[1] Bouyer, op. cit., p. 65.   [2] J. Burnaby, *Amor Dei* (1938), p. 263
[3] *De. Grad. Hum.*, ch. 1, s. 2.

II. THE BLESSED VIRGIN AND ST JOSEPH

It is sometimes said, and written, that St Bernard had a special sense of devotion to the Blessed Virgin as if this was a pleasant whim rather than the theological consequence of his emphasis on the Sacred Humanity of her Son. Devotion to our Lady—and St Bernard probably invented that title—is the obvious safeguard against ascetical Apollinarianism, and our lack of such devotion to her is equally plainly the cause of its modern prevalence.

The Cistercian movement under St Bernard unwittingly gave rise to a good deal of error, of which English religion kept remarkably free. It is important therefore, that these corollaries to Bernardine spirituality are kept in strict theological perspective. A section of the modern Church is inclined to rebel against "Roman customs" or "medieval accretions" such as "devotion to St Mary and the cult of the Sacred Heart". Another section rushes to support these as elements of the true Catholic tradition. I think both sides are wrong in coupling together two kinds of devotion which, as the ascetical application of Christology, are almost diametrically opposed. Devotion to St Mary supports and strengthens orthodox Christology against Apollinarianism: if Mary is his mother, then Jesus is unquestionably man. But the "Sacred Heart of Jesus", although susceptible of theological interpretation, is in danger of supporting this heresy. A little crudity (and the twentieth century is not above that) and the Sacred Heart, even seen as the abstract expression of love, ceases to be quite human. Devotion to our Lady is Cistercian in its true sense, the Sacred Heart is a later accretion; both may be legitimate but, ascetically, they are very different.

St Bernard's devotion to St Joseph completes the idea of the Holy Family, and once again brings the Benedictine "domestic" ethos into effective spirituality. Meditation on the Holy Family, on our Lord, St Mary and St Joseph, and the spiritual and practical relations between them, is inexhaustible in its pastoral significance. Although with roots in Clairvaux, here is an emphasis in modern continental Catholicism we might well borrow, and absorb into our own tradition.

III. *DE CONSIDERATIONE* AND HOLY SCRIPTURE

That the Fathers of the Church were immersed in the Scriptures is a truism upon which Anglicanism bases her doctrinal position. But the patristic use of Scripture *was* theological. St Bernard introduces a new factor. It is misleading to compare the *De Consideratione* with modern meditation. In the twelfth century, "consideration" meant any quest for truth by any intellectual method, but, applied to the mysteries of our Lord's life, and coupled with an unbridled zeal for allegorical interpretation, a new and topical question arises. Is the Bible the ground of doctrine, a theological source-book? Or is it a devotional manual to stir up affection for our Lord's humanity? It may be both, and the relation between them is another problem which we must leave. But two small points of interest arise:

1. If allegorical or imaginative meditations on the Gospel narrative are legitimate means of confronting the Sacred Humanity, then the case for vernacular Scripture is proved. If such meditation is invalid, and a group of modern scholars think it is, then there is no case for an "open" Bible at all. But the Anglican insistence on the unity of the Church prohibits the idea of the Bible as a closed scholarly preserve: it is the book of the whole Church. So we return to the problem of how it is to be used in pastoral practice.

2. We shall see in section V of this chapter that St Bernard's stress on the Sacred Humanity led to two distinct traditions of devotion: imaginative meditation and semi-liturgical cults. Our fourteenth-century writers followed the former approach, thus creating a need for vernacular Scripture. If, therefore, Anglican biblical theology is traceable to the Fathers, English biblical devotion is traceable to St Bernard. The open English Bible is no sudden idea of the Reformers but is a logical development of tradition, arising out of affective devotion to the Sacred Humanity of Christ.

IV. PURITANISM

There is a strong puritan streak in the English character, the English temperament, and in English religion. But "puritanism" is an ambiguous word: it can mean an intense concern for personal morality, it can suggest austerity and iconoclasm, it can mean non-sacramental dualism, or simply a kill-joy dourness. More accurately it means a quest for "pure spirituality" or, to bend the word towards orthodoxy, it can mean ascetical simplicity. This last sense constitutes the "puritanism" of Clairvaux, and is, I suggest, the basis of our own proper tradition. This sort of puritanism means straightforwardness, or plainness. It rebels not so much against colour and gaiety as against extravagance; not against richness, but against complexity. We have noticed that St Bernard disliked Cluny not only because it was rich but because it was too big and too complicated, because it had departed from the Benedictine ideal of domestic simplicity; it had become an organized concern rather than a workman's home.

Both the Cistercian Reform and the English Reformation were movements towards primitive purity. In both cases the appeal is to an essential, workmanlike simplicity and against liturgical elaboration, against "medieval accretions" whether of Cluny or fifteenth-century Catholicism. It is often said that the Prayer Book needs "enrichment", which is a reasonable plea. But we must take care to avoid the errors of Cluny, which we failed to do, to take one example, in the Offices of 1928 with their complicated list of alternatives. The more recent liturgical movement follows the right pattern; away from Victorian Gothic, uselessly elaborate ceremonial, "fussiness", towards Cistercian simplicity. It is Abelard not Bernard who more nearly represents the colourless puritanism of the seventeenth and eighteenth centuries. It is in Abelard that we find the one-sided speculative strain without warmth and colour. Rightly or wrongly, we have sided with St Bernard, with the clear lines of English perpendicular against both the Baroque and the whitewashed shed.

V. THE DOUBLE DEVELOPMENT OF CISTERCIAN SPIRITUALITY

The towering figure of St Bernard overshadows everything else of his age, and his spirituality becomes synonymous with Cistercianism. But that is a mistake. In the first place, the Cistercian Order is far too big and varied to be regarded as a uniform block, basic characteristics notwithstanding. Secondly, there is a discernible division in pastoral emphasis between St Bernard and William of St Thierry, and it is to the latter that English religion inclines. In order to understand this important point it is necessary to look a little ahead.

Writing about the Canons Regular, J. C. Dickinson says:

Unlike the Augustinians, but like certain Protestants of later days, the Cistercians embarked on the perilous course of preaching religion and minimizing theology. It is no accident that both over-employed, and over-simplified, the word "conversion". Cistercianism did, of course, differ from this Protestantism in seeking to convert the world by sheer self-sacrifice within the sanctuary and not in the market place, but it is fundamentally allied to it and distinguished from the Augustinian life by appealing almost exclusively to the heart rather than the head.[1]

That might be true of St Bernard and was certainly true of some of his followers, but it is certainly not true of William of St Thierry, who embodied the remarkable combination of Cistercian spirituality with scholasticism.

This is what happened: St Bernard interpreted orthodox Christology in terms of affective devotion to the Sacred Humanity, centred on the Incarnation and manifested in the Christmas story. The Franciscan emphasis was more penitential, and throughout almost the whole of later medieval Christendom popular devotion moved from Christmas to Passiontide. In a faithful but illiterate age, how was this to find expression in pastoral religion?

The Benedictine school after Bernard gave rise to a group of mystics who can only fairly be described as exotic, and it is here that J. C. Dickinson's charge against what he too broadly calls Cistercianism is true. There were the weird "prophesies" of Joachim of Fiore which produced the heretical *flagellantes*, and the fantastic visions of the German Benedictines, like the angelic whippings of St Elizabeth of Schoenau. This kind of thing produced two effects which are significant to this study.

1. *Popular Devotion.* As a corollary to St Bernard's teaching, an unbridled affectiveness towards the humanity of Christ led to popular devotions centred upon particular aspects of his physical body. St Gertrude the Great initiated the cult of the Sacred Heart, the two St Mechtildes, of Hackborn and Magdeburg, cultivated devotion to the Five Wounds. The Franciscans developed the devotion we now know as the Stations of the Cross, and, rather out of character, the symbolism of the Christmas Crib. Devotional emphasis was placed on the Precious Blood and on supposed relics of the true Cross.

Devotions of this kind may be worthily used and they are susceptible of theological definition, but as the expression of Bernardine doctrine by illiterate people, ill-instructed by a notoriously lax and ignorant clergy, they are certain to be misunderstood. They were no doubt extensively used, and misunderstood, in medieval England,

[1] *The Origins of the Austin Canons* (1950), p. 176.

but if we look into our fourteenth-century writings we find scant reference to them and a different emphasis altogether. To whatever extent these devotions were popular, the English interpretation of St Bernard's doctrine by Hilton, Julian, Rolle, and Margery Kempe remains in general meditative prayer. In Julian and Margery in particular, devoted as they are to the Passion, the emphasis is still on the life of Jesus as a whole, with strong theological undercurrents. However concerned they are with Good Friday, they never lose sight of Christmas. Julian gives detailed descriptions of our Lord's "sweet face" (e.g. *Revelation* VIII), of his "blessed body" and "blessed flesh" (*Rev.* VIII). She "looked into His Side and beheld, rejoicing . . ." (*Rev.* X), but none of this is a special cultus; it is simply part of a detailed, imaginative meditation.

Whatever may be said for and against these methods of interpreting St Bernard, if we choose the first method of semi-liturgical cults to aspects of Christ's Body, then the prior pastoral need is for relics. If we follow Margery and Julian, the prior pastoral need is for vernacular accounts of the Gospel story. While German congregations were offering devotion to what they claimed to be relics of the blood of Christ, Julian was saying "the dearworthy blood of Our Lord Jesus Christ as verily as it is most precious, so verily it is most plenteous".[1] Despite the vividness of this affective devotion, the emphasis is eucharistic and theological. Julian is saying that the true blood of Christ, rather than being tiny drops deposited in reliquaries, is an inexhaustible river flowing from the Blessed Sacrament and washing the world from sin. It is affective devotion, yet it is also atonement doctrine, and, as we shall see later,[2] intensely pastoral theology.

2. *The Priesthood.* St Bernard's main emphasis led naturally to a new devotional approach to the eucharistic "body"; again it is not difficult to see how easily his doctrine could be crudely misinterpreted. Apart from "superstition", the Mass now begins to become dissociated from everything else in the Benedictine scheme; it becomes the sole lay obligation while the daily Office is seen as an entirely clerical matter. Here is the start of the notorious medieval divorce between priest and laity, supplementing the existing gulf between monastic and secular. The gulf is widened by the outpourings of mystical saints like Hildegarde and Bridget of Sweden

[1] *Revelations*, IV.   [2] Ch. 17, section III below.

against an admittedly lax and probably immoral clergy. It was they who tried to improve the position by preaching an extreme and sometimes puerile sacerdotalism: how could priests be so wicked when they "made God" at the altar? when their holy hands touched the very flesh of Christ at the consecration? Thus begins the clerical tradition where the priest, instead of being an ordained functionary within the Mystical Body, becomes a sacerdotal demi-god above and outside it: the tradition wherein the Eucharist is offered by the priest not by the Church, by the priest not by Christ himself.

It is unlikely that the general run of parish priests in England were much better than their brothers in Germany and Sweden, yet the merest glance through the *Book of Margery Kempe* suggests something quite different. Her relations with her confessors and directors, with the curates of King's Lynn, and with the reigning archbishops, show a Church which, whatever its shortcomings, was a united pastoral organism. One can imagine the English village priest digging his garden and getting drunk, but treating his parishioners with affection and not worrying overmuch about his holy sacerdotal hands. Once more the English Church is shown to have rejected "clericalism", not because her clergy are untrained amateurs but because it rejected this particular strain of post-Bernardine spirituality.

Whatever side is taken in the controversy between M. Gilson and Père Pourrat, it is safe to say that St Bernard is certainly not easy either to classify or to formulate into doctrine. He is one of the greatest of the Church's saints, and we must try to understand the true greatness of the other Cistercian and Benedictine saints like Hildegarde, Gertrude, and Bridget. Yet this whole movement sounds the loudest of warnings against the divorce of affective from speculative spirituality. During this period, English religion in general heeded the warning, for its Cistercianism was not so much that of St Bernard as that of William of St Thierry.

8

WILLIAM OF ST THIERRY

I. PSYCHOLOGY

William's conception of the workings of the human soul is formed by a synthesis of the teaching of Origen, Augustine, and Gregory of Nyssa; all of which is concisely worked out and tabulated by Louis Bouyer in *The Cistercian Heritage*.[1] The fundamental position he describes thus:

> Following his Greek sources, William used as his basis to explain the structure of the soul 1 Thess. 5. 23, where St Paul himself distinguished "the spirit, the soul and the body" in man: *pneuma, psyche, soma*. In countless passages elsewhere St Paul mentions the *nous*, i.e., the specifically rational element in the soul. Origen, on this point followed by William, built up a threefold division of the soul. The *psyche* is the soul in its vegetal aspect, in so far as it gives life to the body. The *nous* is the soul in its rational aspect, in so far as it belongs to itself and is conscious of itself apart from the body. The *pneuma* is the soul in its specifically 'spiritual' aspect, in so far as it is made for God and is capable of apprehending Him. In William's usual terminology, *psyche* will be *anima; nous, animus;* and *pneuma, spiritus*.[2]

This is allied to Augustine's theology and may be equally well used to explain the advent of concupiscence and the acquisition of *tranquillitas*. But there is one significant difference. Augustine insisted on the integrity of man; body, mind, spirit in an indissociable relationship, whether in a proper harmony or not. Nevertheless, body, mind, spirit, *mens, cogitatio, amor*, especially when seen in the disharmonious state of concupiscence, cannot but sound like warring factions, like "faculties".

William's teaching is sufficiently distinctive on this point to suggest a religious psychology so modern as to remind us of F. R.

---

[1] See especially ch. 5. [2] Ibid., p. 94; see also p. 100.

Tennant or James Ward. His conception is dynamic, not static; the human soul is characterized by *activity*, by process, and indeed progress. *Anima, animus, spiritus*, rather than being faculties or modes, are forms of the integrated soul's activity, they are stages in its growth; in fact, the Three Ways. In his translation of *The Golden Epistle* (1930), Walter Shewring underlines the point by seeing William in the light of the personal interpretation of the Three Ways which is to be expounded by St Thomas: *anima, animus, spiritus* become equated with Beginners, Proficients, Perfect.[1]

Thus, *anima* is the whole person in its animal activity; "carnal" life. *Animus* is the whole person in the process of reasoning, and *spiritus* the whole person as it is influenced by grace, the soul in contemplation, or the soul loving: *amor*. This modern-sounding psychology, reminiscent of Tennant's attack on the "psychologist's fallacy" ("there is no such thing as the will, only a subject that wills")[2] has plain ascetical implications. In pastoral practice, spiritual guides are still tempted to think of "the will" and "the mind" as "faculties" more or less isolated from the person. Confronted with lust and spiritual sloth in the same penitent, we are still apt to think of two aspects of him rather than of the person confronted with two kinds of temptation. Here William gives us sound psychology, both modern and biblical, framed by the Three Ways properly interpreted as overlapping stages of spiritual growth, not as static states. The four stages of the 118th chapter of *Enchiridion* are again made alive and personal, while the four degrees of the *De Diligendo Deo*, though remaining affective, are kept in hand by reason. William of St Thierry strikes the final death-blow to "spirituality" in the narrow pietistical sense. And he is more practical still: without disappointment we ask how this progress is to be achieved.

II. "EXTERNAL" AND "INTERNAL" FAITH

As the animal soul passes to reason, or if you like, as a child grows up, it is presented with the facts of the faith: catechism. But these facts are "external" to it; the child is shown them as it might be shown a picture. The next step is for this truth to be rendered "internal"; it is to be "absorbed" into the personality by the reasoning soul, *animus*. "Mere belief is not enough; he must model

---

[1] Translation of *The Golden Epistle*, ch. 5.

[2] See Philosophical Theology (1928), Vol. I, pp. 17n, 131.

his whole life on what he loves, and hopes for, and believes in."[1]
Following Augustine, knowledge is inseparable from love because
one cannot love what one does not know. William, moreover,
thinks of knowledge in the intimate biblical sense of Gen. 4.1,
and Luke 1.34 (*ginosko*); and all is acquired, absorbed, made
internal, by a process we should now call "intellectual meditation": we have moved from discursive learning to contemplative
love.

> What, indeed, do we mean by believing in Jesus, unless it be
> going to Him with our love? Those people believed that He was
> Christ, the Saviour anointed for their salvation, but they did not
> love Him as they should have done. That is why Jesus would not
> trust Himself to them, for He knew without being told that they
> did not recognize Him for what He really was. Whereas, if they
> had known His true identity they could not have helped loving
> Him.[2]

Here we have the Cistercian system reduced to order but without
losing its affective warmth. The Sacred Humanity is first known by
meditation on the Gospel story: a picture of Christ is formed
"externally"; composition of place and subject as in the first point of
a three-point meditation. Then, under the inspiration of grace,
knowledge turns to love which forges a unity, St Bernard's *philia*;
love of Christ's manhood becomes "internal". Finally, through the
Humanity as it were, Divinity is perceived and the Godhead adored
in Christ. The ideal

> is faith incorporated into our whole life and refashioning it by its
> influence. It is the shining of faith into a soul which has gradually
> been made capable of penetrating the mysteries of faith by its
> attempt to yield itself to what Scripture calls the "obedience of
> faith". By a lively understanding—that is, the understanding of a
> heart attuned to the heart of God who speaks to it—the soul will
> thereby discover living truths, or better still, a single living truth,
> in what at the beginning seemed a mere conglomeration of
> enigmas.[3]

This is contemplation, the true simplicity, a virtue hard-won by
spiritual struggle and active surrender. William gives important

[1] *The Mirror of Faith*, ch. 4.   [2] Ibid., ch. 13.
[3] Bouyer, *The Cistercian Heritage*, pp. 103f; cf. *The Mirror of Faith*, ch. 11.

practical teaching about meditation in the modern sense of an isolated spiritual exercise, but this is neither enough nor quite what he means. He means, as we shall see better in the next section, no less than an integrated life of religious discipline in which habitual recollection plays a large part:

> Piety is the perpetual mindfulness of God, the continual striving of the will to the understanding of Him, the unwearied affection to the loving of Him; so that—I say not, no day—but no hour may ever find the servant of God save in the labour of exercise and zeal of advancing, or else in the sweetness of feeling and bliss of enjoying.[1]

Here, too, is the affective–speculative synthesis beautifully expressed.

William of St Thierry is assuredly "our" Cistercian, not least when, throughout *The Mirror of Faith*, he demolishes three errors of which English religion to-day must beware. The first is narrow "spirituality", prayer divorced from the rest of life; the second, a lazy quest for a "simple" faith, seen as something comfortably static and almost the direct opposite to hard-won "simplicity"; the third, intellectualism, the pastoral ideal of merely "instructed" Christians. Against all this, *The Mirror of Faith* could be the *locus classicus* of the ascetical approach; of supporting theological thinking against merely knowing a lot of theology.

Bouyer sums it up well: "Faith will never be what it ought to be if it remains an abstract conception of the mind. The whole and entire man must be unreservedly involved in his acceptance of the truth that comes from outside."[2]

It is interesting to note the similarity of this teaching to Tennant's distinction between "belief" as cognitive and intellectual, and "faith" as conative and the source of activity.[3] "Absorbed" faith is also plainly recognized in the Prayer Book Collects for Advent II and Trinity VII.

III. *OBOEDIENTIA NECESSITATIS* AND *OBOEDIENTIA CARITATIS*

William thought in Benedictine terms, where obedience was primarily the third counsel of monastic Order. But as with the

---

[1] *The Golden Epistle*, chs. 1,4, but see note, p. 105 below. [2] Op. cit., p. 105.
[3] Op. cit., Vol. I, pp. 297ff.

Regula, his teaching is easily adaptable—if indeed it needs adaptation at all—to Christian and pastoral terms. Monastic obedience is to the Superior, and we have seen that it is "holy" and "canonical", not servile submission. The Superior embodies the spirit and principle of the Order, in other words the *Regula* itself, so it is no great step to see necessary obedience, whether monastic or secular, as loyalty to the fundamental Rule of the Church. Similarly, if there is any sense in which spiritual directors are to be obeyed, it must be in so far as they direct and interpret ascetical and moral theology. They are called upon to give "counsel", not "advice".[1]

William divides obedience into two kinds in a progression: *necessary obedience*, which is loyalty to the discipline of the Church personally interpreted by a spiritual guide, and *loving obedience*, which is its affective and contemplative result. The first is exercised in the virtues of faith and hope, the second is qualified by charity. St Bernard had hinted at this progression in the second degree of the *De Diligendo Deo*: "yet indeed when he has begun, prompted by his own needs, to worship God and frequently to seek his presence by meditation, by obedience, by reading, by prayer, from a certain familiarity in so doing little by little and sensibly God becomes known to him, and in due course also sweet to him". William works it out much more fully, especially in ch. 3 of *On the Nature and Dignity of Love*: "The constant help of careful and enduring prayer must be sought . . ." And in ch. 13 of *The Mirror of Faith*: "Grace, which is spiritual, is gradually developed in us through the Sacraments which we receive with our bodies." This is simply the doctrine of prevenient grace; we must first respond to God's love before we experience sensible devotion, and we must persevere in obedience to the Church's Rule which is the way of response. Sacramental grace is "gradually developed", it "adds up" with each Communion and affective states may not be achieved for some time: grace is *not* Cassian's dose of tonic.

This teaching is also common sense: young children obey their parents "necessarily"; they have no choice, for they are dependent upon them. But such obedience draws child and parent together and gradually the child understands the benefits he has received by the parental rules laid down for his wellbeing. He develops a more mature affection for his parents and obeys lovingly rather than necessarily.

[1] See *Christian Proficiency*, pp. 42f.

A humble and loving submission to authority brings peace to the soul. It brings security to blind faith, until such time as the Holy Spirit comes, giving understanding of what the ear has heard. . . . But if we neglect to depend on authority at the beginning of our life of faith, we inevitably take the wrong road, being guided by our unaided reason. . . . These are but the first stages in our apprenticeship to the love of Christ, and while we undergo them our faith becomes gradually clearer and brighter.[1]

In such a context, it is natural that *The Mirror of Faith* should continue with teaching on aridity, coldness, desolation and periodicity, for much of this first stage in the spiritual life consists in endurance, stamina, loyalty, discipline and duty.[2] But William raises all these above moralism and convention. They are carefully explained in terms of ascetical theology which, if the Church's experience means anything at all, is certain to attain its object of growth towards affective devotion, the Illuminative Way, or *oboedientia caritatis*: from the obedience of necessary duty to the obedience of loving response.

Here are pinpointed two of the greatest needs in modern Anglican life: the sense of *continuity* in Christian living, and the sane *authority* of the Rule of the Church. Holy Communion, the Offices, periods of private prayer, are not isolated attempts to obtain doses of Cassianic grace, but links in a continuous chain of life in grace; a continuous response to God's never-ending love in a marriage solemnized at our Baptism. When duty is dull we might remember that washing the dishes can be just as much an act of marital love as an embrace.

As spiritual guide, William would not understand a request for a "rule of life"; to him there is only one, the threefold Benedictine system, and the Book of Common Prayer agrees with him. He would see little more than hypocrisy in a prayer for the guidance of the Holy Spirit before a meeting of a Parochial Church Council whose members were irregular at the altar and neglectful of the Office. Our "National Days of Prayer" he would regard as farcical: none of this through emotional feeling against laxity, but because he would see no logic in isolated prayers, no purpose without continuity.

On spiritual guidance itself, this teaching is equally useful. In our natural or carnal state—*anima*—reason is blinded by sin, and

[1] *The Mirror of Faith*, chs. 7, 13.
[2] Ibid., ch. 9; cf. *On the Nature and Dignity of Love*, ch. 4.

although we desire to grow in charity, we are incapable of seeing our real state or the way in which we should go. We must renounce our own view of things for the very practical reason that it is bound to be wrong. We cannot rely entirely on conscience, which, even if well trained, is always fallible.

Faith is just this, to receive from outside a view of things which comes from God and not from ourselves . . . *oboedientia necessitatis* is what gives this reality to faith. In surrendering ourselves into the hands of another who represents Christ to us, the will itself will be penetrated by faith. For the obedience by which the will binds itself to another only extends to the whole of life that initial acceptance of an absolute dependence which is the act of faith.[1]

That of course is monastic, yet it lifts any conception of obedience or spiritual guidance into the sane realms of ascetical theology. Guidance is necessary because we cannot see ourselves, there is no legal authoritarianism, nor any question of evading our responsibilities: it is all part of an honest, practical attempt to respond to the love of God in the face of clearly revealed facts of doctrine. Empirical direction, after the English manner, may soften William's monastic thought, yet it strengthens the ideal of obedience to Christ offered mutually by those in Christ; the ideal of mutual strengthening inherent in the directional relationship itself.[2]

IV. THE EUCHARIST

The foregoing doctrine is clearly linked with, and illustrated by, William's teaching on the eucharistic mystery, for here is the peak of the external–internal faith reaction. In the Eucharist, the whole faith is presented sacramentally and, at first, externally; it is the faith symbolized, pictured, before our eyes. But all this is to be "absorbed", made internal, made part of our very being, overflowing into every minute and every corner of life. And this is what literally happens in Holy Communion: the real presence of Christ is spiritually seen and adored at the consecration, then he becomes part of us in communion.

William would approve the value of attendance at Mass by children, or adults, prior to Confirmation; not simply to "get to know what happens" or "to learn the service", or even to get into a

[1] Bouyer, op. cit., p. 105.   [2] See *The Golden Epistle*, ch. 6.

good habit, but to *see* the faith externally as preparation to its contemplative absorption. He would also approve E. L. Mascall's phrase, that we are to be "liturgical men", for here is the same emphasis on continuity, and on the eucharistic life as the essential life of the whole Church. This doctrine supports the English conception of unity between all members of the Church Militant, and argues against the priest–lay gulf. William could not have been too happy with the idea of "hearing Mass", for that stops short at "external" faith.

Obviously the Mass is at the very centre of the demands of necessary obedience; merely to attend is important, but Holy Communion is also the most efficacious means of attaining *oboedientia caritatis*. William is sometimes regarded as the exponent of "spiritual communion", but this is misleading if it refers to the modern, isolated act of recollection during sickness or other hindrance. What he teaches is a general, habitual recollection of Holy Communion as the central activity of Christian life, not only of the individual but of the whole Church. We should constantly recollect the fact that we have communicated, or rather that we are, every moment of the day, communicants. To absorb, to internalize, that is to *receive*, is the whole point. Again prayer links itself with the Eucharist, for in prayer the sacrament is "digested" and grace becomes crystallized into ideas and resolutions.

The priesthood is functional within the Body of Christ, but the whole Body is Eucharistic:

the right to celebrate the mystery of this holy and awful commemoration belongs to a few men only, to whom this ministry is committed, and that in its proper manner, time and place; but the thing signified by this Sacrament and mystery can at all times and in all places where God is Lord, in the proper manner commanded—that is, with affection and proper piety—be readily accomplished, handled and received into themselves for their salvation, by all men to whom it is said: "ye are a chosen generation, a royal priesthood, an holy nation, a peculiar people . . .[1]

Apart from the unity of the Church, the function of priesthood within it, and the continuity of eucharistic grace, that passage also stresses habitual recollection of a particular type. It is the state of

[1] *The Golden Epistle*, I, 10.

recollection inspired by an internal absorption, thence a deep consciousness of our supernatural status; the habitual knowledge that we are incorporated into Christ at Baptism, that we share in his Sacred Humanity and live on his Body and Blood.

V. MORAL THEOLOGY

Man is made in the image of God. Characteristically, St Bernard interpreted this doctrine subjectively and affectively; he saw the image as elemental free-will, never wholly lost and tending naturally, if sometimes weakly, towards the good. It is this image which is defaced by sin, and which can be obliterated by mortal sin.

William of St Thierry, going back to Irenaeus, distinguishes between the "image" of God in man and his "likeness" to God. The first is ontological, it is an ineradicable imprint upon the soul, like that associated with the initiatory sacraments of Baptism and Holy Order. It is the "likeness" which is blurred or lost by sin. Following Augustine, the image is the imprint of the Holy Trinity upon the soul: *mens*, a subconscious memory of God, *cogitatio*, reason which draws us nearer to the knowledge of God, and *amor*, love, the final consummation or union with God. Concupiscence blurs memory and reason, and destroys love.[1] Christian life, therefore, consists in the gradual restoration of our "likeness" to God, while the "image" remains hidden but intact: "Beloved, now are we the sons of God, and it doth not yet appear what we shall be: but we know that, when he shall appear, we shall be like him; for we shall see him as he is."[2] William seeks support for this in the older and simpler doctrine of Augustine and Gregory of Nyssa: God is omnipresent, therefore indelibly in the human soul; otherwise the soul would not exist, for only by the love of God is all creation sustained in being. Carried over into moral theology, this issues in a fundamental pastoral division of much importance to our own tradition, and indeed, to our own day. It is here that William of St Thierry is to be opposed by St Thomas Aquinas; the English pastoral tradition firmly follows William.

In the fifth chapter of *On the Nature and Dignity of Love*, William teaches that it is possible to commit sin without falling from grace or losing charity. He seeks support from the denial of St Peter: "Peter did not lose charity when he sinned, for he sinned rather against

[1] See E. Gilson, *The Mystical Theology of St Bernard* (1940), pp. 212ff.
[2] 1 John 3.2.

truth than against charity. He lied when he said that he did not belong to the One to Whom he did in fact belong, heart and soul. The truth of charity washed away the lie with his tears." This chapter is notoriously difficult and controversial, but what clearly emerges is that pastoral distinction which the Caroline, and English tradition generally, was to accept: the distinction between sins of "infirmity" and "malice" rather than between sins "venial" and "mortal". The former is clearly expressed in the same chapter:

> The weakness of the flesh often causes it to stumble and fall, causing serious harm and inward pain to the soul. But the soul suffers and submits rather than taking positive action in the exterior evil done. It does not lose charity by its failings; it is charity precisely which makes it grieve and cry out to God: "unhappy man that I am, who shall deliver me from the body of this death."

Here is also support for Caroline moral theology in its strong insistence on the efficacy of personal penitence.

William is denying that definition of mortal sin which speaks of the soul as "cut off from God", or inevitably falling from the state of grace. This is because of the indelible "image" of God with which the baptized soul is endowed; an incorporation into Christ which cannot be undone: "The seed of his spiritual rebirth, which is from God, protects him within" is clearly a reference to Baptism. In pastoral terms, William is taking the classical nuptial metaphor out of the mystical clouds and bringing it down to earth. He is saying, in effect, that if man and woman, or man and God, are ontologically united in marriage or baptism, then no amount of quarrelling, infidelity, or even separation, can break the union: there is no way (not even by "mortal" sin) to become unmarried, unbaptized, or unordained. St Thomas, although he gets over the difficulty in a complicated way by making a series of subtle distinctions between types of grace, nevertheless implies a whole series of divorces and remarriages through the confessional. That, at least, is the only way the ordinary penitent can see it.

William is in tune with, and perhaps an inspiration of, the sane, pastoral optimism which characterizes the fourteenth-century English school. This has a profound effect on English penitential practice. The distinction is that the medieval scholastic and modern Roman systems regard the confessional primarily as restorative and

juridical. William and Anglicanism see confession primarily as an
act of worship, an expression of penitential love. The first deals in
carefully graded juridical distinctions, issuing from the mortal–
venial classification, the second makes a generous prostration at the
foot of the Cross; if there is any question of reinstatement to a lost
position, it is the reconciliation of husband and wife—who have
remained "married" during estrangement—rather than the acquittal
of a prisoner.

This means that self-examination by meticulously graded lists of
questions, and carefully classified penances applicable to carefully
classified confessions, have little place in traditional English pastoral
practice. In William Beveridge's succinct words: "We do not stand
upon fine points with God Almighty". K. E. Kirk typifies pastoral
sanity when he describes the mortal–venial distinction as "unreal
from the point of view of God, dangerous from the point of view of
the sinner, but real and valuable from the point of view of the
priest."[1] Scholastic intricacy, in other words, can be a useful map or
pattern in the back of the confessor's mind, while a smattering of
knowledge of the mortal–venial system continues to do much
harm to penitents.

VI. THE SPECULATIVE–AFFECTIVE SYNTHESIS

It should be clear from the foregoing that William of St Thierry is
concerned to balance the one-sided affectiveness of St Bernard. In
fact, the *Enigma of Faith* is virtually a treatise on this very point:
affective devotion and theology are here shown as interacting
one with another. Devotion will go astray if it is not bridled
by doctrine, and divine learning, if it is truly incarnational, must
lead into affective prayer; reason and love are two parts of one
thing.

Charity, as we have seen, is the soul's natural light, and was
created by the Author of Nature for seeing God. There are two
eyes to this spiritual vision, forever straining to see the light which
is God, and their names are Love and Reason. . . . And when I
say that these two help each other, I mean that reason instructs
love, and love enlightens reason. Reason merges into the

[1] *Some Principles of Moral Theology* (1920), p. 247; cf. T. J. Bigham: "This
definition seems to involve some slight to the Divine holiness, is liable to laxist
abuse, and is of great pastoral use" (*unpublished source*).

affectivity of love, and love consents to be limited by reason. Then it is that they can achieve great things.[1]

VII. THE EREMITICAL IDEAL

As Bouyer points out,[2] it seems curious that a Cistercian should appear so enthusiastic about the solitary life, and one sometimes wonders whether, in this instance, William's loyalty to Origen has not outrun his prior loyalty to St Benedict. But, on consideration, he is looking forward not back, for the solitary life as he conceived it was not that of Origen and the Egyptian Desert, but rather the Carthusian compromise. It was the solitude of the cell within a group or community. It is interesting that the Carthusians themselves made little headway in this country, but the ideal became strongly embodied in the English anchorite. The *Ancrene Riwle*, our earliest significant ascetical treatise, Hilton's *Scale of Perfection*, and some of Rolle, were directions to individual anchoresses, living, like Julian, in cells attached to parish churches. The English anchorite presents a particularly pastoral form of the Carthusian ideal which so interested William of St Thierry: perhaps it has something to do with our inherent individualism.

VIII. ST AELRED OF RIEVAULX

St Aelred well deserves his popular title, "the Bernard of the North", although "the William of the North" might perhaps be even more apposite. The speculative strain in his writings is more pronounced than in Bernard, perhaps rather less pronounced than in William. His chief works, *The Mirror of Charity* and *On Spiritual Friendship*, are spiritual classics of much worth, the former being of pronounced Augustinian flavour. But, to confine ourselves to ascetical doctrine, there is nothing very new in Aelred that cannot be found either in Bernard or William.

His main importance here is in his legendary personification of the humanistic, empirical director of souls, which later was to become so pronounced in the English pastoral tradition. He followed the English fashion by writing a *Rule for Recluses* to an anchoress who was probably his natural as well as his spiritual sister. It is thoroughly Benedictine, steeped in the Bible, and probably the best example we have—certainly to date—of meditation which successfully

[1] See also *On the Nature and Dignity of Love*, ch. 7.
[2] *The Cistercian Heritage*, p. 101

combines restrained allegory with affective, imaginative freedom. The section on the Passion, chs. 10–13, has marked similarities with both Margery Kempe and Julian of Norwich.

NOTE
The Authorship and validity of the "*Golden Epistle*"

Doubts have been cast on the authorship of the *Epistola ad Fratres de Monte Dei de Vita Solitaria*, commonly called *The Golden Epistle*. It has been attributed to St Bernard, William of St Thierry, and others; Pourrat bluntly says that the author is "unknown", *The Oxford Dictionary of the Christian Church* says that William's authorship is "probably correct". It is plainly in line with the Bernard–William development of Cistercian spirituality, and the technical problem need not detain us.

More important are attacks made upon its orthodoxy, notably by Jean Gerson. It seems to teach a doctrine of impeccability, that it is possible to become virtually sinless in this life, shades of which are also found in *On the Nature and Dignity of Love*. I think this could fit in with William's strong optimism about human nature—and his even stronger faith in the efficacy of grace—having here got a little out of hand. It is an important point but one rather removed from the problems of pastoral guidance. Gerson's main criticism is directed against very technical points of mystical theology which do not concern us.

THE SCHOOL OF ST VICTOR

I. THE AUSTIN CANONS REGULAR

The Austin (Augustinian) Canons bear but a tenuous relation to
St Augustine, but their inception, in the eleventh century, was
inspired by the development of his teaching. At Hippo, Augustine
had gathered a group of clergy around him who bound themselves
by the Evangelical Counsels and embraced a common Rule. The
basis of the new "Augustinian Rule" was this example supplemented by the so-called Letter 211; one of the vast quantity of
letters of direction written by Augustine to women religious. The
establishment of the Austin Canons was part of the Gregorian
reform directed against clerical laxity, not least among cathedral and
collegiate establishments. Their foothold in England owed much,
significantly, to St Anselm, while their eventual popularity fitted
well into that pastoral synthesis upon which English spirituality
seems always to thrive. The *via media* here is that between monastic
and secular clergy, between Regular and laity, thus pointing to the
pastoral ideal—like the Book of Common Prayer—of one united
Church Militant.

We have remarked that by this time the "Land of the Benedictines" had almost become the "Land of the Cistercians".
Through the agricultural activities of the latter, fitting in with the
manorial system, England now became more and more parochial.
This made a suitable setting for the Canons Regular, who remained
diocesan clergy living under common but elastic Rule.[1]

The relations between Canons Regular and secular clergy, and
their fulfilment of parochial duties, is a complicated question. It is
probable that the "Regular" aspect of things, that is the maintenance of the Rule as vicarious and intercessory, took precedence over
what we would now call, or miscall, "parish work". But the ideal

[1] Societies like the Company of Mission Priests and the Oratory of the Good
Shepherd are perhaps our nearest modern equivalents to the ideal.

itself is important and there is no doubt that it was congenial to English religious life.[1] On the other hand Robert of Bridlington must have shocked some of his contemporaries—and remember that we are dealing with clerical reform—by stressing the very English conception of the priesthood as partaking of that of Christ the Carpenter: "It is by no means unbecoming that those bound to the Service of the Holy Altar should be chosen for such agricultural labours as to plough, sow, reap, mow hay with a sickle, and make a haystack."[2] The English parson farming his glebe and even disporting himself on the Village Green has a long theological tradition behind him: a point which might be pondered by those Anglicans whose clerical ideal seems to be something between St Bridget of Sweden and the Seminary of St Sulpice.

By their ideals, their popularity, and the number of their houses, the Canons must have exerted considerable influence in English parishes: "Discerning minds . . . realized that the regular canonical ideal, far from being a spiritual second best, as the monks were apt to regard it, was an ideal worthy of the highest admiration".[3] The true *via media* again. But it is their intellectual achievements in the sphere of ascetical theology that really concern us; the influence of which on English spirituality there can be no doubt.

The attitude of the first regular canons, like that of the Elizabethan Reformers . . . strove to lead a life formulated as a result of careful study of the Church's past. They studied previous *canones* as the Anglican Reformers probed the primitive Church. As the Anglican tradition was maintained by an unbroken line of donnish defenders, so the regular canons, at least in their heyday, included within their ranks more than their share of the learned. The delicate balance which the Book of Common Prayer sought to maintain between "true piety and sound learning" was exactly the task on which the regular canons were mostly engaged. . . .

This intensely historical approach to the past—beside which St Bernard's vague appeals to primitive practice appear as amateurish as early Protestant objections to Anglicanism—gives us the whole ethos of the order[4]

[1] See J. C. Dickinson, *The Origins of the Austin Canons* (1950), p. 224.
[2] From the *Bridlington Dialogue*, xiv.
[3] Dickinson, op. cit., p. 179.   [4] Ibid., p. 176.

But:

Had St Augustine returned to the later Middle Ages to witness the varied use made of the Rule which bore his name he might well have been surprised. There is no reason to believe he would have been displeased.[1]

Apart from more important things, those two quotations offer support to the approach I am attempting in this book: any satisfactory spirituality for the twentieth century, especially Anglican spirituality, can only evolve by serious study of our ancient tradition, plus bold experiment.

II. THE SCHOOL OF ST VICTOR

By their ideals and by their nature, the Canons Regular were admirably fitted to rectify two errors which had crept into Christian prayer, and which remain constant dangers.

1. The first is formalism. St Benedict inaugurated the threefold Rule of the Church as absolutely fundamental to all Christian life. But, even when there is no question of omitting any part of it, private devotion itself may become formal and cold. In spite of St Bernard's affective Christology, and of the meditations of saints like William of St Thierry and Aelred of Rievaulx, secular devotion had become formalized. Isolated from the basic Rule, the duty to "hear Mass" was the sole lay obligation. If anything was added to this it was the semi-liturgical devotions into which St Bernard's teaching had hardened. This formalist tendency is countered by that peak of ascetical achievement among the Canons Regular, the School of St Victor in Paris. From now on, this stream of spirituality is to be called not Augustinian but Victorine, and the English fourteenth century is to become saturated with its spirit.

In private devotion, the ideal is a synthesis between ordered method and personal freedom of spirit. Over-emphasis on the first, sometimes associated with St Ignatius Loyola, leads to formalism; exaggeration of the second, the danger inherent in St Bernard, usually ends in sentimentality, or even mere day-dreaming. The Victorines achieved an almost miraculous synthesis which is to be typified in the *Revelations* of Julian of Norwich: an expansive liberty of spirit, yet disciplined by method and doctrine.

[1] Ibid., p. 180.

It is with them (wrote K. E. Kirk) that the word "meditation", with all that it stands for, first comes into prominence as a signpost for the Christian Pilgrimage . . . by their conception of "meditation" the mystics of St Victor introduced orderliness into prayer without quenching individuality . . . the Victorines insist that personal effort is of greater value than the traditional methods in meditation; but they insist as well that what distinguishes meditation from "reverie" is just the substitution of order for chaos. They opened up the way for a manner of prayer which should be at once personal and methodical[1]

Modern Anglican devotion may be assisted by both St Bernard and St Ignatius, but only when they are incorporated into, and disciplined by, the English–Victorine system. This will be more fully discussed in the next section.

2. We now come to the heart of Victorine ascetic: the spiritual significance of the doctrine of creation.

It is foolish to dub monasticism "otherworldly" in the sense of selfish, or irresponsible; yet introspection and pietism remain dangers against which the whole ideal of the Canons Regular militates. Nor is this danger confined to the cloister; it is the error of the "spike" who confines his religion to the sanctuary, and of those to whom "going to church" is the essence of the Christian life. But—and how our age needs reminding of this—the problem is not solved by divorcing ascetic from ethics; by "going to church" on the one hand, and glibly thinking of "Christian principles" in the form of social morality on the other. True Christianity is an integrated life, a continuity of liturgy, devotion, and practical affairs. It is useless to try to "relate religion to life", we have to achieve religious life: "religious experience" wrote William Temple, is the total experience of a religious man."[2]

The Victorines, therefore, stressed an orderliness of mind which grew out of orderliness of life: Rule in the Benedictine sense of a foundation which coloured every moment of every day. And orderliness of life, harmony, *tranquillitas*, logically point to the ascetical implications of creation. "Perhaps, therefore, it is a gain rather than a loss that the Victorines so far deserted the path taken by St Bernard as to prefer meditation upon the harmony of the

[1] *The Vision of God* (1931), pp. 374ff.   [2] *Christus Veritas* (1924), pp. 37 foll.

universe to meditation upon the person of Christ."[1] I think that
needs qualification, yet it pinpoints a truth so vividly expounded by
von Hügel: "that not even Jesus Christ and His Redemption
exhaust God."[2] Redemption cannot be dissociated from Creation.

St Augustine laid the foundation of ascetic by insisting that
spirituality is rooted in dogma; William of St Thierry improved
upon that by finding a place for St Bernard's affective Christology
within a speculative system. The Victorines make a further improvement by seeing spirituality nurtured not only by "religious"
doctrine but by all knowledge and experience whatsoever. And this
is because, by the doctrine of creation, everything is "religious".
The universe is "symbolic" of God, "science" is but one way
among many of probing its mysteries, of "meditating" upon the
created order to find out more and more about the mind of the
Creator. If so wild an anachronism is permissible, the saints of
St Victor would have been as worried as we are about stockpiles of
atomic bombs, but they would have applauded nuclear research.
The scientific facts behind nuclear fission are God's ideas not ours,
and their discovery is but further information about the mind of the
Creator: the moral problem is part of ascetics, science is part of
prayer, because creation and Incarnation are conjoined.

III. THE ASCETICAL THEOLOGY OF
HUGH OF ST VICTOR

Hugh's system for a complete, integrated Christian life consists in
three fundamental stages into which two others are incorporated,
thus giving a fivefold progression. We have a synthesis of two distinct
sources, the first comprising creation and "natural" religion, the
second incorporating the Incarnation and "revealed" religion. The
initial scheme follows Augustinian-Platonic thought which is
indigenous to St Victor, the second stems from St Bernard and
renders "natural" religion into Christianity. Originally there is (1)
The symbolic conception of the universe (2) *Intuitive meditation* upon
it, and (5) *Contemplation*. To this is added: (3) *Prayer*, centred on
Christ as "perfect symbol" and (4) *Progress in Goodness*, judged in
terms of Christian ascetic–moral doctrine. I have offered the thesis
that the whole life of Margery Kempe follows this pattern,[3] so it is of
some interest to English pastoral religion, and, I think, of consider-

[1] *The Vision of God*, p. 378.   [2] *Essays and Addresses*, II, pp. 217ff.
[3] *Margery Kempe*, pp. 28–49.

able relevance to modern spiritual guidance. The five stages are worth examination.

1. Creation is symbolic of the mind of the Creator, and the ascetical approach to it Hugh calls *reading*. To read a book one first looks at symbols, letters and words, followed by "meditation" until their significance, their inner meaning, is absorbed by the mind. Creation is similar; it is the visible expression of divine thought, the book which God has written. We have an idea akin to (but different in some respects from) the "divine visual language" of Bishop Berkeley. For Hugh is more Platonic than the natural religion of eighteenth-century England. Every part of creation, each individual "thing", carries an "idea", a thought which can teach true knowledge of God, not just a general sense of wonder at his harmonious works. Our vision of creation, moreover, is as through a mirror, reflecting the mind of God, which can only be read by constant application and discipline, of which acquired contemplation is the end.

We must, therefore, be very careful if we are to use the popular analogy of the painter and his picture as it applies to the relation between Creator and his creation. If we say that the picture expresses the mind of the artist we are only half-way to Hugh's teaching. Creation is still only mirrored,[1] we have no more than a reproduction of the original, and it is a difficult art-form. If the analogy is to help us, some sort of "abstract" or surrealist picture is needed, it must carry an intellectual meaning to be discovered by "meditation". Mere aesthetics, pictorial representation, even wonder, are not enough. Hugh is a very long way from sentimental nature cults, or from pantheism, while he is not so far from the "analogical discontinuity" of Aquinas.

This is an interpretation of the universe consonant with, and probably inspired by, the allegorical use of Scripture so popular at this time, and sometimes so fantastic to us. As philosophy it is unsatisfactory, but its strong and valid point is that creation, made up of visible and tangible "things", is ascetically important, and to be taken seriously by discipline of mind and body. We are approaching the "first form of contemplation" as an acquired religious and

[1] The popularity of this image is to be noted at this time, especially in the titles of spiritual works; e.g. Hugh of St Victor, *Speculum de Mysteriis Ecclesiae*; Vincent of Beauvais, *Speculum Majus*; Honorius of Autun, *Speculum Ecclesiae*; William St Thierry, *Speculum Fidei*; Aelred of Rievaulx, *Speculum Caritatis*.

moral state, a volitional outpouring of love towards the world of creatures, thence harmony with its God-ordained unity. This is the secret of habitual recollection in the world, and the key to the proper Christian attitude towards it. Any truly Christian sociology must start from here.

2. If Hugh of St Victor's meditation, not being content with aesthetic reverie, contains an intellectual element, it is not, nevertheless, discursive. It is intuitive and contemplative, nearer to St Teresa's "prayer of loving regard" than to St Ignatius' logical reasoning process. It is a disciplined contemplation of some creature in order that grace may guide us to see deeply into its message and purpose in the mind of God. And this, according to Hugh, issues in moral knowledge. Logically, it would seem that he would approve nude painting and sculpture on the assumption that their contemplation, aided by grace, would lead to a true knowledge of what the human body means to God and what it is really for. Mere aesthetics might incite lust, but mere aesthetics are not enough, we must get right through the symbol to the real purpose of creation; and so with all created things, with all scientific research, with all work and life. The moral implications of such a process are obvious and far-reaching.

No single ascetical point could be more important to-day when moral licence so misuses creation and when the Puritan answer is repressive and Manichaean; when the world's goods are so exploited and yet more rightly enjoyed by more people than ever before; when honest affluence pertains in one half of the world and starvation in the other. But these problems will never be solved according to true "Christian principles" without a return to the ascetical implications of the doctrine of creation; that is the real truth about *things*. Hugh of St Victor might well claim to be both the true Christian sociologist and the true Christian scientist.

3. If Hugh of St Victor is a Platonist, with all its philosophical shortcomings, he is also very much a Christian! The next stage is *prayer*, which is a similar process to that already outlined, but centred upon Jesus Christ as the "perfect symbol" revealing the whole mind of God. The scheme is now placed firmly in the framework of Christian theology. Beginning with the doctrine of the Trinity, Christ is seen as the agent of creation, the eternal Word who wrote all the other "words" which make up the universe. If the

analogy is permitted, having read the book here is a personal appearance of the Author, who can more perfectly explain its meaning to us. Christ is made known to us through the Scriptures, through the Sacraments, and through creation, for they all reveal him in different ways and all are necessary to full understanding. The Eucharist, apart from its central place in Christian life, is also the logical centre of this whole idea, for here are simple creatures, the inner essence of which perfectly reveals Christ to us. Apart from all other aspects of eucharistic doctrine, "devotion to the Blessed Sacrament" is hereby justified.

Hugh of St Victor has developed both St Augustine's doctrine of creation and St Bernard's doctrine of Incarnation, and then set them in a composite ascetical system. St Augustine entertained a valid and human love for the world of nature, but, even allowing for a not very successful attempt to see the Trinity mirrored in creatures, it appears to play little part in his devotional teaching. His insistence, against the Manichaeans, that matter is good, appears isolated from his doctrine of the Fall. But: "we know that the whole creation groaneth and travaileth in pain together until now. And not only they, but ourselves also. . . ."[1] If the whole creation, including humanity, is the outward utterance of Christ the Word, then nothing less than the whole creation is to be restored in Christ. To Augustine, creation was good because it was sustained by the Father. To Hugh it is good, even if fallen, because it shares in the redemption of the Son; because it must, in some sense, partake of the mystery of the resurrection of the body. The pastoral and ascetical implications of this doctrine are almost inexhaustible.

It explains the real significance of the "first form of contemplation", of Augustine's harmony with creation, of *tranquillitas* opposed to concupiscence, and of what Albert Schweitzer calls "reverence for life"; the worthwhileness of creatures and the morality of a proper respect for them. It underlies the vicarious principle whereby all creation, including humanity, is a unity, fallen through the first Adam, restored in the Second Adam, thus explaining the doctrine of original sin more satisfactorily than Augustine's hereditary "transmission" theory. It further explains the cosmic significance of the Eucharist, which pierces the eternal realm and gathers all creatures into the one oblation and intercession of Jesus Christ. It shows the Church to be the Vicarious Body, the channel through which grace

[1] Romans 8.22, 23.

flows out on to the world. There is also a hint of the later distinction between the Sacraments of the Church and the sacramentalism of the world, and more than a hint of St Thomas's hierarchy of creatures.

Compared with Hugh, even St Bernard's emphasis on the Sacred Humanity now begins to look curiously narrow. In spite of the strongest insistence on Christ's real Manhood, on real flesh and blood and real human appetites and passions, our Lord seems often abstracted from the world of ordinary men and women. In spite of an objective atonement theory based on the racial solidarity and Second Adam doctrines, St Bernard still portrays Christ dissociated from creation. This raises another topical point: that meditation on the Gospel story is incomplete, and probably ineffective, without the most serious attention to "composition of place". Human nature is inconceivable except in its natural environment, the Sacred Humanity remains but a hazy devotional idea until Christ is seen in the world and in relation to particular creatures: the homes at Nazareth and Bethany, the mountain top and wilderness, the water that turned into wine and the stones that did not turn into bread, the doves in the temple, the fish in the boat, the palms before the ass, and the withered fig tree; how tremendously important all these *things* are!

Hugh can best sum up for himself:

The Incarnation redresses the Fall by teaching us to raise ourselves to God by the help of the senses. The Word took flesh without losing the Divinity, and He offered himself to man like a book, written within and without: externally by the Humanity, and internally by the Divinity, in order that he might be read, outwardly by imitation and inwardly by contemplation; outwardly in order to heal us and inwardly to lead us to happiness. Inwardly we read, "In the beginning was the Word"; outwardly "The Word was made flesh and dwelt among us". This book then is unique, written once within and twice without: first by the creation of the visible world, and then by the Incarnation; the first time in order to afford us a pleasurable sight; the second to heal us. First, in order to create nature, and second, to redress the Fall.[1]

[1] *De Sacramentis*, I. vi. 5; see also P. Pourrat, *Christian Spirituality* (1922), Vol. II, p. 111.

In curiously modern company, Hugh seems more satisfactory than F. R. Tennant, who held that natural theology is a necessary preface to the study of incarnational religion, for if the eighteenth-century rationalists divorced the two and Tennant linked them, St Hugh compounds them into a creative, pastoral entity.

4. "Progress in goodness", progress towards perfection, is the result of this three-dimensional Christian life: meditation on creation, on the person of Christ revealed in Scripture, and both embedded in the sacramental system of the Church. Hugh accepts the prevailing moral theology of his age, but his outlook and system inspire speculation on yet another modern problem. It is that orthodox moral doctrine, based upon the New Testament and the Christian interpretation of natural law, often sounds a trifle rarefied. The capital sins remain the only satisfactory Christian scheme for self-examination, yet the list, as such, consists of seven abstractions. The usual alternative is a long list of little questions, often silly sometimes heretical, and usually incompatible with Anglican doctrine, which rejects fine juridical points and gives much authority to the maturing conscience. Hugh provides the hint that the capital sins might appear more real if linked with the doctrine of creation.

Thus, pride becomes the rejection of creaturehood, the sin of Satan, the supreme lie. Humility is essentially the strong quest for truth—and the great Christian virtues are apt to sound even more unreal than the sins—it is not so much a moral attitude as the expression of a fact, the fact of creation, of existence wholly and continuously dependent on the love of God. Habitual recollection of and in creation can be a more effective inspiration to humility than any amount of conscious moral effort. Margery Kempe, sublimely humble as the Lord's "darling", finds this virtue by seeing herself, without abasement of self-consciousness, as "this creature".

Envy and anger spring from the lack of harmony between people failing to see creation as unity. Both sins refuse to seek God's purposeful design in the dispensation of his gifts. Jealousy and anger may be selfish, immoral, and unjust, they may hide ambition and vanity, but they also manifest a failure to understand creation; to see all things and all people as, ideally, a unity of praise to the Creator.

Covetousness is plainly a misguided idea of the real value of things, springing from both materialism and idealism, for the first exploits creation and the second rejects it; neither respects and loves it.

The implications of lust and gluttony in this context are too obvious to need explanation; suffice it to repeat that Victorine meditation, inspired by grace, upon the human body, a bottle of beer, or a pork chop, may well prove a more potent antidote to these sins than the abstract, negative way: the "reject the temptation" approach. It is better to keep sober because you love and respect whisky than because you hate it. Finally, if pride rejects creation, sloth refuses to look at it at all; it is basically a lack of interest, that awareness which can be stimulated only through the senses.

This could be much expanded, which would be no bad meditative exercise. In brief, the doctrine of creation, and re-creation in Christ, might almost be defined as the ascetical basis of the purgative way. The whole purpose of mortification, fasting, almsgiving, and discipline, is to replace concupiscence by *tranquillitas*, to re-establish harmony with people, creation, and God.

5. *Contemplation* is one of the most ambiguous of terms, especially in a medieval context. Hugh clearly allows elementary forms, the sense of harmony, but here it is a mystical, and in the technical sense ecstatic, quality. It is perfection; the single, comprehensive union with God himself.

The scheme as a whole has much to recommend it for practical purposes. As St Thomas is to insist later, spiritual life is a comprehensive whole which begins with sense-experience. Prayer, like our Lord's experience in Bethany, the Upper Room and Gethsemane,[1] is always initiated in the world of human affairs. Then follows a general, disciplined approach to this life in creation, Hugh's "meditation", or as we should say, habitual recollection; then "prayer", the more formal approach to and colloquy with Christ; next, "progress in goodness", both the result of communion with our Lord in creation and the test of spiritual growth. And finally perfection, the Vision of God. All is set within the sacramental Church, within Rule; and with its sane "world-affirmation", its emphasis on recollection, and common-sense simplicity, there is no wonder that Hugh found such favour in fourteenth-century England.

---

[1] As treated in Ch. 3.

IV. RICHARD OF ST VICTOR

Compared with Hugh, Richard is a more mystical theologian. His best known scheme, the six degrees of contemplation, is not without interest. It runs thus:

(*a*) Following Hugh, the first step is a simple, sensible awareness of created things, leading to awe and wonder, perhaps to a numinous sense. (*b*) is the aesthetic stage, a deeper awareness and sensibility for beauty and design in creation. (*c*) is the sacramental stage, wherein the inner reality of creatures is sought and perceived. (*d*) leads into a mystical state in which intellect, imagination, and symbol play a decreasing part. This is the beginning of the Pseudo-Dionysian "negative way", the threshold of the "dark night of sense". (*e*) and (*f*) are purely mystical. Three brief comments are relevant to our purpose:

1. The three earlier stages may be classed as "acquired", the three later stages as "infused", which provides a link between ascetical and mystical theology. Pastoral guidance is mainly concerned with the former, yet it must ever remain aware of the latter, and should be capable of discerning it. Richard of St Victor gives us important clues for this discernment.

2. The first three stages correspond to a natural progression which every parish priest has confronted, and perhaps sometimes failed to understand. The first is the emotional stirrings of a new convert; a childlike sense of wonder, a groping for supernatural experience, a subjective and often immature zeal. Secondly comes an aesthetic sense, often expressed in an ingenuous enthusiasm for ceremonial and music. Then comes sacramentalism, or Proficiency, qualified by balanced Rule, by "necessary obedience", by "progress in goodness". In young Christians it may be wise to wait patiently for this third stage before the whole principle of Rule is introduced, or too strongly insisted upon. Under wise guidance, the first two stages are lived through fairly rapidly, but no less a person than Richard of St Victor regards them as important.

3. Richard continues to insist on repentance; everything remains firmly grounded in moral theology. Even when treating of the sixth and most perfect state, he can write:

> In order to reach this contemplation, compunction of heart is more needed than deep investigations of the mind, yearning of

the soul more than reasoning, groanings more than proofs. We know, indeed, that nothing renders the heart more pure, nothing brings greater purity of soul, nothing more effectively drives away the clouds of error, nothing gives greater calm, than true repentance and compunction.[1]

That is an improvement on William of St Thierry's too optimistic hints at impeccability. And it, too, has kinship to Caroline moral theology.

[1] *Benjamin Major*, iv. 6. See also Pourrat, op. cit., Vol. II, p. 123.

10

THE FRANCISCANS

In spite of the impact and popularity of the Friars Minor in thirteenth-century England, they must be regarded as but a subsidiary influence in the development of its spirituality. As with the Austin Canons, it is difficult to assess the direct influence of the Order in the parishes of their time, yet so knowledgeable a Franciscan champion as J. R. H. Moorman admits this influence to have been comparatively short-lived. It may be said that while English spirituality *followed* St Augustine, St Benedict, the Cistercians, and the School of St Victor, it merely *borrowed* one or two Franciscan characteristics and made them its own. St Francis, we have seen, put his affective emphasis on the Passion rather than the Incarnation, and all Christendom, including fourteenth-century England, followed him. But the penitential rigour of St Francis is utterly unlike the penitential optimism of Julian of Norwich, even if they are both concerned with the Passion of Christ.

This is hardly surprising when it is realized that, with a series of contradictions, the Franciscans cut across nearly everything that English spirituality stands for. If St Bernard rode rather lightly on theology, St Francis scorned it; yet the Franciscan Order included "illuminists" like Joachim, John of Padua, and Jacopone da Todi, on the one hand, and scholastics like Alexander of Hales, Duns Scotus, William of Occam, and St Bonaventure, on the other. Here is dangerously extreme affectiveness and somewhat stolid speculation, but—with the possible exception of Bonaventure—no attempt at synthesis. St Francis preached mendicancy and the Order ended with stability; it began with an evangelistic zeal which minimized formal Offices and ended by composing them. It taught an affective approach to the Sacred Humanity as thorough as St Bernard's, yet it was mainly manifested in popular devotion of a formal kind: whatever the value of these devotions, it is significant that they always seem to arise when theology is cast aside. Perhaps because he was a layman, St Francis was no less severe than St Bridget and St Hildegarde in his castigation of the lax clergy, issuing in the same distortion of the sacerdotal function and isolation of the Mass. It may well be asked what a spiritual tradition of *via media* could possibly make of all this. St. Francis himself is a glamorous figure who catches the public imagination, but in general, the English have been content to honour his image—in statuettes looking like a monk in Trafalgar Square—rather than follow his spiritual teaching. Nevertheless, our Franciscan borrowings have their importance.

I. ST FRANCIS OF ASSISI

In his life and example, St Francis offers four points of which we should take note.

1. *Poverty and creation.* We saw how the School of St Victor interpreted creation as "symbolic" manifestation of the mind of God. The world is God's painted picture, God's printed book, but known to us only as the reflection in a mirror. That implies idealist philosophy, which is one of the weak points in Victorine ascetic, and one which St Francis rectifies with characteristic abandon. In fact, St Francis achieved exactly what Hugh of St Victor taught: a perfect contemplative harmony with creation. His nature poems, like the *Canticle of the Sun*, are more than pleasant little hymns; they are expressions of this contemplative unity, and it is only against this background that his teaching on poverty can be understood. When Francis talks of "brother sun and sister water" he means it contemplatively and almost literally: is not God our Father because he created us? Did he not create all things, sun, moon, stars, birds, and flowers? So he is their Father too, and they are our brothers and sisters.

Creation is still symbolic in that it speaks to us of God, but it is also "real", no mere mirrored reflection; it is not to be analysed, but embraced, loved, and sung to. Further, still following St Victor, creation is one with the Christian because it shares in the mystery of redemption; it is restored in Christ.

To Francis, then, ownership of property takes on something of the horror we associate with slavery; exploitation of creatures by men is not so far from the exploitation of men by men. This is rather far-fetched but it has its ascetical importance. If materialism is the end-product of pride, idealism might be the end-product of sloth;

the Christian ideal, the sacramental ideal, is to love all things and possess nothing, or to possess everything in love alone. St Francis did not defy the world of sophisticated pomp and wealth because he was too "spiritual" to be bothered with creatures, but because he was so spiritual that he loved them more than anyone.

But if St Victor was wrong in seeing creatures as mere symbols, St Francis was wrong in seeing them as almost human: the greatest ascetical importance is that these two extreme attitudes are synthesized in the Thomist hierarchy of being, and from that viewpoint, both can still teach us practical lessons.

2. *Sonship and suffering.* One of the most neglected of St Francis' messages is the biblical theme that "whom the Lord loveth he chasteneth". We may, with St Peter, truly rejoice in suffering for Christ's sake,[1] because we may draw near to him in his Passion, and for sinners it is easier to share his Passion than to share his glory. If the saints know Christ because of their perfection, we can know him only because of our penitence. St Francis saw, without bothering to explain, that peace, harmony, *tranquillitas*, could only be won in abandonment to the will of God; and he saw it long before Caussade or anyone else turned it into a system.

Because of this typical Franciscan affectiveness which under-valued reason, some of his followers may have indulged in the in-human and unhealthy quest for suffering for its own sake. But the important fact remains that vicarious suffering, in Christ, is an essential part of the Christian vocation. It can be creative and inter-cessory, and if God does not send physical punishment as the direct result of sin—though I see no reason why he should not—then affliction may be more of a divine compliment than a sign of dis-favour. It was against the opposite idea, that riches and well-being were a sure sign of righteousness rewarded by God, that St Francis first rebelled. The 1662 Office for the Visitation of the Sick contains more sound doctrine than our sentimentalists can see. St Francis not only defies such shallowness but points to a supremely positive approach: suffering of whatever kind, whether the chasten-ing of a loving Father or the vicarious sharing in Christ's Passion, is to be *used* not *borne*.

3. *World-defiance.* It has been pointed out that an important aspect of ascetical doctrine is its adaptation to circumstances and

[1] *Acts* 5.40, 41.

temperament. We have also noted that the parables of the leaven and the candle show the two ways in which Christian influence may be exerted on the world. The normal method, and the one inherent in Anglicanism, is the subtle pervasion of the lump by the invisible leaven of hidden prayer. St Francis is the most spectacular exponent of the candle, shouting defiance to the surrounding gloom from the height of its candlestick. He manifests a supreme Christian heroism, in which there is no compromise with the poverty, humility, and agony of the redeeming Cross.

The English tradition, with its prudent, domestic ethos, is a legitimate spirituality, but we must not forget that the opposite, Franciscan, method may sometimes be required by circumstances. With our affective–speculative synthesis, we realize that religion is neither "simple" nor easy, but St Francis warns that it can become far too sophisticated.

4. *Penitence and the Passion.* In seeking to emphasize the Sacred Humanity, St Bernard not unnaturally laid stress on the Incarnation and on the Advent–Christmas season. So did St Francis, as witness the introduction of the Christmas Crib—complete with ox and ass— but he extended a much greater emphasis to the Passion, especially as an aid to penitential devotion. Here it is only necessary to credit Francis with this development, whereby he fearlessly confronted the Passion and Death of Christ in all its horror. It seems strange to-day that this type of affective prayer was so neglected in past ages, but it is also important to notice that in a good deal of Franciscan writing —especially in the *Rules*—there is an element of extreme harshness against the sinner. This is another truth in the Franciscan message so often overlooked by the sentimental.

II. ST BONAVENTURE

If St Bernard needed William of St Thierry to bring his affective devotion into some order, St Francis was even more in need of the speculative mind of St Bonaventure. But if the teaching of the Cistercian pair grew into a unity, the Franciscans only illustrate their own notorious complexity. St Bonaventure is himself something of a paradox: he follows St Bernard yet becomes almost Abelardian in speculative technique; he can be doggedly doctrinal and gloriously affective, but seldom both at once. One sometimes wonders how he can possibly be Franciscan; then it seems that he could not possibly be anything else. Within the scope of this study, four points are of interest.

1. *The Three Ways.* We have explained the absurdity of claiming that St Bonaventure "invented" the Three Ways, for they are fundamental to Christian spirituality from the New Testament onwards. But he should be given the credit for its first detailed treatment. All succeeding exponents of the scheme—we shall study it more fully under Walter Hilton—owe a good deal to him.

Bonaventure continues the Augustinian–Platonic line of thought and, like the school of St Victor, is influenced by the Pseudo-Dionysius. The purgative way is governed by the fight against concupiscence in which victory brings "peace of soul", or harmony. The illuminative way remains thoroughly penitential, and is qualified mainly by thanksgiving for sins forgiven and for the efficacy of grace in fighting temptation: "there but for the grace of God go I" is a typical Bonaventuran idea. The unitive way is expressed in Dionysian mysticism.

Especially important is the teaching on the appropriate forms of spiritual exercise for each way; purgation, illumination, and union, are governed by meditation, prayer, and contemplation. The first comes from St Victor, and can mean either consideration of creation as symbol, or of the Gospel story centred on the Sacred Humanity. On the "mirror" of God in creation, he goes a stage further than both Augustine's vague analogy of the Trinity and Bernard's image–likeness distinction. The image of the Trinity leaves *vestiges* in created things, its *image* in rational beings, and *resemblance* in the perfect. The last two stages follow St Bernard's image and likeness.[1] In meditation on the Person of Christ, Bonaventure is as affective, and as bold, as St Bernard, and some wonderful examples of this form are to be found in the *Tree of Life* and the *Mystical Vine*. In the *Itinerary of the Mind to God*, we are given the classic definition of meditation in the modern sense: "In meditation the soul should apply to the subject all its faculties—reason, judgement, conscience, will: the reason puts a question, the judgement gives an answer, the conscience draws a practical conclusion, the will makes a resolution."[2] Prayer, in the illuminative way, is colloquy with Christ, qualified

---

[1] See L. Bouyer, *The Cistercian Heritage* (1958), pp. 53 foll., cf. P. Pourrat, *Christian Spirituality* (1922), Vol. II, pp. 180ff.

[2] *Itin. Mentis in Deum,* I. 3.

by a typically Franciscan stress on penitential devotion to Christ in his Passion. Contemplation is the way of union.

Modern spiritual directors cannot be reminded too often that this plan puts things the right way round. Meditation is the essential *first* step, colloquy, "saying your prayers", is the *second* step. Meditation introduces Christ to the soul, and gives it some knowledge of him; and you cannot hold a colloquy, or conversation, with someone you do not know and have never met. So many beginners are still taught to say prayers into thin air, to open their hearts to nobody in particular.

2. *Departmentalism.* But if St Bonaventure gives us valuable teaching on the Three Ways, he is probably the unwitting cause of that unreal, departmental interpretation of them to which we have referred. As his trinitarianism sometimes degenerates into a facile game with the number "3", so the three ways become rigidly fixed periods of life. The proper prayer for the purgative way, whether meditation or colloquy, is almost confined to confession and penitential sorrow, while the higher stages are nearly confined to thanksgiving and praise. But William of St Thierry has shown that intercession, thanksgiving, adoration, and petition for enlightenment are incumbent upon all Christians in whatever state, and Richard of St Victor has insisted that there is no contemplative state which precludes the need for penitence.

The Three Ways remain fundamental to Christian spirituality, and essential in spiritual guidance, but as a map or chart of the spiritual country, as a "back-cloth", not as a rigid programme.

3. *Death and the "four last things".* If St Bernard stressed the Incarnation and St Francis narrowed it to affective meditation on the Passion, St Bonaventure is inclined to narrow this still further and concentrate on the Cross. He may be responsible for the tradition of meditating on the "four last things" in Advent. The form of the Crucifix remains the central Christian symbol, it is at the heart of the Gospel. Nevertheless St Bernard is unquestionably right in seeing the Sacred Humanity in terms of the whole life from the Conception to the Ascension. On the other hand, there is the need for ascetical theology to be crowned by contemplation; however remote the Vision of God, no lesser goal will do. But, without rejecting hope or overthrowing the restrained optimism of the English School, death, hell, and judgement are as important

subjects for speculation as heaven: we should think of Christ in judgement as well as Christ in glory.

This element is not lacking in the English tradition, and it is treated in a creative way; death is something to be *achieved*, not simply succumbed too; it is one step in the soul's progress and judgement is another. The positive idea of a good death comes into the fourteenth-century writings, and is more pronounced in the Caroline age. To quote a famous title, there are *"Rules and Exercises for Holy Dying"*, but many others of this period, Bayly, Nelson, Stanhope, Walton, as well as Taylor, wrote in the same vein.

4. *The affective nature of theology.* I do not think St Bonaventure achieved any pronounced synthesis of the affective and speculative elements in a full ascetic. But whereas many are aware that doctrine should underlie affective prayer, he taught the important truth that reason itself, and theology as such, have their own affective side. As we speak rather vaguely about the "beauty of truth", he saw it as an almost emotional fact; he saw beauty in theological truth as a musician might see beauty in mathematics, music and numbers being closely allied. So to Bonaventure the actual doctrine of the Trinity was more than an intellectual expression of the Christian doctrine of God, it was beautiful, lovable in itself. Thus "intellectual meditation" is more than a counterbalance and guide to affective prayer, it can be an affective exercise in itself. Struggling theological students with final examinations in the offing, might be excused for thinking this a little far-fetched, yet it has practical implications.

In an age when all intellectualism is regarded as cold and dull, this ideal might well be cultivated. Ascetical or "occasional" theology appears as a stepping-stone towards it. Against "academic" learning, it makes dogmatic facts interesting and when translated into Christian action, they can become "lovable". A further pastoral stage is to see moral doctrine in the light of the attributes of God. All forms of dishonesty, lying, embezzlement, theft, are wont to be seen as merely anti-social; as part of a utilitarian ethic. Or they are regarded as the breach of some impersonal law. Bonaventure would see truth primarily as an attribute of God—"I *am* the Truth"—and so as lovable, in itself, as the inherent virtues of a beloved person. A man can be said to love, not only his wife, but her faithfulness, sense of humour, good temper, or any other characteristic. The truth, therefore, whether scientific, personal, or theological, is lovable as part of God; to live in the truth is, in part at least, union with God. Dishonesty is rejection of divine love, and almost a marring of his beauty; it is not only immoral but ugly. Intellectual meditation thus becomes of the first practical importance, for we tend to grow like the beloved and partake of his character. The truth has not only to be "told" but absorbed.

III. CONCLUSION

This section might almost be called "confusion", for the Franciscan movement will ever remain an asceticist's headache. It is so diverse, and in many ways so contradictory, as to be irreducible to any sort of order.

On the one hand, it gave rise to popular devotions like the recollective *Angelus*, devotion to the Holy Name, the Crib, and others associated with the Passion. On the other hand, the Friars Minor started the fashion of popular "Lives of Christ", some of which are sufficiently removed from the text of the Gospel to remind us of to-day's biblical novel. These, naturally, are affective in character, and again raise the point of the validity of free imaginative interpretation in mental prayer.

Later Franciscan writings vary from the *Examples* of St Bernardino of Siena ("the Apostle of the Holy Name") which read something like Victorian moral tales and are still admirable for the Sunday school, to the "*Golden Treatise*" of St Pedro Alcantara, which could have come from the pen of Ignatius Loyola, complete with a love of military analogy.

The Tertiary movement is of obvious pastoral significance, but, if we are to concentrate on English spirituality, I think we must be content to give thanks for the Franciscan inspiration, while humbly regarding it as a "subsidiary influence" to the main stream of development.

11

ST THOMAS AQUINAS

Paradoxically, St Thomas is another "subsidiary influence" in English spirituality, but this time because he is altogether too big to be an incorporative factor in any particular school. As there is no single Benedictine tradition so there is no single Thomist spirituality, for the whole of Catholic Christendom owes a good deal to them both.[1] No Christian therefore, Anglican or otherwise, would be prudent to undertake the guidance of souls without some reference to the main principles of Thomist ascetical theory.

St Thomas has a more particular place in the English tradition in that he is at the peak of a development that starts with St Anselm, and is a considerable source of post-Reformation thought, especially in the case of Richard Hooker. He is thus linked with the precursors of our two greatest ages.

On the other hand, English spiritual theology retains a loyalty to the Augustinian–Platonic stream, and, while honouring St Thomas as probably the greatest Christian thinker of all time, it refuses to grant him infallibility. In the St Thomas–William of St Thierry conflict on mortal and venial sin, Anglican moral theology has consistently followed the latter.

The barest minimum of Thomist ascetical theory is all I can hope to introduce. It comprises five particular doctrines.

I. CREATION

With God at its peak, or rather, beyond its peak, and matter at its base, creation consists in an ordered hierarchy of being. All orders of being, inanimate matter, plants, animals, humans, angels, form a unity, but each has its own particular characteristic and function. In one sense the whole creation has a single function, to glorify its Creator; but this is achieved by each creature being true to itself, by fulfilling its own specific purpose in its own unique way. On the

[1] See Jacques Maritain, *The Angel of the Schools* (1936), pp. 68 foll.

surface, the mammals appear to be like men in many ways, and in other ways men resemble angels, but this likeness is only "analogical":[1] dogs are dogs, men are men, angels are angels.

> The ladder of learning involves a transmutation of knowledge at each rung. But it is a real ladder not an illusion . . . each rung in it has a character specifically and uniquely its own, though derived from the One Eternal Being towards knowledge of which it leads; and every rung leads on to the next. Thus, though we cannot know God by the direct operation of reason, nor attribute to him existence in the sense in which we predicate it of His Creation, we are not wholly at a loss. Analogy provides a key for speculation.[2]

We may say, then, that we climb the hierarchy of creation which leads to God, by a ladder and not by a ramp, and that the parallel rungs of the ladder are just too far apart to be comfortable. We neither walk a gentle incline to heaven nor climb a simple staircase; we must take an analogical jump each time, a jump of faith and a jump of love.

This completes an ascetic of creation by rectifying the errors of both the Victorines and of St Francis. The sun and the moon and all created things are neither mere "symbols" which mirror the mind of God, nor our "brothers and sisters" on a level with us: they are the sun and the moon and the creatures, uniquely and "really" in their own right. Because they manifest the mind of God, and glorify him in their own way, they can tell us of his Being, character, and love. Thus are creatures to be reverenced in their own order, and indeed loved; they are not merely to be utilized as symbols, and yet, however poetic and pleasant the Franciscan image may be, it is just not true. We can love and learn from the sparrows while being of more value than many of them: they are neither symbols nor sisters but sparrows. As G. K. Chesterton so succinctly points out, St Thomas insists, by sublime theology, that eggs are neither complexes of sense-data, nor embryonic hens, but eggs.[3]

God is perfect Being. Creatures have potential being, in that they

---

[1] See e.g. D. M. Emmet, *The Nature of Metaphysical Thinking* (1949), ch. 8; E. L. Mascall, *Existence and Analogy* (1949), chs. 5, 6.

[2] K. E. Kirk, *The Vision of God* (1931), pp. 380 foll. See also D. J. B. Hawkins, *A Sketch of Medieval Philosophy* (1946), pp. 78 foll.

[3] *St Thomas Aquinas* (1933), ch. 6.

are naturally inclined to move towards their perfection, of which unity, wholeness, truth, and beauty are aspects: beauty is qualified by wholeness, harmony, and radiance. Thus creation is dynamic not static, God's creative activity is a continuous process, and he is in all creatures by essence, power, and presence: to some degree all things partake of the divine essence, they develop by God's power, and all is regulated by providence. For the tidy-minded, these groups of categories may provide a kind of "three-point" system for the contemplation of creation.

Man, too, is to move from potentiality to actuality, from imperfection to perfection. As in Augustine, sin is a privation of this progress, it is a lack of right use of the powers of the soul, so K. E. Kirk is right when he defines sin simply as "that which impedes spiritual progress".[1] Ugliness and evil consist essentially in wrong order, as Gerald Vann says: "a bunion is being, and therefore of itself good, and doubtless beautiful, but in its context it denotes a lack, a privation of the proper shape and texture and complexion of a foot, and is therefore in that sense a lack of being."[2] There is sound Thomist doctrine in the farmer's definition of a weed as a plant growing in the wrong place. But Hugh of St Victor is wrong when he sees all things, good and bad, merely as ideal symbols, and St Francis is wrong, not for loving brother louse, but for assuming the human body to be his proper habitat.

Thomism, therefore, like Augustinianism, is essentially *ascetical* theology because, though less "occasional", its whole principle is movement, becoming, progress towards perfection. In pastoral practice it provides that most fundamental of all progressions: being–knowing–doing. Confronted with a complete stranger seeking counsel, how many of us begin by asking if he has been baptized? by inquiring, that is, not what the person thinks, or has done, but what, ontologically, he *is*? It is another aspect of the ascetical doctrine of prevenient grace; God acts first by giving existence, then by giving grace, and only after that may we bother with thoughts and actions: the good fruit depends on the goodness of the tree. Once again we are forced to the conclusion that the sacraments of grace, which with the Rule of prayer develop a *person*, have absolute first priority in Christian living. Christian action is the result, not the cause, of Christian character. That is one of the reasons

[1] See *Some Principles of Moral Theology* (1920), pp. 221-8.
[2] *Morals and Man* (1959), p. 34.

why spiritual guides should be very reticent in giving purely practical advice. Matters of education, careers, finance, work, are generally speaking, outside his province.

11. MAN AND PERFECTION

Following the doctrine of creation, St Thomas uses the word "soul" in the sense of vital principle; thus a plant acts through its "vegetative soul", an animal through its animal or "sensitive soul", and man through his "rational soul". In Thomist terms, the soul is to the body as "form" to "matter", the soul is the form of the body, so the two are inseparable: man is a unity.

> . . . . the soul is what makes the body a human body . . . soul and body are together one substance. The human being is not composed of two substances, soul and body; it is one substance in which two component factors can be distinguished. When we feel, it is the whole man who feels, neither the soul alone nor the body alone. Similarly, when we understand something we could not do so without the soul, but it is the man who understands.[1]

Here is development and completion of the psychology of William of St Thierry.

It is also the whole man who prays, worships, and commits sin, and this is a fundamental principle of ascetical theology. There is a sense in which we can distinguish between "physical" and "spiritual" sins, but only the total man commits them, and we have seen that both are closely linked with the doctrine of creation. Thus, mortification is no answer to "physical" sin unless it is linked with the mind, and spiritual exercises are of little avail unless the body is recognized as having its part in them: St Thomas too, has killed "spirituality" in the narrow sense.

St Thomas's doctrine of perfection is very complicated. All I can try to do is to fit it in with what has been said so far, and link this with the next section. To start with the famous, and intensely pastoral, definition: "a being is perfect in so far as he attains to his proper end, which is his highest perfection. Now it is charity which unites us to God, the last end of the human soul, since, according to St John, 4.16, 'he that abideth in charity abideth in God and God in him'".[2]

Incorporated into the doctrine of creation, each form of being has

[1] F. C. Copleston, *Aquinas* (1955), p. 155.   [2] *Summa*, II.II.184, i.

its own perfection, which is the development and final fulfilment of its own potentialities. Therefore our prayer, worship, and life are to be *human*. We miss our vocation when we are content to live as the brutes; man is equally, if less obviously in error when he tries to pray as the angels. That is the fundamental mistake of what is properly called Puritanism, the quest for "pure spirituality" which precludes the use of the senses, the body, and mental imagery. It is significant that in the traditional celebration of the Eucharist all five senses—sight, taste, smell,[1] feeling, and hearing—are employed. And the Eucharist is the extensible centre of the whole Christian life within creation.

Absolute perfection is the Vision of God which is only possible in the next life; so, pastorally, perfection is a process of growth, the development of our potentialities. St Thomas follows an unbroken line from St Augustine, or even from St Paul, in which spiritual progress, movement, development, is absolutely fundamental to every single Christian life. Ascetical theology and spiritual direction, far from being esoteric subjects on the fringe of Christianity, are at the very heart of all theology which can claim to be incarnational, and of all pastoral practice whatsoever.

It is far from sufficient to herd people into church; on the contrary, if once there they are presented with vapid statues and vapid sermons, and are made to sing of mindless yearnings to flee from this wicked world and rest in a somewhat negative and super-latively comfortable deity, their instincts are in fact being set precisely in the wrong direction: they are being suggested into subhumanity instead of helped towards divinity.[2]

I doubt if many English parishes are quite so bad as that, yet the *static* idea prevails, a comfortable mediocrity is the norm, with "progress" as a curious novelty.

To ask exactly how this progress is to be achieved is to approach the core of St Thomas's spiritual theology.

III. THE ASCETICAL MAP

As creation consists in an ordered hierarchy of being, so the Christian pilgrimage consists in a five-fold ladder up which we climb towards God. These five steps or rungs are:

[1] Which is the most sensible, pastoral argument in favour of incense. Cf. Julian of Norwich, ch. 17, iv, 2 below on the *14th Revelation*.

[2] Vann, op. cit., p. 102.

1. Human existence begins with "sense life" and all knowledge is gained through sense-experience. In plain language, the journey towards the Beatific Vision starts not with some rarefied devotion or spiritual exercise, but with the experience of *things*. This is akin to the Victorine "reading" and although St Thomas was suspicious of certain "scientific" speculations of the School of St Victor, they would both be bewildered by the modern exhortation to "relate religion to life": religion *is* life because both start with creation, and it cannot be otherwise.

2. Next comes "natural life" qualified by intellect and will. This natural though fallen state is that of the "acquired virtues", the ordinary goodness, the natural inclination towards perfection, inherent in all men and manifested in well-established habits. It is here that St Thomas is rightly regarded as more "optimistic" than St Augustine. Following this teaching, there need be no surprise when moral excellency is found in non-Christian people. But it should also be remembered that, in a Thomist context, what we call moral excellence is not always "goodness"; the good is that which fulfils its essential purpose, which, in man, is the conscious and volitional worship of God.

3. Accepting the doctrine of analogy, the spiritual life is a series of jumps rather than a steady climb, but it is between the second and this third stage that the biggest jump, the most marked "discontinuity", occurs. For the third stage is the supernatural life of grace, the life not of nature but of redemption; in other words the fully Christian life. There is, indeed, an important relation between the two stages, between *gratia Dei* and *gratia Christi*, since all goodness of whatever kind is initiated by God. And "grace perfects nature", neither destroying nor suppressing it. But however rosy a view is taken of human nature in its natural and fallen state, it cannot make the jump from nature to grace by its own efforts. We are back to prevenient and sacramental grace, to the new life by Baptism, of incorporation into the Sacred Humanity of Christ.

It is impossible to apply the ascetical principles of this stage, however sensible and moral they may sound, to the unbaptized. Nor does it make very much sense to try to apply them to any but regular communicants. This is of pastoral relevance: "you should make your communion a little more often" has come to imply an incompetent director who cannot think of anything else to say.

Regrettably the little joke has point, yet it can be exactly the right counsel. There is also a prevalent practice of "hearing confessions" of adults *prior* to Baptism. Whatever psychological or directive value this may have, it cannot be the sacrament of penance nor is it a channel of grace. This theology is not always understood.

That "grace perfects nature" is one of the most pastoral of doctrines, ever to be borne in mind in every act and aspect of spiritual guidance. There are four special points relevant to the contemporary situation.

a. To examine one's conscience and dislike what one sees is a healthy thing, yet the answer is not to turn oneself into somebody else. Without puritanical repression, devout Christians are always trying to do just that. Theology, no less than psychology, treats of the analysis of the human soul and attempts a classification of temperament, yet it insists that, in the last resort, every person is unique. And each unique nature is to be sanctified as it is. An arrogant extrovert must try, by the help of grace, to become a humble extrovert, but he must not try to be a humble introvert. He must be himself.

It is difficult to distinguish between innate characteristics, our "nature", and acquired habits formed by circumstances. This difficulty must be accepted and its subtlety recognized, but the doctrine remains. Homosexuality is an example, for this can be almost subconsciously acquired, as a developing tendency, or it can be an innate characteristic. In the former case, the tendency should be fought, for it is but an excrescence upon nature; in the latter case it is part of nature, which can be accepted and ultimately sanctified. What must be avoided is the abominable heresy that the "Christian character" implies a rigid uniformity; that rather than sanctifying our own God-made selves we should ape some other real or imaginary character. Thomas Merton sums it up well:

Many poets are not poets for the same reason that many religious men are not saints: they never succeed in being themselves. They never get around to being the particular poet or the particular monk they are intended to be by God. They never become the man or the artist who is called for by all the circumstances of their individual lives.

They waste their years in vain efforts to be some other poet, some other saint. For many absurd reasons, they are convinced that they are obliged to become somebody else who died two hundred years ago and who lived in circumstances utterly alien to their own.

They wear out their minds and bodies in a hopeless endeavour to have somebody else's experiences or write somebody else's poems or possess somebody else's sanctity.[1]

A Catholic poet should be an apostle by being first of all a poet, not try to be a poet by being first of all an apostle. For if he presents himself to people as a poet, he is going to be judged as a poet, and if he is not a good one his apostolate will be ridiculed.[2]

The same applies to ploughmen, bankers, and housewives; the first duty of a Christian film actress is to be a good film actress, not to change into a nun. This is the trouble with "priest-workers", and most "parish work". It is all a matter of being and doing, potentiality and actuality, grace and nature; all in the right order and relation.

But if grace perfects nature, I have a quite personal idea that St Mary Magdalene is the most glorious example of all. If we can trust tradition as to her early life, it is apparent that her innate characteristics remained to the end. Her sensuousness, her physical generosity, her passionate, impetuous self-giving, her sexuality and femininity; all this was once given to her revolting clients, then to the Son of God. Her kisses and caresses began in sin and ended in sanctity, at the feet of Christ, but they were still kisses and caresses. Her generosity started with harlotry and ended with precious ointment, but it was the same generosity. Her passionate love was first carnal and then contemplative, but it was the same love, the same nature, only sanctified. It is a meditation worth making.

Having said that, the other three pastoral points need be but mentioned.

b. If nature is to be sanctified and if it is unique, then its guidance *must* be personal: whatever their pastoral use, sermons and group-instructions can never be adequate. Further, although we need ascetical theology, the teaching and inspiration of the experience of the Church, it *must* be applied. Here is further argument against the "case" system, and against a too rigid, juridical, text-book technique, and an argument for the empirical tradition.

c. Theological training and pastoral approach are apt to become stereotyped. Country clergy are frequently depressed because their

[1] *Seeds of Contemplation* (1949), p. 57.   [2] Ibid., p. 63.

people, of limited intellectual powers, cannot "understand" the
faith: perhaps they are not meant to. Perhaps the faith should not be
taught in "simple sermons" but *applied*. Anglican speculative
emphasis means that such application should be based on doctrine
and reason, not that all natures, as God has made them, should be
predominantly intellectual.

d. But grace is not magic. It implies response: "It is possible to
receive the sacraments with great frequency and emotional piety but
to gain relatively little benefit from them because of this lack of
effort. Similarly, with regard to growth of personality in general:
grace here as elswhere perfects nature, presupposes nature, and
cannot make good a privation of natural means."[1] We are back to the
necessity, not just of the sacraments, but of total Rule of which they
are part. Response means "necessary obedience": the sacraments
and the Office, generously given like Mary's ointment of spikenard,
and the effort needed for the development of private devotion.

This important third stage, then, is a participation in the divine
nature given by Baptism, wherein the soul is energized by what St
Thomas calls the *infused virtues*, added to the acquired virtues of
natural life. The infused virtues are of two kinds, the *theological
virtues*,[2] faith, hope, charity, and the *cardinal virtues*,[3] fortitude,
temperance, justice, and prudence. It is prudence which St Thomas
somewhere calls the "charioteer", which controls the other three
in a reasonable way, and which prevents them from degenerating
into foolhardiness, extreme austerity—encratism—and merciless
rigour. It is the strong virtue of prudence which would have all
things not lax, not moderate, but *right*: this is the hall-mark of the
true synthesis, the real *via media*, the spirit of both Benedictinism
and Anglicanism.

The infused virtues are free gifts of God which, when responded
to, make up the life of the *precepts*[4] of the faith. This is what St
Thomas also calls *Proficiency*, the life of ordinary Christian
maturity midway between *Beginners* and the *Perfect*: the illuminative
way.

But it is here that St Thomas conflicts with William of St Thierry,
and with the tendencies of the English tradition. St Thomas explains that although the distinction is a real one there can be no

---

[1] Vann, op. cit., p. 103.
[2] F. P. Harton, *The Elements of the Spiritual Life* (1932), pp. 30–61.
[3] Ibid., pp. 62–70.   [4] See Kirk, *The Vision of God*, pp. 243–8.

isolation of acquired from infused virtue; there is both distinction and connection between nature and grace. A natural man acquires the virtue of truthfulness by habitually telling the truth, and although faith, hope, and charity can never be acquired but must be infused by God, they nevertheless develop through constant acts of prayer and of volitional effort. To St Thomas, therefore, the acquired virtues are more constant and the infused virtues more easily lost. The latter are given by supernatural means and cannot co-exist with "mortal" sin; in such case restoration is only possible by further infusion of grace by sacramental confession. The difficulties of this doctrine have already been referred to,[1] and St Thomas solves them by further distinctions between different sorts of grace: "sanctifying" and "actual", "efficacious" and "sufficient". This is subtle and ingenious, and it is logically difficult to disprove; the most serious criticism is that it is too complex and too false to experience to be pastorally useful. It is difficult to give much pastoral meaning to a "state of grace" when, through subtle distinctions of sin, we pass from one kind of grace to another. Experience suggests that a faithful person, living sacramentally within the Church, might commit serious sin, while he cannot be said to have "lost" faith and hope, or indeed, as William of St Thierry insists, charity. For penitence implies it. On the other hand, I think St Thomas and William would agree that a baptized soul with no spiritual or sacramental life at all might well "lose" the infused virtues and be "out of the state of grace". But the reason would not be isolated acts of sin, "mortal" or otherwise, but a habitual lack of necessary obedience.

In pastoral practice, therefore, the English tradition of moral theology, with the infirmity–malice distinction, and with sacramental confession as a channel of grace, love, and worship rather than as a juridical restorative, seems more in keeping with experience and with the doctrine of redemption through Baptism and continuous spiritual growth. On the other hand, we must be careful of exhortations to "have faith" or "have hope", for these virtues cannot be acquired by effort. Such exhortations can only mean "be baptized and use the sacraments"; not so much "have hope" but "acquire it from God and respond to his gift." In short, may we use St Thomas' ascetic as an invaluable spiritual map which can be interpreted in a Caroline rather than post-Tridentine way?

[1] See also ibid., pp. 249 foll.

4. The fourth stage is that of the *Gifts of the Spirit*,[1] which develops from the life of the *precepts* and is called the life of the *counsels*. The Gifts of the Spirit, traditionally associated with the list in Isaiah 11.2,3,[2] spring from the direct action of God within the soul. The life of the precepts tends to Christian Proficiency, the life of the counsels to perfection. There is some confusion over the various lists of the Gifts of the Spirit. Guibert follows St Thomas with *Wisdom, Understanding, Counsel, Knowledge, Godly (Holy) Fear, Ghostly Strength*, and *Piety*. Harton calls the last *Godliness* and changes the order. The pastoral point is that the Gifts imply an advanced and hard-won spiritual state. Although "the Word of God is not bound", and God bestows his graces where he will, we speak far too glibly about the Gifts, especially where the terms are also common words with different meanings, as with *Knowledge* and *Wisdom*.[3] There is also much confusion between the Gifts and the "leading of the Spirit". The inspiration of the Holy Ghost is possible to any Christian, but it is not just a "hunch", yet we should not expect to find the Gifts of the Spirit well developed in anyone who has not lived loyally within the Church for some years.

In a valuable but insufficiently known book *Mental Prayer According to the Teaching of St Thomas Aquinas*,[4] Fr Denis Fahey interprets this teaching pastorally and concisely.

Sanctifying Grace, participation in God's own nature, appears to us, then, enriched with three groups of principles of action. At the summit of the structure are to be found the Gifts of the Holy Ghost: at its centre, the Theological virtues; at its base, in close contact with our rational human life, the infused moral virtues. . . . The Theological virtues are, absolutely considered, at the summit of the structure, for, besides other reasons, perfection of life lies in Charity, and the action of the Gifts is ever directed towards the perfecting of Charity. Looked at, however, from the point of view of their proximate rule of action, which is the Divine Reason, for by them the Holy Ghost acts directly in the guidance of our souls, the Gifts are superior to the Theological Virtues.[5]

That explains a great deal. It explains the error of too rigid

---

[1] Harton, op. cit., pp. 71–85.
[2] Guibert, *The Theology of the Spiritual Life* (1954), pp. 121 foll.
[3] e.g. Harton, loc. cit.　　[4] Dublin, 1927.　　[5] Op. cit., pp. 24f.

interpretation of ascetical hierarchies in general, and it explains why perfection does not depend on intellect or upon any other particular gift: it is the actualization of a unique man's potentiality, no more, no less. Fahey also points to another misconception. We hear, *ad nauseam*, that we must "rely on the Holy Ghost", for "only the Holy Spirit can teach us to pray". That is true because God always acts first and only in God do we exist at all. But it is a blatant *non sequitur* to deduce from this that a human guide is unnecessary. A spiritual director must be self-effacing, recollected in the Spirit and on the alert for signs of his leading, but it is only on the higher levels of Proficiency that a clear and direct leading of the Spirit is to be expected. To assume plain and easily discernible guidance by the Holy Ghost is arrogance on the part of the ordinary Christian and irresponsibility on the part of his director.

Fr Fahey continues with a valuable analysis of the types of mental prayer suitable to each stage. The prayer of the infused moral virtues [1] is discursive meditation, the prayer proper to the active life, since its normal end is the *praeceptum* or resolution. It is the prayer of the practical reason or conscience, and its effect is what is rather ambiguously known as "following Christ". [2] Fortitude, Temperance, and Justice are the virtues concerned with practical living, with Prudence, their "charioteer", as the over-all factor of control.

Next comes the prayer of the Theological Virtues, [3] which starts with a simple act of Faith, issuing in further acts of humility and penitence. It is maintained by Hope and consummated by Charity. Faith and Charity are reciprocal: Faith illuminates the soul while Charity strengthens Faith, since it is a mutual loving, a "friendship" between man and God—St Bernard's *philia*. Though nurtured by spiritual reading and study, this type of prayer is less discursive, more intuitive, more objective and theocentric, and it leads into habitual recollection. The prayer of the Gifts of the Spirit is contemplative.

We have been led once more to the Three Ways. Meditation, the initial meeting with God, followed by active resolution, is essentially purgative, though here presented in a most healthy and positive way. Intuitive prayer plainly depends on illumination, and contemplative prayer is the way of union.

[1] Ibid., pp. 25–9.   [2] See E. J. Tinsley, *The Imitation of God in Christ*.
[3] Fahey, op. cit., pp. 29–51.

5. The final stage in the Thomist schemes is perfection, the Beatific Vision.

IV. TEMPTATION AND THE PASSIONS

According to St Thomas the basic human state is one of self-love of a somewhat negative kind. Properly understood and developed this becomes wise self-love, which is not so far from the "cool self-love" of Bishop Butler. From this state there arises the *sensible appetite* or fundamental desire for one's own good. This is divisible into the *concupiscible* and *irascible* appetites, from which arise the *Passions*. From the former appetite come *love, desire,* and *joy* and their opposites *hate, aversion,* and *sadness.* From the latter are derived *hope* and *fear* and their opposites *despair* and *boldness,* as well as *anger.* The eleven passions of the soul are morally indifferent, becoming good or bad as they are, or are not, controlled by *reason* and the *law of God.*

Temptation arises from three causes, two outward or objective causes, the *world* and the *devil,* and the inward or subjective cause, *concupiscence :* the *lust of the flesh,* the *lust of the eyes,* and the *pride of life.* From this originally Johannine scheme the *capital sins* are deduced: *pride, envy, anger, covetousness, gluttony, lust, sloth.* Sin arises when human self-love, confronting temptation, is divorced from reason and defies the law of God. Wise self-love is overridden and self-love becomes *inordinate.*

In view of the loose way in which we speak of St Augustine's "pessimism" and St Thomas's "optimism" about human nature, together with the traditional English leaning towards the former, we should notice the similarities, as well as the real differences, between them. The initial similarities are quite clear. St Augustine was no dualist: God created all things and declared them very good; there is nothing basically wrong with the body and its appetites, the soul and its passions, the mind and its desires. Evil is but disorder, concupiscence, a loss of control by reason; it is a privation of the good. This is the fundamental position of St Thomas as well, yet there is one important difference. While Augustine assumes concupiscence to be an innate weakness, St Thomas somewhat reluctantly expects it to arise. To the latter, the Fall has stripped human nature of its supernatural gifts only; it is a real privation, not a kind of inherited moral disease.

In both cases, the only real answer to the human problem is

prevenient grace flowing from the redemptive life and Passion of the Incarnate Lord. Here is the core of the modern pastoral problem of "indiscriminate Baptism" and all the directorial questions that go with it. Whatever the circumstances, an Augustinian cannot charitably defer Baptism, for its lack means damnation. A Thomist can defer Baptism, for the "nature" is no bad state in which to be, and the Church is a redemptive organism, efficacious beyond its own membership. Curiously, it is the Thomist who cannot, in charity, defer absolution, for it is the only method of restoration after serious sin; followers of William of St Thierry can so defer absolution, for the soul's true benefit, because it does not change supernatural status.

In pastoral practice perhaps we may see Augustine's *homo vulneratus in naturalibus* as a wild animal, which of course is good, but which must be barred and bolted in a strong cage; there is no doubt what will happen if it escapes. To St Thomas, man is also *homo gratuitis spoliatus* which is more like a domestic dog that may get into mischief and might go mad and run amok, but not quite so inevitably.[1] Needless to say, this does not turn St Thomas into a Pelagian! The possibility of life "in grace" is ever the presupposition of his optimism; watchfulness and discipline are always needed.

"The passions are two-edged swords; they may be suggestions of evil as well as helps towards goodness."[2] To Augustine, perhaps one side of the sword is a good deal sharper than the other. "It therefore behoves the Christian to watch attentively over his passions; for, on account of their spontaneity and their violence, they often forestall the judgement of reason." So by means of mortification and asceticism they are curbed and kept in the path of duty. Again, "attentively watched" may be a little too weak for the thoroughgoing Augustinian.

V. MORAL THEORY

St Thomas's whole conception of human life is teleological. It is a movement, a progress, towards our true end in God, which is attained by cultivating the virtues in response to grace. The Christian ideal is not self-control but divine-control, therefore there *cannot* be—not *should not* be—any separation of morals from ascetic: "The whole basis of teleological ethics, is the idea of moral

[1] *Summa*, I.II.80.3 *et al.*   [2] *Summa*, I.II.24.iii.

action as a striving after an end to be attained rather than the achievement of conformity to a rule of right."[1] This kind of progress is interpreted in terms of *natural law*, but meaning the natural inclination to fulfil our essential purpose, and not the Kantian idea of obedience to God as a lawgiver, which so often presents the idea of God as a sort of over-sized schoolmaster laying down rules for no particular purpose: "Aquinas believed that actions which are contrary to the natural moral law are not wrong simply because God prohibits them; they are prohibited by God because they are wrong".[2] Because, that is, they inhibit spiritual progress towards the final goal.

Our good is our true happiness, therefore we naturally incline towards it, although, in a particularly moral situation, we may be in error as to what our true good really is. To St Thomas, original sin is not so much a natural inclination to evil as an inclination to good misinterpreted by false judgement. The thief steals, not because he is evilly inclined but because he sees his true good in possessing the stolen property, but without understanding all the other factors involved in the action. This does not justify theft, but it does incline to make it "venial", which leads to yet another difficulty in the mortal–venial distinction. "Mortal" sin implies three things: a clear knowledge of the evil intended, full consent of the will, and gravity of matter. Coupled with this is the Thomist teaching wherein any deliberate human act involves a complicated deliberation through no less than twelve stages. Having unravelled all the subtle distinctions of grace, and explained with equal subtlety what "mortal" sin is, the pastoral guide might be excused for wondering if it is really possible to commit one.

I have no doubt that the Thomist scholar can put me right about all this; but I have little confidence that the information would be of much pastoral use. What experience makes quite plain is that we commit sins, sometimes inadvertently, sometimes of comparatively small matter, often through weakness and sometimes by ignorance. And sometimes, no doubt, we fall into serious sin through our own most grievous fault, with no excuse whatever: the former are of infirmity, the latter of malice, and the distinction must remain blurred.

What Thomist moral theology makes plain to pastoral practice is that Catholic moral doctrine is teleological and must always be

[1] Vann, op. cit., p. 50; see also Copleston, *Aquinas*, pp. 192–210.
[2] Ibid., p. 218.

interpreted as such. Even in the Confessional, it is not sufficient to eradicate sin; that is but the initial step to spiritual progress. It is not sufficient for a drunkard to become temperate, he must use his temperance for the fulfilment of his true end; it must be linked with prayer. On the other hand such progress towards our fulfilment cannot seriously be regarded like a game of snakes and ladders: for venial sins you miss a turn, for mortal sins you go back to the beginning.

VI. FURTHER DOMINICAN ASCETIC

1. *The Rosary.* The Dominican Order is closely associated with, if not responsible for, the Rosary, which is unique among popular devotions. Its origin and purpose are obscure, but there are strong suggestions that it was always intended to fulfil the function it now achieves for modern Roman Catholicism. As a devotion used daily by the whole communion, by Pope, priest, and peasant, it forges a pastoral unity throughout that Church. It expresses, in other words, what the Mass creates. The great distinction, therefore, is that whereas most popular devotions—whether the cult of the Sacred Heart or special services for Boy Scouts—are inclined to be separative, to emphasize a group rather than the whole, the Rosary is unitive.

The English equivalent is a twofold Office, especially designed for use by the *whole* Church. This maintains a primitive Catholic tradition from which the Rosary is generally admitted to be something of a climb-down. Dom Cuthbert Butler writes: "of all non-liturgical prayers it is the one that approaches most nearly to the Canonical Office, by reason both of the formal nature of its authorization, and of the public manner of its recitation by the Faithful in common in church, as well as for private prayer."[1] And Pourrat notes: "A great number of the faithful, living in the world, wished to imitate the monks. Instead of the Psalter, which they had no time to recite, they invented the *Psalter of Our Lady*, in which each one of the 150 psalms is represented by an *Ave Maria*."[2]

On all counts, theological, historical, and ascetical, the Anglican twofold Office is the better way of achieving the agreed end: the pastoral unity of the Church Militant. The alternatives confronting us are clear: either we must accept the Office for what it is, especially in future revisions, or reject our traditional ideal in favour of the

[1] *Ways of Christian Life* (1932), p. 103.   [2] Ibid., II, p. 330, n.2.

Rosary or its equivalent—if we can! The proper course for Anglicans could not be more obvious.[1]

A great deal has been written about the devotional and psychological value of the Rosary, and the foregoing in no way contradicts it. But if Anglicans choose to use it, and many would be wise to do so, they must recognize the essential difference of approach. To us, the Rosary must be a private devotion, though possibly forging a charitable unity with the Roman Church; it cannot be a substitute for the daily Offices.

2. *St Catherine of Siena.* I started this chapter by saying that Thomist theology is too big and influential to be expressed in a single, clearly defined school. It develops, in fact, along three separate, and disparate, lines. It leads into the supreme ascetical and mystical achievement of St John of the Cross and St Teresa of Avila, and also of St Ignatius Loyola. It is interpreted—and misinterpreted[2]—in the affective mysticism of the German Dominican school. And it is expressed in its sublime purity by St Catherine of Siena who, alone of these three groups, impinges upon the English school to any great extent.

St Catherine has a marked resemblance to Julian of Norwich, and, in certain sections of the *Dialogue*, with the colloquies of Margery Kempe. Mr Algar Thorold describes the *Dialogue* as "nothing more than a devotional exposition of the Creeds", which is precisely what ascetical theology should be. Though similarly "unlettered", therefore, St Catherine has a wider range than Julian, and a far greater theological depth than Margery: St Catherine is ruled by "Know, my daughter, I am he who is, and thou art she who art not"; Margery by "Daughter, have mind of my goodness and thy wickedness". If St Thomas is to guide English devotion, it seems more reasonable to seek his teaching in Siena than in Germany or Spain.[3]

[1] See Ch. 20, iv, below.
[2] Tauler, for example, teaches an unmediated mystical union between the divine essence and the essence of the soul. This is in direct contradiction to St Thomas, who taught that the object of contemplation is divine truth revealed and known by faith, but *not* the divine essence. In this life, communion with God is *always* mediate.
[3] See further R. Garrigon-Lagrange, *The Three Ages of the Interior Life* (1960) vol. I, pp. 3-97.

CONCLUSION TO PART TWO

Ascetical theology consists in making classifications and schemes, maps, models, and plans of the spiritual life as it grows out of dogmatic theology and is manifested in the living experience of the Church. The resultant theory is to be applied to individual Christian people, and also to Christian communities, according to their particular needs and circumstances.

The student of ascetical theology is constantly beset with the temptation so to stretch points and strain conclusions that his plans and schemes take on a false character. He is in danger of presenting Christian prayer with a tidiness that is not true to experience. These schemes and maps are both theoretical and useful, but they must be properly interpreted and applied. Having said that, I do not claim it to be more than interesting to look back on our studies so far to try to find a pattern of relationships amongst the teachers we have considered, and to seek further relationships between them and the fully formed English School.

The first point of interest is that the four great names in our story offer pastoral doctrine only when interpreted by four lesser-known but equally important writers. The two speculative saints, Augustine and Aquinas, need to be complemented by Hugh of St Victor and Catherine of Siena before their ascetical doctrine lives. The two affective saints, Bernard and Francis, give us little more than edification until they are reduced to order by William of St Thierry and Bonaventure. All the while, to some extent, each of these eight lives his life in association with the practical doctrine of St Benedict, itself nurtured on the theology of St Augustine.

Secondly, these four great pairs give a different slant to Christian spirituality; each emphasizes a different aspect which plays a major part in the English tradition. The outlook of St Augustine and the School of St Victor is repeated in the writings of Walter Hilton. The bold approach to the Sacred Humanity in daily life, experienced by St Bernard and taught by William of St Thierry, is the basis of *The Book of Margery Kempe*. The romantic lyricism, the penitential emphasis, and some of the almost arrogant individualism of St Francis of Assisi finds an English counterpart in Richard Rolle of Hampole. And the spiritual doctrine of St Thomas, made vividly alive by St Catherine of Siena, forms a speculative–affective synthesis which is the hall-mark of the *Revelations* of Julian of Norwich.

Plainly things are not quite so tidy as that. Hilton contains a large Thomist element, there are both Cistercian and Franciscan elements in Julian, and Margery Kempe bears a kind of small-sister relation to Catherine. And these four English writers present a marked family resemblance to one another.

Such classification should not be taken too seriously, yet even such a scheme, sensibly used, may not be entirely without value in pastoral guidance. If an Anglican were temperamentally inclined towards Thomist spirituality, it would surely be wise to nurture his prayer on Julian and Catherine. It would be very unwise to give him only the works of Tauler and Suso, although they too, would claim to be Thomist and Dominican. In practice, I suspect that such an Anglican would soon find himself immersed in St John of the Cross, who is also Thomist and whose works are admirable, but they make things more difficult for our English parishioner than they need be. The English Christian with an attraction for St Thomas may happily take Catherine and Julian to church with him; Suso and *The Ascent of Mount Carmel* seem somewhat out of harmony with parish Communion in Leeds. It seems curious, to say the least, that Anglicans who are sensibly devoted to St Augustine's *Confessions*, St Bernard's *Sermons*, and St Francis' *Canticle*, should pay such scant attention to Hilton, Margery, and Rolle.

In the middle of the period that we have been considering stands the all-important figure of St Anselm, and while we are playing a little game of plan-making, two things might be noticed about him. The first is that, amongst the medieval galaxy of saints and doctors, he alone needs no obvious interpreter. Anselm is in no sense an insular figure, but he achieves the speculative–affective synthesis in a personal way which has never been surpassed. Secondly, it might be noticed that had we tried to invent some composite figure as the father-founder of English spirituality, we could hardly do better than imagine a deeply affective Benedictine of Augustinian leanings,

11—E.S.

employing the scholastic method as a loving director of souls; and then make him Archbishop of Canterbury.

As we approach the English School itself, we find the specifically monastic tradition Anglicized into the Gilbertines, and the perennial ideal of solitary life flourishing, not so much within the Carthusian Order, but in a very pastoral interpretation of the anchorite life.

PART THREE

The English School

THE CELTIC CHURCH AND WHITBY

I. YORK AND ROME

Certain English historians assume that the Council of Whitby, in 664, was an unmitigated tragedy. It is implied that the adoption of the Roman date of Easter, the question of the tonsure, and so on, led to a total Romanizing of our Church. Participants like Wilfrith and Benedict Biscop are represented as traitors selling their heritage to a foreign power. In an attempt to counter this implication, other historians, still seeing Whitby as a disaster, reach the curious conclusion that the English Church was Protestant before the Reformation and Catholic after it. The more reputable view is neatly put by J. H. Overton: "to Gregory (and the mission of St Augustine of Canterbury) belongs the credit of laying the foundation of the English, as distinguished from the British Church".[1] This fact is worth a little elaboration.

Starting from the characteristics of the English School of which we are now aware, it is tempting to try to trace their native antecedents further back than is reasonable. One might look for a warm "domestic" tradition in the lives of saints like Ninian, Aidan, Columba, and Chad; one might see something solidly English as well as Benedictine in St Cuthbert's refusal to allow his monks either rich clothing or ostentatious rags. With a little more conviction it is possible to see our scholarly tradition in Alcuin and the affective–speculative synthesis in Bede, the devout monk preaching homely sermons combined with scholarship of remarkable restraint for an historian of his age. Yet all that seems a little strained and artificial, and I do not think such speculation is of much importance to this study.

What is necessary is to see, following Overton, how the manifold branches of the English spiritual tradition were successfully engrafted to the British stock. There was no recognizable English

[1] *The Church in England* (1897), Vol. I, p. 30.

School of Spirituality before the fourteenth century, but if we have traced the trends and movements which combined to make it up, there must have been some underlying principle of selection; some native instinct which accepted some teaching and rejected others. This British, or Celtic, stock was unquestionably there, deep-rooted and alive. One imagines Wilfrith, overwhelmed by the glories of Christian culture he had seen in Rome and Gaul, becoming a little dissatisfied with the homespun religion of his native Northumbria. He may be likened to a village boy, returning from his first visit to London convinced that his village could do with the qualities of the capital. The important thing is that, however hard he tries to put this idea into practice, his village, the deep-rooted parent stock, will accept some of London's ways and reject others. The village girls might adopt the latest fashions from Bond Street, but the proprietor of the village store will not sell them in a tail coat.

So upon the Celtic stock was to flourish the glorious branch of St Bernard's affective prayer, but the stock would not support the extravagances of later Cistercian devotion. The heirs of the old Celtic priests happily adopted the Roman tonsure, but they never propagated the type of priesthood preached by St Hildegarde or St Bridget. England produced her mystics, who no doubt learned much from the Rhineland, but it was English mysticism stemming from the Victorine tradition. The actual make-up of the Celtic stock, and how it got there in the first place, are obscure; all we need to know is that it will support some things and not others: strains of spirituality like the Carthusian ethos and Rhineland mysticism "just won't take" (as the gardeners say).

According to ecclesiastical history, in the popular sense of Church history with a political bias, the results of the Whitby decision were unfortunate. Had things gone the other way the Middle Ages in England might have been less turbulent. But from the point of view of English spiritual growth any other result would have been a disaster. From whatever motive, it was St Augustine and the "Romanizing" party which made possible the glorious spiritual lineage which has been traced in Part Two of this book. Without this expansive movement, the British stock might have remained alive and healthy, but it is unlikely that it would have developed into the sublimely fruitful tree of the English fourteenth century.

II. THE CELTIC PENITENTIAL SYSTEM

Once the small native Church was brought into the main stream of Catholicism, it is to be expected that the former would grow and develop under the influence of the latter. That is what happened, but with one significant exception. In the matter of penitential doctrine and practice, things are curiously reversed. Rather than the Celtic tradition moulding itself upon the main Catholic stream, it is the main Catholic stream which brings itself into line with the Celtic Church: it is a case of the boy teaching the school. Five points of difference are worth considering in the light of penitential development as we know it.

1. Rome regarded penance as the reconciliation of serious sinners, often only of the excommunicate; in the Celtic Church it was remedial, applying to all Christians and all types of sin.

Reconciliation differs from remedy in that the one is a juridical term and the other pastoral. The first implies the legal reinstatement of the excommunicate or of a grave sinner who has "fallen out of grace". The second implies healing and therefore growth, which gives it an ascetical rather than a merely moral implication. The defendant of a lawsuit gains nothing on acquittal; at best he is back where he was before. A patient who is healed and strengthened may be better than he was before treatment.

2. Rome allowed absolution once only, with the proviso that it could be repeated on the death-bed of grave or excommunicate sinners; the Celtic Church permitted confession at need, with absolution at recurrent intervals throughout life.

Here the Roman system is not merely rigorous; it underlies a different outlook on the doctrine of the Church. Death-bed absolution after a second serious fall is a charitable attempt to get the sinner, by hook or by crook, into the "ark of salvation" before it is too late. It is a pastoral attitude not wholly to be despised, but it leaves out of account the creative life of the Christian within the Church Militant: it is concerned with status rather than with progress. The idea behind frequent confession and absolution is not laxity but gradual progress towards perfection. Its immediate aim is to get the sinner back, not into the *state* but into the *stream* of grace; back into the daily work of the Church.

The Celtic system started in the monasteries, but it was in advance of the rest of Christendom in extending the fruits of penitential discipline to all people: "with regard to the penance of sinners, which is the medicine of the soul, we deem it to be useful for all men: and that the penance be assigned to the penitents by the priests when confession has been made; let the assembled priests be understood to agree".[1]

3. In Rome, confession was both private and, on occasion, public. The fulfilment of penance, and final absolution, were often of a public nature. In Celtic practice, confession, penance, and absolution were always private.

These last two points led naturally to what is now called "confession of devotion", that is, confession as a regular part of normal Christian life, whether or not grave sin has been committed. It is a generous profession of sinfulness and self-oblation before the healing Cross. In this Alcuin is both pastoral and peculiarly modern:

> Come then, O penitent, confess thine own sins, lay bare by confession the secret of thine iniquity. Known unto God are those things which thou hast wrought in secret, which if the tongue have not spoken, yet the conscience will not be able to conceal. Tell thy sins by confession before thou feel the anger of the Judge. Believe me, all that thou hast sinned will be found pardonable if thou do not blush to confess it. God awaits the sacrifice of confession from us that he may accord to us the delightful boon of pardon. Accordingly, my dearest sons, hasten to the remedy of confession. Lay open your wounds in confession that the medicaments of healing may be able to take effect in you.[2]

That is Anglican enough to remind us of Jeremy Taylor, or even of a modern sermon on the Prayer Book exhortation. Alcuin is clearly thinking of "confession of devotion" as he writes: "Diligently purge the slightest soils of words and thoughts . . . before a faithful and prudent confessor, according to thy conscience, so that nothing remain, wherein the Evil One may have to accuse thee before the highest Judge."[3]

4. According to modern standards, penances were severe under both systems, but in the Celtic schemes they were less so, and could be commuted. But there are strange anomalies: three years' fasting

[1] Council of Chalon, A.D. 640.   [2] Opusculum, 7.   [3] Letter 188.

seems a light penalty for homicide,[1] and fifteen days not unreasonable for serious drunkenness,[2] yet theft may also carry a three year penance, and perjury seven.[3]

That a penance is commutable has pastoral significance, but it also points to another fundamental difference of approach. The Roman penance was not commutable because it was a legal sentence; the Celtic attitude is that of just punishment, penitentially borne in love of the divine justice. This, of course, is present practice; the penance has to be *accepted* and freely offered to God with thanksgiving for absolution. This underlines the devotional approach, for one cannot freely accept a juridical penalty.

5. Under the Roman system, the minister of the sacrament was generally the bishop; under the Celtic system it could be the monastic superior or parish priest.

It follows that when confession becomes the regular thing for all Christians, its administration must be delegated from the bishop to the parish priests. But this, too, is more than a practical necessity. In the nature of the case, the bishop dealing with serious sins is apt to become a legalist judge; the priest dealing with all cases must be a pastor. The one belongs to a part of the Church administering the law to another part, the other to a united Church sanctifying itself. Is it over-stretching the evidence to see here the beginning of the later medieval priest–lay gulf of Continental Christendom, and the comparative lack of such a clerical caste in the English Church?

The whole of the Celtic system presupposes the interrelation between morals and ascetic; or it presupposes a teleological moral theology. The differences between Celtic and Roman in the seventh century were much the same as those between England and Rome a thousand years later. It is the same fundamental divergence between Caroline and post-Tridentine Roman moral doctrine, and through all this the Anglican approach to penance remains constant. For twelve centuries, it has been no juridical haggle, no means of easy acquittal, but a generous act of worship.

At the risk of pedantry, I plead that modern Anglicans should take more care with devotional phrases relating to the sacrament of penance which belong to another tradition and to an alien pastoral

[1] *Penitential* of Columbanus.   [2] *Penitential* of Theodore.
[3] *Penitential* of Finian.

theology. Why speak of the "sacred tribunal" when we mean, or ought to mean, an objective act of penitence? Why "the ministry of reconciliation", implying a rejected scholastic doctrine, when we mean a remedial channel of grace and absolution? And in a united Church Militant, why are we so reluctant to point out that a good confessor must himself be a good penitent rather than a judge over against a prisoner?

Finally, it is interesting that at least two Celtic authorities admit the validity of non-sacramental or "private" confession. The *Penitential* of Theodore contains: "But it shall be lawful that confession may be made to God alone". More fully the first *Capitulary* of Theodulf reads:

> For the confession which we make to the priests brings to us this support, that we wash away the stains of our sins when we receive at their hands salutary counsel, the very wholesome observances of penance, or the exchange of prayers. But the confession which we make to God alone is helpful in this, that in so far as we are mindful of our sins, so far God is forgetful of them; and conversely, in so far as we forget them, so far God remembers them.

That sounds very Anglican, especially the little sting in the tail, which offers a strong argument in favour of sacramental confession, while allowing the validity of "private" confession. But the latter is absolutely safe only for the truly contrite: "for these and all my other sins which I cannot now remember . . ." is of much importance. It should also be noticed how Theodulf supports a mutuality of priest and penitent—"or the exchange of prayers"; here are no judge and culprit, but two brothers in Christ.[1]

III. THE TENTH CENTURY

As with Whitby and the School of York, so with the tenth-century monastic revival: it would be unreal to seek from it any developed English spirituality. We are told that King Alfred mourned the demise of English scholarship, and that the revival under St Dunstan did much to restore it. There continue to be close relations between Church and monarchy, exemplified by the Council of Winchester, called by King Edgar, presided over by St Ethelwold, and inspired by St Dunstan. The result of this synod, the *Regularis*

---

[1] For the whole question, see O. D. Watkins, *A History of Penance* (1920), Vol. II, pp. 587–631.

Concordia Angliae, points to a common English monastic use, and might just hint at the ideal of pastoral unity. England no doubt suffered from all the monastic difficulties of the age: expanded and complicated liturgy, and a decline in manual labour. But it remained aloof from the exaggerations of Cluny, and never submitted to its growing influence; its monastic heritage was to continue along the opposite line from Cîteaux.

J. Armitage Robinson describes the *Regularis Concordia* as an example of "the national aptitude for taking the best from all quarters, tempering extravagance with a fine discretion, adapting rather than copying the customs of other lands."[1] That hints at the principle of development the English school was to follow; but we must not force a preconceived scheme further than it will rightly go. The one certain point in this early period is that when England looked to a religious revival its overriding principle remained solidly Benedictine:

> Then, lest individuals by acting on their own presumptuous choice should forfeit the fruits of obedience, they bound themselves by a solemn vow to observe these Customs in their common practice, whilst all should be free to use in secret parts of the church such private prayers as the Holy Spirit might inspire.[2]

That is the principle of the *Regula*; and it is the principle of the Prayer Book.

[1] *The Times of St Dunstan* (1923), p. 145.   [2] *Regularis Concordia*, Preface.

14

ST ANSELM

St Anselm occupies a place in English spirituality not unlike that of
Chaucer in English letters. He is the father-founder who first
brought all the essential elements together, who gave the school its
clear character and stamp. In Anselm, English spiritual theology is
embodied and potentially formed; formed as a young man who still
needs to mature but who is no longer a child; who still has much to
learn and whose best work is yet to come, but who is complete,
equipped, and adult. For the needs of pastoral practice, Anselm is
not our greatest asceticist; in the narrower sense he is hardly an
asceticist at all. Yet true English ascetical theology springs from him,
and without him it is difficult to see how it could have developed at
all.

If Anselm may thus be compared with Chaucer, there is another
sense in which he might be compared with Samuel Johnson: his
influence, power, and perception were probably more important
than his actual writings. For our present purpose, however, Anselm's
writings are by no means without value.

I. THE AFFECTIVE–SPECULATIVE SYNTHESIS

The affective–speculative synthesis does not mean an exact
fifty-fifty balance, nor is it attained either by adding an occasional
devout phrase to a theological work, or by interposing one or two
quotations from the Fathers in an affective meditation. It is a synthesis, not merely a mixture, and the true synthesis is possible to
different temperaments. Everyone has a natural bias to one side or
the other, and spiritual health is attained by allowing this bias to be
permeated by the other aspect through mental and emotional
discipline. Nobody would wish to curb St Bernard's affectiveness,
yet had he brought doctrinal discipline to bear more fully on his
nature, the Church would have been saved much trouble. So it was
with St Francis. Conversely, had Abelard allowed the humility of

affective devotion to have warmed his speculative genius, he would have saved a good deal of trouble for himself. By this criterion, St Anselm is greater than either. His natural bent was as speculative as that of Abelard, yet all his works are full of an affective devotion as real and deep as St Bernard's. Anselm is less Christocentric and more theocentric, but the affective strain is unmistakable; he achieved in fact what St Bonaventure taught in theory. "No one", wrote C. C. J. Webb, "has ever more strikingly shown how the disinterested search for metaphysical truth can be offered as a service of passionate devotion to God."[1] "Disinterested" is an important word: it is no mere quest for "pure scholarship" or "academic" knowledge, but the Augustinian search for the truth about God because such truth leads to love, and ultimately the two are indissociable. As Dr Webb goes on to explain in his useful introduction, Anselm is neither evangelist nor apologist; his "disinterested" search is for divine truth which stimulates praise, not for that which would convert the heathen or refute his opponents. Anselm would be out of place leading either a mission or a heresy-hunt. He is supremely the ascetical theologian in the wider, adjectival sense, if not in the narrower sense. To him, all theology is applicable to worship, in fact it has no other use, but he gives us no methods of prayer or ascetical schemes other than his underlying Benedictinism.

It is in this way that I think the writings of Anselm should be approached, certainly if we are to benefit from him as a pastoral guide. He cannot be classified or departmentalized in the modern fashion: and if the "ontological argument" is boxed up under "philosophy of religion", and *Cur Deus Homo?* chained to the shelf marked "dogmatics", then he is bound to be misunderstood. This should become clearer as we look at some of his works.

II. *MONOLOGION* AND *PROSLOGION*

The original title of the *Monologion* was *Exemplum meditandi de ratione fidei*: an example of meditation on the reasonableness of faith. Mr Martin Rule gives an important footnote on the meaning of this phrase,[2] and is surely right in objecting to Dean Church's over-literal "an example of meditation on the reason of faith". The important point is that the *Monologion* supplies a method of harmonizing faith with reason. The subject of the discourse, as

---

[1] *Devotions of St Anselm* (1903), introd., p. xvii.
[2] *Life and Times of St Anselm* (1883), Vol. I, p. 176.

Rule points out, is not the reason of faith but the Being of God; this is first affirmed by faith and then subjected to the method—*de ratione fidei*—of thinking something out for oneself in prayer: *credo ut intelligam.*

Mr Rule goes on to say that this is not "meditation as that word is usually understood", but the word is very often misunderstood. What Anselm offers is a superb example of what is generally called "intellectual meditation", here based on the *De Trinitate* of Augustine, and one which provides a pattern for others. It is a free yet disciplined attempt to elicit from *a priori* reasoning the idea of God held by faith. It is, as Anselm calls it, *soliloquy.*

If the *Monologion* is *soliloquy*, the *Proslogion* is *colloquy*. Subtitled *Faith in search of understanding* or the *Address*, it begins, as all true colloquy must, with a hymn of praise to God; to "that than which no greater can be conceived", yet with whom one can converse, and from whom one may receive enlightenment:

> I seek not, O Lord, to search out Thy depth, but I desire in some measure to understand Thy truth, which my heart believeth and loveth. Nor do I seek to understand that I may believe, but I believe that I may understand. For this too I believe, that unless I first believe, I shall not understand.[1]

That is prayer, the *Address* to God, but such an address demands an answer, or a series of answers, from God to the mind. It is not uncommon to find philosophy or theology presented in dialogue form—Aquinas, Spinoza, Hume spring to mind—but with Anselm, in both the *Proslogion* and *Cur Deus Homo?* the dialogue is not between fictitious protagonists, but between himself and God. It is colloquy, prayer.

The key to my suggested approach is simply this: that as one reads affective devotion—Bernard, Francis, Aelred—the author is assumed to be preaching to an audience, attempting to stir up a response. With most speculative theology, one imagines the author sitting at a desk surrounded with books, trying to impart knowledge. But whatever one reads of Anselm, he can only be visualized on his knees, not trying to do anything but worship God. Approached in this way, Anselm still has much to say to modern English spirituality.

1. Anselm was in the forefront of a new theological movement which was to culminate in scholasticism, and which tends to counter the

---

[1] *Proslogion*, ch. 1.

"blind faith" of purely affective spirituality. For an eleventh-century Benedictine to propound a specific method of personal reasoning about the dogma of the Church, of thinking things out for oneself and boldly facing the possibility of doubt, must have been regarded as original and not a little dangerous. To be consistent, St Bernard must have been as suspicious of Anselm as he was of Abelard: yet what a difference between the two. In Anselm, there is neither rationalism nor arrogant humanism, but a respect for human reason as the ally of faith and the promoter of love. Tertullian's *credo quia est absurdum* becomes *credo ut intelligam*, which F. R. Tennant, with a somewhat rare smile, delightfully translates as "nothing venture, nothing have".[1] Credulity has become "faith-venture", as faith remains an infused virtue rather than an intellectual assent; it is seen as something dynamic, active, ascetical, rather than passive and static. It is, in other words, a gift to be *used* not *held*.

As on the one hand, right order requires that we believe the deep things of the Christian religion before presuming to subject them to the analysis and test of reason, so on the other hand it looks to me like indolent neglect if, already established in the faith, we do not take the trouble to gain an intellectual intimacy with what we believe.[2]

Thus Anselm speaks to modern Anglicanism: we are right to grapple with the deep mysteries of the faith; "blind faith" is not loyalty but sloth. If doubts arise in the mind, they are to be calmly faced and resolved as the struggle continues, they are hurdles to be jumped as we progress towards understanding and love. That is truly Anglican, for it is neither "free thought" in the sense that anyone has the right to believe what he likes, nor does it make dogma anything but dogmatic, but it does not impute sin to honest inquiry.

Thus the pastoral answer to intellectual doubt is not that it is wicked to doubt the dogmas of the Church, nor that it does not very much matter. The answer is in the acceptance of a creative challenge. So, to a spiritual guide, such difficulties should be neither shocking nor unimportant. They should be seen as positive not negative, a call to further action: it should be "let us see how to use this" rather than "oh but you must trust the Church" or "try not

[1] *Philosophical Theology* (1928), Vol. I, p. 263   [2] *Cur Deus Homo?*, I. 2.

to worry". What Anselm is saying, in Sunday school language, is when in doubt go and tell God about it, and keep on arguing: the result could be another *Proslogion*.

The Anglican Church, therefore, is wise not to promulgate a series of new dogmas, to be held on pain of ecclesiastical censure. It is very *un*wise to allow contrary opinions on fundamental doctrine. Anglicanism needs no Index of prohibited books, not through lack of discipline but because of its Anselmic spirit. But it is both foolish and unfair not to give positive pronouncements as to what Baptism, Confirmation, the Real Presence and the Virgin Conception really mean, because such dogmatic statements, rather than inhibiting reason and understanding, are the basis of them. One cannot "believe in order to understand" when one does not know what to believe in the first place; one cannot even indulge in the creative process of doubting.

2. This kind of exercise, "intellectual meditation" in its widest sense, results not only in an increased knowledge and love for God, but also in the "absorbed" or contemplative faith of William of St Thierry.[1]

"What faith is to religion, experience is to science."[2] Faith, like observed phenomena, begins with an external object, which has to be tested, examined, and absorbed into the personality. C. C. J. Webb adds an important note to ch. 12 of the *Proslogion*, to the effect that God *is* life, wisdom, goodness; qualities of which we can only partake: we *have* life, virtue, and truth; God *is* life, virtue, and truth. But we may *have* faith in different degrees, we may simply "hold" it, or agree with it, or try to live by it as a code of laws, but it is still external. It can, and must be absorbed, so becoming the spontaneous source of action and praise. To put it in scholastic terms, faith is a God-given virtue infused into the depths of the soul, which is to be nourished and developed by prayer; which is to be fed with doctrine. As so many saints have discovered—St Catherine, Julian, the Curé d'Ars—prayer is the proper way to learn theology. Strictly speaking, therefore, a baptized person cannot "lose his faith"—except possibly by continuous sin and laxity—but he can fail to feed it. Faith is supernatural and not to be confused with intellectual assent, of which it is the parent. The one is essentially internal,

---

[1] Discussed in Ch. 8, ii above.
[2] Anne Freemantle, *The Age of Belief* (1957), p. 138.

the other essentially external until it is, as it were, digested by faith.[1]

It is against this background that the so-called "ontological argument" can best be appreciated. As philosophy it is unsatisfactory and generally discredited, and Karl Barth makes a strong case against its being even ontological.[2] But it is not philosophy at all; Anselm is not interested in "proving" the existence of God *a priori*, or for purposes of evangelism or apologetic. He begins with faith and ends with greater faith because faith has been wedded to knowledge. The "ontological argument", or rather the early chapters of *Proslogion*, is an intellectual meditation about God starting with an *Address*, not to proselytes or to a philosophical society, but to God himself. It begins with the dogma of the existence and attributes of God and ends with adoration; which is what it is meant to do. It is affective–speculative prayer, not a D.D. thesis.

III. THE ATONEMENT

Like the "ontological argument", the atonement doctrine set out in *Cur Deus Homo?* is now largely discredited. But this involves the same misunderstanding of Anselm's purpose. If the "ontological argument" is not philosophy, neither is this legal, "account-book" image of atonement dogmatic theology in the modern, departmental sense. The *Proslogion* is colloquy leading to adoration, *Cur Deus Homo?* is colloquy leading to penitence. The first is prayer centred on the transcendent Father, the second is prayer centred on the Passion of the Son.

The doctrine of *Cur Deus Homo?* was, however, an important step in the history of atonement theory, and an advance on the current "ransom-to-the-devil" theories. It is objected that it is crudely legalistic, with redemption worked out only in terms of the owing and payment of debts. But, as pastoral theology, this objection needs a good deal of qualification.

1. Christians know that their redemption depends on the sacrificial death of Christ and not on their own works, but they also know that good works are, in fact, good. Judgement involves a total life, in which good works and sins have their importance as well as "faith". The idea of the owing and payment of debts, the "account-book"

[1] As in the Advent II collect.
[2] *Fides Quaerens Intellectum* (1931), p. 171.

image, is therefore, like heaven above and hell below, basic symbolism which most mature Christians do in fact use. In everyday life the commission of sin subconsciously suggests a debt to God, just as injustice suggests a debt to the one injured: on penitence we feel we must "make up for it". Crude as it may appear to the cloistered theologian, all this is normal, and valid, pastoral symbolism; the most intelligent of laymen cannot carry the latest atonement theory around with them. That is why nine out of ten sound modern sermons on the atonement—good, practical sermons—contain a considerable amount of Anselmic doctrine. Granted both the shortcomings and the pastoral value of the image, Anselm deserves our gratitude for putting it accurately. Although no modern Anglican would "hold" the theory, as intellectual explanation, it is all too easy to slip into Pelagian thinking, even in a recollected life. Anselm prevents this by firmly teaching the impossibility of any "credit balance" in the best of human lives: our "debt" to God is unredeemable except by Christ. In a sublime speculative-affective idiom, the account-book symbol here leads to humility and love. In practice, it avoids the errors, not only of Pelagius, but of antinomianism and "justification by faith alone".

2. As its title implies, *Cur Deus Homo?* is not only an explanation of the atonement but also a devout meditation on the Incarnation. Medieval popular devotion over-emphasized the idea of Christ as judge of mankind, just as the present age so flagrantly forgets this true and chastening fact. Anselm's doctrine puts proper stress on Christ as both judge and saviour through a pastoral re-appraisal of Christology. This involved a reconsideration of the Sacred Humanity which developed into the glorious devotion of the Cistercian and Franciscan schools. In the context of atonement doctrine, concentration is obviously fixed on the Passion, and the Anselmic synthesis is consummated with the *Revelations* of Julian of Norwich, in which our Lord may be seen as both sympathetic judge and suffering saviour. Such meditation inspires penitential love, but it also leads to, and develops, the virtue of hope. With no trace of sentimentality or laxity, all this adds up to that subdued optimism which, initiated by Anselm and completed in Julian, remains a marked characteristic of the English school.

3. If Christ is seen only as judge, whose adverse decision means the vivid, fiery, demon-infested hell of the medieval frescoes,

then popular devotion will seek a mediator other than the judge himself; it will seek some other "advocate with the Father". It is but a short step to the heretical and unintelligent (those adjectives are important!) cults of our Lady, saints, and angels, and another short step to an over-exalted idea of priesthood.

The influence of *Cur Deus Homo?* on fourteenth-century England [1] did much to save us from some of these excesses. England never quite submitted to the mediation of a sacerdotal caste flagrantly abusing the powers of the Keys: Chaucer laughed at the idea and Margery Kempe's confessors would have joined with him. Anselm's meditations and prayers to our Lady and the saints are quite different from those addressed to our Lord, and also different from St Bernard's. Margery Kempe provides the perfect example when her prayers and colloquies are addressed to Christ, judge, advocate, and redeemer, while he is surrounded by his saints and angels. The host of heaven is essential to any fully mature spirituality, but with Margery, as with Anselm, the saints are put firmly in their proper place; they are our contemporaries and our friends, looking on and offering their considerable support. That is very important but it is not mediation in the sense reserved for Jesus Christ.

4. The relation between mercy and justice is a problem inherent in atonement doctrine. To Anselm, this is also a problem of ascetical synthesis. Justice is primarily a speculative idea, it is an objective attribute of God manifested in Christ the judge; a certain "legalism" is here justified and necessary. Mercy is an affective concept, also an attribute of God, manifested in the Passion. Again the *Revelations* of Julian provide a synthesis.

There is an apocryphal story told by St Anselm in a sermon at Bec: Justice and Mercy were arguing in heaven as they looked down upon the fallen world in the year 1 B.C. Justice insisted that it should be destroyed, for how else could his position be maintained? Mercy replied that, in that case, how could his position stand? They were joined by the divine Logos who, embracing them, said "leave it to me and I will satisfy you both". Apocryphal or not, that is what *Cur Deus Homo?* means.

[1] Walter Hilton reproduces the whole argument in Book II, ch. 2, of the *Scale of Perfection.*

IV. MEDITATIONS AND LETTERS

The Meditations and Prayers of St Anselm might reasonably be
expected to contain the most usable of his ascetical teaching, but
that is not necessarily the case. Mr Rule criticizes Dom Gerberon's
edition of Anselm for making too rigid a distinction between the
"meditations" and the "prayers".[1] I do not think this criticism
goes far enough: none of Anselm's works can be so tidily split up
into "subjects"; place any of his books anywhere you wish on the
shelves of a religious bookshop and nothing could be out of place.
His prayers are meditative, his theology is prayer, his philosophy is
devotion, his letters of counsel are pastoral theology; all is biblical,
all is doctrine, all is praise. That is the whole point. And it is well
demonstrated by the subject matter of the Meditations themselves.
The first, in Gerberon's edition, is the *Monologion* in a different
form, the eleventh is based on *Cur Deus Homo?*, and the twenty-
first contains hardly a phrase which is not in the *Proslogion*.[2]

The significance of this is brought home when we consider that
such a process to-day is barely conceivable: take a modern devotional
manual, or a series of retreat addresses, and try to turn it into a
treatise on philosophical theology; take the latest book on dogmatics and try to turn it into a prayer. Yet St Anselm found such
alternation easy and natural; and it remains the Anglican ideal. His
particular perfection is in the virtue that ascetical theology knows as
"simplicity" and which moral theology calls "purity"; it is an
integrity, a working harmony between body, mind and spirit
because every facet of his personality points in the same way:
Godward. As Dean Church has pointed out, it is not difficult to
think of a greater theologian, philosopher, or administrator, a
better abbot or archbishop, but it is hard to find a more perfect
Christian soul: that, too, points to an Anglican ideal.

The *Letters* abound with this same wisdom which is a compound

[1] Rule, op. cit., Vol. I, p. 421.

[2] Not unnaturally, doubt has been cast upon the authenticity of some of the
Meditations attributed to Anselm. The technical problems need not deter us
since all 21 in Gerberon's edition are of the same type and are plainly influenced
by Anselm's thought. Mr Rule makes the interesting point that Anselm's
Latin is very difficult to translate into English, while in certain of the *Meditations*
"sentence after sentence turns itself, as it were, into English . . ." If these are
the work of an English disciple, thinking in English and writing in Latin, they
are more significantly "Anselmic" than ever; see ch. 15, iv below and also
Rule, op. cit., Vol. I, pp. 421–8

of doctrine, philosophy, devotion and love, and they breathe the
easy "domestic" spirit of English optimism.[1] These letters, like
those of Bernard and Aelred, are always quoted in support of the
truly human affection between brethren which is characteristic of
Benedictinism; of the family ideal which has so special a place in
English pastoral relationships. And it is Anselm who also opposes the
cold theory of "detachment" to which reference has already been
made.[2] Modern Anglican directors and parish priests must seriously
consider which side they are on; are we to side with Anselm,
Bernard, Aelred, Hilton, Herbert, and Keble, or with St John of the
Cross, Ignatius Loyola, and M. Olier? The letters of our father-
founder give an emphatic answer.

As archbishop, Anselm remained a strong Papalist, but because
he saw the Church as one and indivisible, yet as a true Benedictine
he was quite capable of seeing the significance of racial families and
schools within it. This theology of the one pastoral Church is
illustrated by another of his sublimely practical stories:

In Benedictinism, *nutriti* were child oblates, brought up in the
community, while *conversi* were adult converts from the world.
The former were wont to claim greater seniority and purity, the
latter greater experience and depth of faith gained through struggle.
It was the perennial argument between "once-born" and "twice-
born", between the regular soldier and the volunteer, between
Magdalene and the Little Flower. Anselm's answer to one such
dispute was reputed to be: "my brothers, can you imagine St Michael
blaming St Peter for his denial of the Lord? And had he done so,
can you imagine St Peter retorting that an Archangel could hardly
be expected to understand human temptation?" That is deep
domestic theology; the real unity of the Church local wherein
not only bishops, priests and laity, but saints and angels as well,
have their diverse gifts and functions within the unity of the
Body.

The final message is the basis of all. Anselm the archbishop was
not unmindful of pastoral responsibility, yet he ever remained, like
Bernard, primarily the monk. He disliked the world because he
liked the cloister better; he was no evangelist, no preacher, no
apologist, yet he was one of the most renowned spiritual directors of
all time, and his spiritual children were of every type; rich and poor,

[1] See Rule, op. cit., Vol. I, pp. 147–50.
[2] See C. Butler, *Benedictine Monachism* (1919), pp. 56f.

secular and religious, beggars and kings. His biographer, Eadmer, writes:

> Hence it was, that, illumined by the searching light of an inner wisdom and guided by a discriminating reason, he could analyse characters of every age and sex with such an accuracy that when he came to speak you perceived that he had lifted a curtain and was showing each one his own heart.[1]

The lesson is plain: to be pastorally effective and competent in spiritual guidance, to serve, love, and understand men and women, we are first to seek and to love God, in whose image all are made.

[1] See Rule, op. cit., p. 135.

PRELUDE TO
THE FOURTEENTH CENTURY

In order to understand the first glorious flowering of the English School it is useful to glance at four general aspects of English religion during this period, or immediately before it. The pastoral background to the fourteenth century is well absorbed by a study of the *Book of Margery Kempe*, while the preceding century— roughly the period between St Anselm and Hilton—is admirably described in J. R. H. Moorman's *Church Life in England in the Thirteenth Century*. From this background emerge the four points relevant to English spiritual theology.

I. THE SOLITARY LIFE AND
SPIRITUAL DIRECTION

The religious life of solitude is as old as the Desert Fathers, or as old, perhaps, as Elijah, but like monasticism in the Middle Ages, it developed into a wide and complex range of types. St Benedict's preference for cenobite organization was now everywhere accepted as the norm of Christian life, suited as it was to feudal government. But the solitary life continued throughout the Christian world and it holds a special place in English religion. There may have been no more solitaries in England than elsewhere—in the nature of the case statistics are difficult to come by—while in these islands monastic houses were probably thicker on the ground than in most European countries. The singular difference was that while most of the ascetical theology of the medieval schools sprang from the monasteries, every significant English treatise was related in some way to the solitary life. In other words, while continental spirituality sprang from monastic order, English spirituality grew out of personal direction. The *Ancrene Riwle* (which we will consider in a moment), written by an unknown author for three anchoresses, is the first truly English spiritual treatise.[1] Walter Hilton's *Scale of Perfection* was similarly addressed to an anchoress; Julian of Norwich was such a one, Margery Kempe was first guided by "an Anchorite of the Preaching Friars of Lynn", Richard Rolle was a hermit and spiritual guide,[2] and, by general consent, the anonymous author of the *Cloud of Unknowing* was a solitary of some sort.

In thirteenth- and fourteenth-century England we have therefore, the parishes with their secular clergy; the monasteries, predominantly Benedictine and Cistercian; Franciscan and Dominican friars exerting their particular pressures on the Church at large; the Austin Canons Regular, of which Hilton was one; and the solitaries, less in number than any other group, but upon whom pastoral spirituality seems to have converged. Whatever the work, influence, and value of all other sides of the Church, it was the solitaries who produced the doctrine and writings, either directly, like Julian's *Revelations*, or indirectly by being guided by others.

The point is even more significant when it is realized exactly what an English medieval solitary was. Medieval terminology on the point is, as usual, ambiguous, but it is sufficient to distinguish two main types. The "hermit", usually male, was one living the solitary life unattached to any particular place or cell, who went about preaching and giving counsel; he was, like Rolle, a sort of free-lance friar. The "anchorite" or frequently anchoress, lived permanently in a cell, often attached to a religious order, like Margery's confessor, or to a parish church like Julian.[3]

The "cell" was a little cottage and garden adjacent to the church. The *Ancrene Riwle* speaks of the "church-ancress" and gives sensible instructions about clothes, furniture, curtains (which should be double to prevent gossip and idle window-gazing), food, work (copying manuscripts, needlework, making and repairing vestments), and the entertainment of friends and relations. It is all very domestic in the English and Benedictine spirit: special psalms and prayers are provided for "the anniversaries of your dearest friends". One need not seek far for traditions which would be horrified at the idea of dedicated Religious having any!

---

[1] C. 1230. *Aelred's Rule*, containing wonderful devotion, was hardly a treatise.

[2] Rolle's *Form of Perfect Living* and some letters were written to "Dame Margaret".

[3] Julian's cell is now the Lady Chapel of St Julian's, Norwich, and is perhaps the best extant example of the usual arrangement.

The church-ancress is to spend most of her time in prayer and in giving spiritual counsel to any who consult her, which all are free to do. She is not to "turn herself into schoolmistress", she is not to "look like a housewife". Domestic servants to look after her are taken for granted, and are subject to Rule and discipline like lay sisters or externs of a community. There are no restrictions on private possessions and the *Ancrene Riwle* firmly insists, in both first and last chapters, that all practical rules are for purposes of utility only: "you should certainly not promise to keep anything of the exterior rules as if under a vow". In this, as in the whole spirit of the enterprise, there is a vast difference between the English Rules— Aelred, Hilton, and Rolle—and the German of Grimlaic (an appropriate name!) which was the basis of continental solitary life.

These Rules are also intensely English in that they combine unimpeachable orthodoxy with individualism. Although their value is relevant to the whole Church's mission, they are compiled for particular people, and are quite different from monastic constitutions. There was no "order" of anchoresses, the Rules were more individualistic than those of present-day deaconesses: "The recluse's Rule of Life consisted of friendly counsel rather than rigid regulations."[1] It is not monastic order but secular guidance of a very personal and empirical kind.

The minutiae of the Rules are somewhat fussy and elaborate by modern standards,[2] yet they include spiritual reading and study for those sufficiently educated to profit by them; a good many anchoresses were, like those to whom the *Ancrene Riwle* was addressed, "high-born". This book may need adaptation as from the thirteenth to the twentieth century, but it does not need adapting from monastic to secular religion. Much of its teaching retains its value to-day.

Ch. 2 and 3, dealing with the relation between external and internal discipline, contain sublime ascetical theology: "the custody of the senses"—fasting and mortification—are only useful in so far as they tend to "the regulation of inward feelings". The subject is treated under the delightful metaphor of "the Lady"—prayer—and "her handmaid"—practical discipline: "so this [external] rule exists merely to serve the other [internal] devotion. The other is the Lady, this her handmaid, for all those actions which belong to the outer rule serve only to govern the heart within."[3]

---

[1] R. M. Clay, *The Hermits and Anchorites of England* (1914), p. 96.
[2] E.g. *Ancrene Riwle*, ch. 1.   [3] Ibid., Introduction.

Practical teaching follows about temptation and the fight against sin,[1] all given in a down-to-earth way, the gentility of the high-born ladies notwithstanding. It is all intensely sane: as Margery Kempe would say, "full homely and full boisterous".

In spite of some typical and far-fetched biblical allegory, ch. 5 is still probably the most comprehensive pastoral treatment of confession there is in the English idiom. It foreshadows the Caroline approach and looks back to the Celtic tradition; confession is generous oblation based on atonement doctrine, there is no shred of legalism, artificiality or mock piety. Confession is to be "complete, naked, speedy,[2] humble, ashamed", but also "hopeful, prudent, true, voluntary". Altogether sixteen such qualities of a good confession are treated thoroughly but with pastoral simplicity. "Voluntary" must not be taken to overrule ecclesiastical regulation, but it does mean generous and non-legal: "confession must be voluntary, that is, it must be made willingly and unasked, not drawn out of you as if against your will".

The *Ancrene Riwle* thus forms something of a bridge between St Anselm and the fourteenth century, but it is no exceptional document; it sets the fundamental pattern of English spiritual writing. Here is the traditional vehicle, personal, pastoral, empirical, domestic, and non-monastic, which is to create and carry English ascetical doctrine. Apart from its actual teaching, has this fact any message for modern pastoral practice? Two points come to mind which may be less far-fetched than they appear at first sight.

1. As we look back on the ordinary, not outstanding, anchoress, we visualize a single lady of some spiritual acumen, living a life of prayer, study, work, and spiritual guidance, in a cottage by the church, while she herself submits to the guidance of the parish priest. There are no "vows", no exaggerated austerity or poverty, no special habit. Age for age, is it over-straining the facts to see a hint at the much-needed vocation for the many devout Anglican ladies whose spiritual gifts are now so shamefully wasted? It is very wrong for these ladies to force themselves to aspire to a monastic vocation which they know they do not really have. It is worse still when their gifts are squandered on "parish work" of very doubtful value. Is the possibility of some modern adaptation of the anchoress, primarily the spiritual guide of others, so very remote? It

[1] Ibid., ch. 4.   [2] Modern confessors please note!

is, after all, a typical English compromise to which not a few loyal laywomen are already leaning. But, without pride of position, they need authority and recognition.

2. The solitary vocation may, or may not, underlie an English desire for compromise and for individualism; a racial trait militates against both ostentation and regimentation. The question to be faced is this: if there is to be a new phase in Anglican spirituality, if the English School is to flower once more, then from where is the impetus to come? Can the twentieth century create its own ascetical theology and spiritual technique? If it can, and such hope is reasonable, will it evolve from the work of ascetical scholars, or from a commission on spirituality; from parochial experiment or from our religious orders? If historical tradition has any logical meaning, the most likely source is none of these. If the present revival is to gain impetus, the most hopeful activity would appear to be for many spiritual guides to work out, and perhaps write down, their counsel for many different people. That is the traditional English method.

II. ST GILBERT AND THE GILBERTINES

Dom David Knowles describes the Gilbertines as "a purely English institute which arose out of the practical needs of the country."[1]

Gilbert of Sempringham, when a parish priest in Lincolnshire, found himself in the position of director to a number of dedicated women; at the suggestion of William, first Abbot of Rievaulx, who happened to stay with him while on a journey, he added to his nuns a second branch of the order, that of lay sisters. Next, it was found that as the houses gained possessions and estates regular labour was needed for the cultivation of the land and the collection of revenues. Here again Cistercian influence was at work, for Gilbert was solicited by those who had seen or heard of the white lay-brothers at work and wished to imitate their example. He therefore attached *conversi* to his nunneries.

The Order grew with unexpected rapidity. . . . Gilbert decided to add a fourth member to his order by grouping together a number of chosen priests as canons who should be chaplains to his nuns. Finally, at a still later date, he consented to assume the title of Master.[2]

[1] *The Monastic Order in England* (1940), p. 205.   [2] Ibid., pp. 205f.

As background to this study, two more points are to be noted:

1. This "purely English institute", which never left our shores, set a pastoral, domestic seal on English monasticism which was to be continued by the Little Gidding experiment, and which is not without influence on modern Anglican communities.

2. The genesis of the Gilbertines bears a similarity to the anchorite movement. At the start, St Gilbert is said to have had seven devout girls under his guidance, for whom he built a lodging against the wall of the parish church. There are, therefore, seven instead of three in the same position as those for whom the *Ancrene Riwle* was written. There are also the lay sisters, closely akin to the anchoress's servants. The lay brothers were of a similar type, living to the very modified rule of Cistercian *conversi*, and spending most of their time in practical work.

This is a good example of how all the inter-related elements in English religion combined together in a united Church and all pointed to personal spiritual direction as the pastoral norm. In the Gilbertines, with guidance at the heart of it all, we see aspects of Benedictinism, the nun's Rule, Cistercian *conversi*, the anchorite movement, the Canons Regular of St Augustine, and a secular parish, all interacting to form "a purely English institute".

It is tragic that, with the possible exception of an interesting but not very distinguished treatise called *Handlyng Synne*, the Gilbertines left no major treatise in writing.

III. FOREIGN INFLUENCE

Schools of spirituality are not insular coteries going their own way and rejecting all outside inspiration. St Gilbert is typical, in that nothing could be more English than his order, yet, as Knowles points out, "it nevertheless borrowed almost all its constitutional framework from abroad". Not only had it the various elements just mentioned but it owed much to the experiment in "double monasticism" of Robert of Arbrissel at Fontevrault.

The English fourteenth century was a similar synthesis: unique in character, the consummation of a long development, it continued to receive added inspiration and impetus from many sources of this remarkable Christian era. It was the age of St Gertrude the Great, Bridget of Sweden, Angela of Foligno, Catherine of Siena, Jean Gerson, Thomas à Kempis and the *devotio moderna* movement.

There was also the German Dominican School: Eckhart, Suso, Tauler, Ruysbroek, and Mechtilde of Hackeborn. All these had some influence on English religion; exactly how much can be argued interminably: Knowles, for example, gives the Rhineland mystics a more prominent place than is usual,[1] and I have tried to show how the influence of Bridget of Sweden on Margery Kempe is a rather superficial one.[2] Two things are reasonably certain: first, that this influence would trickle into England through the trade routes, hence the prominence of the Rhineland and Scandinavia, and also the remarkable prominence of Norfolk, especially King's Lynn and Norwich, in the fourteenth-century movement.

Secondly, we can be certain that, whatever the extent of these foreign importations, they were comparatively minor ones compared with the main stream of tradition: Augustine, Benedictinism, St Victor, Anselm.

IV. THE ENGLISH LANGUAGE

It has often been pointed out that it is impossible to study early English literature without absorbing a good deal of early English religion. That the two developed together is not without significance, for vernacular devotion and liturgy imply much more than convenience or edification. Middle English became the proper and necessary vehicle for the promulgation of specifically English spirituality. If, in spite of the literary setback enforced by the Norman Conquest, there is some connection between the seventh-century Celtic Church and fourteenth-century religion, there is also a connection between Caedmon, protégé of St Hilda, and Langland. It is interesting to see how the literary and theological scholars are here of one mind: "The first masterpiece of religious guidance, unrivalled for almost two centuries afterwards, scarcely ever surpassed, and certainly never displaced, during the Middle Ages, was the anonymous *Ancrene Riwle* (the Anchoress's Rule; 1175–1200?)[3] which had probably a greater influence on subsequent writing than anything else of English origin."[4] The pastoral and domestic ethos of this movement is again shown up: monastic rules and chronicles are not usually influential as prose composition.

---

[1] *The English Mystical Tradition* (1961), pp. 34ff.
[2] *Margery Kempe*, ch. 6.
[3] These dates are earlier by half a century than other scholars hold.
[4] A. I. Doyle, *The Age of Chaucer* (1954), p. 70.

From the theological viewpoint:

> In the fourteenth century a great change began. Treatises and prayer books written in Latin and French were translated into English, and the vernacular was used increasingly for original work. The early translators at the turn of the century were followed by the English writings in prose and verse of Richard Rolle and others, and these in turn by the magnificent flowering of Middle English in the works of Langland and Chaucer. . . . in the realm of spiritual direction, the four writers whose works are described in the chapters which follow[1] are unsurpassed in their use of words by those of any nationality in any age of great mystical and spiritual teachers.
>
> Finally, the age was the first in which we catch a glimpse in our fellow countrymen of those characteristics of language and mind which we recognize as English. They are no longer concealed behind the formalities of Latin or French. Just as the inhabitants of Langland's hovels and taverns, and the characters who exchange words in the prologues and connecting links of Chaucer's Canterbury Tales, are racy of the soil of England, so the Author of *The Cloud*, Walter Hilton and Julian of Norwich speak a language and show personalities that we can feel to be English, and the counsel that they give can be, and is, as valid for us as for those for whom it was first intended.[2]

The use of the vernacular, therefore, far from being a Reformation issue, is embedded, as an essential part, in English ascetical theology itself. It is the perfect medium for expressing affective-speculative doctrine, it conveys the domestic tradition of St Benedict in a single phrase more vividly than pages of stolid explanation, and it is a common devotional language in empirical direction which itself helps to bind priest and layman into a united family in Christ.

There are many terms in many languages for "approaching the Sacred Humanity in private prayer". It is called petition, vocal prayer, and colloquy, yet Margery Kempe's "homely dalliance" means something unique and untranslatable. One could try over and over again to translate foreign phrases which mean, literally, "beloved of God", "God's betrothed" or "Christ's virgin spouse", but one would never reach "Christ's own dearworthy darling",

---

[1] Rolle, *The Cloud of Unknowing*, Hilton, Julian.

[2] Knowles, *The English Mystical Tradition*, pp. 46f.

which is to be found in both Margery and Rolle. Nor is the idiom confined to the affective side: it is a theological fact that God works in mysterious ways, that there is "analogical discontinuity"; Rolle writes: "To us it longs not to know God's privy doom." It is regrettable that the phrase "spiritual direction" has itself come to imply Counter-Reformation authoritarianism; no English layman of whatever persuasion could object to "full merry counsel with his ghostly father".

In short, English religion is "homely and full boisterous", and if these phrases mean little to the reader, then it is useless to try to explain them. The fact remains that, even for the uninitiated, a struggle with the original Middle English works is itself a valuable exercise in English ascetical theology.

Whatever our judgement, or the Church's judgement, on Wyclif (Hilton is violently condemnatory), the idea of a vernacular Bible is neither heretical nor Protestant. It is an inevitable, and logical, development of fourteenth-century religion.

16

WALTER HILTON

Walter Hilton, Austin Canon Regular of Thurgarton, near South-well, is at the centre of English ascetical theology, and remains, to my mind, our prime source of teaching on spiritual direction. He is a kind of sheet-anchor for the other fourteenth-century writers, consummating the Catholic tradition in the English School, and providing a foundation for everything that was to come.

The Scale of Perfection, as the title implies, is a comparatively systematic work; a practical exposition of the spiritual life written for an English anchoress. It is a minor *Summa* in that it brings together all the elements of English spirituality and synthesizes the fundamental teaching of those who have made it up. The theological basis is from St Augustine, its ascetical emphases and religious psychology are Victorine, it has a Benedictine warmth, prudence, and optimism, and the devotional–speculative balance of St Anselm. Written in the unique devotional idiom of the Middle English language, its teaching remains impeccably orthodox within the framework of the Three Ways.

The *Scale* is *comparatively* systematic; the adverb is important if the student is not to be disappointed and bewildered. Medieval writers are notoriously unsystematic, and to call Hilton more careful than most of his contemporaries is no great claim. One must not expect the careful, point by point analyses of Ignatius Loyola or St John of the Cross. Nevertheless a clear pattern of pastoral guid-ance emerges from the book, and a lack of too rigid order is an ascetical virtue, since it is nearer to experience and is inevitable in a book which consists in the actual guidance of a particular person. It is, therefore, worth trying to unravel the structure of Hilton's teaching as introduction to the necessary study of the book itself.

I. THE ASCETICAL FRAMEWORK
From manuscript and historical evidence it must be assumed that the second book of the *Scale* was written some years after the first had

been delivered to, and used by, the anchoress in question. The clue
to the ascetical position of Hilton is to consider Book II as an expansion or even reappraisal of Book I rather than its sequel. The
first chapter of Book II bears this out: "For as mickle as thou
covetest greatly and askest it by charity, for to hear more of an
image the which I have before times in party discried to thee . . . I
shall open to thee a little more . . ." Thus the early chapters of the
second book form a general framework to the doctrine contained in
the early part of the first. The whole thing, therefore, is not only
spiritual guidance from Hilton to the anchoress, but also empirical
direction worked out by mutual experiment. In effect, Hilton
produced the first book and asked the anchoress to "try it out", and
after some years the second book grew out of her questions on the
problems that had arisen. The two books must be seen as parallel
and to some extent repetitive.

Book II begins with a résumé of fundamental doctrine. We are
made in the image of God after the Augustine–St Victor–William
of St Thierry tradition:

The soul of a man is life,[1] made of three mights, mind,[2] reason,
and will; to the image, and the likeness,[3] of the blessed Trinity,
whole, perfect, and righteous. In as mickle as the mind was made
mighty and steadfast, by virtue of the Father Almighty, for to
hold him without forgetting, distracting, or letting of any creature,
and so it hath likeness of the Father. Reason was made clear and
bright without error or murkness, as perfectly as a soul in a body
unglorified might have; and so it hath the likeness of the Son,
which is endless Wisdom. And the love and the will was made
clean, burning into God without beastly love of the flesh or of any
creature, by the sovereign goodness of God the Holy Ghost, and
so it hath the likeness of the Holy Ghost, the which is blessed
Love. So that a man's soul, which may be called a made trinity,
was fulfilled in mind, sight, and love, of the unmade blessed
Trinity which is our Lord.[4]

This forms a pastoral summary of Catholic teaching from St

[1] See Ch. 8, I above.
[2] After Augustine, "mind" is memory or imagination; Ch. 5, III above.
[3] Following St Bernard–St Bonaventure; Chs. 7, I; 10, II above
[4] *Scale*, I. 43, cf. II. 1,2,31. Footnote references in this chapter are to *The Scale of Perfection* unless otherwise indicated.

13—E.S.

Augustine onwards, bringing in the relevant points of development from the other sources. It well illustrates Hilton's orthodoxy and the extent of his theological studies.

But: "This is the dignity, the state and the worship of a man's soul, by kind of the first making."[1] Now, by the Fall, the human soul is "disfigured and forshapen".[2] "Forshapen" means knocked out of shape or disarranged: "two manner of sins makes a soul to lose the shape and likeness of God."[3] This is the disharmony or concupiscence of Augustine. But Hilton does not follow Augustine into the "transmission theory" of original sin; he substitutes the much more satisfactory theory based on racial solidarity. Fallen humanity is recapitulated in the first Adam, redemption is won by Christ the Second Adam, who recreates humanity into a new status: "Now is it sooth mankind, that was wholly in Adam the first man",[4] yet "For then shall the soul receive the whole and the fulfiling of God in all mights of it, without medley of any other affection; and it shall see mankind in the person of Jesu."[5]

Redemption, however, is no automatic process, it demands a continuous life-struggle of response to grace and love: "Two manner of men are not reformed by virtue of this passion. One is of them that trow it not. Another is of them that love it not."[6] Truth and love, the speculative and the affective, are both necessary parts of the response to grace, which is the substance of ascetical doctrine and Christian living. And the key to it all is to be "nourished in the bosom of Holy Kirk":[7] the channel of grace.

The basis of the doctrine is plainly Augustinian, while Book II, 2 is a pastoral summary of the atonement doctrine of Anselm's *Cur Deus Homo?* But if we recall the ascetical doctrines of those teachers treated in the preceding part of this study, it will be seen that they all contribute to the Hilton synthesis. This will become more apparent as we proceed.

II. THE THREE WAYS

Having traced this fundamental doctrine, Hilton now gets down to the practical business of co-operation with grace, and considers the state of the human soul in various stages of the life-process.[8] The principal division or progression is that between souls "reforming

[1] I. 43.   [2] II. 1.7.   [3] II. 6.
[4] II. 2.   [5] II. 4, cf. Augustine, *De Civitate Dei*, XXII. 28, 29.
[6] II. 3.   [7] Ibid.   [8] II. 5–19.

in faith" and "reforming in feeling". These are equivalent to the purgative and illuminative ways of the classical scheme. The first is purgative, discursive, disciplined and dutiful; the "necessary obedience" of William of St Thierry. The second is affective illumination, following the Christological progression of St Bernard from love for the Sacred Humanity to the worship of the Incarnate Godhead. This eventually leads to contemplative union. Hilton, however, makes two significant developments of the orthodox Three Ways doctrine.

1. "Reforming" is an Augustinian term; "re-forming" of the soul which has been "forshapen" by concupiscence. This is more comprehensive than the usual meaning of "purgation" as a purging of sinful tendencies. Hilton not only refuses to split up people into "faculties" but maintains the moral–ascetical synthesis which the Three Ways are ever in danger of dissecting. "Reforming", either in "faith" or in "feeling", always means reorganizing the whole man which concupiscence has disordered. Despite frequent warnings, there is a constant risk of seeing purgation as a different life from illumination; *first* one is rid of sin, *then* one starts serious prayer. To Hilton, the Christian life is a continuity; there are stages, steps up the ladder of perfection, but it is one ladder and one's feet not unnaturally overlap during parts of the climb. It is here that, despite complications for the student, the *Scale's* lack of meticulous order presents a truer picture of spiritual experience. And it is here also that Hilton anticipates the Caroline ideal.

2. The second development issues from the startling statement that "reforming in faith may be had lightly and in short time. The second (in feeling) may not be so, but through length of time and mickle ghostly travail."[1] Purgation is not usually regarded as something to be achieved "lightly and in short time"; the conquest of even gross sin is apt to be a hard and long drawn out business. But this is where Hilton's sane pastoral sense prevails: "The first may be had with the feeling of the image of sin; for though a man feel nothing in himself but all stirrings of sin and fleshly desires, notwithstanding that feeling, it he wilfully assent not thereto he may be reformed in faith to the likeness of God."[2]

That is near to the Thomist doctrine of venial sin, but Hilton

[1] II. 5.   [2] Ibid.

tends strongly to side with William of St Thierry in the "mortal–venial" dispute, and he follows his "necessary obedience" teaching. His point here is that "reforming in faith", the Purgative Way, is essentially struggle and loyalty, which may be had "lightly and in short time" by any Christian of sincerity. Neither in the Purgative nor in the Illuminative Ways is sin fully conquered, but we are not "thrown out of grace" by an occasional fall; sins of infirmity do not necessarily preclude charity.

"Reforming in feeling", roughly the Illuminative Way, is a wide term covering the whole range of Christian life which is usually placed under the general heading of Proficiency. This leads to the Unitive Way, designated "contemplation"—of all terms the most ambiguous. But the text of the *Scale* makes it clear that Hilton uses this word in a very wide sense. It includes the first affective experiences that all faithful Christians know, and it ends with mystical union of, as is to be expected, a Pseudo-Dionysian type. It is therefore the first broad process of "reforming in faith", overlapping the earlier forms of contemplative and affective prayer of "reforming in feeling", with which we are here concerned. In order to understand this in pastoral detail it is necessary to return to the opening chapters of the first book.

III. "REFORMING IN FAITH"

Hilton uses another blurred distinction, borrowed from St Gregory the Great, between the "'active" and "contemplative" lives, although "contemplation", in one form or another, plays its part in both. This, and other ambiguities, are resolved if we remember to whom the books were addressed. The English anchoress, though technically "enclosed", was very different from a member of what we would to-day call an "enclosed order". Her business was prayer, yet active work, especially spiritual guidance, was central to her vocation.

In pastoral practice, it is necessary to keep on reminding the faithful that Christian life begins with Baptism. In his down-to-earth way, Hilton makes the point with Augustinian bluntness:

A soul of a child that is born and is unchristened, because of original sin has no likeness of God; he is nought but an image of the fiend and a brand of hell. But as soon as it is christened, it is reformed to the image of God, and through virtue of faith of

Holy Kirk suddenly is turned from the likeness of the fiend and made like an angel of heaven.[1]

In context, this seems to be a somewhat rhetorical passage, but Hilton is obviously trying to keep loyal to Augustine. Notice, however, his careful use of the words "likeness" and "image", following the development through St Bernard and St Bonaventure, and also the vicarious nature of the united Church and the efficacy of its faith. But the message could not be clearer.

All depends on grace, after which comes our response to it. The psychological centre of this response is humility—"meekness"— which nurtures volition. After Baptism, the active Christian life starts with a purposeful act of will to conform to the "laws of Holy Kirk". Hilton is far too wise to assume that the "laws of Holy Kirk" will always be obeyed, or that after Baptism, or after Confession, temptation and sin will be done away. Nevertheless he insists upon what modern evangelists call a "decision for Christ",[2] a firm commitment to submit, in humility, to the Church's order; an acceptance of "necessary obedience" which nurtures love. This is the subjective element of Confirmation.

But the struggle continues: "other men that stand in the common way of charity, and are not yet so far forth in grace, but work under the bidding of reason, they strive and fight all day against sins and for the getting of virtues; and sometimes they be above and sometime beneath, as wrestlers are. These men do full well."[3] Following William of St Thierry, it is the struggle that matters: a fall is not total defeat; a marital quarrel is not divorce.

Ontology and psychology, the objective and subjective elements in religion, are now combined. By Baptism we are lifted into the Church's stream of grace; the sacraments, Confirmation, Confession, and the Eucharist, maintain the flow of actual grace. By humility and will, we make our personal response and firmly resolve to remain loyal to the new status; to fight temptation, perhaps to fall, but never to despair. Prevenient grace runs through the whole Christian life. Now come the four main stages in the life of prayer—"contemplation".

1. "The first lieth in knowing of God and of ghostly things, gotten by reason, by teaching of man, and by study in Holy Writ; without ghostly affection and inly savour felt by the special gift of the Holy

[1] II. 6.   [2] "A whole and stable intention", I. 22.   [3] II. 36.

Ghost."[1] This is William's "external faith", the initial process of
Catechism. It is possible to "heretics and hypocrites"; mere
intellectualism is useless, theology not loved and absorbed is of no
avail. Hilton goes on to castigate those whose intellectual attainment
is used for personal ambition and vain-glory.

The point is elaborated in II.3, yet knowledge remains the starting
point in prayer, and it is truly loved, humbly and willingly but still
not necessarily affectively, even by "simple and lewd souls who are
nourished in the bosom of Holy Kirk".[2] This is that "necessary
obedience" whereby even the chores—getting the coal and washing
the dishes—is a real expression of love, even if it is not very exciting
or romantic.

2. The next stage "lieth principally in affection, without light of
understanding of ghostly things; and this is commonly of simple
and unlettered men . . . who . . . in meditation of God, by grace
of the Holy Ghost feeleth fervour and love and ghostly sweetness, by the mind of His Passion or of any of His works in His Manhood".[3] This may well be the initial state of some people, for
it is the Bernardine–Margery Kempe type of affective devotion,
later to become known as "the prayer of loving regard". It is notice-
able that Hilton widens the Franciscan emphasis on the Passion
alone, so prevalent in fourteenth-century Christendom, to the whole
of our Lord's life: the secret of Margery's habitual recollection,
and again consonant with Caroline ideals.

3. In the active life, this infused affectiveness is usually spasmodic,[4]
in the third stage it is habitual,[5] and more usual in "contemplatives"
—here covering anchoresses. These are in "great rest" (*tranquillitas*).
This quality is no sentimental peacefulness, but something which
partakes of that active contemplation taught by Augustine and called
"rest" in the *City of God*.[6] In Hilton's glorious phrase it is "Holy
idleness and a rest most busy".[7]

The blurred division between these two stages is the distinction
between "reforming in faith and in feeling". We arrive at the
important pastoral concept that progress depends not so much on
spasmodic fervour but on moving from actual to habitual spiritual

[1] I. 4, cf. I. 14.   [2] II. 3.   [3] I. 5.
[4] I. 6.   [5] I. 7.   [6] *De Civ. Dei*, XXII. 29, 30.
[7] *Scale*, II. 40.

states, or from the discursive to the contemplative. A person habitually, if coldly, aware of his Christian status and of the presence of God is more advanced than those who occasionally experience affective fervour and then forget all about it. This has an important bearing on the English preference for habitual recollection over formal meditation.

4. The fourth stage "is perfect as it may be here, lieth both in cognition and affection: that is to say, in knowing and in perfect loving of God".[1] Here is the final speculative–affective synthesis: the mystical knowledge and love of God, leading "through length of time and mickle ghostly travail"[2] to the mystical marriage.

Hilton's mystical theology, following the Pseudo-Dionysius, the School of St Victor and *The Cloud of Unknowing*, is nevertheless influenced by the more positive mysticism of St Augustine. The traditional negative terminology of the former group becomes softened into paradoxes: we find lovely ideas and phrases like "rich nought" and "lightsome darkness".

The prayer proper to the first three stages, those with which ascetical theology is concerned, is meditation—in a very wide and ambiguous sense,[2] personal colloquy,[3] and what would now be called "affective prayer of simplicity".[4] This is matter for personal guidance, and will be discussed later.[5] But underlying it all, following St Benedict and preceding the Caroline Divines, is "the Paternoster, and also more generally by the ordinance of Holy Kirk, as matins, evensong and hours".[6] The prayer of the third stage, the advanced state of habitual affectiveness, is characterized, not by a rejection of the Church's common Rule but by a greater love and fervour for it: "the Paternoster, or the Ave, or hymns or psalms and other devout sayings of Holy Kirk are turned as it were into a ghostly mirth and sweet song".[7]

Such is the fundamental pattern of the Christian pilgrimage: "reforming in faith", doctrine turning into love by grace, or affectiveness stabilized by doctrine, according to initial temperament and gifts, all nurtured by prayer proper to each and always beginning with co-operation with sacramental grace by loyalty to the "laws and ordinances of Holy Kirk". The pastoral characteristic of this

[1] I. 8.   [2] II. 5.   [3] See section VI. 2 below.
[4] I. 29.   [5] I. 32.   [6] I. 27.
[7] I. 7.

habitual loyalty is found in the great English ascetical term
"homely".

IV. THE CHURCH

Thirty or forty years ago, commentators on the English fourteenth
century overstressed its "mysticism"—often leaving the word
undefined—and concluded that Hilton, Julian, and Rolle were
quite unconcerned with the daily routine of the Church's life.
"Formalism" was the arch-enemy, and Puritan circles were even
known to invoke these three asceticists to detract from the value of
"set prayers". On the other wing Miss Evelyn Underhill speaks of
"the English Mystics' almost exclusive interest in personal religion",[1]
and goes on to discuss "the interior life of love and prayer . . .
which it is the business of external religion to support and preserve".[2] It is just possible to twist that sentiment into orthodox
channels, but the implication remains that the Offices, and even the
Eucharist—which is presumably "external religion"—are but
useful supports to private devotion. I do not believe that that was
Miss Underhill's true position and I am quite certain it is not
Hilton's. It is true that, in spite of its recurrent refrain about "the
laws and ordinances of Holy Kirk", the *Scale* contains little direct
teaching about the Office or the Mass, but then it is personal
direction which, like many spiritual treatises from the fourth
Gospel onwards, takes the basis of Christian life for granted.

Hilton's view of the Church, however, is anything but autocratic;
its laws and ordinances are not the dictates of a tyrant but the joyous
customs of a privileged family: all is "homely". In these days
especially, it is necessary to stress the demands of Christian duty,
but we must avoid the idea that the obligations of prayer and worship
are slightly unpleasant. "Homely", whether in Hilton, Julian,
Margery or Rolle, means Benedictine domesticity, and therefore
"stable" or "habitual". "Homely dalliance" means not so much
"friendly" or "easy-going" but *habitual* colloquy or recollection
of Christ in his Body. The Church is "our Father's house" where
we should be "at home", implying the comfortable stability of sons
and daughters rather than the fleeting visits of guests. The Church
is what we are, the parish church is where we belong. "Reforming
in faith" is upbringing within that Church; it certainly demands
struggle, constant efforts of humility and will, but by Baptism "it

---

[1] Introduction to the *Scale*, Watkins edition, p. xvi.   [2] Ibid., p. xxxi.

may be had lightly", and the status is not easily lost. We may be unruly children, we may need punishment, but we belong to the family of God and are not likely to be shown the door.

The Church is our true Mother, protecting her children in a permanent relationship:

> the second thing which thee behoves to have, is secure troth in all articles of the faith, and the sacraments of Holy Kirk, trowing them steadfastly with all the will in thine heart. And though thou feel any stirring in thine heart against any of them by suggestion of the enemy, for to put thee in doubt or in dread of them, be thou steadfast, and not too mickle a-dread of feeling of such stirrings, but forsake thine own wit without disputing or ransacking of them, and set thy faith generally in the faith of Holy Kirk, and charge not the stirrings of thine heart which as thee thinkest is contrary thereto. For that stirring is not thy faith; but the faith of Holy Kirk is thy faith, though thou neither see it nor feel it.[1]

That is neither medieval obscurantism nor authoritarianism: it is not "How dare you doubt the Church?" but "Trust Mother". And it is the doctrine of baptismal incorporation, plus some very sound teaching about the vicarious efficacy of the Church—"regard not my sins but the faith of thy Church"—and about intellectual scrupulosity. In other words, faith comes before feeling and faith comes before understanding: *credo ut intelligam*. Again:

> If thine enemies say to thee first thus, by stirrings in thine heart, that thou art not shriven aright, or there is some old sin hid in thine heart that thou knowest not, nor were never shriven of, and therefore thee must turn home again and leave thy desire, and go shrive thee better: trow not this saying, for it is false, for thou art shriven.[2]

Hilton was loyal to the Church of his day and maintained its penitential discipline, but Confession, like all other Christian duties, is a privilege not a sanction. For the benefit of absolution, one does not plead in a law-court but one "turns home"; this is no ecclesiastical legalism but "a great courtesy of our Lord, and an endless

---

[1] *Scale*, I. 21; cf. the delightful treatment of the story of the Canaanite woman in II. 10.

[2] II. 22.

mercy, that so lightly forgives all manner of sin, and so suddenly gives plenty of grace to a sinful soul that asks mercy of Him. He abides no great penance doing nor painful fleshly suffering, or He forgive it."[1]

Penance must be, if not "voluntary", then at least generous: "Therefore shall he go and show him and shrive him to his ghostly father, and receive penance enjoined for his trespass and gladly fulfil it."[2] This applies to: "all Christian men that will know Holy Kirk as their mother and will be buxom to her bidding".[2]

So pronounced is this domestic pastoral ethos, yet so scrupulously orthodox does Hilton wish to be, that he cannot always avoid an undercurrent of conflict here and there. He condemns Jews, heretics, and unbaptized infants to hell,[3] and is abusive to the Lollards,[4] yet he is Anselmic about honest doubts, and sometimes rides lightly to current ecclesiastical disciplines. He is unattracted by the tight moral distinctions of Scholasticism, and, while accepting the mortal–venial sin classification in theory, is nearer in spirit to William of St Thierry and the Carolines than to St Thomas.

> But we Christian men have this privilege of His mercy, such feelings are no sin, but they are pain of original sin. Nevertheless when by negligence and blindness of thy self this feeling is received unwarily in thy thought and turned into a love and liking, then is there sin, more or less after the measure of thy love.

That is basically Thomist, but softened towards the infirmity–malice distinction; then Hilton gets delightfully impatient with the scholastic categories:

> [Sin is] sometime venial and sometime deadly. When it is venial and when deadly, fully can I not tell thee.[5]

Stop quibbling and get on with the job!

V. MORAL THEOLOGY

Hilton's moral theology is mainly concentrated in Book I, chs. 52–93, although this is elaborated throughout the work, especially in the central chapters of Book II. This comparative lack of system is again something of a point in favour of a writer who refuses to dissociate moral from ascetical doctrine. Apart from the relation

[1] II. 7.   [2] Ibid.   [3] II. 6.
[4] II. 26.   [5] I. 56; cf. I. 81.

between the two books already discussed, moral and ascetical theology, tidily contained in watertight compartments, would be foreign both to Hilton and to English spirituality as a whole.

This point is borne out in his masterly treatment of the capital sins.[1] Here is a concise pastoral exposition of an orthodoxy to which we all pay lip-service but often forget in practical guidance.

Pride is, literally, the "root sin" and the source of all others: that we all know, yet, confronted with a drunkard or an adulterer, few modern confessors open the attack against *pride*. Hilton does. It is not simply that the so-called "spiritual sins" are more lethal than the fleshly ones—though Hilton is adamant on the point—but that pride is the direct cause of them all, and humility—"meekness"—is their one certain conqueror. Pride is the root sin, first because it puts self before God: "love of thine own excellence; that is, of thine own worship".[2] It is not so much "immoral" than untrue. Secondly, pride denies the need for grace. They are both theological reasons and Hilton is not particularly concerned with any others. Vainglory, presumption, ambition, envy, jealousy, and all such objectionable qualities, are but symptoms of pride in the depths of the soul. It is the "black image" which only grace can reach. So, too, gluttony, lust, and sloth, though real and deadly, are reduced almost to symptoms of pride: "a man sinneth not commonly deadly in gluttony, but if he be encumbered with other deadly sins before done".[3] Keeping close to Augustine, Hilton avoids both errors which are prevalent to-day: he refuses to see lust and gluttony as the most serious of human failings, yet he regards them as "symptoms" of the utmost gravity. They are deadly because pride is deadly, they manifest an irreligious self-love. It is always pride that must be attacked, and it can only be conquered by grace; co-operation with victorious grace remains, in essence, the common Christian life according to "the laws and sacraments of Holy Kirk".

Envy, anger, and covetousness thus become, above all else, *distractions* from our active co-operation with grace. Envy of another's gifts and qualities distracts from the development of one's own. Anger upsets that peace, harmony, and quiet integration of the soul which is the prerequisite of contemplation. Covetousness distracts attention from "Jesu-God" who is the only worthy object of love.[4] The social, ethical, and political relevance of these

[1] I. 55–76.   [2] I. 56.   [3] I. 72.
[4] Cf. The Sermon on the Mount, examined in Ch. 3, IV above.

sins has little interest for Hilton; not that he is blindly other-worldly, but because of his wise and undeviating purpose to get to the very root of the matter.

This insistence on the sacraments and the Church's Rule does not make Hilton a determinist. Grace is not magic; the Church's Rule is the necessary foundation for the exercise of the strengthened will. The moral struggle must issue in charity. Love for God is ever the goal; Christian morality is teleological. Two stages of this struggle arise which are similar to the general faith–feeling progression. Virtue is first embraced out of duty, then it is loved because it is pleasing to God.

> There is many man that hath virtue, as lowness, patience, charity to his even-Christian and such other, only in his reason and will, and hath no ghostly delight nor love in them. For oftime he feeleth grouching, heaviness and bitterness for to do them . . . but when by the grace of Jesu, and by ghostly and bodily exercise, reason is y-turned into light, and will into love, then hath he virtues in affection, for he hath so well gnawen upon the bitter bark of the nut that he hath broken it, and feedeth him on the swete kernel . . . the virtues which were first heavy for to do are now turned into very delight and savour.[1]

Recollective "homeliness" prevents tension and panic, but the slow struggle continues; there is the principle of periodicity with its alternating series of consolations and desolations, of resistance to temptation and falls, of pleasant duty and dull duty; all so aptly illustrated by the image of the wrestlers already quoted (p. 181). This struggle, qualified by "homeliness" rather than heroics, habitual loyalty rather than spectacular austerities, creates a "general will" which is a deep, constant, mature faith. Will is not so much strengthened as directed, firmly set on God and unshaken by the ordinary ups and downs of life. It is a habitual love for Christ, expressed sometimes affectively, sometimes in dutiful loyalty, sometimes by penitence. It implies a status far less easily lost than the Thomist teaching on infused virtue suggests.

"Mortal sin", reluctantly accepted as a category, comes to depend not on a carefully classified gravity of any particular sin, but on the status of the sinner. The following perfectly expresses William of St Thierry's position:

[1] I. 14.

For this is sooth, he that chooses the lust and the liking of his flesh in delices and welfare of meat and drink as a full rest for his heart, that he would in his heart never have other joy nor other bliss, but live aye in such lust of his flesh if he might, it is no doubt that he sinneth deadly, for he loveth his flesh more than God. . . .

But another man or woman which is in grace and in charity hath always a good general will to God in his soul, whether he sleep or wake, eat or drink, or what deed that he doth, so that it be not evil in the self. . . . This will, though it be but general, is of so great virtue by the grace of our Lord Jesu, that though he fall by frailty in lust and liking of meat and drink, or such other sickness, either in excess of too mickle eating, or too often, or too greedily, or too lustily or delicately . . . it saveth and keepeth him from deadly sin.[1]

This is wise pastoral guidance, incorporating the Caroline malice–infirmity distinction. But it is neither lax nor negative. It implies a "good general will" constantly maintained by Rule, by spiritual stamina, and by strong loyalty to the Church. And it implies positive acquisition of virtue; humility and love follow the volitional attack on the root sin, which, it may be remarked, is not necessarily true of the other sins. The proud cannot become humble without growing in charity, yet it is possible to defeat, say, drunkenness and remain in the shackles of pride. To Hilton, with his unbreakable ascetic–moral relation, such merely moral victory would mean very little. On the other hand:

For wit thou well, he that hath in his desire and in his travail none regard to none other thing but to meekness and charity, aye craving after them how he might have them, he shall in that desire with working following after, profit and wax in all other virtues, as in chastity, abstinence and such other though he have but little regard to them.[2]

It is the same inviolable pastoral principle: attack at the root, and aim at the heights.

Hilton goes on to attack exaggerated physical austerity for the best of all possible reasons: it does not work. And, on theological grounds, it cannot work; we miss the whole point if we regard

[1] I. 72.　　[2] I. 76.

Hilton's, or St Benedict's, so-called "moderation" simply as humane and enlightened. It is rather the logical conclusion to the ascetical application of the doctrine of prevenient grace, allied with Victorine religious psychology. Thus Hilton objects to flagellation simply because it is neither a sacrament of grace nor is it conducive to deep charity or humility.

> But this travail against the ground [of lechery] namely shall be ghostly, as by prayers and ghostly virtues, and not bodily by no bodily penance. For wit thou well, though thou wake and fast and scourge thyself and do all that thou can, thou shalt never have that cleanness and that chastity without the gift of God and the grace of meekness. Thou shouldest be able rather to slay thyself than thou shouldest slay fleshly stirrings and feelings of lusts and lechery, either in heart or in thy flesh, by any bodily penance. But by the grace of Jesu in a meek soul, the ground may be stopped and destroyed, and the spring may be dried; and that is very chastity in body and in soul.[1]

"Meekness" is the practical weapon, charity the end-product, of all Christian life, but love and knowledge are still together in the Augustinian synthesis: the final test is as clear as it is blunt:

> As mickle as thou lovest God and thine even-christian and knowest Him, so mickle is thy soul; and if thou little love Him, little is thy soul; and if thou nought love Him, nought is thy soul.[2]

VI. SUBSIDIARY ASCETICAL TEACHING

1. *Progressive love.* In I.35, Hilton refers to St Bernard, by whom he is obviously inspired, yet his degrees of love are even more practical than in the *De Diligendo Deo.* They are:

a. William of St Thierry's necessary obedience expressed in dutiful loyalty to the Church. Here intention is as important as fervour, the marital love implied by helping with the household drudgery; such habitual intention and help, the "general will", is better than isolated acts.

> The prayer of other men that are busied in active works is made of two words. For they oft times form in their hearts one word through thinking of worldly business, and sound in their mouth another word of the psalm sung or said; and nevertheless if their

intent be true, yet is their prayer good and needful, though it lack savour and sweetness.[1]

This substantiates the real value of *reciting* the Office, in the train or on the bus, objectively with the intention of praising God with the Church, and without paying too much heed to "devotion". We shall see that further support for this principle is to come from the Caroline defence of "set prayers", especially by William Beveridge.

b. Central to the whole of fourteenth-century religion is the affective love for Christ in his Sacred Humanity. But differing from Cistercian example, such affective devotion in Hilton, Julian, and Margery is always interlaced with doctrine. This theological under-current turns such affective prayer into a stage in a progression, almost a proximate preparation for the next degree which is:

c. Contemplative love for the Godhead as seen in the Incarnation. This is more than a simple transference of thought from Christ's humanity to the divinity—which risks Nestorianism—but is nearer to the "perfect symbol" doctrine of Hugh of St Victor. The progression and relation between these two stages is beautifully illustrated in some of Margery's colloquies, and also in Hilton's lovely treatment of the Resurrection appearance to Magdalene in II.30.[2]

2. *Meditation.* This follows the pattern of progressive love, since meditation is the proper prayer for the first three stages of the Christian life. But there are four methods of meditation which roughly correspond to the four stages of Christian life as set out in section III above.

a. First comes self-examination, a search into the sinful soul with honesty and courage, but inspired by the fact of redemption. The Passion is simply looked at, "externally", while moral theology in some simple form is used as an objective guide. It is meditation which might be called the way of acquired penitence.[3]

b. Meditation on the Passion, on "the Lord Jesu in a bodily likeness"—a phrase typical of Julian. This is very similar to the modern "three point" meditation, which aims at affective devotion. It is "an opening of a ghostly eye into Christ's Manhood",[4] which leads to a more "internal", or contemplative, experience of him.

[1] II. 42.　　　　　　　　[2] Cf. *The Book of Margery Kempe*, I, ch. 81.
[3] *Scale*, I. 34, cf. I. 15.　　[4] I. 35.

c. Next comes meditation on God as manifested in the Sacred
Humanity: "For a man shall not come to ghostly delight in contemplation of Christ's Godhead, but he first come in imagination by
bitterness and compassion and by steadfast thinking of His Manhood."[1] Here Hilton, the asceticist and spiritual director, is analysing
what Julian of Norwich achieves in synthesis. It might almost be
called meditation on the Passion from the Father's point of view.

d. This is the contemplative state[2] leading to union with Christ
in the depths of the soul cleansed by grace and penitence.

It is interesting to see that the three "means" of meditation listed
in I.15 are "Holy Writ, ghostly meditation, and busy prayer with
devotion". Then Hilton regretfully admits that "Reading of Holy
Writ, may thou not well use": another hint at the *need* for an
English Bible.

3. *Aridity, distractions, discernment of spirits.* Hilton deals with these
common problems with his usual sanity, and gems of teaching crop
up throughout the book. In I.36 he has some important teaching on
the causes of aridity. It is a sign of growth, a trial given or permitted
by God whereby the soul deepens and matures: "Our Lord with-
draweth it and all other devotions sometime from a man or a woman,
for He will suffer him for to be assayed by temptations of his enemy,
and so will He dispose a man to feel Him more ghostly." This is
Hilton's interpretation of John 16.7: "It is speedful to you that I go
from you bodily . . ."

It is now often forgotten that aridity is also caused by sin,
especially unchecked habits of venial sin: "If a man wax proud of it
in his own sight, or for some other sin by the which he maketh
himself unable for to receive the grace." It is right that growing
souls should be consoled by the fact that aridity is a normal Christian
experience and usually a sign of progress. But it must not be forgotten that venial sin is another cause. Confession may, therefore,
be a cure for aridity, but it must be English confession: free, full,
and generous. The juridical approach, restricted to "mortal" sins,
is inadequate in this instance. Once again, Hilton is careful to avoid
too rigid distinctions: aridity arises out of a mixture of causes.
Pastoral warmth, encouragement, and above all theological application, are the fundamental needs.

Hilton has a thorough understanding of the general state of the

---

[1] Ibid.   [2] I. 42, 50–2.

ordinary Proficient Christian in the process of "reforming in faith".
In these days the word "aridity" is used very loosely, and frequently
in the negative sense of simply lacking devotional fervour. In Hilton
it appears to imply some degree of desolation, of definite spiritual
pain. The important thing is that lack of sensible devotion, a certain
coldness, or even boredom, is the ordinary state of many Christians
and cannot rightly be called aridity. Modern guidance sometimes
suggests that sensible fervour is the normal state, with "aridity"—
either as negative lack of this feeling or as positive desolation—as a
spasmodic but common experience. Hilton teaches that ordinary
Christian duty according to "general will", without great devotional
fervour, is the normal state, with both sensible consolation and
desolation as the spasmodic occurrences. Many modern Christians
speak of being in a state of "aridity" for months on end, when,
according to Hilton, they are perfectly normal. Sensible devotion
must always be treated as a gift from God, not as an ordinary state
to which loyal people have some kind of right. The pastoral importance of this teaching can hardly be exaggerated.

I.33 is a little masterpiece on distraction, emphasizing the prime
value of general intention. The subject is continued on a deeper
level in II.21, stressing the need for humility, volitional love, and
quiet struggle but without fuss, anxiety, and tension: given a right
general will, distractions matter little. Christian life should be ruled
by "I am nought, I have nought, I covet nought, but One". Aridity
and distraction, difficulty and desolation, are put firmly in their
place in a single glorious exhortation: "What so thou hearest or
feelest that should let thee in thy way, abide not with it wilfully, tarry
not for it restfully, behold it not, like it not, dread it not; but aye go
forth . . ."

I.10,11, and II.11,22,42, all contain doctrine on the discernment
of spirits couched in the same pastoral–theological idiom. This
specific teaching is important, but underlying it all is the general
ascetical background, the maps and patterns of orthodox experience,
used and worked out by empirical direction. Hilton's delightfully
humble little asides, "or so me-thinketh", "what little I can say",
and his frequent hints that the anchoress to whom he is writing
knows so much more than he does himself, is no mock
modesty but an expression of the essential empiricism of Anglican
guidance. The relation is a mutual one, a common working out of
ways and means by two people knit together in the love of Christ and

guided by the Church's teaching. In I.71 and 83, Hilton impresses on
the anchoress that this must be her approach in her dealings with her
own spiritual children: a good director must himself be well
directed. The pastoral ethos is well summed up in II.31:

> Now I have said to thee a little of reforming in faith, and also I
> have touched to thee a little of the forthgoing of that reforming to
> the higher reforming that is in feeling. Not in that intent as I
> would by these words set God's works under a law of my speak-
> ing; as for to say, thus worketh God in a soul and none otherwise.
> Nay, I mean not so: but I say after my simple feeling that Our Lord
> Jesu worketh thus in some creatures as I expect. And I expect well
> that He worketh otherwise also, that passeth my wit and my
> feeling . . .

VII. SYNOPSIS OF THE *SCALE*

In II.28, following Romans 8. 29,30, Walter Hilton gives his own
summary of his system. It begins with a reminder of the doctrine of
prevenient grace, and of the necessary connection between creation
and redemption: "For He doth all; He formeth and reformeth. He
formeth only by Himself, but He reformeth us with us; for grace
given, and applying of our will to grace, worketh all this." Then come
the four stages from St Paul: "*Calling, Righting, Magnifying*, and
Glorifying", which are made to correspond with Hilton's plan.
Calling is vocation, the prevenient election of the soul by God and
the soul's response by a definite commitment: the "decision for
Christ". This is the stage of the new convert's romantic excitement,
it is "often easy and comfortable", "but this softness passeth
away after a time". *Righting* is reforming in faith, the Purgative
Way, which is "travailous", demanding stamina to fight doubt,
temptation, and laxity. I do not think this necessarily contradicts
Hilton's teaching that this stage "may be had lightly and in short
time" but rather complements it. The ontological status is given in
Baptism, the subjective response is a simple, firm decision; that is
the "easy" part. Although this status is not easily lost—only, if at
all, by habitual neglect of the sacraments of grace and spiritual
exercise—progress implies a struggle which is "travailous". Hilton,
like all sound directors, assumes good will on the part of his spiritual
children: the lax cannot be legislated into holiness. *Magnifying* is
reforming in feeling or illumination, this is "a time of quiet rest"

but the quiet of *tranquillitas* and the active, contemplative rest of the *De Civitate Dei*. It is more than holy reverie. *Glorifying* is union, when the soul is "fully reformed in the bliss of heaven."

Everything remains firmly grounded on "the laws and sacraments of Holy Kirk"; each stage has prayers and meditations proper to it, and its own particular difficulties and disciplinary needs. Bodily mortification is played down, legalism avoided, and Rule expressed in the strict Benedictine spirit: "Bind thee not to wilful customs unchangeably, that should let the freedom of thine heart for to love Jesu if grace would visit thee specially."[1] Rule is liberating, and a means to an end only.

The whole spirit is pastoral, not legal. Hilton's system is a usable map, a background against which Christians in all states may safely be guided; yet it contains specific and very definite teaching on all the aspects of ascetical theology. His stages and progressions overlap, his definitive edges are blurred. This is typical of medieval writing, but it is also plain that Hilton is not content to theorize and speculate against the facts of pastoral experience.

The real point is that, to return to Patrick Thompson's terms, Hilton is a true ascetical "scientist" who nevertheless knows that spiritual guidance requires a modicum of "art". St Ignatius Loyola and St John of the Cross give us much tidier plans, which are useful if properly applied, but which risk a too formal approach to Christian people; direction "by the book". St Bernard inspires but teaches nothing very practical, he is all "art" and little "science". Hilton is synthetic in yet another sense, avoiding the dangers and combining the values of these two opposing groups. But for this reason he must be read and studied more thoroughly than either. One can almost memorize Loyola like learning mathematical tables—which is not without use. One absorbs Bernard like music. Hilton is more difficult, but for Anglican guides (if I dare say so) much more worthy of study.

However, the *Scale* cannot be called unsystematic by fourteenth-century standards. The simplest classification for ordinary purposes is as follows:

The *fundamental system* is found in I.1–23 and II.1–19. *Moral theology*, though never divorced from ascetic, is mainly in I.52–93. Particular teaching on *prayer and meditation* comes in I.25–51. The

[1] II. 21.

larger portion of the remainder of Book II deals with the advanced
stages of contemplation of a pseudo-Dionysian type.[1]

VIII. HILTON AS EDITOR:
THE GOAD OF LOVE AND THE EUCHARIST

The Goad of Love is a composite work based on the *Stimulus Amoris*,
once attributed to St Bonaventure but more probably by the
thirteenth-century Franciscan, James of Milan. This work was
edited, expanded and translated into English by Walter Hilton. The
edition published by Faber and Faber in 1952 contains an enlighten-
ing introduction by Clare Kirchberger, who shows how Hilton's
character and outlook are well illustrated by comparing his translation with the original. This interest is heightened by the fact that,
according to the custom of his age, Hilton takes editorial liberties
which would be considered outrageous to-day.[2] An examination of
this freedom with another's text demonstrates both the spirit of
Hilton and of the English School in general.

1. First, Hilton inserts a great deal of theology, especially insisting
on a proper understanding of St Augustine's doctrine of concupiscence, with its relevant moral doctrine. James of Milan's
exaggerated devotional imagery is toned down, brought under the
influence of reason, and often omitted altogether. Spiritual experience is rationalized into ascetical categories. Hilton omits all
traces of the false mystical idea of "absorption into God", which
would destroy individuality, and into ch. 27 is inserted a long warning on the dangers of reliance on feeling.

Like most strongly affective writers who occasionally attempt
ascetical theory, James's patterns and plans tend to be far too exact
to be true to experience. Hilton goes out of his way to blur the
boundaries between the Three Ways, and to overlap other categories. In the apposite words of Clare Kirchberger, "he cannot abide
the spiritual spider-webs spun of beautiful fine logic".[3]

The value of physical penance, prescribed by James with typical
Franciscan gusto, is much moderated or omitted. Hilton leaves out
"an assumption that manual work is not suitable for a contemplative,
and an unkind reference to a 'rusticus'":[4] the Church Militant is
one.

---

[1] See section IX below. [2] *The Goad of Love*, ed. Kirchberger, p. 27.
[3] Ibid., p. 27. [4] Ibid., p. 29.

2. Hilton is more Christocentric. The word "God" is frequently translated "Christ", and a good deal of new material is added which emphasizes the Incarnation, the progression from devotion to the Sacred Humanity to the Divinity, and which teaches the recollective value of these doctrines. This could almost have been written for Margery Kempe: much of it is expounded and substantiated by New Testament quotation. A good deal of Scripture is inserted by Hilton throughout the work, which is itself significant, and which Clare Kirchberger appears to have overlooked.

3. James of Milan almost revels in the wickedness and corruption of human nature, and indulges in the sort of grim self-judgement which incites one to despair. Hilton either omits these passages or softens them under the plain influence of St Thomas. James's thoroughly unchristian exhortation to "hate thyself" is changed to "nought thyself", which is something very different indeed! The one is self-abnegation, allied to the heretical mysticism of "absorption" theories, the other is humility. English domestic optimism is summed up in the glorious phrase that "we should hope for mirth without measure and joy without end".[1]

The book itself contains little ascetical doctrine which is not in the *Scale*. Neither need the other minor works detain us, although they should be read and prayed with for the sake of the occasional stimulating insight if not for new doctrine.[2] It is interesting to see confirmation of Hilton's pastoral approach in the fact that his most important work after the *Scale*, written for an anchoress, is the *Treatise on Mixed Life*, addressed to those "the which have sovereignty", those, that is, of worldly responsibility: the "busy layman". But again, most of the particular ascetic is to be found in the *Scale*, which is the *Summa* of his fundamental doctrine.

The one possible exception is the teaching on preparation for Holy Communion, to be found in ch. 22 of *The Goad of Love*. Hilton's six concise points are still very usable, more practical in fact than those more elaborate schemes of the Caroline period which are here anticipated. There are four points of what we would now call "remote preparation" and one each for the traditional division of the Mass itself.

a. The communicant should be armed with some *knowledge* of

---

[1] *The Goad of Love*, ch. 38.
[2] *Minor Works of Walter Hilton*, ed. D. Jones, Orchard Books (1929).

eucharistic doctrine according to his capacity. Hilton would be the last person to exaggerate the need of intellectualism, nevertheless knowledge leads to love. Everyone must make the attempt at thinking out the mystery; the devout Christian need not be a theologian but there is no excuse for mental sloth. The more he can understand the better he can worship.

b. "Devotion of heart" is a good general intention. The communicant is to make an act of oblation, a serious and disciplined act of will, long before the actual Mass. This will carry him through any superficial distractions which may occur at the time: here is a brilliant solution to a very common dilemma. Undue worry about wandering thoughts and distractions at Mass is scrupulous and silly because it makes things worse, yet counsel to take these nuisances too lightly may invite laxity: Hilton's act of general will beforehand solves both problems.

c. "Reverence of heart" deals with the dilemma of the "worthiness" of the communicant, with which Caroline thought was to become preoccupied. Communion should not be made casually but scruples about "worthiness" are also to be avoided. Hilton's teaching is crystal-clear and theologically safe: "unworthiness" is lack of spiritual discernment more than moral weakness, "reverence of heart" means penitence whereby "His goodness and pity is more than our wretchedness . . . His worthiness shall make us worthy."[1]

d. "Love and desire of heart": preparation is to be taken seriously; we communicate, primarily, in obedience to Christ's command, but reception should always be *joyful.* Too great a stress on Christian duty tends to turn worship into a dull obligation instead of a joyous privilege.

e. The *Missa Catechumenorum* should be attended with "meek and devout prayer", mainly of petition and penitence.

f. The *Missa Fidelium* is to be qualified by "nought thyself"; objective surrender to Christ and the Church, humble self-oblation and adoration. But the communicant should not be disturbed by the lack of sensible devotion.

IX. DOM GERARD SITWELL'S PLAN OF THE *SCALE*

The simple classification of *The Scale of Perfection* I have given in section VII above is intended to facilitate the serious study of the work. In Burns and Oates's Orchard Series edition, Dom Gerard

[1] Cf. The Caroline teaching in Ch. 20, VII below.

Sitwell provides a more detailed analysis, which cannot be improved upon for purposes of easy reference. I reproduce it for convenience:

PLAN OF BOOK I

Section I

Chs. 1–14   The end for which we are striving, union with God in contemplation.

Section II

Ch. 15   1. Introduction.
Chs. 16–23 2. The Virtues of humility, faith and charity.
Chs. 24–36 3. Prayer and meditation.
Chs. 37–9   4. Difficulties and how to overcome them.
Chs. 40–1   5. Necessity of knowing God's gift to us.

Section III

Chs. 42–5   The transformation that must be brought about in us before union with God can be attained; the reforming of the image of God in us.

Section IV

            Means of bringing this about:
Chs. 46–54 1. To seek Jesus.
Chs. 55–92 2. To obtain knowledge of the roots of sin within us, and to destroy them.

PLAN OF BOOK II

Section I

Chs. 1–20   Comparison between the state of ordinary Christians and of contemplatives:
Chs. 1–3   1. The Fall and the Redemption.
Chs. 4–16   2. Reform in Faith.
Chs. 17–20 3. Reform in Faith and in Feeling.

Section II

Chs. 21–32 The Contemplative Life.

Section III

Chs. 33–5; The Nature of Contemplation.
   40–1

Section IV

Chs. 36–9; The effects of Contemplation:
     42–6 1. General effects of Contemplation, which may be connected with:
Chs. 36, 43   (a) Gifts of the Holy Spirit, and
Ch. 42   (b) with prayer.
Chs. 37–9 2. The effects of Contemplation in relation to particular vices and virtues.
Chs. 44–6 3. Various supernatural experiences which are "mystical" in the more commonly accepted sense of that term.

X. EDITIONS OF THE *SCALE*

There are various editions of *The Scale of Perfection* obtainable, in which slight variations of chapter divisions may occur, according to manuscript sources used.

Of modernized versions, my personal preference is for the John M. Watkins edition [1] which is easy to read yet which manages to retain a good deal of the original idiom. Most of the other editions suffer, in varying degrees, from being too modernized. They are almost translations from a foreign tongue, leaving very little fourteenth-century flavour. My own references and quotations are from the Watkins edition.

[1] Ed. and introd. E. Underhill, 2nd imp. 1948.

17

JULIAN OF NORWICH

Introducing St Anselm, I tried to explain that the affective–
speculative synthesis implies neither exact proportions nor a simple
admixture. Hilton and Julian achieve the ideal but in their own
particular ways, and they should be approached differently. Hilton
can inspire us with affective piety, but he is primarily an ascetical
theologian, a director of souls, to be carefully studied. Julian's
theology, like that of St Catherine of Siena, is certainly not to be
despised, but it is best understood by meditation. *The Revelations of
Divine Love* supplies the English Christian with all that is best in
"spiritual reading".

I. INTRODUCTION TO THE *REVELATIONS*

The Revelations of Divine Love grew out of a supernatural experience
granted to Julian on 8 May 1373, when she was thirty years old.[1]
The inevitable arguments about the exact nature of this experience,
its genuineness as "mysticism" and so on, need not detain us. No
authority denies her a place among the true mystics of the Church,
however much they argue the fine points of the case.[2] And no devout
Christian can read her book without finding sublimely simple
"meditation" on the Passion. Whatever the experience with which
Julian began, and to whatever the heights she finally rose, the
Revelations remain the fruits of lifelong reflection upon the Passion
as a central point of Christian theology.

The authorities agree in dividing the experiences underlying the
Revelations into three main types. These are:

1. "In bodily sight", which is ordinary, imaginative meditation.
The sublimity of this meditation is no doubt heightened by the
original experience, but it remains perfectly "ordinary" prayer.

[1] *Revelations*, ch. 2; all references in this chapter, unless otherwise indicated,
are to the 13th ed. of Grace Warrack's translation (1949).
[2] Knowles seems to have modified his view between *English Mystics* (1928),
and *The English Mystical Tradition* (1961).

2. "In bodily likeness: ghostly", is an intermediate stage wherein imagination and intellectual understanding become fused. This, too, is the same in kind if superior in degree to a "three point" meditation leading into contemplation.

3. "In ghostly sight", is an intuitive or mystical perception of divine truth.[1]

In practice, it is impossible clearly to distinguish between imaginative meditation leading to doctrinal considerations, and "intellectual" meditation helped by imagery and symbol. Julian supplies both: vividly affective meditation on the Passion itself, always coupled with intuitive–theological pictures of what it means in terms of atonement doctrine. We may believe that her intuitive and mystical insights are also reducible to the same pattern. Like her spiritual father, Anselm, Julian ultimately refuses to be "classified". "She differs from many modern and medieval ecstatics, such as Catherine Emmerich. Their visions derive what value they may have from their claim to be glimpses of the Crucifixion; with Dame Julian the material showing (in this second stage) is no more than a taking off point for the words and meditations."[2] In other words, Julian will not have affective experience, however sublime, without theological support.

We should heed the warning given by Julian herself: "with many fair shewings of endless wisdom and teachings of love: in which all the shewings that follow are grounded and oned".[3] With even more vigour, the scribe of the Sloane manuscript adds: "And beware thou take not one thing after thy affection and liking, and leave another: for that is the condition of an heretique. But take everything with other."[4] The medievals foresaw the dangers of too elaborate classifications and analyses. Julian sums up her own viewpoint: "Truth seeth God, and Wisdom beholdeth God, and of these two cometh the third: that is, a holy marvellous delight in God; which is Love."[5]

The *Revelations* have come down to us in two versions, a fact which raises other technical questions which need not bother us. It is generally accepted, and fairly obvious, that the *Shorter Version*

---

[1] For a full treatment of the question, see Paul Molinari, s.j., *Julian of Norwich* (1958), pp. 60–70.
[2] *The English Mystics*, pp. 140f.   [3] *Revelations*, ch. 1.
[4] Ibid., Postscript by Sloane MS. scribe.   [5] Ch. 44.

was compiled soon after the original experience of 1373, while the *Longer Version* resulted from twenty years' reflection and meditation upon it.[1] While the former may well be used for devotional purposes, the latter is to be preferred for general use. This contains important additional matter, notably chs. 44–63 and 71–86,[2] consisting of Julian's ascetical–theological reflections on the revelation itself, which is essential to a full understanding of her doctrinal position.

This doctrine is introduced in *Revelations* 1–3, and elaborated in the two additional sections of the *Longer Version*. *Revelations* 4–12 occupy the central meditation on the Passion, of which the long 8th *Revelation* is the peak. The 13th *Revelation* is a thorough devotional treatise on sin and grace, the 14th is devoted to a discussion on prayer, while the 15th and 16th present the only fitting conclusion: spontaneous outburts of adoration. While heeding the warning against too much analysis, there are certain fundamental points which could be helpful in making the *Revelations* more usable.

II. THEOLOGY

Like Hilton, Julian perfectly expresses the English spiritual tradition because she is not in the least bit insular; rather she combines all the strands of our patristic lineage into a synthesis altogether new. Hilton and Julian teach the same thing, but whereas the former is guiding an anchoress, the latter is living the anchorite life; the one guides according to English spirituality, the other prays in the tradition itself. But Julian also teaches if we pray seriously with her, for all the doctrine is embedded in her prayer. Here is the same Augustinian–Victorine basis, the affective Christology of St Bernard, and the supreme English source of Benedictine optimism flowing from a rather more pronounced Thomist element. Her similarity to Anselm has already been noted. The beginning of Christian life is still prevenient grace, the basis of all prayer, however affective in nature, is still the Creeds.

The scribe of the Sloane manuscript aptly lengthens the title to "The Revelations of Love of the Blissid Trinitie shewed by Our Savior Christe Jesu".[3] In spite of the most moving depiction of the

---

[1] "twenty years after the time of the shewing, save three months . . ." (ch. 51). We may therefore date the *Longer Version* as starting in February 1393. See Dom Roger Hudleston, introd. to Burns, Oates edition, pp. xiiiff.

[2] In Warrack's (Methuen) edition, subtitles "Annent certain points" and "Sundry teachings".

[3] Postscript.

Passion, in the best loved of the *Revelations*, it is a mistake to regard Julian as Christocentric. Not merely references but deep insights into the mystery of the Holy Trinity abound throughout the whole book. The peak is reached in the lovely parable of the Lord and servant in ch. 51, although later, especially in ch. 58, Julian gets carried away by the idea of three-in-one in a way reminiscent of St Bonaventure. Nevertheless, ideas like Nature–Mercy–Grace, Father–Mother–Lord, Almighty–Allwise–All–love, The Father is pleased—The Son is worshipped—The Holy Ghost is satisfied; and similar examples repay much meditation. Man, too, is trinitarian, created in the image of God: "our soul is made-trinity, like to the unmade blissful Trinity".[1] "For as the body is clad in the cloth, and the flesh in the skin, and the bones in the flesh, and the heart in the whole, so are we, body and soul, clad in the goodness of God and enclosed."[2]

But man is fallen and concupiscent; the soul has to become "oned" in itself and "oned" to God: "the soul is oned to God when it is truly peaced in itself".[3] Sin remains *deprivatio boni*: "sin is no deed";[4] "sin hath no manner of substance nor no part of being".[5] And our end is God himself: "our soul shall never have rest till it cometh to him";[6] it is "the love-longing that lasteth".[7] It is not very difficult to disentangle both the Augustinian and Thomist elements in such ideas, yet how English are the actual expressions! And how English is the whole!

When it comes to creation and human nature, Julian rejects St Augustine for St Thomas, and thereby sets her most characteristic seal on the doctrine of optimism; on the virtue of hope. Creation, redemption, and the sustaining love of God are ever joined together —"oned": "The first is our excellent and noble making, the second our precious and dearworthy again-buying; the third, all-thing that He hath made beneath us, He hath made to serve us, and for our love keepeth it."[8] "Again-buying" hints at Anselmic atonement doctrine, while Julian, like Catherine of Siena, is well acquainted with scholastic terminology: she speaks of the Holy Trinity as "everlasting Being",[9] and phrases like "nature-substance",

---

[1] Ch. 55.
[2] Ch. 6; see also chs. 10, 58, and the important note (2) in Warrack appended to Ch. 57.
[3] Ch. 49. [4] Ch. 11. [5] Ch. 37.
[6] Ch. 5, cf. ch. 26. [7] Ch. 31. [8] Ch. 42.
[9] Ch. 58.

"sense-soul", and "sense-nature" are used naturally and accurately. "For all our life is three: in the first we have our Being, in the second we have our Increasing, and in the third we have our Fulfilling: the first is Nature, the second is Mercy, and the third is Grace."[1] That might be called a Middle English translation of the doctrines of potentiality and actuality, being and becoming, nature and grace.

But if Julian rejects the Creation–Fall doctrine of St Augustine, neither will she slavishly follow St Thomas. When it comes to the meaning of actual sin, she sides, as might be expected, with William of St Thierry. Here, indeed, Julian's irrepressible optimism becomes a little dangerous: this will be discussed later.

The whole is pervaded with a plain Benedictine spirit, which, as Molinari points out,[2] may be due in part to her association with the Benedictines at Carrow, but this cannot be the only influence. Not only her optimism, but her prudence and "domestic" doctrine of the Church, all imply that Benedictinism inherent in all English spirituality. She is ever loyal to "the common teaching of Holy Church, in which I was informed and grounded."[3] Miss Evelyn Underhill is no less in error with Julian as with Hilton when she speaks of the English fourteenth-century writers' "almost exclusive interest in personal religion".[4]

III. APPROACH TO THE *REVELATIONS*:
EUCHARISTIC DOCTRINE

The student of English spirituality is advised to "live with" the *Revelations* continually, perhaps setting aside an initial period, say one Lent, to pray carefully through them.[5] The first three contain the doctrinal basis, but also the ascetical approach which is to pervade them all. The first, for example, moves straight from a vivid glimpse of the thorn-crowned head of Christ—"who was both God and Man"—to the fact of the Holy Trinity. Humility, ever the basis of good prayer, is introduced as a theological fact: God is Creator, sustainer, lover of all things, as exemplified in the famous illustration of the hazel-nut.[6] This is "the strength and ground of all". Then follows naturally an expression of the central Christian paradox of immanence and transcendence, inspired by a sight of the Passion: "This shewing was quick and life-like, and horrifying

---

[1] Ch. 58, cf. ch. 11.   [2] *Julian of Norwich*, pp. 8ff.
[3] Ch. 46.   [4] Introd. to the *Scale*, p. xvi.
[5] See Appendix.   [6] Ch. 5.

and dreadful, sweet and lovely." The paradox is resolved by our
approach to the God-man who "is so reverend and dreadful, so
homely and courteous". That sets the tone of the whole book. In
ch. 8, Julian gives six points of summary of all necessary theology:
prevenient grace offering the theological virtues is "the ground
of our life", humility before God the Creator is the logical,
not merely pious need. Ch. 9, concluding the first *Revelation*,
leads to the Church, and our unity in love with all our "even-
Christians".

The second *Revelation* stresses the facts of the Fall and, with the
third, the recurrent need of grace flowing from the Passion. Little
need be said about the main section on the Passion itself, chs. 4–12,
except that much will be missed, and probably misunderstood, if
this essential synthesis of devotion and doctrine is not always borne
in mind. Thus the fourth *Revelation*, while stirring and disturbing
in its imaginative detail, could so easily be dismissed as but a
typically medieval exaggeration of the scourging. But if we look, we
find ourselves deeply involved in atonement doctrine of eucharistic
significance. It is worth seeing how curiously *untypical* of medieval
affective devotion this doctrine really is.

While most of medieval Christendom was worshipping what were
believed to be relics of Christ's actual blood, or fragments of the
true Cross, Julian was writing "the dearworthy blood of Our Lord
Jesus Christ as verily as it is most precious, so verily it is most
plenteous". By worldly standards, value depends on rarity, so the
honouring of relics, devout and legitimate as it may be, follows
worldly standards. But the Cross contradicts worldly conceptions,
and it is this supernatural scale of values that Julian honours.
Through the Eucharist, the redemptive blood of Christ becomes an
everflowing river in which, overthrowing economic logic, its
inexhaustible plenteousness increases rather than diminishes its
preciousness.

Julian offers no support to the Protestant idea, which seeped into
Caroline thought, that the Blessed Sacrament would be more
honoured by infrequent celebrations. That, curiously, is the same
devout error which typifies the cult of relics; it is an attempt to
raise the value of supernatural things by reducing them to natural
terms. The redemptive river of blood must constantly flow in the
daily Mass, because its preciousness increases with plenty; all the
psychological difficulties which arise from daily celebration and

communion have to be met, but they are subservient to the ontological facts.

The seventh *Revelation* deals with some of these difficulties;
periodicity, aridity, desolation, and consolation, in a kind of in-
structive interlude in the Passion meditation. This teaching follows
Hilton: "these I had in faith, but little in feeling". Then, in the
wonderful eighth *Revelation*, Julian accepts complete imaginative
freedom; she has no fear of being "unbiblical" yet every detail
means something in full accord with Christian doctrine. While
tradition suggests, for example, that the pain of the Passion was
enhanced by heat, Julian sees "blowing of wind and cold"; this is no
mere fancy, but a significant symbol of spiritual dryness and desolation. Our Lord's final experience of being forsaken by the Father
was not "warm" but "cold".

The ninth *Revelation* is pervaded by that devout optimism, so
typical of Julian and so incomprehensible to the sentimental,
whereby the Passion is seen as joyful in its redemptive fulfilment:
"it is a joy, a bliss, an endless satisfying to me that ever suffered I
Passion for thee . . ." We are inevitably led back to the Trinity: "All
the Trinity wrought in the Passion of Christ." In the tenth Revelation, which has associations with the sixth, popular devotion to the
five Sacred Wounds are also lifted out of a one-sided affectiveness
towards a calm doctrinal meaning: "Our Lord looked into His
wounded Side, and beheld, rejoicing . . . Lo! how I loved thee . . .
This shewed our good Lord for to make us glad and merry." The
next three *Revelations* (11–13) deal with the Blessed Virgin, the
sovereignty of God, and reach the peak of prudent optimism. The
last three are adoring, deep, and sublime: but they may also be
prayed as affective-intellectual meditation.

IV. DOCTRINE OF PRAYER

Julian's doctrine of prayer is scattered throughout the book, and,
because she is both English and medieval, closeknit schemes and
methods are not to be expected. She does, however, devote a
considerable part of the fourteenth *Revelation* to a short treatise on
the subject. Prayer is, like Christian morals and Christian life,
essentially teleological: "Prayer is a right understanding of that
fulness of joy that is to come, with accordant longing and sure
trust."[1] St Augustine and St Thomas embrace one another in that

[1] Ch. 42.

brilliantly curt definition. But it begins with grace: "I am the ground of thy beseeching";[1] grace "quickeneth the heart and entereth it, and maketh it pray right blissfully".[2] If that sounds idealistic, we must realize that aridity is due to our frailty, especially to lack of hope, but it is to be dismissed as unimportant:

> Pray inwardly, though thou thinkest it savour thee not: for it is profitable, though thou feel not, though thou see nought; yea though thou think thou canst not. For in dryness and in barrenness, in sickness and in feebleness, then is thy prayer well-pleasant to me, though thou thinkest it savour thee nought but little.[3]

That is necessary obedience, leading to the purpose of all prayer; to be "oned" to God. From this orthodox setting arise six characteristic points relevant to modern guidance.

1. Prayer depends on *facts* not moods, so we must avoid *tension*. Ascetical theology itself does not preach a doctrine of justification by works. Yet misguided personal effort can degenerate into a kind of spiritual Pelagianism; the idea that all depends on us and that, if we fail in a tense concentration for a moment, then our prayer must be ineffective. The impression is sometimes given by devout priests that, unless they are very careful, unless they expend all possible mental energy, their Mass will be invalid. Devotion and recollection are, of course, necessary, but they are very different from tension. The real key to prayer is doctrinal fact, not subjective feeling: "the greatest deeds are already done".[4] Prayer does not so much achieve something as fulfil our baptismal status, it is our proper activity, manifesting and consummating what, in fact, God has made us to be.

2. There is the expected stress on recollection rather than formal techniques: "it pleases Him that we work both in our prayers and in good living, by His help and His grace, reasonably with discretion keeping our mights[5] turned to Him".[6] We are to come to God in this life "in our own meek continuant prayer . . . by many privy touchings".[7] "Homely" means "habitual", and it is significant that, at the close of this section where the final bliss of heaven is

---

[1] Ch. 41.   [2] Ibid.   [3] Ibid.
[4] Ch. 42.   [5] i.e. powers or faculties.   [6] Ch. 41.
[7] Ch. 43.

described, all five bodily senses are used as symbols: "Him verily seeing and fully feeling, Him spiritually hearing, and Him delectably smelling,[1] and Him sweetly drinking.[2] And then shall we see God face to face, homely and fully."[3] But it is Margery Kempe who carries this art of symbolic recollection to its conclusion.

3. Prayer is not a plea from servant to master—usually rejected—but a habitual intercourse between child and Father, between redeemed and Redeemer. Christ wants and loves our prayer: "Full glad and merry is Our Lord of our prayer".[4] That is St Bernard's *philia* rather than St Augustine's *agape*, and it makes prayer a joyfully optimistic thing: "For this is Our Lord's will, that our prayer and our trust be both alike large."[5] That, too, is what I have called English generosity; total oblation, not formal duty.

4. Our prayers are eternal, they are the link between earth and heaven, partaking of the qualities of the latter. "Our Lord Himself, He is the first receiver of our prayer, as to my sight, and taketh it full thankfully and highly rejoicing; and He sendeth it up above and setteth it in the Treasure, where it shall never perish."[6] Perhaps it is only our prayers which make up that incorruptible treasure, laid up where rust and moth cannot corrupt and where thieves cannot reach?

5. None of this is "personal religion" in an individualistic sense. All Julian's teaching is set against the unchanging background of the corporate Church. Ch. 61 contains a passage to which we must refer in a later section

> And He willeth that we take us mightily to the Faith of Holy Church and find there our dearworthy Mother, in solace of true Understanding, with all the blessed Common. For one single person may oftentimes be broken, as it seemeth to himself, but the whole Body of Holy Church was never broken, nor never shall be, without end. And therefore a sure thing it is, a good and a gracious, to will meekly and mightily to be fastened and oned to our Mother, Holy Church, that is, Christ Jesus.

[1] See Warrack's note to ch. 43, p. 92.
[2] "swelowyng": tasting; see also n. 1.
[3] Ch. 43.   [4] Ch. 41.   [5] Ch. 42.
[6] Ch. 41.

6. There follows from this doctrine—though not in the order of the book—some significant teaching about intercession. It is legitimate to intercede "either in special or in general",[1] but the latter is to be preferred:

> I desired to learn assuredly as to a certain creature that I loved, if it should continue in good living, which I hoped by the grace of God was begun. And in this desire for a *singular* Shewing, it seemed that I hindered myself: for I was not taught in this time. And then was I answered in my reason. . . . Take it *generally*, and behold the graciousness of the Lord God as He sheweth to thee: for it is more worship to God to behold Him in all than in any special thing.[2]

Devout Anglicans are reluctant to learn that loyal life within the Church is the supreme intercession for "all-thing, special as well as general". The most impassioned prayer for a loved one is then permissible and good, but it is still subsidiary to, and less efficacious than, the Office and the Eucharist. Intercession without Rule would be meaningless to Julian, to whom the test of all prayer, petition and intercession included, is "that it is more worship to God".[3]

V. THE ATONEMENT

Like most contemplatives, Julian is absorbed with the doctrine of creation, which gives her a strong pastoral sense. The *Revelations* are concerned at every point with the fact of Atonement. These two together lead inevitably to the problem of evil, which Julian is unable to solve and which she wisely leaves in the hands of God: "it is a great mystery reserved to Our Lord's privy counsel, and it belongeth to the royal Lordship of God to have His privy counsel in peace".[4] Nevertheless her grappling with the problem, as all serious Christians must, helps us to understand some of her most characteristic qualities.

Julian's atonement doctrine is a racial solidarity theory similar to that of St. Bernard: "For in the sight of God all man is one man, and one man is all man."[5] From this comes the curious idea that Adam's sin virtually comprises all other; the "original" sin is the

---

[1] Ch. 61.   [2] Ch. 35.
[3] Cf. Simon Patrick: "whatsoever doeth Him most honour, will certainly do us most good". See Chs. 19, VI, 20, III below
[4] Ch. 30.   [5] Ch. 51.

only sin, and men's actual sins are but part of it. So such actual sin is "right nought", which is true in the sense of *deprivatio boni*, but very dangerous in any other sense. The argument follows the line of the Epistle to the Romans; where sin abounds, grace abounds more, thus sin becomes almost "useful". It makes us humble, while resistance to temptation expresses Christ's love towards us. In ch. 38, Julian mentions some of the sinful saints—David, Magdalene, Peter, Paul, Thomas, and, topically, John of Beverley—as examples of the glory of sin forgiven. It follows that evil leads us to compassion for our fellow men, and that such is a real participation in the virtue of Christ: "each kind compassion that man hath to his even-Christian with charity, it is Christ in him".[1]

That is good enough pastoral doctrine but Julian's optimism makes it dangerous; to the query "Shall we then sin that grace may abound?" she more than once suggests an affirmative answer. Later, this error is recognized and put right:

> If any man or woman, because of all this spiritual comfort that is aforesaid, be stirred by folly to say or think: "If this is sooth, then were it good to sin (so as) to have the more meed,"—or else to charge the less guilt to sin,—beware of this stirring: for soothly if it come it is untrue.[2]

That is something like Margery Kempe's trick of starting off a colloquy with admitted error and arguing it round to orthodoxy, but Julian, here, is much less convincing. This intellectual struggle, with both right and wrong plainly set out for the purpose of pastoral teaching, is also found in Rolle. With the possible exception of the very careful Hilton, all the English writers lay themselves bare to that scourge of authors: being quoted out of context. If this point is not recognized, much fourteenth-century writing can be misunderstood.

VI. JULIAN'S OPTIMISM

The refrain pervading the thirteenth *Revelation* and indeed the whole book, is: "All shall be well, and all shall be well, and all manner of thing shall be well." It is the deepest expression of hope understood as a permanent virtue infused by God:

> But our good Lord the Holy Ghost, which is endless life dwelling in our soul, full securely keepeth us; and worketh therein a peace

[1] Ch. 28. [2] Ch. 40.

and bringeth it to ease by grace, and accordeth it to God and maketh it buxom. . . . Our failing is dreadful, our falling is shameful, and our dying is sorrowful: but in all this the sweet eye of pity and love is lifted never off us, nor the working of mercy ceaseth. . . . For grace worketh our dreadful failing into plenteous, endless solace; and grace worketh our shameful falling into high, worshipful rising; and grace worketh our sorrowful dying into holy, blissful life.[1]

This optimism springs from St Thomas, but enriched by the *philia* concept from St Bernard: "He shall never have His full bliss in us till we have our full bliss in Him, verily seeing His full Blissful Cheer. For we are ordained thereto in nature, and get thereto by grace."[2] But, still following St Thomas, there is the problem of sin to contend with: "a monstrous thing against nature . . . for as verily as sin is unclean, so verily it is unnatural . . . but He shall heal us full fair".[3]

Julian is constantly troubled by the problem of predestination. In chs. 32 and 33 she makes a submission to the teaching of the Church that "many creatures" are doomed to damnation. This worries her, but she leaves the mystery in the hands of God and continues to preface her optimistic remarks with such a phrase as "those who shall be saved by grace". But difficulties arise because her teaching now seems to apply to a minority of high sanctity, which is an attitude quite incompatible with her optimistic charity to "all her even-Christians". This difficulty is insoluble, since the idea of the vicarious nature of the Church is not strongly in evidence.

As is to be expected, Julian follows William of St Thierry and the English tradition on the pastoral meaning of actual sin. She will have nothing to do with "mortal sin cutting off the soul from God": "in the sight of God the soul that shall be saved was never dead, nor ever shall be".[4] The same arguments follow: it is the love of God which keeps all things in being, to be "cut off" from God means annihilation, and Julian reproduces the nuptial analogy in her own inimitable style:

And thus in our making, God, Almighty, is our Nature's Father; and God, All-Wisdom, is our Nature's Mother; with the Love

---

[1] Ch. 48.   [2] Ch. 72.   [3] Ch. 63.   [4] Ch. 50.

and the Goodness of the Holy Ghost: which is all one God, one Lord. And in the knitting and the oneing He is our Very, True Spouse, and we His loved Wife, His Fair Maiden: with which Wife He is never displeased. For He saith: I love thee and thou lovest me, and our love shall never be disparted in two[1]. . . . For strong and marvellous is that love which may not, nor will not, be broken for trespass.[2]

Julian elaborates this relationship from both sides. From God's side, although

we are sinners: wherefore we deserve pain and wrath. . . . I saw soothfastly that our Lord was never wroth, nor ever shall be. For He is God: Good, Life, Truth, Love, Peace; His Charity and His Unity suffereth Him not to be wroth. For I truly saw that it is against the property of His Might to be wroth.[3]

That sounds a little sanguine, and not wholly compatible with the biblical revelation, but here again Julian puts the other side later. We must continue to heed the Sloane scribe's warning and "take not one thing after thy affection and liking, and leave another. . . . But take every thing with other."

The human side is more dangerous still. In the thirteenth *Revelation*, ch. 37, Julian teaches that there is a depth in the soul, a "supreme point", which is ever free from sin and in which God dwells. This appears to arise out of a piece of rather mixed-up Thomism, or from a clumsy attempt to reconcile St Thomas with William of St Thierry.[4] The ambiguity continues in chs. 52 and 56, where our "higher and lower parts", that is, grace and nature, are "oned in Christ". That "our substance and our sense-part, both together may rightly be called our soul",[5] and that "they shall never dispart", is good Victorine psychology, but it is doubtful whether, in this life, the distinction between nature and grace can be eliminated as "right nought".[6] In glory, nature will be wholly perfected by grace, but in ordinary experience they are constantly at variance. It is even more doubtful that "in every soul that shall be saved is a Godly will that never assented to sin, nor ever shall".[7]

It must be understood that this is mystical theology, and Julian

---

[1] Ch. 58.
[2] Ch. 61.
[3] Ch. 46, and cf. ch. 49.
[4] See Warrack's important note, pp. 121f.
[5] Ch. 61.
[6] Ch. 52.   [7] Ch. 37.

herself was no doubt nearer to God than most of us, yet she knows
the pastoral facts about sin as well as anyone. Here she is rejecting
both the tight, juridical categories of scholastic moral theology, and
the exaggerated penitential rigours of the Franciscans. Nevertheless,
"sin is the sharpest scourge that any chosen soul may be smitten
with: which scourge thoroughly beateth man and woman, and
maketh him hateful in his own sight, so far forth that afterwhile he
thinketh himself he is not worthy but as to sink in hell".[1] The
trouble, of course, is that it does nothing of the kind, our sins are all
too easily borne. But to Julian, no pain is of any account compared
with the love of God. Significantly, she says practically nothing about
attrition; the smallest sins of frailty carry her straight to the most
exquisite contrition. It presents a glorious ideal, but pastorally, it
needs supplementing from other sources.

It is important to understand these difficulties in the *Revelations*,
because the optimism of Julian is of supreme worth, and is central
to the English tradition. It means, predominantly, that the Christian
life is a long, hard struggle, but a joyful struggle, even a gay one. It
means joy in creation and joy in redemption, earned through the
fullest development of the undervalued virtue of hope. It underlies
the Christian fact that the real difference between a saint and a
sinner is that the one falls, repents, and moves hopefully on towards
heaven, while the other falls and stays down. Penitence is an active
quest for truth, hope, and love; almost the exact opposite of self-
centred shame. In an age when the Christian life is seen either as
sentimental convention, or as something frigid and grim, it is most
necessary for Anglicans to pray the Passion with Julian and to
imbibe her spirit of deep optimism and joy. Her ambiguities and
possible dangers must therefore be properly discerned. It would be
tragic if her optimistic gaiety were misconstrued as lax and superficial.

The fifteenth and sixteenth *Revelations* move along to pure
adoration. If God is "never wroth", he nevertheless "willeth that we
reverently dread Him".[2] Love and compassion are completed by
awe:

And thus we shall in love be homely and near to God, and we
shall in dread be gentle and courteous to God: and both alike
equal. Desire we of our Lord God to dread Him reverently, to

[1] Ch. 39.   [2] Ch. 65.

love Him meekly, to trust in Him mightily; for when we dread Him reverently and love Him meekly our trust is never in vain.[1]

VII. DOMESTICITY AND THE MOTHERHOOD OF GOD

Julian's optimism is a theological concept rather than a temperamental attitude; so her "domesticity" is much more than a spirituality warm and cosy. "Homely" means habitual, and therefore constant, calm, and, in the Benedictine sense, stable. If Hilton counters anxiety about aridity by teaching that the lack of sensible fervour is our normal state, Julian goes further still. Feeling is "right nought" because emotional experience, in any context, is spasmodic, therefore it cannot be "homely". Christian joy is truly expressed not primarily in ecstasy but in *tranquillitas*, in domestic harmony, in sure hope and devotion expressed by Hilton's "rest most busy". To Julian, consolation becomes an habitual state rather than an occasional vivid experience of sensible devotion. Modern Anglicans are rapidly growing out of their uninformed anxiety about feeling, or its lack, which arose out of the former Anglican exaggeration of "personal devotion" and a somewhat puerile fear of "formalism". Aridity is no longer fearsome but we are still inclined to over-theorize about it. Julian's teaching guards against this self-consciousness: husbands and wives in a stable, habitual state of love do not argue and theorize about romantic feeling; they either accept it or do without it.

So "homeliness" means that the ontological facts of the faith are to be taken seriously as the constant background of Christian life. It underlies the fact that Christian living and Christian prayer are concerned not so much with the fulfilment of aims as with the expression of what Christ has achieved in us: "the greatest deeds be already done".

All this is worked out in the family-domestic analogy, and we must be careful not to let these rich illustrations detract from their deep theological meaning:

And thus I saw God rejoicing that He is our Father, and God rejoiceth that He is our Mother, and God rejoiceth that He is our very Spouse and our soul is His loved Wife. And Christ rejoiceth that He is our Brother, and Jesus rejoiceth that He is our Saviour. These are five high joys, as I understand, in which He willeth

[1] Ch. 74.

that we enjoy; Him praising, Him thanking, Him loving, Him
endlessly blessing.[1]

The crux of the matter is in Julian's working out of the conception
of the Motherhood of God. The idea is not original; it is found in
St Bernard and St Anselm, amongst others, but Julian's elaboration
is all her own.

Our Father willeth, our Mother worketh, our good Lord the
Holy Ghost confirmeth: and therefore it belongeth to us to love
our God in whom we have our being: Him reverently thanking
and praising for our making, mightily praying to our Mother for
mercy and pity, and to our Lord the Holy Ghost for help and
grace. . . . I understood three manners of beholding of Motherhood in God: the first is grounded in our Nature's *making*; the
second is *taking* of our nature,—and there beginneth the Motherhood of Grace; the third is Motherhood of *working*,—and therein
is a forthspreading by the same Grace, of length and breadth and
height and of deepness without end. And all is one Love.[2]

It is through this concept that the Passion should be seen, for it
explains the essential joy which Julian sees in it, and enlightens the
otherwise disturbing ninth Revelation:

Then said our good Lord Jesus Christ: Art thou well pleased that
I suffered for thee? I said: Yea, good Lord, I thank Thee; Yea,
good Lord, blessed mayst Thou be. Then said Jesus, our kind
Lord: If thou art pleased, I am pleased: it is a joy, a bliss, an
endless satisfying to me that ever suffered I Passion for thee; and
if I might suffer more, I would suffer more.[3]

Without the Motherhood teaching, that is disturbing and almost
blasphemous, but the Passion is turned to joy through Christ's
"Motherhood of working in ghostly forthbringing". It is the birth
of the new humanity, the child-bearing of the Second Adam which
incorporates the suffering of our Lady the Second Eve. In the rebirth of mankind, "our Holy Mother Christ" . . . "forgets the
anguish for joy that a man is born into the world".
This family figure is no mere analogy, for the local Church is
truly a family; love and service to our "even-Christians" is no
isolated duty or worldly morality. It is another constant, "homely"

[1] Ch. 52.   [2] Ch. 59.   [3] Ch. 22.

manifestation of the ontological facts. With Julian, common Christian ideas like "our Mother Church", devotion to the Mother of our Lord, and the fatherhood-in-God of the priesthood, cease to be pleasant conventions and become theology.

The English pastoral tradition of a united Church Militant, of empirical direction, of priest–lay unity; all that is far more than a matter of English temperament and custom. We reject the concept of priesthood as a sacerdotal caste because it represents the wrong type of father and rejects Christ's Motherhood as its source. It is all a question of theology.

18

RICHARD ROLLE AND
MARGERY KEMPE

I. RICHARD ROLLE

Of our five principal writers of the fourteenth century, Richard
Rolle of Hampole (1295–1349) was the earliest in time, the best
known and honoured in medieval England, and, from our special
point of view, by far the least important. It seems curious that, of
this group, the process of canonization was initiated, though not
realized, on behalf of Rolle only. His similarity to St Francis of
Assisi has been mentioned, and if St Francis needed St Bonaventure
to explain and order his spirituality, then Rolle's greatest work may
well be in his influence and inspiration on Hilton and Julian.[1] It is
only fair to remember that the value of a spiritual guide (and Rolle
was renowned as such) cannot always be assessed by his writings.

Like St Francis, Rolle distrusted learning: "wherefore I offer
this book to be seen: not to philosophers nor wise men of this world,
nor to great divines lapped in infinite questions, but unto the
boisterous and untaught".[2] "Knowledge without charity builds not
to endless health but puffs up to most wretched undoing."[3] To
guide souls irrespective of their mental ability is admirable, and
warnings against the idolatry of learning are always necessary, not
least in our own day; but again and again in Christian history the
results of well-meant opposition to intellectualism have been
mischievous.

Rolle followed Francis as a wandering hermit. Apart from Rolle's
greater academic achievement, their early lives were remarkably
similar. No doubt he did great work in preaching, or rather singing,
the love of God, and in the spiritual direction of the under-privileged.

---

[1] But see Knowles, *The English Mystical Tradition*, p. 65; "both these
writers (Hilton and the author of the *Cloud*) are at some pains to counteract his
(Rolle) influence on their disciples".

[2] *Fire of Love*, Prologue.   [3] Ibid., I. 5.

Both lives were inspired by an almost arrogant rebellion against a lax secular clergy and an opulent monasticism. Both boldly embraced poverty, but Rolle lacks that mystical love for creation which typifies the Franciscan. In his longer and better-known treatises, *The Fire of Love* and *The Mending of Life*,[1] his denunciation, not only of worldliness but of creatures, becomes unreal and tedious. His strictures against ecclesiastical evils were no doubt warranted, but there were some good clerics and monks, and the solitary life is not the only way to serve God. His championship of the eremitical ideal is as vigorous as some of the Desert Fathers, which, in his age, is both inaccurate and not a little silly, while his invective against women and marriage is either objectionable or comic according to how one looks at it. St Paul suggested that the pagan woman could be sanctified by a Christian husband; with a characteristic twist, Rolle says that a faithful man is bound to be perverted by an unbelieving wife! "If a true man be united with an untrue woman, it is full near that his mind be turned to untruth".[2]

Both Rolle and St Francis were of the type of individual genius who inevitably divide their contemporaries. Rolle gained much support and made many enemies, who caused him much distress. Yet, to my mind, his personal defence and his attitude towards his detractors, compare unfavourably with the calm, courageous charity of Margery Kempe. His typically medieval presentation of hell and purgatory hint at that peculiar type of spiritual sadism, so characteristic of the age, which is utterly incompatible with the restrained optimism of Julian. Julian is loyal, but plainly uncomfortable with the Church's teaching about eternal damnation; Rolle seems rather to enjoy it!

Strongly affective spiritual writing can only be subjectively judged, and I must admit that I have never achieved a deep sympathy with Rolle. The minor works, *On the Holy Name*, the *Ego Dormio*, and the poems and lyrics, contain passages of much beauty and depth, while the symbolism of colour and music cannot fail to attract. The *Meditation on the Passion* remains, by common consent, one of the finest pieces of affective spirituality we have.

Rolle's idiosyncrasies can be appealing, so long as he is not defending them too arrogantly, and they can be comic. His first hermit's habit, made out of two of his sister's garments, must have

---

[1] Written in Latin but translated into English by Richard Misyn in *c.* 1435.
[2] *Fire of Love*, I. 24.

made him look something like a continental goalkeeper, and the girl's frantic "My brother is mad, mad" was not entirely unjustified.[1] His complete inconsistency can also be either infuriating or endearing. He follows a virulent attack on learning with a complex interpretation of the *Quicunque Vult*.[2] He quotes with much approval from St Benedict against the instability of "runners about, that are the scandal of hermits",[3] when that is precisely what he was himself! Such lack of logic matters little to a singer of the joys of the love of God, but it does not give much to ascetical theology. For that we must be content with Rolle's influence on Hilton, Julian and Margery. There are, however, four points of some practical, and topical, worth, which come out of his teaching.

1. In spite of everything, Rolle gives us a much-needed example of creative individualism: "He does not do things because they are done, or because others have done them, such as excessive fasting or always kneeling in prayer. He is careful to subject his methods to the achievement of the best results. He therefore boldly goes his way, despite criticism."[4] Rolle's famous and curious choice of the sitting posture in prayer is typical: "I have loved to sit, not for penance nor for fancy that I wished men to speak of me, nor for any such thing; but only because I loved God more and the comfort of love lasted longer with me than when moving or standing or kneeling. For sitting I am most at rest and my heart is most uplifted."[5] In Rolle we see the exponent of what I have called "devout experiment" in prayer, and of empirical direction. He is typical of the traditional good Anglican who combines faith and loyalty with freedom of spiritual expression.

To-day we face a dilemma: the apathetic masses, loosely attached to the Church, exaggerate "liberty of conscience" out of all proportion. The idea of corporate loyalty to the Church's Rule, or of fundamental orthodoxy in relation to the religious life, wholly escapes them. On the other hand, the modern faithful tend to become stuck in the narrowest of conventional grooves. The simplest and sanest liturgical experiment disturbs them, and they are shocked by such common-sense ideas as addressing our Lord in

---

[1] Described in the *Legenda* in the Office prepared for the Canonization process.
[2] *Fire of Love*, I. 6,7.   [3] Ibid, I. 14.
[4] G. C. Heseltine: Introduction to the *Selected Works*, p. xxiv.
[5] Ibid., quoted p. xxiii.

modern idiom or reciting the Office in the train. In this much-needed combination of orthodoxy and boldness, of loyalty and personal experiment, Rolle is a worthy exemplar.

2. Perhaps more than any of his contemporaries, Rolle is interested in the Scriptures. He not only quotes them freely in the course of his writings, as indeed did Hilton, but he compiled a considerable number of commentaries on parts of both Testaments, the best known being on the Psalter. This may imply his recognition of the value of the Church's daily round of prayer for lay devotion, and he certainly regards the Scriptures as the proper meditative source for all Christian people. He explicitly advises Bible-reading, even if, with his characteristic lack of logic, few of his lay contemporaries could do very much about it! But his advice is still sensible, probably more so now than then: "be not negligent in meditating and reading holy Scripture; and most in those places where it teaches manners, and to eschew the deceits of the fiend, and where it speaks of God's love, and of contemplative life. Hard sayings may be left to disputers and to wise men used for a long time in holy doctrine."[1]

These commentaries comprise the most theological part of his work, more restrained and carefully thought out than usual, and they clearly show his knowledge and acceptance of the fundamental English tradition: Augustine, Bernard, and St Victor.[2] If Rolle influenced Hilton and Julian, he no doubt also inspired Wyclif: more than anyone, he proves the point that English spirituality itself demanded vernacular Scriptures.

3. Rolle is in complete conformity with his tradition in insisting upon actual and habitual recollection as the necessary link between formal worship and private prayer. His particular contribution is a characteristic development of devotion to the Holy Name of Jesus.

4. The English *via media*, with its central idea of synthesis: speculative–affective, priesthood–laity, corporate–individual, law–liberty, is ever in danger of degenerating into a facile doctrine of "moderation". Rolle is by far the most "heroic" of the fourteenth-century school, and his never flagging insistence "that God demands all" is a welcome safeguard. Against a warm domesticity, his tirades against sinners, even his horrific descriptions of hell and purgatory, may have a rightful place as warnings against laxity.

[1] *The Mending of Life*, ch. 9.
[2] See Knowles, *The English Mystical Tradition*, pp. 52–3.

Rolle and the *Cloud of Unknowing*, with their varying degrees of mystical doctrine and purely affective prayer, offer comparatively little to the narrow confines of this study. Yet in no sense could the fourteenth-century English School be considered complete without them. To our present study, they form the necessary background music; which is an apposite metaphor.

II. MARGERY KEMPE

Hilton and Julian, with Rolle and the *Cloud* in the background, provide a complete plan of English spirituality as it is fully formed in the fourteenth century. With the exception of symbolic recollection, Margery Kempe adds no new facet to the School. Even this important exception is not really new, for although Margery is the supreme exponent of habitual recollection after the Victorine pattern, both Hilton and Julian clearly recognized and taught it. But the *Book of Margery Kempe* is of unparalleled importance in clothing the system with living flesh and blood. It gives not just a plan, but a living, talking, singing moving-picture of the system in action. Margery gives us Hilton's ascetical theology from the receiving rather than the teaching end, as spiritual child rather than as spiritual director. She gives us Julian's affective devotion to the Sacred Humanity, her insight into the redemptive Passion, her domestic optimism, but from the market-place and the family kitchen instead of from the anchoress's cell. The bold individuality of Rolle is worked into a secular life, while Margery's courageous humility in the face of professional rivals, heresy-hunting prelates and even angry mobs, is an example to all. Her active works of mercy and her charity towards slanderers and detractors, her joy in adversity and her wit in danger, are examples in practical Christian living which are hard to surpass.

It is agreed that, by the cool criteria of spiritual theology, Margery is cast in a lesser mould than her great contemporaries, and as inspiration we are again forced to subjective judgements. Many sensible Anglicans find her *Book* infuriating, many more are amused and some greatly edified. But her value to this type of pastoral study is unique, for whether the *Book* is read with delight or fury, it contains the solid core of English spirituality vividly alive. It is also an important bridge between the English fourteenth and seventeenth centuries; Margery helps to carry the living stream of our pastoral and ascetical tradition through the Reformation period.

Admitting my personal attraction to Margery, I must confess that, during my research and planning of this book, she got quite out of hand—which is not uncharacteristic! I thought her importance was such that it could not be confined to a single chapter of proportionate length. Since so little serious study had been given to her rediscovered *Book*, and since I found myself forced to disagree with a good deal of what there was, a separate little book proved the only answer to the dilemma.[1] Readers who are attracted to Margery might perhaps see my small study as an offshoot of the present work, which indeed it is. For other readers I will try briefly to summarize my main conclusions.

Margery Kempe's Christian life is whole and integrated, yet of remarkable *breadth*. Her prayer is orthodox, grounded on that theological tradition which we have traced from St Augustine and St Benedict, yet it is of a far wider range and variety than either Hilton or Julian. She is boldly experimental, like Rolle, and it is impossible to tie her down to any single technique or method; she takes hints and teaching from the whole School, which may be due, in part, to the variety of her spiritual guides: an anchorite of Dominican connection, several secular clergy, an Austin Canon Regular, a German priest, and various accomplished women including Julian of Norwich.[2]

Her life is truly progressive, yet we are presented with all the ups and downs, struggles and falls, which are common to experience. There is none of the artificially gentle incline so often suggested by the text-books, and progress is always tested by moral theology, especially in deepening penitence and practical service to her "even-Christians".

But in spite of this breadth and liberty of spirit, the effective basis of Margery's prayer is the fivefold progression of Hugh of St Victor, which I have described in Ch. 9, III, above. (1) "Reading", or the symbolic interpretation of the created world. (2) "Meditation"—with Margery, always on the Person of Christ as "supreme symbol", and based on a clearly recognized Christology: the progression from the Sacred Humanity to Christ's Divinity, and thence to the Holy Trinity. (3) "Prayer", which is expressed in hard, honest colloquy with our Lord, the Father, or the saints. These colloquies take up a good deal of the *Book*, and are of a rich variety: some are beautifully

[1] *Margery Kempe: an Example in the English Pastoral Tradition*, S.P.C.K. 1960.
[2] Ibid., ch. 7 and Appendix 3.

affective prayers—"full homely dalliance"—some are sublime
expressions of penitence and joy in forgiveness, and some are
"intellectual meditations" of supreme worth. Margery is a great
exponent of the art of gaining theological insight by prayer. (4)
"Progress in Goodness" is both growth in the knowledge and love
of God, and its manifestation in charitable service to society. (5)
"Loving Contemplation" is mystical experience in some of its
multifarious forms.[1]

Margery develops (1) and (2) into her special art of habitual
recollection. Every creature and every human situation encountered
in daily life spontaneously carries a symbolic reference to some aspect
of the Gospel story. This plays an important part in the medieval–
modern link to be discussed in the next section. Margery's recollective technique is traceable to Rolle, although more practical and,
in the right sense, worldly. In his quasi-mystical devotion to the
Holy Name, Rolle recollects a "symbol", while Margery goes
straight through the symbol to the living Christ in human life. The
optimism of Julian pervades the whole.[2]

As an illustration of the Church Militant in action, of empirical
direction, and of a deeply loving, sane pastoral relation between
priest and spiritual child, the *Book of Margery Kempe* is unsurpassed.
The love and loyalty of Margery's various confessors, her relations
with bishops, archbishops, monks and friars, above all, her love and
friendship with Master Aleyn, her constant protector; all that is as
relevant to Anglican pastoral practice to-day as anything in this
week's *Church Times*.

III. LINKS BETWEEN THE FOURTEENTH
AND SEVENTEENTH CENTURIES

It is exactly a century from the death of Margery Kempe to the
publication of Luther's Schmalkaldic Articles, and almost another to
the death of Lancelot Andrewes. Much can happen in two hundred
years, and in the story of English religion there are no more complicated centuries than these. At each end of this complex period we see
English Spirituality in one of its two greatest phases: is there any
relation, or continuity, between them?

In spite of the Anglican insistence on tracing doctrine, orders, and
polity back to the primitive Church and the Bible, it is still held by
some that "Anglican" devotion began in the seventeenth century.

[1]Ibid., chs. 4, 5.   [2] Ibid., ch. 9.

It is implied that while the sixteenth-century upheaval was merely a "reform" of theology and liturgy, it meant a complete break with the past in terms of ascetical doctrine and spirituality. But this is an impossible position in a tradition wherein doctrine and devotion are always intertwined. Theology based on the Bible, Orders flowing from the apostles, loyalty to the historic Creeds, and spirituality starting in the seventeenth century, all in a context of the speculative–affective synthesis, add up to a series of contractions which are difficult to count.

The problem of a postulated continuity of tradition between the fourteenth and seventeenth centuries involves the difficult problems of "social", as opposed to political or ecclesiastical, history. With these problems I am not competent to deal, but, against the theory that any modern spirituality means a clean break with the Middle Ages, the position should be stated. It is that, in ascetical theology, the important data are not so much what this or that leading Reformer taught, but what the ordinary parish priest taught and what his people actually did. And we know that, whatever the theological convulsions, the English faithful continued to be nurtured on *The Scale of Perfection*. It is suggestive that Hilton's *Scale* was printed four times between 1494 and 1533, and three times more between 1659 and 1679. Although these later editions were probably initiated by the exiled English Benedictines, it is interesting that, after more than a century, its revival coincided with the Prayer Book period.[1] No doubt "medieval abuses" had crept in through the German Dominicans, and through the popularity of ecstatics like Dorothea of Prussia and Angela of Foligno.[2] No doubt many English clergy were ignorant and lazy, and not above a profitable sideline in indulgences and false relics, although many more were solidly with their people against monastic and political exploitation, and enclosure.[3] And yet, if we forgo politics and sociology and look deeply into ascetical theology, we find all the fundamental characteristics of English spirituality common to both great eras. I suggest that Caroline devotion was a return to primitive example *through* the fourteenth century, and in some ways it was a return to the fourteenth century itself. As one example, the English Reformation did more than merely eradicate abuses connected with the confessional;

---

[1] See E. Underhill's introduction to the *Scale*, Watkins ed., pp. l–lii.
[2] See M. D. Knowles, *The Religious Orders in England*, II, p. 223.
[3] J. R. H. Moorman, *History of the Church in England*, pp. 117ff. A. Tindal-Hart, *The Country Priest in English History*, pp. 16–17.

it brought back priest and laity into that domestic unity which Margery Kempe describes so well. It is often said that the Caroline divines broke away from medieval legalism and autocracy, and reemphasized the authority of the individual conscience. But what this means, shorn of Reformation controversy, is the reuniting of ascetical and moral theology and the fusion of corporate loyalty with individual responsibility, which all the fourteenth-century writers plainly taught: Rolle and Margery hardly cringed under the oppressive weight of authority!

In the absence of positive proof, I like to believe that beneath the political, intellectual, social, and ecclesiastical factors of the Reformation, the English spiritual tradition, after a thousand years of development, continued to flow on in its unobtrusive, or even underground, channel. I suggest that the deep, pastoral religion of the Church, the maturing ascetical integrity of the faithful, retained their native instincts and qualities whatever kings, popes, and prelates may have said or done. Whether by accident or design, Taylor and Ken inevitably succeed Hilton and Rolle just as they succeeded Anselm and Francis. Julian is spiritual mother to George Herbert and grandam to Keble; Margery Kempe is sister to John Donne, and Little Gidding bears the family resemblance of Sempringham. There are great differences because a tradition lives and moves, but it is the same living stream, the same lineage.

This is of more than academic interest because our concern remains not so much with the fourteenth or seventeenth centuries but with the twentieth. And, to reiterate my much firmer belief, a revitalized spirituality to-day can only come through a continuation of a tradition, together with devout experiment. I am not advocating a "return" either to the Caroline or medieval periods, but a fresh development from them. Preoccupation with the past, whether in ascetics or liturgy, can become no more than a nostalgic stunt, yet, on the other hand, we must avoid the woolliness of the popular type of *non sequitur* that suggests that nuclear energy somehow invalidates the Nicene Creed. A modern Margery Kempe would make her pilgrimages by jet plane instead of wooden ship, but her doctrine of pilgrimage, her communion with the saints of the shrines she visited, her relations with fellow pilgrims, and her recollection of the Divine Presence in danger, would remain as valid now as they were then. It is in the nature of ascetical theology to change with circumstances, yet the fundamental spiritual needs of human souls remain remarkably constant. My contention that a combination of fourteenth- and seventeenth-century teaching is the proper basis for twentieth-century ascetic is illustrated by one composite example: the technique of habitual recollection.

In the Middle Ages the day was held together and offered to God by means of the sevenfold daily Office. But this was monastic and clerical. Laity and *conversi* were encouraged to say simple prayers— barely "offices" in any real sense—in the morning, evening, and at midday. Margery Kempe used parts of the Little Office of Our Lady, the Angelus, and the Rosary. Such devotions and prayers, however, do not "consecrate the day to God" in the same way as the seven-fold Office. Margery met the need by the development of her recollective technique, based on the symbolism of Hugh of St Victor. She saw Christ symbolized in "seemly men", human suffer-ing led her straight to the Passion, mothers and babies to our Lady and the Holy Family. Every ordinary incident in daily life, every commonplace thing, was spontaneously linked with recollection of the Sacred Humanity. From this Margery developed the technique of recollecting the presence of Christ, and holding colloquy with him, in thanksgiving for the day's successes and joys and in penitence for its sorrows and failures: a scheme sometimes presented in modern retreat addresses as startlingly novel!

Generally speaking, the replacement of the clerical and monastic sevenfold Office by the twofold Office of the united Church is a brilliant piece of ascetical theology. It is something that Margery, Hilton and Julian would have welcomed, but excellent pastoral practice though it is, it does not in itself solve the problem of sanctifying the whole day. Every serious Anglican knows how easy it is to start the day with Mattins and Holy Communion and pay little more heed to God until the time of Evening Prayer. The English Office must be supplemented by habitual recollection. In an attempt to provide this need, some of the earlier Carolines adopted a compromise between Margery Kempe and the Prymer. The Christian was bidden to say appropriate prayers on waking, dressing, eating and so on throughout the day. These prayers were composed with the idea of linking, in C. J. Stranks's words, "trivial incidents with great themes, and to bring the mind to prayer and meditation".[1]

[1] *Anglican Devotion*, p. 25. The idea is implicit in Jeremy Taylor, *The Whole Duty of Man*, and especially John Bradford's *Private Prayers and Exercises*, see Stranks, ibid., pp. 22ff.

It is the same symbolic principle as the priest's formal prayers while vesting for Mass. Compare, for example, the traditional prayer at putting on the chasuble, "grant that I may carry that which thou dost now impose upon my shoulders in such a manner as to merit thy grace", with Bradford's more secular "grant therefore that as I compass this my body with this coat, so thou wouldest clothe me wholly with thine own self".

The idea is sensible, devout, and recollective in its attempt to carry the presence of God into every aspect of daily life, but it can become stiff and formal. *The Whole Duty of Man* returns to the medieval idea of saying at least the *Our Father* at four "hours" during the day, while Taylor and Traherne return to the Victorine symbolism of creation.[1] The important point is that, in the attempt to link daily life with a twofold Office and the Eucharist, Margery Kempe's recollective technique is far more compatible with twentieth-century conditions than the Caroline methods. If modern Anglicans wish to cultivate habitual recollection, I think that the *Book of Margery Kempe* will offer inspiration and teaching of greater practical value than anything else we have. Recollection, however, is largely a matter of temperament, and for many people the more formal Caroline approach may be easier. In this case the disciplines of modern life, the catching of trains, set hours of work and so on, are advantages which the seventeenth century lacked. In other words, some temperaments will now find Margery's technique more creative than that of three centuries later, while others will find Caroline methods more compatible with the present age than with their own.

There is a further point. Margery's recollection is an affective sense of Christ's presence in daily life, without any *necessary* practical or moral content. Later Caroline recollection tends towards the solution of moral questions by a conscience trained in casuistry, without any *necessary* affective content. Following Margery, it might be possible to recollect the presence of Christ while robbing the till at the same time. Caroline recollection *could* become an academically moral debate about stealing with no reference to our Lord at all. The Calvinistic *Practice of Piety* taught that moral understanding and action was itself union with God; affective experience was of no account.[2] But the ideal of daily life is obviously a synthesis of these two methods: to refrain from robbing the till *because* of an affective

[1] See Stranks, ibid., pp. 73-4, 106-9.   [2] See Stranks, ibid., pp. 35ff.

recollection of the presence of Christ. No doubt both Margery and the Caroline casuists frequently attained this ideal, but their recollective systems, as such, do not necessarily point to it.

The plain message is that to teach the habit of recollection in the twentieth century, that is to develop responsible, everyday Christian living, we need to combine fourteenth- and seventeenth-century elements, and boldly experiment with them. A truly revitalized Anglican spirituality for to-day will not just arrive from nowhere: it will not be the ascetical system of Margery Kempe, nor that of Jeremy Taylor, but I think it might well be the new-born child of their marriage.

19

THE CAROLINE DIVINES

I. METHOD OF STUDY

The first four books of Richard Hooker's *On The Laws of Ecclesiastical Polity* were published in 1594 and William Law's *A Serious Call to a Devout and Holy Life* in 1729. The intervening period of 135 years has come to be loosely known as the "Caroline" age, and it is characterized by a spirituality which I have also loosely called "seventeenth-century English".[1] Compared with the fourteenth century this presents the student of ascetical and pastoral theology with difficult problems of selection and classification. The spiritual emphases are far more varied, and its literature is vast. The former period was overshadowed by five writers, two of which are peripheral to this study, and considerable insight into its teaching may be gained by seriously reading three books.[2] The Caroline symposium compiled by Elmer More and F. L. Cross, *Anglicanism*, gives extracts from ninety-five writers. The collected works of most of these would be longer than all the fourteenth-century writings put together. And at the centre of Caroline devotion is the Book of Common Prayer, which has a vast bibliography of its own.

On the other hand, modern Anglican commentary on the Caroline period is available in a rich variety of forms, from meticulous studies of single writers to popular summaries of its fundamental teaching. Compared with the more neglected fourteenth century, the student may select Caroline reading according to his tastes and particular interests. He may also gain much insight into the spirit of the age by prayerful use of some of the many devotional manuals it produced. With a little practice, these manuals are easily adaptable

[1] Strictly, of course, "Caroline" only refers to the reigns of Charles I and Charles II; Authorities differ as to what extent the theological movement can be said to precede 1625 and extend beyond 1685. There seems little point in bothering with the arguments in a book of this kind.

[2] *The Scale of Perfection, Revelations of Divine Love*, and *The Book of Margery Kempe*.

to the present age; they are written in comprehensible language and are all firmly based on the Prayer Book.

It is, therefore, more necessary here than in any other section of this book, to keep our limited aims in mind. I hope only to place the Caroline teaching in its context of the evolving English School of Spirituality, all for the sole purpose of pastoral competence in the guidance of Anglicans to-day. At this point I should make it clear that, although I have found it convenient to arrange this book in a roughly chronological way, it makes no claim to be a technically historical study. It is not history but ascetical theology, written for a practical purpose, and, for reasons stated above, it will be more convenient to examine the Caroline age according to subject-matter rather than with individual writers in historical sequence.

II. SOURCES AND INFLUENCES

Caroline spirituality presents a fine example of the principle of the maintenance of a pure tradition without insularity. I have expressed my belief in its fundamental continuity with the fourteenth-century tradition, even if this continuing stream was more of a pastoral, underground current, than a conscious theological development. The Caroline divines went directly to primitive and patristic sources, embodying facets from this teaching into their system, and absorbing ideas from the newer spiritualities of Spain and France. The later Middle Ages, including fourteenth-century England, were inclined to be by-passed, but the characteristics of the school remained constant if expressed in a different idiom: the threefold Rule, the speculative-affective synthesis, the unity of priest and people, biblical meditation, recollection and spiritual guidance, all retained their importance. If it was argued that the continuity from the fourteenth century is a delusion, and that there was a complete break in the tradition, then there are still our two golden eras, growing out of the same sources and embodying exactly the same principles. However one looks at it, there is an impressive argument in favour of the solidarity of the English School itself.

This new synthesis arising out of a quest for primitive purity was also inspired by the better elements from the Continental Reformers, and, perhaps even more, by reaction against their excesses. Thus Hooker, softening both the subjectively affective elements in Lutheranism and the rationalism of the Puritans, sought the obvious ally in St Thomas Aquinas. *On the Laws of Ecclesiastical Polity* is probably the nearest we shall ever get to an Anglican *Summa*, setting the tone of the movement it was to initiate. Following Aquinas, Hooker bases his doctrine on natural and divine law, conceived as the all-pervading reason of God. There follows the close relation between creation and redemption, or Nature and Grace. Christian life is governed by divine laws, but these are the fundamental facts of human life, not deistic "commandments".[1] The approach is therefore *ascetical* in the wider sense of the term, and the doctrine-prayer synthesis remains central to the whole huge treatise.

Not only is the Church's Common Prayer firmly defended against Puritan objection, but the Prayer Book constitutes an integrated system. The Office is linked with the Sacraments within the organic threefold Church,[2] and Christian life is essentially recollective.[3] The Office is held to be superior to personal devotion, though they too are connected,[4] and—fundamental to Caroline ascetic but frequently overlooked—preaching can not only become exaggerated but is incomplete without the support of personal guidance.[5]

The Liturgy and Recollection form the twin pillars of Hooker's ascetical system, the latter being underlined by some original teaching on the Kalendar. Both the continuity of Christian living and natural law demand the Kalendar, but what we would now call the temporal—eternal relation is illustrated by the motion of sun and moon, which, like heaven itself, are but aspects of God's creation. There is a relation between Holy Days and heaven since both types of experience—the temporal and eternal—derive from the one Creator.[6] Like Aquinas, the whole treatise is intensely and constantly sacramental.

It follows that because God is both immanent and transcendent, omnipresent yet omnipotent, places, such as consecrated churches and shrines, are important.[7] Margery Kempe would have agreed with this, and she would have been grateful for such a reasonable explanation.

Hooker, like Augustine and Aquinas, is therefore an asceticist in the wide but not the narrow sense. He does not give any precise methods or techniques of prayer, yet useful ascetical theology is

---

[1] See L. S. Thornton, *Richard Hooker* (1924), pp. 42–9.
[2] *Ecc. Pol.* V. 23, 50–1.   [3] Ibid., V. 55.   [4] Ibid., V. 24.
[5] Ibid., V. 21, iv.   [6] Ibid., V. 69.
[7] See L. S. Thornton, op. cit., pp. 51f.

dotted about his work, especially in Book V, 23–40 and 55–72, of the *Ecclesiastical Polity*, while Book VI, 3–4, contains sound doctrine on repentance and confession.[1] He is important to Anglican spiritual theology both as the foundation of Caroline ascetic and also as something of a link with medieval spiritual thought. His teaching on angelology, especially on angelic mediation between the Church Militant and the Church Triumphant,[2] on penance and fasting, and on divine punishment,[3] is almost more medieval than Caroline; one feels that it could be more acceptable to Hilton than to Jeremy Taylor. Yet, and this is the important point, Hooker can hardly be described as medieval any more than he can be called Thomist, though these are his sources and inspiration: doctrine is not copied and added to Anglican spirituality but absorbed into it.

In the same way, popular Catholic books of devotion like the *Imitatio Christi* and *Introduction to the Devout Life* were as widely read in England as anywhere, but their inspiration was incorporated into the system. Caroline writers say the same things as à Kempis[4] and François de Sales but their spirit and approach are different:

> Taylor had read à Kempis's *Imitation of Christ* and obviously admired it, for there are glances toward it in most of his devotional works, and here and there some definite borrowings, but à Kempis's mood of withdrawal and abnegation was not one which Taylor wished to instill.[5]

Again:

> It is sometimes said that *Holy Living* borrows largely from the *Devout Life* of St Francis de Sales, but only in one passage is there evidence of direct quotation, and for the rest only such resemblances as are bound to arise when two men of the same temperament write on the same subject for similar readers.[6]

It is also said that Taylor was influenced by the new spiritualities of St Ignatius Loyola and St John of the Cross. This is true only so long as we make "influenced" the operative word; in no case do we

---

[1] See Vernon Staley, *Hooker*, pp. 178–88; the authorship of Book VI has of course been questioned.

[2] *Ecc. Pol.* V. 23; Sermons I, II, VII (Keble's edn.).

[3] Ibid., VI. 5.   [4] The authorship is in doubt.

[5] C. J. Stranks, *Anglican Devotion* (1961), p. 85.   [6] Ibid., p. 85.

find the crude lifting of these doctrines out of context and planting them haphazardly upon Anglicanism, which became a popular game towards the end of the nineteenth century. Let Taylor speak for himself: ". . . but yet our needs remains, and we cannot be well supplied out of the Roman store-house; for though there the staple is, and very many excellent things exposed to view; yet we have found the merchants to be deceivers, and the wares too often falsified."[1] Again:

> my endeavours will be the better entertained, because they are the first entire Body of directions for sick and Dying people that I remember to have been published in the Church of *England*. In the Church of *Rome* there have been many; but they are dressed with such doctrines which are sometimes useless, sometimes hurtful, and their whole design of assistance which they commonly yield is at the best imperfect, and the representment is too careless and loose for so severe an employment.[2]

Anglican interest in Greek theology is traditional, and the Carolines prove no exception. The Eastern liturgies provide much inspiration for the devotional writings of Anthony Sparrow, Thomas Comber, and Simon Patrick. Lancelot Andrewes borrows freely from Greek sources, and the famous *Preces Privatae* provides a comprehensive example of the point I am trying to make: no book of prayers could be more obviously English, yet more varied in its sources.

Another notable example of a tradition enriched by a consciousness of its own roots is the Caroline return to the ascetical implications of the doctrine of creation. For it is this, rather than social or moral considerations, which underlies its recollective life in obedience to divine law, wherein all things and all daily circumstances are to be consecrated to the glory of God. Fourteenth-century spirituality suffered from under-emphasis on this point; Hilton held a sensibly optimistic view of human nature, Julian saw the importance of creation in a rather academic way, and Rolle returned to the dualism of the pre-Bernardine period wherein wonderful hymns to creation are found side by side with tedious ranting against all things worldly.

Caroline theology returns with full force to the great saints of creation doctrine: the School of St Victor, St Francis, and St

[1] *Ductor Dubitantium*, preface.   [2] *Holy Dying*, the epistle dedicatory.

Thomas. Jeremy Taylor adds a moral content to Margery Kempe's habitual recollection in the world, and supports it with a more Thomist attitude to human nature and to created things.[1] Thomas Traherne is Victorine through and through:

> Traherne turns continually to the glories of the visible world as the wonders which may be most readily understood by those who have eyes to see, and which will lead them to a right apprehension of the deep mystery of the cross. It is rare that these two approaches to an understanding of the nature of God are so completely combined as they are in Traherne.[2]

It is a short step to the sane optimism of the English tradition exemplified in Julian: "For it is infallibly certain that there is heaven for all the godly, and for me amongst them all, if I do my duty."[3] Or on Traherne again, Stranks writes: "Traherne's eyes are not fixed on the damnation from which the Passion of Christ saves mankind, but on the felicity into which it admits us".[4] . . ."and all manner of thing shall be well".

If patristic and biblical roots produced the fourteenth-century tree, the Carolines enlarged the trunk by refertilizing those same roots and then grafted selected branches from other traditions into it. All grew in profusion but it remained the same tree. On the dubious tenet that the exception proves the rule, the period ends with the grim example of William Law's unbalanced interest in the German Dominicans and his final surrender to the exotic heresies of Jacob Boehme. That is an attempt to absorb the unabsorbable, to graft buds to which the parent stock is allergic, and it is the error of the early twentieth century.

So, whatever the answer to the thorny question of continuity, the fundamental thesis of this book is supported by Caroline example. If the seventeenth-century greatness grew directly from fourteenth-century doctrine, then the modern need is to continue developing the living stream. If Caroline thought constituted a breach with the fourteenth century, if it was largely new thought, then its inspiration came from an even deeper probing into our past tradition. The error of the Protestant Reformers, ascetically speaking, was to reject too much that was ancient. The error of some Catholic Schools is

---

[1] See Stranks, op. cit., pp. 73f.   [2] Ibid., p. 106.
[3] Taylor, *Holy Living*, ch. 4, ii.   [4] Stranks, op. cit., p. 105.

fear of new experiment. And the Preface to the Prayer Book supports the conclusion that our present need is experiment based on our heritage: a synthesis of fourteenth-century and Caroline ascetic again looks like our most fruitful source of living religion.

III. SPIRITUAL DIRECTION

Spiritual direction is inherent in the English pastoral tradition, not simply as a useful addendum to the life of prayer but as the creator of its ascetical theology. The Celtic penitential system, the centrality of the fourteenth-century anchoress, the doctrine–devotion synthesis, the unity within the Church Militant, are all facets of a spirituality which could never have arisen and matured without personal guidance. The Caroline divines continue and develop this tradition, but this fact is not always recognized.

Not without reason, the seventeenth century is regarded as the golden age of Anglican preaching, but it is a misconception to regard the sermon as the be-all and end-all of Caroline pastoral practice, replacing both personal guidance and confession. Such misconception conceals some important conclusions.

1. The sermon was literally central to Caroline pastoral practice because it was preceded by catechetical instruction and followed by spiritual guidance. The first stage of this threefold process is established by the vast numbers of manuals written in this form. Against the exaggeration of preaching, Hooker defends catechism as an integral part of the ministry of the word.[1] Hammond, Andrewes, Nicholson, Nowell, and Wilson all wrote at length on the subject, and it is difficult to find any writer of the age who omitted it altogether.

Next comes the sermon, and it is important to see it in its contemporary setting. Seventeenth-century Christians were generally either illiterate or leisured, and even in the first category theology was a common topic.

> Some of the choicest divinity of the age is scattered up and down the many volumes of sermons from this period when theology was as common a topic of conversation as association football is today. . . . Sermons were at once instruction and entertainment and into them was poured the best thought of some of the finest minds of the day. Particular events evoked different treatises and

[1] *Ecc. Pol.* V. 18.

theologians wrote to supply the present demand or because events required theological explanations.[1]

It has been seen how current world events must force thoughtful people into a similar position.

But even in these ideal circumstances the sermon was no end in itself. Jeremy Taylor is emphatic:

> Let every minister teach his people the use, practice, methods and benefits of meditation or mental prayer. . . . Let every minister exhort his people to a frequent confession of their sins, and a declaration of the state of their souls; to a conversation with their minister in spiritual things, to an enquiry concerning all parts of their duty: for by preaching, and catechizing, and private intercourse, all the needs of souls can best be served; but by preaching alone they cannot.[2]

It would be both easy and tedious to pile up quotation after quotation in support of that view. Thomas Wilson, Sanderson, Joseph Hall, Simon Patrick, even the Puritan Richard Baxter who kept open house on Thursday evenings to discuss the previous Sunday's sermon, could all be quoted in agreement with this principle. As in the case of the necessity of catechetical instruction, it would be hard to find a writer of this age to whom personal spiritual guidance was not a normal and necessary part of Christian living.[3] As an illustration of the principle that out of evil cometh forth good, it is not always realized that Taylor's *Rules and Exercises of Holy Living*, published in 1650 and followed by *Holy Dying* in 1651, were only written because Anglicans were unable to get personal guidance under the Puritan Commonwealth.

We have, therefore, a clear-cut pastoral pattern consisting of three inter-related forms of instruction: catechism, preaching, personal guidance. The position offers three points of criticism to modern pastoral practice.

a. As we shall see in the next chapter, this total pastoral method is firmly based on the integrated ascetical system of the Book of Common Prayer. Reference to any of the Caroline catechetical instructions makes our "Confirmation Classes", crammed into a

---

[1] H. R. McAdoo, *The Structure of Caroline Moral Theology* (1949), p. 8.
[2] *Episcopal Charge*, 1661.
[3] See Thomas Wood, *English Casuistical Divinity* (1952), pp. 41 foll.

few weeks, look a little amateurish, yet nowhere do these manuals depart from the Prayer Book Catechism. Our error would appear to lie in the prevailing departmental attitude, of seeing "catechism", or some substitute in "Confirmation Classes", as a particular stage in the Christian life, or a particular part of the pastoral ministry, divorced from everything else. To the Caroline parson, catechism was linked with the Office, which was itself linked with the Eucharist, which was in turn related to Baptism, Marriage, and everything else. Catechism was part of an integrated system; it was that aspect of the pastoral ministry which added sound learning to true piety.

b. Although the Caroline writers insist on personal guidance, they rarely use the phrase "spiritual direction" and never in the restricted modern sense. Catechism, preaching, guidance, together constituted "the ministry of the word", which becomes almost synonymous with spiritual guidance itself in the wide, empirical, Anglican sense. Neither catechism nor preaching were concerned with intellectual, or "academic", teaching, but with Christian living: it is all ascetical theology, "practical divinitie", spiritual direction. The underlying basis of the whole system is still the speculative–affective synthesis.

c. The Caroline Church did not need a Pope to make authoritative decisions on current questions of faith and morals, because such decisions were hammered out by the Church, loyally united by the Prayer Book system. The modern Church has to face such questions as nuclear armament—or disarmament—birth-control, gambling, industrial relations, and so on, and it is justifiably accused either of saying nothing about them or of speaking with a divided voice. Two bold bishops will make honest, sincere, forthright, and contradictory pronouncements about any of these things, but this is not the opinion of the Church, nor even the Church giving a lead. It is but the view of a Christian individual against which the decisions argued out in the Reverend Mr Baxter's house on Thursday evenings carry far more moral authority. For that was at least the microcosmic Church, comprised of individuals grounded in the Rule of the Church, living daily within the channel of grace. Do all members of the average Diocesan Conference, or of the House of Laity, live seriously and loyally by the Prayer Book pattern? Unless, or until they do, those bodies are theologically incapable of making decisions of any real weight.

In the seventeenth century, individual liberty of conscience was firmly guarded, yet the "opinion of the Church" had real meaning. To-day it has not; not because individual Christians lack integrity or courage, but because they are not acting as, are not *being*, the Church. Our need is the same: spiritual guidance according to the Caroline pattern, based on the Catholic ascetical theology which the Prayer Book pattern embodies. To attain efficiency, we must either be true to our adult spirituality, or we must constitute a Sacred College through which the Archbishop of Canterbury can exercise total power!

2. Another popular idea is that moral instruction in the Caroline sermon replaced, or became opposed to, the confessional. This is a dangerous half-truth. Caroline doctrine of confession is varied and rather muddled, but as pastoral practice, in some form or other, many authorities could be quoted in favour of it: Taylor, Cosin, Francis White, Hall, and Sanderson, to name but a few.

The practical point is that the pulpit replaced the confessional, not in pastoral practice, but as the medium for the working out of moral-ascetical principles. Three aspects of ascetical theology and practice are governed by this change of emphasis.

a. If the confessional is the medium for the development of moral theology, then that moral doctrine must be juridical and to some extent artificial. The confessional deals only with sins, so its experience can only produce "moral" theory divorced from ascetic. A great deal of Caroline casuistical divinity was, in McAdoo's phrase, "hammered out in the pulpit" by preacher and hearer; sometimes by question and answer at sermon time, more often by discussion between priest and layman later or by empirical guidance. It was, therefore, the product not of clerical moralists but of the Church; it arose out of the experience of the worshipping community and was "occasional", that is, practical and pastoral. This Caroline method produced the integrated science of moral-ascetical theology, the art of full co-operation with grace in a total Christian life. It emphasized progress towards perfection rather than keeping on the right side of the law.

b. Seventeenth-century Roman practice, which is still prevalent in Anglicanism, more or less equates confession with direction. Guidance then becomes "spiritual" in the wrong sense, and even when it is widened to include the development of prayer, it tends to issue in methods and devotional exercises of a somewhat rarefied kind.[1] Caroline direction places more emphasis on recollection in the world than on techniques of formal prayer, which is Benedictine, fourteenth-century, and English.

"Pray frequently and effectually" is Taylor's succinct advice to a new convert; "I had rather your prayers should be often than long".[2]

> Only it becomes us to remember, and to adore God's goodness for it, that God hath not only permitted us to serve the necessities of our nature, but hath made them to become parts of our duty; that if we, by directing these actions to the glory of God intend them as instruments to continue our persons in His service, He, by adopting them into religion, may turn our nature into grace, and accept our natural actions as actions of religion.[3]

Or: "Every good and holy desire, though it lack the form, hath notwithstanding in itself the substance, and with Him the force of a prayer, who regardeth the very moanings, groans, and sighs of the heart of man."[4] That is a return to the Victorine–Thomist ideal, which interprets "spirituality" in the right way; as the whole human life of reason and action governed by grace found in prayer.

Anglican empirical guidance is, therefore, closely and logically linked with that habitual recollection which is so characteristic of the English School. Again it is shown to be not just a pleasant way of conducting pastoral relations but an ascetical principle.

3. By limiting both the use and purpose of the confessional, the Caroline Church enlarged rather than diminished the concept of personal guidance. This total pastoral scheme, catechism-preaching-guidance, offers the laity a full and creative place in the united Church. The tremendous principle involved is that it is the Church, not just the priestly minority, which creates its own theology, liturgy, moral doctrine, and policy. Empirical direction, consisting in give-and-take argument and experiment, is the principle of progress. The heavy stress Anglicanism lays on personal conscience and individual responsibility, far from minimizing the need for personal guidance, greatly increases it. For to enter into empirical

---

[1] Although modern Roman doctrine draws a sharp distinction between Confession and Direction, it appears that, in pastoral practice, the ordinary laity receive more guidance in the confessional than in the home or presbytery.

[2] See *Anglicanism* (1935), p. 615; cf. *Holy Living*, ch. 4, vii.

[3] *Holy Living*, ch. 1, i.   [4] Hooker, *Ecc. Pol.* V. 48. ii.

direction, playing one's proper part in the mutual relation, is but the right exercise of responsible churchmanship; it is advantageous, not only to guide and guided, but to the creativity and influence of the whole Church.

> A mean would do well [writes Joseph Hall] betwixt two extremes: the careless neglect of our spiritual fathers, on the one side; and too confident reliance upon their power, on the other. . . . The Romish Laity makes either oracles or idols of their ghostly fathers; if we make cyphers of ours, I know not whether we be more injurious to them or ourselves. We go not about to rack your consciences to a forced and exquisite confession, under the pain of a no-remission; but we persuade you, for your own good, to be more intimate with, and less reserved from, those whom God hath set over you, for your direction, comfort and salvation.[1]

There can be no doubt that such spiritual friendships as between Jeremy Taylor and Lord and Lady Carbery, Bishop Ken and the Misses Kemeyse, William Law and Hester Gibbon, were productive of devotional and ascetical doctrine. It is also certain that the learned and experienced laity of the day played their full part, not only in the creation of practical theology but in the guidance of others. Men like Henry Dodwell, Izaak Walton, and Robert Boyle, women like Mary Astell, Susanna Hopton, and Margaret Godolphin, were employed in this way. Mary Caning is described as one who "understood the grounds of religion as thoroughly as most",[2] and we are told how Lady Ranelagh acted as spiritual guide to the Earl of Clarendon: "He often visited her, especially on Sunday afternoons, for the purpose of religious counsel. Indeed she seems to have been a spiritual counsellor to many, preserving all the while the utmost humility and feminine softness";[3] shades of Julian and Margery: "full, homely dalliance"! Here is the natural continuance of an ascetical tradition springing not from the cloister but from the vocation and guidance of the English anchoress.

When I suggest, as I have already done in this book, that spiritual guidance could be the proper work of many devout lay-women

---

[1] *Resolutions and Decisions*, III. 9; cf. Hooker, *Ecc. Pol.* V. 81; See also Wood, op. cit., pp. 56f

[2] See J. H. Overton, *Life in The English Church* (1885), pp. 154 foll.

[3] Ibid., p. 142.

17—E.S.

to-day, I am regarded as either daringly original or eccentric: I am certainly not original.

From this situation, four more points of topical relevance arise.

a. We must avoid that type of emphasis on the sacrament of penance which equates it with spiritual direction, not because it is "Roman" or medieval, but because it gives rise to a juridical and artificial morality and because it narrows the creative limits of direction itself.

b. Full empirical direction is an absolute necessity if the Church is to solve its current problems of moral and ascetical theology. In view of our greater knowledge of human psychology, and confronted with new problems of international and sociological significance, neither the moral orthodoxy of St Thomas nor that of Jeremy Taylor and Sanderson is completely adequate. Our moral theologians can add their contributions to these problems, but only the Church can solve them. Similarly, if we are to create a new spirituality consonant with the twentieth century, if we are to enter a third Anglican golden age, then our fourteenth- and seventeenth-century exemplars can inspire and our ascetical scholars can advise, but again only the Church of Christ can create.

c. In conclusion to the first point of this section we have seen that only mutual spiritual intercourse between loyal members of the Church can hope to give an authoritative voice to current "occasional" questions. A conclave of clergy, solemnly debating the Christian policy towards industry, is not only ineffective but it is a travesty of proper action of a united Church. Nor are the problems likely to be solved by priest-workers or industrial chaplains. They can only be solved by the Church, which means clergy, Christian industrialists and workers, bound together by empirical guidance in prayer based on loyalty to the Prayer Book ascetic.[1]

d. A subtle and intriguing problem underlies the whole matter. A large majority of Anglican priests, and an even larger proportion of the laity, would give vigorous assent to the theory of empirical guidance. But it is not easy to practise. The relations involved are subtle and complex. Because of his Orders, commission, and learning, the parish priest is, and must be, autocratic in matters of liturgical and dogmatic theology: in one sense he must "run the parish". But in Caroline practice, it is the autocracy of the captain of a

[1] For an important treatment of the question, see F. A. Cockin, "Ministers of the Priestly People", in *Theology* (January 1962).

cricket team (and nobody's decisions are more dictatorially final) rather than that of a tyrant. And even in personal guidance, the priest, again through Orders, commission, and learning, must retain a final decisiveness: there can be no compromise with the truth. But private prayer is unique to the individual, and Christian morals imply a casuistry whereby temperament and circumstances are taken into account. It is here that empiricism and experiment are essential.

No doubt because of unfortunate mistakes in the recent past, this situation can easily be overthrown: while a few arrogant laymen reject all guidance and try to usurp the priest's proper authority, many faithful people are so meek as to fear expressing an opinion even about their own prayer. Even the factory worker, confronted with an industrial moral problem, and plainly knowing more about it than his spiritual father ever will, is reluctant to give his own view.

The point is that, in the English ascetical tradition, mutual discussion and argument is not the layman's privilege but his duty. I doubt if the group in Mr Baxter's house was backward in recounting its moral and spiritual experience. Those who interrupted the Caroline sermon with a question were not hecklers but serious theological students. And, earlier in our tradition, Margery Kempe never hesitated to oppose her ghostly father—or the Archbishop of York for that matter—when she thought his counsel was wrong for her; yet, once a decision was mutually made, she would be obedient to it in the face of death.

Here is the creator of moral and ascetical theology, the inspiration of both our golden ages, and the most constructive hope for the expansion of influence by the Church to-day. Only against such a background can the clerical conference and the commission of scholars work effectively. And this, of course, is the much discussed "layman's job".

IV. MORAL THEOLOGY

1. Moral theology, as such, is but peripheral to our study, but the whole Caroline approach militated against the very idea of moral theology "as such".

Casuistical Divinity meant the practical application or interpretation of Christian moral principles to all the conditions of men's lives, in order that they might be led on to the Christian ideal of holiness: it included not only the resolution of hard cases of doubt and perplexity and all the juristic side of moral theology, but also the entire range of ascetic theology, the whole being regarded as one comprehensive science.[1]

To place the matter in its historical context:

Post-scholastic and post-tridentine moral theology displays a juristic and legalist bias, the inevitable outcome of an authoritarian system. The delicate task of ministering to souls is performed by means of a minutely-detailed code. The primary aim of this comprehensive legislation . . . would appear to be the formation of the decision in the priest's mind as to whether a given act in a particular person is lawful or not. Two criticisms of this will at once arise in the mind of the Anglican student: first, the chief defect in the system resides in its disregard of freedom and consequent heavy stress on the authoritarian element, and in the low ranking of the authority of the individual conscience. Secondly—and this criticism goes deeper—the very content and aim of moral theology in the Roman Communion is narrower than in traditional Anglican views of the science. After Trent, the Roman Church made the great mistake of separating moral and ascetic theology, so that instead of one comprehensive science of preparing souls for heaven, two distinct sciences emerged, the one occupied with the question of the legality or illegality of human acts, and the other concerned with spiritual progress and holiness.[2]

Modern Roman practice tends to react against this trend, yet a modern writer can still say:

The object of moral theology is not to place high ideals of virtue before the people and train them in Christian Perfection . . . its primary object is to teach the priest how to distinguish what is sinful from what is lawful . . . it is not intended for edification, nor for the building up of character.[3]

The distinction is between a hierarchical Church and a united Church in which all orders are regarded as mature and responsible. Only against this Anglican ethos can the Caroline writings be properly used and understood.

[1] Wood, *English Casuistical Divinity*, p. 65; cf. p. x on Baxter's view.
[2] McAdoo, *The Structure of Caroline Moral Theology*, pp. 9f.
[3] T. Slater, s.j., *Cases of Conscience* (1919), Vol. I, p. 36.

2. The logical outcome of this position is a strong emphasis on the authority of conscience, and this is based on another return to primitive and scholastic sources. In Anglicanism, authority means what it meant to Augustine and Aquinas: natural law guided by reason and grace, with right action depending on reason and will. Moralists like Taylor and Sanderson, though opposing contemporary Rome, nevertheless returned to scholastic categories. They describe conscience in terms closely akin to those used by St Thomas, as contrasted with those associated with the later Franciscans, who located conscience in the conative or "emotional" side of man's nature. Conscience is cognitive. It is, as Aquinas said, "a certain pronouncement of the mind"; or, as Taylor puts it, it is "the mind governed by a rule".[1] Yet, says Sanderson, "conscience is not an Autocrat". The Caroline casuists would have distrusted the semi-idolatry of conscience, to become associated with Bishop Butler, as much as they distrusted legalism and emotionalism. Conscience needs training and the underlying aim remains not just human goodness but holy perfection dependent on grace.

> Not least important for our day [writes McAdoo], is their repeated admonition that piety becomes a meaningless burden of rules unless we go first to the heart of the matter, the life of God in the soul of man, because the goal of all spiritual progress is the realization that man can be a partaker of the Divine Nature. For moral and ascetic theology is concerned with nothing less.[2]

And it must be repeated that, in context, this Christian life leading to perfection is life within the Church's redemptive stream: the life of the total Prayer Book system. This fact can easily be overlooked because of the style and presentation of Caroline writing.

At first sight, tomes like the *Ductor Dubitantium* and Sanderson's *Lectures on Conscience and Human Law* look very much like the legalist medieval case-books to which they were set in opposition and which they were meant to replace. But their purpose was quite different; the older books were manuals for confessors, the Caroline works were directed towards the training of the individual conscience by both personal study and spiritual direction. They were to help adult Christians to meet daily problems theologically and to train spiritual directors to make competent decisions in cases of grave doubt.

[1] *Ductor Dubitantium*, ch. I, vii.   [2] Op. cit., p. xii.

It is a pity that, from the modern view-point, these works look so unsuited to their purpose. Taylor's *bon mot*, "what God has made plain, men have intricated", is singularly ill-placed in the preface to *Ductor Dubitantium*, itself one of the longest and most complicated books on casuistry ever written!

It is also easy to regard this teaching as mere worldly morality if the underlying moral–ascetical synthesis is forgotten, if we lose sight of the comprehensive pattern which points unequivocally towards perfection, however far off it may be. In English seventeenth-century religion, the danger is enhanced by the scarcity of anything that can properly be called mysticism. Once more a compound of Caroline with fourteenth-century spirituality is shown to be the ideal. But Taylor himself is quite plain on the totality of Christian life, and on the moral–ascetic relation:

> When God sent the blessed Jesus into the world to perfect all righteousness, and to teach the world all his Father's will, it was said and done, "I will give my laws in your hearts, and in your minds will I write them": that is, you shall be governed by the law of natural and essential equity and reason, by that law which is put into every man's nature; and besides this, whatsoever else shall be superinduced shall be written in your minds by the Spirit, who shall write all the laws of christianity in the tables of your consciences.[1]
>
> Now there are two ways by which God reigns in the mind of a man, 1. faith, and 2. conscience. Faith contains all the treasures of divine knowledge and speculation. Conscience is the treasury of divine commandments and rules in practical things.[2]

That boils down to nature ruled by grace and contains nearly all the English syntheses: speculation and affection, prayer and action, loyalty and responsibility, moral integrity as the practical prologue to ascetical perfection. But at p. 875 of the *Ductor Dubitantium*, we might perhaps be excused for forgetting what is on p. 8!

3. Following the Benedictine and English emphasis, the purpose of Caroline casuistry is the training of the conscience to be used mainly in habitual recollection. It is concerned with the practical art of making moral decisions during daily life rather than with formal "self-examination" prior to sacramental confession. This links up

---

[1] *Ductor Dubitantium*, Bk I, ch. 1, rule I vii.   [2] Ibid., I, ch. 1, rule I 10.

with the recollective techniques of the fourteenth and seventeenth centuries which were compared in the preceding chapter, and with the Caroline relation between pulpit and confessional. Contemplative recollection was naturally central to the "professional" religion of anchorites and anchoresses, and we have seen how Margery Kempe, as "laywoman", developed her own technique. But, in the fourteenth century, moral and penitential theology were still largely concerned with formal prayer. Although Margery is led to penitence by certain symbolic events—cruelty, disease, misfortune, and so on—morality was still applied by self-examination at set times followed by confession. This change of emphasis also links up with some of the Caroline teaching we have already discovered.

a. The Caroline trained conscience, dealing with moral problems as they arise, diminishes the need for very frequent confession for ascetical reasons which have nothing to do with quarrels with Roman practice or medieval abuses. Margery, habitually recollective of the Sacred Humanity, appears to have gone to confession on every possible occasion. This may have been devotional, yet, with an affective rather than moral recollective emphasis, it was also a need.

b. Thus, to the Caroline Christian, self-examination was extended into a continuous process, an aspect of recollection, as well as a formal exercise. Formal self-examination alone tends to the juristic attitude as much as moral theology based on confessional experience. Thus the Caroline ideal of a properly trained and recollected conscience diminishes the need for formal pastoral self-examination by graduated lists of questions. In modern pastoral practice this type of formality may sometimes be useful, but it is greatly exaggerated.

c. In two further ways a combination of fourteenth- and seventeenth-century method is indicated. With a daily emphasis on moral integrity and recollective repentance, "private", or non-sacramental, confession becomes a natural and proper procedure, and its efficacy is not to be doubted. But this is part of recollective life and technique which in no way opposes the confessional as a sacramental channel of absolution and grace. The right Anglican procedure would seem to be the proportionate use of both methods: "private" confession as the daily discipline with occasional resort to the sacramental method either in the case of serious sin or as "confession of devotion".

d. Neither method alone is adequate in terms of Trinitarian doctrine. Christocentricity, as in Margery, is in danger of paying too little attention to the divine law of God the Father transcendent, and to the moral struggle carried on under the inspiration of the Holy Spirit. "Love God and do as you please" may be an expression of very great sanctity, but it is no normal pastoral maxim. On the other hand, although a life lived in a perpetual casuistical debate is the last thing Taylor or Sanderson would have wished, over-emphasis on divine law can easily lead to moralism, scrupulosity, and even, ultimately, antinomianism. Over-emphasis on conscience can become just as unhealthy as over-emphasis on the confessional: we can be too subjective or too objective.

The need is for a completely Trinitarian system of habitual recollection with a moral content: the Caroline teaching on divine law based on reason, interpreted by conscience trained and guided by the Holy Spirit, but with the whole coloured and inspired by affective devotion to Christ who is both God and man, lawgiver and Redeemer. Again the two golden ages of English spirituality complement and enrich one another. The balance achieved is no compromise but a synthesis, based, not on "moderation", but on ascetical logic.

4. It is necessary to remember that the Caroline approach to moral theology was, like its patristic precursor, "occasional". It was dictated by the current needs of the living Church, and even such an imposing—and somewhat terrifying—tome as *Ductor Dubitantium* was written, not as a D.D. thesis but for everyday use by both clergy and laity. This "occasional" nature of Caroline moral doctrine was demanded by two needs: (1) to counter medieval legalism, to reunite moral with ascetical theology, and to train the individual conscience; (2) to counter laxity, which had arisen through the abuse of *probabilism*. But this presents the modern spiritual guide with a dilemma: on the one hand, the Caroline system is the main source of Anglican moral theology, and its practical, down-to-earth outlook is attractive to English Christians. On the other hand, its basis in *probabiliorism* gives a certain harshness, and is generally rejected by modern moralists. *Probabiliorism* is a modified rigorism, and rigorism in morals has seldom proved a good ally to Christian devotion.

Very roughly, *probabilism* allows a man to resolve his conscientious doubt by acting on a probable opinion in favour of liberty even when it seems more probable that he is under an obligation to observe the law. On the other hand, *probabiliorism* requires a man to take into account all the relevant considerations, so far as he can, and, when there is a greater probability in favour of liberty or in favour of the law, to act according to the greater probability.

The former system can very easily be abused, and it was the Caroline objection that, by its misuse, almost any act short of mortal sin could be justified. This objection was not simply against laxism but against the legal or static conception of morals. With Aquinas, the Carolines stood firm on the teleological principle: the human end is not moral goodness but glory; morals and ascetics are inseparable. Yet the Caroline pastors may have been wise to teach a modified rigorism to a laity but recently emancipated from authoritarianism and who were still unused to personal freedom of decision.

But *probabiliorism* also has its dangers. In ordinary life, where moral decisions have to be made expeditiously, it becomes too complicated and exacting. Demanding a full assessment of all the relevant details, it tends to turn life into a continuous moral haggle. The theory of *probabiliorism* inclines to rigorism (or tutiorism) in practice; to an unhealthy emphasis on choosing the "safe" course where pleasure is suspect. As Lindsay Dewar puts it: "The doubtful conscience is often unable to decide which *is* the more probably right course; and this means inevitably that on Probabiliorist principles it is driven to the Rigorist conclusion."[1] This dilemma is resolved to some extent by the application of two pastoral principles which derive from it.

a. In the context of the Anglican tradition, one cannot legislate for the lax; pastoral guidance must assume adult responsibility and good will. *Probabilism* has now returned to favour with most modern moralists, who rightly affirm that the possibility of abuse is no argument against the system as such. Christians of vocation and good will can be trusted not to stretch probabilism into laxity, while the lax themselves cannot be dragooned into sanctity. The greatest safeguard, however, remains in the English moral-ascetical synthesis in which moral decision is indissociable from life within the Church's stream of grace.

It is failure to recognize this ascetical principle that leads to false arguments against, for example, legalized Sunday amusements.

[1] *A Short Introduction to Moral Theology* (1956), pp. 4of.

Whatever the rights and wrongs of the matter, the possibility that people might thereby be dissuaded from public worship is a poor argument. Similarly, it is sometimes held that daily celebrations of the Holy Eucharist, or evening Communion, might lead to slackness of preparation. These arrangements may need further ascetical thought but the possibility of abuse is no valid argument against them.

More directly relevant to this thesis is the prevalent misconception of the principles of Rule which arises out of the same error. I have tried to explain elsewhere [1] that Rule is a technical thing consisting, basically, of Office, Holy Communion, and personal devotion, *and nothing else*. Although a good many other things, like almsgiving and fasting, are bound to come into any serious Christian life, they need no tight legislation; yet we continue to come up against so-called "Rules of life" consisting in anything up to twenty clauses. One such "Rule" especially compiled for ordination candidates legislates for a weekly meditation on the office and function of the priesthood: if an ordinand needs a firm rule on such meditation, he is hardly fit for the priesthood and he cannot be legislated into vocation.

b. The difficulties of both *probabilism* and *probabiliorism* may also be alleviated by the addition of that fourteenth-century recollection of the Sacred Humanity which has been discussed as a Caroline omission. Under *probabilism*, legal laxity—the attitude of trying to "get away with it" or of keeping just on the right side of the law—is incompatible with contemplative recollection of the crucified Redeemer. Under rigorism, to choose the harder course, or even to forgo legitimate pleasure, for the love of Christ, is very different from making the same decision for "safety".

5. This "occasional" context illuminates the Caroline opposition to the distinction between "mortal" and "venial" sin. Rather differently from William of St Thierry, Caroline morality, although accepting the pastoral distinction of sins of "malice" and "infirmity", remained rigorist rather than humanist. Taylor, for example, uses scholastic terms in the treatment of the subject, especially in *Unum Necessarium*,[2] and appears not to object to the idea of sin "cutting off the soul from God". His objection is rather

[1] *Christian Proficiency*, ch. 5.
[2] See Thomas Wood, op. cit., p. 123.

that no sin, "venial" or otherwise, can ever be regarded as anything but heinous against the loving majesty of God. In other words, William of St Thierry objected to the scholastic teaching on "mortal" sin and Taylor to that on "venial" sin. The emphasis is still on progress towards Perfection rather than lawfulness, and the underlying pastoral principle is still continuity, or habitual recollection.

As with prayer and morals in Caroline thought, repentance is not so much a question of isolated acts but of a habitual state. And, characteristically returning to patristic authority, Taylor insists that true contrition itself wins the divine forgiveness. The practical difficulty, of course, is to know whether or not such true contrition exists in any particular person at a particular time. Repentance is a matter of reason rather than emotion, yet "attrition begins with fear, contrition hath hope and love in it."[1] The distinction between the two is a subtle one, and medieval practice overcame the difficulty with the teaching that sacramental confession, as well as bringing back the soul into a state of grace lost through mortal sin, also made up for any lack of true contrition on the part of the penitent. Taylor and most of his contemporaries never rejected confession as such, which offers further support for the Anglican view of "private" and sacramental confession as complements, especially when "private" confession grows out of the habitually recollected state. Repentance, in other words, is part of the total Christian *ascesis*. Acts of contrition are important, but only that penitence may become a habitual state. The relation, therefore, between habitual repentance and acts of repentance, like, for example, private or sacramental confession, is as the relation between habitual recollection and formal meditations. The one serves the other, but, in the Caroline tradition, formal periods either of prayer or confession are subservient to the habitual state of the human soul: in Thomist terms, what the soul *does* is dependent on what it *is*.

The Caroline moralists did not uphold the parity of sins; there is still the distinction between those of malice and infirmity, neither, within these categories, are all sins equal. The objection was against the mathematical exactness with which scholastic and contemporary Roman moral theology tried to classify sin, and the objection was sustained not simply because of the resultant laxity but because law had replaced teleology. Caroline thought was interested not so much in rigorous moral life as in the glory of God whose service is perfect

[1] *Unum Necessarium*, ch. 3. iv.

freedom. We must conclude, therefore, that in English spirituality, discussions on the appropriate penances to fit particular confessions, as well as complex systems of self-examination and mental prayer, are quite out of place.

The pastoral distinction between attrition and contrition remains a problem; certainty that repentance is sufficient to win forgiveness is never possible. Once more the problem may be solved by a union of private and sacramental confession, and once more a synthesis of Caroline and fourteenth-century ascetic is needed. If habitual penitence is the aim and if "contrition hath hope and love in it", then the sublime unity of atonement doctrine and affective devotion to the Passion found in Julian's *Revelations* constitutes the ideal. Jeremy Taylor's objection to laxity over "venial" sin is upheld only by constant reference to the redeeming love of God manifested in the Passion. And I do not think Taylor's outlook precludes it. H. R. McAdoo seems a little inconsistent when he writes: "The deliberate return of Anglicanism to the patristic fountain head could have no other result, for devotion to the Sacred Humanity is not to be encountered among the fathers. . . . Richard Rolle and Julian of Norwich are separated from Lewis Bayly and Jeremy Taylor not only by time and theological upheaval but by a view of liturgy in which the balance had shifted."[1] On the other hand, preceding a specially affective passage from *The Great Exemplar*, McAdoo exclaims: "Who, reading the following words may say that Bernard is forgotten?".[2] Taylor may have received his affective inspiration straight from Bernard, but English religion can hardly by-pass Julian.

Finally, the "occasional" context of seventeenth-century ascetic contains the English insistence on the unity of the Church Militant, and the integrity and responsibility of its laity. However the anti-Romanist may attack the abuses, laxity and legalism of the medieval Church, it should be recognized that these were forced upon it by the gulf between priest and layman. Once lay spirituality is taken seriously, once perfection is accepted as the Christian end for all men in their various states and capacities, then something like the Caroline system is inevitable. In fairness, Roman and medieval casuistry, and its doctrine of Penance, spring from a charitable desire to get the laity into heaven somehow, without taking their spirituality too seriously.

[1] *The Structure of Caroline Moral Theology*, pp. 138f.   [2] Ibid., p. 155.

Given a gulf between priest and laity, it is not too bad a human trait to treat "inferiors" with a good deal of loving condescension. A sane rigorism is natural when the priest-lay gap is narrowed, and in Caroline practice the priest may rightly function as a confessor while he remains essentially a habitual penitent: the whole Church is One.[1]

The rigour of Caroline moral theology was inspired, not by the wickedness of the world or the evil of creatures, but by the glory of God. Sometimes our relation to creatures must be qualified by stern renunciation, sometimes by a more affirmative attitude, but the purpose is always growth towards perfection, not the evil, or even danger, of created things. The position is summed up in a balanced way in the first two chapters of *Holy Living*. Some of this teaching, especially on food, drink, and the right use of time, is a little "tense", but through reverence for, not abuse of, creatures, which remain aids to the recollected life. This attitude is to be found in Donne, Traherne, and Joseph Hall, but Hall, teaching how every creature and circumstance should be linked with a verse of Scripture or Psalm, again appears a little stilted by comparison with the recollective freedom of Margery Kempe.[2]

Traherne especially insists on the Christian ascetical principle so often missed: that discipline and mortification in the use of creatures is part of the quest for true happiness. "I chose rather to live on ten pounds a year, and to go in leather clothes, and feed upon bread and water, so that I might have all my time clearly to myself, than to keep many thousands per annum in an estate of life where my time would be devoured in care and labour"

Traherne speaks of himself as a social creature, and that is what we might expect of one who saw everything except sin as the gift of God. Delighting in humanity as he did, he is not likely to have refused whatever company, and quiet pleasure, his life afforded. He was a close observer of both people and nature because the glory of God is revealed in both.[3]

That is true Franciscanism: a renunciation of the poorer for the sake of the richer, therefore a deep principle of poverty in order that

[1] But moral theology remains a special difficulty in Anglicanism: see Wood, op. cit., pp. 103–47; Kirk, *Some Principles of Moral Theology* (1920), pp. 244–70.
[2] See *Anglicanism*, ed. More and Cross, p. 617.
[3] See Stranks, *Anglican Devotion*, pp. 99–100.

creatures should be loved in absolute freedom. This attitude is found in most of the Caroline Divines, many of whom tend to sound, at first reading, thoroughly renunciative. It is linked with the teleological against the legal approach to morals; morality, rigorist or humanist, is valid only in so far as it leads to human perfection; creatures, whether enjoyed or renounced, must always be seen in terms of the glory of God.[1]

V. FORMAL PRIVATE PRAYER

Caroline piety returns to the liturgy as its basis and moves away from the more affective devotion of St Bernard and St Francis. There are glorious exceptions, but the stress is on the more practical duties of Christian living. Further, formal private prayer and recollection tend to change places; the former is only a help to the latter. It is not surprising, therefore, to find comparatively little teaching on techniques and methods of mental prayer. This creates two paradoxes which are important to modern practice.

1. The need for meditation is everywhere taught: Taylor, Hall, Patrick, Nelson, Hammond, Horneck, Beveridge, are all insistent upon it. Occasionally, especially in Taylor,[2] terminology suggests acquaintance with St Ignatius Loyola and St John of the Cross, but rigid techniques and methods are avoided. To Joseph Hall, meditation "begins in the understanding and endeth in affection", but it is more the affection for virtue itself than affective devotion towards the Person of Christ. Caroline meditation is, therefore, what we would now call "intellectual"; sometimes it is not unlike that of St Anselm. Simon Patrick's treatment of the attributes of God is a clear example of this strain.[3] The results of this meditation are "resolutions", mostly in the form of moral teaching based on a deeper grasp of divine truth.

The dilemma is that, even in the seventeenth century when "theology was as common a topic of conversation as association football is to-day", such meditation for all Christians seems a little ambitious. Here is where simpler affective prayer centred on the Sacred Humanity would be more satisfactory, and it is precisely here that adaptation from the newer systems from Spain could be most useful. It is significant that, even in *The Great Exemplar*, where

[1] See also Hooker, *Ecc. Pol.* V. 55.   [2] *The Great Exemplar*, I. v. 3.
[3] *A Discourse concerning Prayer*, 2.

it might reasonably be expected, there is very little use of imagination. It should also be recognized that, if we are to borrow from St John or St Ignatius, the Caroline rejection of much of their teaching is due not to its intricacy but to its incompatibility with the primacy of habitual recollection. Elaborate techniques tend to limit prayer to set periods and to detach it from ordinary life. St Benedict and Hilton would have made the same objection.

2. This very intellectual type of meditation, enjoined on the whole Church, is coupled not only with the liturgy but with the Bible. But again, to say that the majority of seventeenth-century Christians were capable of deducing doctrine and morals from, say, the Epistle to the Romans, seems a little too optimistic. The Carolines are responsible for the modern difficulty of confusing "meditation" with "Bible study". After the biblical upheaval of the nineteenth century the question is more serious than ever, and again I would suggest that, in normal lay practice, a meditative and affective approach to our Lord in the Gospel story is the better and safer way.

On the other hand we must admire, and retain, the Caroline sense of both the reality and transcendence of God. Nowhere do we find the error—both ancient and modern—of turning God into a mere super-man and of interpreting prayer in terms of utility. Simon Patrick, and many others, is constantly insisting that the reason for prayer is God himself. But the Caroline idea of God is transcendental and much coloured by the Old Testament, which may overshadow the idea of approaching the majestic Divinity through the Sacred Humanity of Jesus. The result, compared with the fourteenth century, is that prayer becomes a little stilted and "tense".

In brief, Caroline "intellectual" meditation, its sane reserve, its strong moral and recollective element, and its sense of divine reality and glory must all be carefully guarded. Simon Patrick's "whatsoever doth Him most honour, will certainly do us most good"[1] makes an admirable slogan for modern direction. But a little less "tension", duty not quite so grim, even a little less respectability and a mite more humour, all imported from the fourteenth century, might be more in keeping with modern needs.

Two small but important points remain:

[1] Op. cit., 12. ii.

a. The Carolines are no exception to the English tradition, starting from St Augustine, wherein the doctrine of prevenient grace forms a constant background. The emphasis on the moral life can sometimes sound Pelagian, but the sacramental Rule of the Church is everywhere and always assumed.

b. This spirituality is generally non-mystical, often with very downright counsel against anxiety for consolation and sensible experience. Such a characteristic could lead to Pelagianism or Deism, but this risk is diminished by constant reference to the doctrines of heaven and of death. All is treated with sanity and optimism, there is neither morbidity nor sentimentality, for teleology remains firm: all is directed towards the Thomist "end", to the final purpose of human life, to the Vision of God to which it is our joy and duty to aspire.

THE BOOK OF COMMON PRAYER

The book of Common Prayer is fundamental to our understanding of all ages of English spirituality. It is the development and consummation of our patristic and biblical tradition, it embodies principles for which the fourteenth-century asceticists had been groping, and in its final form it is the product of the Caroline age. Whether the Prayer Book is a compilation of "superstitious rags of Popery" or whether it is "schismatically new" is part of the debate as to whether we can claim a continuity of ascetical tradition or not: I must continue to advance the claim that we can.

The historical and liturgical make-up of the Prayer Book continues to receive a great deal of attention, and we know that its composition, like Caroline spirituality itself, is made up of a complex mass of different sources. Orthodox reformers like Cardinal Quiñones on the one hand, Luther and Calvin on the other, together with prayers from ancient liturgies both Eastern and Western, and borrowings from Missal, Breviary, and Prymer; all have their parts and places. Our present task is to try to look through this predominantly liturgical study to the ascetical principles inherent in it; to examine not only its superficial composition but also the theology behind it and the characteristic spirituality which inspired it.

I. THE PRAYER BOOK AND THE RULE OF ST BENEDICT

At first sight, the 1662 Prayer Book might appear to be even more than its thousand years apart from the *Regula*. The ages and circumstances are as different as they can be: Monte Cassino seems an entirely different world from the parish of St Mary, Manchester. But that is only the judgement of social history. From the point of view of ascetical theology, these two documents have a remarkable amount in common, and in a very real sense Caroline and modern England remains "the land of the Benedictines". There are five points of practical interest.

18—E.S.

1. The basis of both the Prayer Book and the *Regula* is the fundamental, and biblical, threefold Rule of the Catholic Church: Office–Eucharist–personal devotion. The Prayer Book Office is twofold instead of sevenfold, and is more elaborate, but both sets of Offices are based on the Psalter, both constitute corporate worship, the main emphasis of which is objective praise. Both presuppose a weekly celebration of the Eucharist although provision is made for more frequent services as required.

2. Both documents point to the ideal of a life of contemplative recollection, with private prayer as but a support to this. Jeremy Taylor writes, "I would rather your prayer be often than long", St Benedict says prayer should be "short and frequent": neither provides much direct teaching on formal prayer and neither gives any semblance of a "method". Recollection is not just a religious exercise but that which controls and colours practical daily life: to the Carolines all the duties of one's station, to the Benedictine, manual labour. The 57th "Instrument of Good Works" is simply "to apply oneself frequently to prayer"; the 48th and 49th are "to keep guard at all times over the actions of one's life" and "to know for certain that God sees one everywhere". Those are "Caroline" phrases if ever there were any. In fact the whole of this fourth chapter of the *Regula* is of recollective significance, moral rather than affective, and could be almost a skeleton syllabus for Caroline moral and ascetical theology.

   Both *Regula* and Prayer Book couple recollection with repentance and progress towards perfection, and both extend daily recollection into the setting of the liturgical year.

3. Both systems are designed for an integrated and united community, predominantly lay. Ch. 62 of the *Regula* makes it clear that there is no distinction between priest and lay-brother "except with regard to his office at the altar". The Rule is for everyone within the united community, while the priest is exhorted to set a good example of obedience to it to encourage the others.

4. Both books breathe a sane "domestic" spirit, and are noted for prudence, especially over physical discipline like fasting and mortification. St Benedict's *Prologue* speaks of "a school of the Lord's service, in the setting forth of which we hope to order nothing that is harsh or rigorous". The *Regula* is "a little rule for

beginners" aimed at the needs of the less gifted. *The Whole Duty of Man*, arranged as a companion to the Prayer Book, is "laid down in a plain and familiar way for the use of all, but especially the meanest reader". Simon Patrick's *A Book for Beginners, or A help to Young Communicants*, another Prayer Book guide, goes even further with "directions for such as cannot read"; it is requested that "their masters and mistresses, or some good neighbour or relation, to be so charitable as to read them their duty about the matter". Like the Christian faith itself, both St Benedict and the Prayer Book are capable of nurturing saintly doctors and saintly illiterates.

5. Liturgical revisers and pastoral planners do not always realize that the Prayer Book, no less than the *Regula*, presupposes a comparatively compact and very stable community. Whatever the difficulties we face to-day, and whatever reorganization may be necessary, the geographical parish is as much part of the Prayer Book ascetic as the monastery was to the Benedictine Rule. The Common Office, empirical guidance within the "family" unit, as well as rubrics relating to Baptism and the residential qualifications for marriage and burial, all presuppose "Benedictine" stability. Whatever the answers to our practical problems, we should realize that huge parishes, group-ministries, industrial chaplaincies, eclectic congregations, and so on, are basically ascetical matters which are opposed to the Prayer Book system of spirituality.

II. THE PRAYER BOOK AND THE FOURTEENTH CENTURY

To what extent, if any, the Prayer Book developed out of the fourteenth-century pastoral and spiritual undercurrents poses another question of "continuity" to which there can be no positive answer. The original compilers, like nearly all Caroline theologians, appear to have paid little attention to this period, yet the questions involved, even if the answers can be little more than guesses, are not without interest. The over-all question is, to what extent is the fourteenth-century ascetic compatible with the Prayer Book system? My guess is that it fits the Prayer Book well. Or to put it into another, hypothetical way, how would the fourteenth-century writers have received the Prayer Book? I think that Hilton, Julian, Rolle, and Margery would have welcomed the revision. If this is so, it implies not only a deep spiritual continuity, but that we can use the fourteenth-century teaching to-day without resorting to ascetical contortions in order to adapt it. Five more points are worth considering.

1. The first and obvious point of contact is that both ages are developed from the same patristic sources and remain markedly Benedictine in character. The Prayer Book and its Caroline setting tend to reduce the Cistercian and Franciscan affective elements, but the main stream of development, Augustine, Benedict, Anselm, the Austin Canons, and St Thomas, is strongly represented in both cases.

2. The main English emphases are common to both: the doctrine–devotion synthesis ("true piety and sound learning"), the stress on habitual recollection, the unity of the Church Militant, and a "domestic" sanity and optimism. Both are strongly yet sanely penitential and, age for age, neither exhibits any great enthusiasm for formal methods of prayer or for extra-liturgical devotion.

3. I have suggested that the fourteenth century clearly pointed to the eventual need for vernacular Scriptures and liturgy: Wyclif was the product of his age. Richard Rolle saw fit to devote most of his biblical teaching and commentary to the Psalter and Office Canticles, which suggests that he would have approved of a fully vernacular Office. Margery Kempe's recollective technique depended upon her knowledge of the Gospel narrative, gained through sermons and from finding a clerical friend to read and translate the New Testament to her. It was this knowledge which made her suspect as a Lollard and led her into considerable danger. She would have preferred to gain this necessary knowledge through an English Bible or by hearing the eucharistic Gospel in a comprehensible language. Hilton hints at the same need. All these writers—with the possible exception of Rolle—were firmly orthodox and loyal to the Church of their day, and would never have demanded reform (Hilton was violently anti-Wyclif) but their spirituality itself would have eventually made the demand necessary.

4. As an experienced laywoman, Margery saw the need for some sort of formal Office, shorter and less onerous than the sevenfold scheme of monk and cleric. She used the Little Office of Our Lady, the Rosary, and the Angelus. Surely she would have welcomed an Office which she could have shared with her confessors and priest

friends, for this would have expressed the spiritual and pastoral unity which did, in fact, exist. Julian, like other "Church-anchoresses", would equally have wished to share the formal worship of the Church with those to whom she ministered and with her parish priest. It would have fitted well with the ethos of the anchorite movement.

5. Mainly, if not entirely through the priest-lay gulf, Margery and Master Aleyn got into trouble for being a little too friendly, although there was no breath of scandal. I think both would have welcomed the sane pastoral relations which the Prayer Book assumes as consonant with a united Church.

All that is guesswork, but I think that it is based on some semblance of ascetical logic. My own experience, for what it is worth, is that the Ignatian Exercises can be useful to an Anglican only after adaptation involving a series of spiritual gymnastics. The *Revelations* of Julian form an ideal and straightforward complement to the Prayer Book services for Passiontide: especially if you admire the Norfolk dialect.

III. THE PRAYER BOOK AND THE CAROLINES

By a curious irony our understanding and use of the Prayer Book *as an ascetical system* was greatly enhanced by the Puritan attacks upon it. Whatever the learning and intention of the compilers, the development of the Prayer Book from 1549 to 1662 must have contained a large pragmatic element: basically and pastorally it was a practical method of celebrating sacraments and services in an orderly and edifying way. The Puritan attack produced two important reactions.

1. It led Anglicans to defend the Prayer Book and so give its meaning, structure, and method of use far more scholarly scrutiny than it would otherwise have received. Without Puritan opposition it is doubtful if books like Anthony Sparrow's *Rationale upon the Book of Common Prayer*, William Beveridge's *Necessity of Public Prayer*, and Hooker's comprehensive defence in *Ecclesiastical Polity*, V. 24–75, would ever have been written.[1] As it is, no Caroline divine, and few of the many lay manuals of the period, omit careful consideration of the Prayer Book scheme.

[1] See further G. W. O. Addleshaw, *The High Church Tradition* (1941), pp. 29–38.

2. During the Puritan Commonwealth, the Prayer Book was proscribed and inevitably driven underground, driven, that is, into private and household use. Private devotion and family prayer, accepted by all sides, became based on the Offices of the Church. In that way the Book became more familiar to many Anglican laymen than it would have been by open use in formal Church services. It also became greatly loved, through familiarity, and also no doubt, by taking on the added relish of forbidden fruit.

From this situation two important principles arise.

a. "Going to Church", however regularly, suggests participation in a "service", and the Prayer Book takes on the character—so regrettably prevalent to-day—of a series of heterogeneous rites for various times and occasions. But when the Prayer Book is studied and used, publicly, privately, and constantly, then it takes on its true character of a comprehensive system. And the more it is used privately, the more it is seen to be the basis of an integrated religious life; something to be found not neatly stacked in the church bookcase but in the kitchen and in one's pocket. It is possible to attend Mattins and Holy Communion for months or years without seeing any connection between them, but it is impossible to say Mattins privately, or as family prayer, without reaching the conclusion that the Collect for the day is to be found with the eucharistic Epistles and Gospels: there is an immediate connection. The Book grows into a system: regularity of worship leads into Continuity of Christian living.

Thus in Caroline teaching the Prayer Book is everywhere conceived as a whole, as a liturgical-ascetical plan. Following the Preface to the Book itself, Taylor, Laud, Hooker, Prideaux, and nearly everyone else, speak of the "liturgy"—in the singular—in this composite sense. The "liturgy" is not a service but a system. Take, for example, John Durel:

> Our Liturgy is an admirable piece of devotion and instruction. It is the marrow and substance of all that the piety and experience of the first five centuries of Christianity found most proper to edification in the public assemblies. It is a compound of texts of Scripture, of exhortations to repentance, of prayers, hymns, psalms, doxologies, lessons, creeds, and of thanksgivings; of forms for the administration of Sacraments and for other public duties of Christians in the Church; and of comminations against

impenitent sinners. And all this mixed and diversified with great care expressly to quicken devotion and stir up attention.[1]

This coherence, this sense of a living ascetical framework and system of Christian living, is to-day's pastoral need.

I cannot improve on an analogy used in another book: that the Book of Common Prayer is like a sublimely proportioned mansion, indeed a seventeenth-century mansion built on classical lines. Most of its rooms need a good deal of redecorating and refurnishing, the plumbing might need attention and there is no reason why the butler's pantry should not be adapted for more modern needs. All that is work for the living Church, for the worshipping community being boldly experimental under the guidance of sane authority. Let us, guided by the liturgical experts, proceed with the job—new Offices, revised Eucharistic liturgy, new rites for occasional services. But for goodness' sake let us leave the basic structure alone; undermine the foundations, the overall plan, the classic proportions, and the whole pile will fall. That was the error of 1928 and it is still the error in much spiritual guidance.

In 1627 John Cosin summed up the Prayer Book system thus:

THE PRECEPTS OF THE CHURCH

1. To observe the Festivals and Holy Days appointed.
2. To keep the Fasting Days with devotion and abstinence.
3. To observe the ecclesiastical customs and ceremonies established, and that without frowardness or contradiction.
4. To repair unto the public service of the Church for Matins and Evensong, with other holy offices at times appointed, unless there be a just and unfeigned cause to the contrary.
5. To receive the Blessed Sacrament of the Body and Blood of Christ with frequent devotion, and three times a year at least, of which Easter to be always one. And for better preparation thereunto, as occasion is, to disburthan and quit your consciences of those sins that may grieve us, or scruples that may trouble us, to a learned and discreet priest, and from him to receive advice, and the benefit of Absolution.

Following the Lambeth Conference of 1948, and the Report on "The Spiritual Discipline of the Laity" (1948), the two English

---

[1] Sermon, 1662: see More and Cross, *Anglicanism* (1935), p. 179.

archbishops issued the *Short Guide to the Duties of Church Member-ship*. This originally comprised seven rules:

1. To follow the example of Christ in home and daily life, and to bear personal witness to Him.
2. To be regular in private prayer day by day.
3. To read the Bible carefully.
4. To come to Church every Sunday.
5. To receive the Holy Communion faithfully and regularly.
6. To give personal service to Church, neighbours, and community.
7. To give money for the work of parish and diocese and for the work of the Church at home and overseas.

Two further rules were added later:

8. To uphold the standard of marriage entrusted by Christ to His Church.
9. To care that children are brought up to love and serve the Lord.

Now, at first sight, the two schemes appear to have a good deal in common, both are based on the Prayer Book, and both display Anglican common sense and lack of legal rigidity. But on closer examination one can see what has happened between 1627 and 1948. The first is a *Rule*, an ascetical system; the second is a list of rules. The first is Benedictine in principle, the second—omitting all mention of the daily Office—is open to an infinite amount of private interpretation. The first, in other words, is the Caroline and Prayer Book mansion; the second is a row of little houses, to which more can always be added. The first is *composed*, the second is diffused.

b. That the Prayer Book is the ascetical basis for a Christian community is taken for granted by all Caroline writers. *The Whole Duty of Man* is perfectly clear that the daily Office is the prayer of the whole Church, and that its use may be public, private, or as "family prayer".[1] Or in the words of William Beveridge: "When we pray by a form prescribed by the Church, we pray the prayers of the whole Church we live in,[2] which are common to the minister and people, to ourselves, and to all the members of the same Church."[3]

The daily Office is so important to Caroline and Prayer Book ascetic that it must be given fuller consideration in the next two

[1] 5th Sunday, secs. 11–14.   [2] not "go to"!   [3] Sermon 1681.

sections. Here it must suffice to insist, as strongly as possible, that everything is overthrown by regarding it as the "priest's Office", which is exactly what it is *not*. To the faithful Anglican layman, this can never be an optional extra, or even a mere buttress to private prayer. Everywhere in the seventeenth century it is regarded as linked with personal devotion, but unquestionably superior to it. Simon Patrick is insistent as he argues in favour of the Office by considering "the Nature of Prayer, the Nature of Man and the Nature of the Church".[1] All is in line with the traditional principle that true individuality is better nurtured by the common life in the Body of Christ than by subjective self-culture.

But we have noted that, to meet modern needs and to supply a Caroline deficiency, the meditative techniques of St Ignatius and the Spanish Carmelites can offer an enrichment if properly incorporated into the English system. The risk lies in allowing the Prayer Book system to be not enriched but choked by such devotions. "Three point" meditations, extra-liturgical devotions, and particular intercession, all enrich the bare bones of the Prayer Book foundation, but without the bones the body collapses, without the Office all is lost. Yet how reluctant we are, when time presses, to give up personal petition for Mattins and Evensong; all no doubt for sincerely pious but hopelessly wrong reasons: "whatsoever doeth Him most honour, will certainly do us most good".

IV. CAROLINE THEOLOGY AND THE DAILY OFFICE

1. There is no doubt that the importance of the daily Office, and its supremacy over private prayer, arose as counter-attack to Puritan objections to any form of "set prayers", to their emphasis on extempore prayer, and to their exaggeration of preaching. Beginning with Hooker,[2] book after book and sermon after sermon takes up the challenge. Patrick, Beveridge, and Horneck were all unstinting champions of the cause. No major Caroline writer neglects the subject, and scores of lesser figures add their contributory support. And the Caroline Church practised what it preached.

Laymen like Sir Thomas Browne, Lord Digby, and Robert Nelson all took the Prayer Book with intense seriousness. We are told how ladies like Mary, Countess of Warwick, "very inoffensively, regularly and devoutly observed the orders of the Church of England in its liturgy and public service, which she failed not to attend twice

[1] *A Discourse concerning Prayer*, II, secs. 11–19.   [2] *Ecc. Pol.* V. 24–8.

a day with exemplary reverence",[1] while Susanna Hopton produced a charming little treatise called *Devotions in the ancient Way of Offices*. There were constant outcries against "lecturers" who omitted "the full service of Common Prayer" before preaching,[2] and episcopal charges continually urge the absolute necessity of providing the daily Office in all parish churches.

> Have, as the rubric directs, Morning and Evening Prayer every day of the week in your church ... if by any means in the world you can prevail with at least a few of your parishioners, which sure cannot be wanting in most parishes, where there are either some devout gentry and persons of quality, or at least some piously disposed people; and to all such I could almost kneel, begging them to do their parts towards so good a work, perhaps the best and most public good they can ever do in the places where they live; and where there are either poor widows, who may well afford to be at prayers, for those whose pensioners they are; or children taught by the schoolmaster or mistress, there it is very hard if some little daily congregation might not be found, would but the minister attempt and labour at it with as much application and zeal as the thing itself mightily deserves.[3]

Modern incumbents (and bishops) please note well!

The Religious Societies of the seventeenth century offer most practical and important witness. Associated with Anthony Horneck's ministry at the Savoy Chapel, London, and later with William Beveridge and Robert Nelson, these societies arose as an attempt—and a successful one—to practise the full teaching of the Church as enshrined in the Book of Common Prayer. The initial influence of these societies, these "Faithful Remnants", was enormous, and history supports their sanity and zeal. The recitation of the daily Office was central to their activity, a priest-director was an essential part of the system, while works of charity towards the poor were a natural outcome. It is significant that their demise came when extraneous interests in politics and sociology overbalance the original Godward intention. For most of our modern parochial organizations, the writing on the wall could hardly be plainer.[4]

If that is sufficient to establish the importance placed on the Office

[1] J. H. Overton, *Life in the English Church* (1885), pp. 143 foll.
[2] Ibid., pp. 190ff.   [3] Bishop Turner of Ely, *Episcopal Charge*, 1686.
[4] Overton, op. cit., pp. 207–13.

in Caroline practice—and if it is not deemed sufficient the additional evidence available is almost inexhaustible [1]—we must now ask why it was considered so important and how its value was interpreted. The answers to these questions comprise an illuminating mixture of ancient theology and the pastoral needs of the age, the consideration of which has much relevance to modern guidance, and indeed to pastoral theology and liturgical revision.

2. Enough has been said about the patristic, and especially Benedictine, influence on the formulation of the Prayer Book ascetical system; the ancient ideals of the Office are still held. Our quotation from Bishop Turner's Episcopal Charge contains a strong *vicarious* element; the daily Office is "perhaps the best and *most public* good they can ever do *in the places where they live*". The "poor widows" in particular are to see their part as a vicarious offering for their benefactors. In other words, the Office is no personal devotion but the corporate praise of the whole, threefold Church, and consequently of great intercessory power.

> In our Baptism, wherein we gave up our names to Christ, we became denizens and freemen of heaven. All the difference between them [the saints] and us is only this, that we are abroad, and they are at home; we on this, and they on the other side of Jordan; we in the acquest and they in possession of the heavenly Canaan . . . shame will it be to us not to copy their behaviour, we who are belowstairs in the same house. [2]

The relation between the Office and the Communion of Saints is stressed and all is linked with the Kalendar as the temporal–eternal link. [3]

The ministry of the angels in "carrying the public prayers up to God" is another favourite idea of the age. "Prayers are made by the whole Church; and not by the Priest only. They all say one and the same prayer . . . and what wonder is it if they pray with the priest, when they send up the holy Hymns of the Church, in common with the Cherubim, and the Powers above . . . ?"[4] "The public service

---

[1] See Anglicanism, pp, 628ff, esp. Cosin, Fell, Walton.

[2] John Scott; see Overton, op. cit., p. 273.

[3] e.g. Hooker, *Ecc. Pol.* V. 69–72; *Whole Duty of Man*, 2nd Sunday, 19–21; Nelson, *Fasts and Festivals*; Francis White, *Treatise on the Sabbath Day*; Taylor, *Holy Living*, 4, vi.

[4] Patrick, *A Discourse concerning Prayer*, II, 12.

of the Church . . . is so acceptable unto God; that the Angels, God's heavenly ministers, attend in such Holy Assemblies, and make a part of them."[1]

Simon Patrick, and many others, constantly stress this classical attitude: the adoration of God is the height and end of all life, and the Office is the most perfect praise we can offer because it is the prayer of Christ, through his Church, to the Father. Despite moods and feelings, the Common Prayer, shared with saints and angels, is that prayer in which our frailties and infirmities are made up by Christ himself. The proper technique of offering this prayer is, therefore, qualified by objectivity, selflessness, and obedience. Let William Beveridge sum it up:

> Moreover, that which conduceth to the quickening our souls and to the raising up our affections in our public devotions must needs be acknowledged to conduce much to our edification.[2] But it is plain that as to such purposes a set form of prayer is an extraordinary help to us. For if I hear another pray, and know not beforehand what he will say, I must first listen to what he will say next; then I am to consider whether what he saith be agreeable to sound doctrine, and whether it be proper and lawful for me to join with him in the petitions he puts up to God Almighty; and if I think it is so, then I am to do it. But before I can well do that, he is got to another thing; by which means it is very difficult, if not morally impossible, to join with him in everything so regularly as I ought to do. But by a set form of prayer all this trouble is prevented; for having the form continually in my mind, being thoroughly acquainted with it, fully approving of every thing in it, and always knowing beforehand what will come next, I have nothing else to do, whilst the words are sounding in my ears, but to move my heart and affections suitably to them, to raise up my desires of those good things which are prayed for, to fix my mind wholly upon God, whilst I am praising of Him, and so to employ, quicken, and lift up my whole soul in performing my devotions to Him. No man that hath been accustomed to a set form for any considerable time, but may easily find this to be true by his own experience, and by consequence, that this way of praying is a

[1] Ibid., II, 17.

[2] To the Carolines, *edification*, of course, means the building up of the whole man, morally, spiritually, and mentally; see McAdoo, op. cit., p. 144.

greater help to us than they can imagine that never made trial of it."[1]

That quotation, in spite of a certain naivety, contains a good deal of English spiritual theology: the unity of the Church, the speculative–affective synthesis, the Benedictine emphases, are all there. And it contains some admirable advice on the technique of saying Offices: of a fundamental objectivity in order "to fix my mind wholly upon God". It also teaches the invaluable lessons that Offices can only correctly be used when they are completely familiar, and that practice is the real proof of their value. But the passage hints at other things which introduce the next heading.

3. Although I think the foregoing is sufficient to prove Caroline loyalty to the ancient and Benedictine emphasis on the Office as the Church's daily praise of God, the Prayer Book services, plainly and rightly, have an eye to seventeenth-century pastoral needs. The Office is conceived as an essential pillar in the threefold Rule of Christian life, but it also becomes a pattern for all other prayer. The pastoral situation was still that of a recently emancipated laity learning to play their full part in a united Church Militant. This led to four additional elements in the construction and interpretation of the daily services.

a. Although the praise of God is still paramount, all other types of prayer are brought in: confession, thanksgiving, petition, intercession, and so on. Many a Caroline writer praised the comprehensiveness of the Prayer Book Offices, which, with the general emphasis still on habitual recollection rather than on formal private prayer, supplied a complete balanced diet in themselves. This, as will be discussed shortly, has proved something of a mixed blessing, but it was good ascetical theory for its age. The need for such comprehensiveness was determined by:

b. A preoccupation, sometimes almost a fetish, with the idea of the "acceptability" of prayer to God. The laity were still largely illiterate and might not be trusted to make their own petitions "acceptable". Jeremy Taylor, amongst others, discusses at length what may and may not worthily be prayed for,[2] and the idea of "acceptable" prayer is very strong in the Prayer Book collects.[3] The

---

[1] *Sermon on the Excellency and Usefulness of the Common Prayer*, 1681.

[2] *Holy Living*, 4, 7, i–vi.

[3] E.g. Epiphany I, II, Septuagesima, Lent III, Easter III, IV, Trinity I, III, X, XII, XXIII.

prayers in the Offices, therefore, fulfilled three purposes: they were "acceptable" (1) because they were in the Church's formal prayer; (2) because they were the careful compositions of theologically sound doctors of the Church; (3) they acted as patterns upon which private petitions could be based.

c. With this type of laity in mind, and with the vernacular Bible now established in English spirituality, it had to be read publicly and at length. The daily services were the obvious occasions for this: the Lessons accorded with both primitive practice and pastoral need.

d. From here, it is but a short step to the exposition of the Scriptures in sermons, which became associated with the Offices, due no doubt to the comparative infrequency of the celebration of the Eucharist.[1]

A reappraisal of these principles is one of to-day's most important pastoral needs, and it presents itself under two main heads. First, we must re-examine our ascetical and pastoral needs in the light of ancient and orthodox usage. And secondly, in view of our constant doctrinal emphasis, we must reconsider the theology behind the Church's Rule and try to give it meaning to the modern mind.

V. THE PRAYER BOOK OFFICES AND PRESENT PASTORAL NEEDS

1. The comprehensiveness of the Offices was a pastoral need in the seventeenth century, although what it sought to gain was probably hampered by the resultant complexity. I would suggest that the pastoral reasons for this complexity no longer pertain, and for several reasons.

a. Modern churchpeople may not discuss theology in favour of association football, but they are literate and comparatively well educated. They are thus quite capable of bringing proper personal petitions and intercessions into their formal private prayer.

b. Although Anglicans should be encouraged to keep to the traditional proportion between recollection and private prayer, a sensible use of modern techniques borrowed from other traditions gives a rather greater emphasis to private prayer.

c. During the last century, serious self-examination, the Sacrament of Penance, and more especially the Eucharist, have become much more frequent. When it is remembered that the Eucharist

[1] See section VII below.

is the only parochial service in which absolution is pronounced, confession before every Office becomes a little superfluous.

d. The doctrine of "acceptable" prayer, though a worthy one, is part of that Caroline "tension" of which we do well to beware. And it grows from a comparative neglect of the Bernardine emphasis on the Sacred Humanity which, again possibly through new meditative techniques, is much more pronounced in modern spirituality. Healthy modern colloquy, like Margery Kempe's prayers, is less concerned with fine points of "acceptability" than with a devout but free access to God through the Sacred Humanity of Christ. Almost anything can thus be devoutly "discussed" in prayer with our Lord, and this, as I have attempted to show, has meditative, penitential and theological value.[1]

Such modern freedom makes the Office, as such, more necessary than ever, but in a simplified, Benedictine form: comprehensiveness is no longer necessary since all these points discussed above—personal petition and intercession, confession, colloquy, thanksgiving—naturally come into the Christian life at other and more convenient times. The more comprehensive recollection and private prayer become, the less complex the Office need be.

e. Similar arguments apply to the use of Holy Scripture. It is no longer so necessary for a largely illiterate Church to have the Bible read to it, and the nineteenth-century biblical upheaval makes mere reading of little value to any but Fundamentalists. The Bible must now be either carefully studied or slowly meditated upon. Both require leisured thought and, again, perhaps the sensible use of new methods such as the "three points" based on the teaching of St Ignatius Loyola. In short, Richard Rolle's advice to concentrate on practical sections of Scripture and omit "hard sayings" is a more sensible and modern approach than Lewis Bayly's dubious idea of reading the whole Bible once a year irrespective of chronology and devotional value. The greater frequency of Holy Communion, and thus the reading of the Epistles and Gospels, makes our elaborate and unwieldy Lectionary even more unnecessary.

2. Two main objections to the simplification of the 1662 Offices will doubtless arise: one from the liturgist and another from the parish priest.

a. The former will defend the Prayer Book Office on the weighty

[1] See *Christian Proficiency*, pp. 88–97.

grounds that is follows primitive practice to which the Reformers quite properly looked. I would reply that such primitive, pre-Benedictine, or even Jewish example presupposed a pastoral situation not so dissimilar from the seventeenth century but very different indeed from the twentieth; and however firmly Anglicanism is tied to primitive example, ascetical technique must, by its very nature, develop. A return, not to the first and second centuries but to the seventh, not to the Jewish-Christian era but to St Benedict—which ought to be orthodox and primitive enough to satisfy the purists—would be much more in keeping with modern pastoral needs.

b. The parish priest's argument is that, now as in the Caroline age, comprehensiveness ensures that nothing is omitted from a full life of prayer; that without such comprehensiveness the layman—or cleric for that matter—might *not* read the Bible, make his confession and so on. That is the old fallacy of trying to legislate for the lax. Ascetical principle and guidance must assume the good will of the faithful. The Caroline ideal was sound because most people were uneducated and illiterate, not because they were lax.

3. My arguments against these main objections may be elaborated into three further factors in support of a simplified Office and Lectionary.

a. As the daily praise of God by the Church, to be offered through Christ by its individual members, the *authority* of the Office is of greater significance than of any other part of the total Rule. Whatever we may think of an Anglican priest who uses the full Latin rite in his parish Church, there is no doubt that his Eucharist is valid and that his people have communicated. But the Office stands or falls by authority; it should, therefore, be so simple as to make omissions or alternatives impossible. That is in accord with both St Benedict and Beveridge. Further, when a layman's time is restricted, and when he wants time for newer methods of meditation and private devotion, then a shorter Office is but pastoral common sense.

b. We have to rethink the validity, or desirability, of private recitation when public worship is impossible. Simon Patrick and others make impressive use of the fact that *ecclesia* means *assembly* and that the Office of the Church therefore implies the Church assembled. No one can deny that this is primitive, orthodox and ideal. It nevertheless presupposes, like much modern apologetic for "parish Communion", a rather shallow idea of the Church's

THE BOOK OF COMMON PRAYER

corporate unity. As A. M. Ramsey[1] and E. L. Mascall[2] have recently pointed out, a large and heterogeneous congregation around one altar at one time may offer a pastoral picture of the corporate nature of the Church, but it does nothing to create it. Ten parishioners, communicating (or reciting the Office) in ten different places at ten different times, are expressing their deeper unity in Christ just as truly as if they were all together.

The Caroline divines began by assuming corporate recitation, based on the assumption of small rural parishes with their houses clustered around the parish Church. We have seen that Puritan objection, culminating in the Commonwealth, drove the Prayer Book into private use as "family prayer": advantages soon became apparent and private or family recitation was henceforth assumed to be permissible. The modern situation offers a rough parallel. Not the Puritan Commonwealth, but large parishes, mobility, the regimentation of modern labour and administration, make private recitation a pastoral necessity. But the advantages remain the same; the Prayer Book, through the Office, becomes a normal part of daily life, it is "in the world", to be used sometimes in Church, sometimes at home, sometimes in the train or on the 'bus. But if this ideal is to be further developed, the Office must be simplified and brought together into one smallish book.

c. Perhaps the most impressive point of all is consideration of what is, in fact, happening in pastoral practice. A significant number of the faithful laity have seen and proved the value of the threefold Rule; they see the need for Offices and use Mattins and Evensong without the Introduction or state prayers (as do most priests by common custom) and without lessons; Bible reading or meditation having its proper place as part of private devotion. On the principle propounded by Dom Gregory Dix that liturgy is what the Church does, rather than what it is told to do, that spirituality demands growth and change within a tradition, I can only conclude on all grounds—ascetical, pastoral, and theological—that we must boldly rethink the whole question of a "consecutive" lectionary. To my own mind its purpose is now obsolete.

With Dom Gregory in mind, I would repeat the plea to modern revisers that, in any future revision, Morning and Evening Prayer are accepted for what they indubitably are: the daily Office of a united Church. They are not weekly services for the edification of

[1] *Durham Essays and Addresses* (1956).   [2] *Corpus Christi* (1953), p. 8.

19—E.S.

an eclectic congregation; Sunday Evensong cannot be understood in isolation from Monday Mattins. The prevalent error is to regard Mattins and Evensong as Sunday services which may be simplified on weekdays. Ascetical theology, from the New Testament onward, insists that they are daily Offices which may be elaborated on Sundays and Festivals.

VI. THEOLOGY AND THE CHURCH'S RULE

For reasons discussed above, the Prayer Book system was acceptable to the seventeenth-century laity on the grounds of common sense. To-day the position is different. To loyal Churchmen, the Prayer Book is still an attractive heritage, and its threefold pattern, so fundamental to all schools, ages, and aspects of orthodox Christianity, is more than sufficient to justify its authority. After some doubtful experiments with the newer techniques of private prayer from Spain, there is now a return to the ancient ascetical system. More and more of the faithful are embracing the Rule of Office–Eucharist–devotion for the best of all possible reasons, *vide* Beveridge: it works. Many Anglicans remain sceptical, and all must ask why and how does this scheme work? The Anglican emphasis on piety and learning, on the speculative–affective synthesis, demands that these questions be answered. However weighty, mere authority is not enough, and to-day's great need is for a serious restatement of the ascetical theology behind the Prayer Book scheme.

Over the last seven or eight years I have done my best to make some contribution to this need. To repeat it would be tedious and it would stretch this section of the book out of all reasonable proportion. But for the sake of completeness I will try to summarize the main points; if any are unacceptable as they stand, my fuller arguments may be referred to elsewhere.

1. The threefold Rule of the Church provides an ascetical expression of our faith in God the Most Holy Trinity. The correct conscious attitudes to the three inter-related parts of the Rule create an awareness of the theological attributes of God. Acceptance of the transcendence of the Father, or in H. H. Farmer's terms, of God as "ontologically and axiologically other", is manifested in the objective offering of the daily Office of praise. The absolute demand made, and the perfect succour offered, by God the Son, form the basic ascetical attitude of worship in the Holy Eucharist. The immanental and rightly subjective religious element in personal

devotion is inspired by the Holy Ghost conceived as indwelling Spirit: the Paraclete.[1]

The health of our prayer depends upon the adequacy of our conception of God, especially as our conception of the Christian doctrine of God becomes "absorbed" after the teaching of William of St Thierry. The Rule of the Church provides for this process and, conversely, various forms of spiritual ill health appear so soon as its balance is disturbed by the omission of any part of it. Thus the elimination of the Office diminishes our sense of the divine transcendence and usually issues in some form of spiritual eudemonism: subjectivism, sentimentality, pantheism, Quietism, and the like. The elimination of personal devotion inspired by the indwelling Spirit leads to the opposite errors: legalism, formalism, and all the dangers of the Pharisees. The modern error is all too plain; neglect of the Office has produced Anglican introspection, which, by a vicious circle, leads to a greater neglect of the formal Office.[2]

In short, only the complete Rule expresses a living and creative faith, as against a mere external belief, in the doctrine of the Holy Trinity.

2. The threefold Rule emphasizes our membership of the threefold Church; our real communion with the saints and with the Church Expectant. It prevents "earth-bound" religion and, coupled with the Kalendar, forges a sacramental relation, not only between matter and spirit but also between time and eternity; it thus perfects our prayer by making it part of the prayer of Christ to the Father.

The Office in particular gives pastoral expression to the unity of the Church Militant. It is that which binds individual Christians into a corporate whole, thus expressing what Baptism and the Eucharist create.[3] It is, therefore, the Anglican equivalent to the Rosary because it is the daily prayer used authoritatively by all members of the Church. Whatever the value of the Rosary in private devotion, and I think it is considerable, it remains in Romanism a somewhat artificial bond between Religious, priest, and laic. Anglicanism needs no such artificial bond since its unity is expressed by the Rule of the Church itself.[4]

[1] *Pastoral Theology: a Reorientation*, pp. 192–204; see especially n.1, p. 194.
[2] Ibid., pp. 205–17, 218–47.   [3] Ibid., pp. 248–54.
[4] *Essays in Pastoral Reconstruction*, pp. 48–59; see also "Some pastoral thoughts on the revision of the Office", in *Prism* (April 1961).

3. The Rule of the Church is the means towards the working
efficiency of the local Body of Christ. It is that which keeps the
Church demonstrably alive as the creative channel of grace within
a community. It is, therefore, from both private and corporate points
of view, the most efficacious of all evangelistic and intercessory
factors.[1]

These three general theological points are followed by four more
personal ones:

4. In personal use, the Rule maintains spiritual health, and therefore progress, by resolving a series of paradoxes. It synthesizes the
subjective and objective elements in religion, the speculative and
affective, discipline and freedom, the quest for grace and the use of
free will. It induces sensible devotion while forbidding reliance
upon it, and brings the whole personality into play: body, mind,
spirit; conation, intellect, will; *mens, cogitatio, amor*; imagination,
reason, emotion. Through the Rule the whole man worships the
Christian God.

The Rule, moreover, forces us to live in the light of theological
fact; it seeks to give expression to what God has, in fact, made us to
be. In it we seek redemption in the knowledge that by the Cross we
are redeemed; we seek to live with Christ while acknowledging that,
by Baptism, we are in him; we seek heaven, which is the perfect
praise of God, while, here and now, we perfectly praise him because
through the Rule our deficiencies are made up by Christ himself.
So in the Rule of the Church, we have, in a sense, attained our
true end.[2]

5. The Eucharist and Office form an essential prerequisite for
private devotion, again both psychologically and ontologically. The
Office, offered objectively to God the Father, is the perfect preparation for eucharistic worship, and also for the rightly subjective
aspects of personal prayer. Eucharist and Office, moreover, because
of their theological status as the prayers of Christ through his
Mystical Body, win for us the right of access to him in personal
colloquy: "which private worship is then acceptable unto God, when
performed by a true member of Christ's Body: that is, by one who
attends upon the public assemblies: by which he procures acceptance

[1] *Christian Proficiency*, pp. 16–22 and *passim*.
[2] *Christian Proficiency*, pp. 67–70.

for his secret and private services ".[1] But in spite of this and kindred quotations, we have discovered a stilted tension in Caroline prayer, which is still prevalent. This comes through a devout and admirable sense of the Divine Majesty to be approached with reverence and awe, but, because of the Incarnation, we are offered a new freedom of approach to the Sacred Humanity. Private petition in stilted devotional idiom is understandable but theologically wrong; and it is often subconsciously dishonest.[2] This supports my general thesis that this error belongs to a spirituality which stresses the objective Office and undervalues meditation and affective Christology.

But this freedom of approach to Christ, as Patrick has shown, is only won by membership of his Body expressed by necessary obedience to the Rule of the Church. It is ironical that an impious "palliness" with God is so often assumed by the undisciplined and lax while Proficients, faithful to the Rule, having both won and been given liberty of spirit in Christ, are reluctant to use this freedom because of false piety. The total Rule, therefore, allows for a true, honest, and free approach to our Lord while guarding against a false Christocentricity.

6. The Office is the supreme remedy for aridity and periodic spiritual sluggishness. There are times when any attempt at affective meditation or colloquy is impossible, and when habitual recollection degenerates into acts or even ceases altogether. At such times, the Office objectively said, "recited" even with boredom, constitutes necessary obedience: a satisfying discipline upon which the weary soul may rest. All thoughts, affections, and devotion may be thrust upon the Church itself; the arid soul has praised God, it is truly knit with Christ, lack of fervour notwithstanding. The Office is our daily gift to God, through Christ, and the value of a gift lies in its acceptability to the recipient, not in its effect on the donor. And there are times when we all need a spiritual rest, sensible modification of daily Rule. In such cases, recollection plus the Office is a comforting and adequate exercise.

7. Without obscurantism, it is worth giving this last point back to William Beveridge. As Anglicans we have a healthy right to ask why the Church's Rule is what it is. But we may not always want to; then two thousand years of uninterrupted tradition is impressive

---

[1] Simon Patrick, *A Discourse concerning Prayer*, II. 14.
[2] See *Christian Proficiency*, pp. 88–97.

evidence for its value. Over that period, the Rule of the Church has been proved to work: "this way of praying is a greater help to us than they can imagine that have never made trial of it".

VII. THE CAROLINES AND THE EUCHARIST

At first sight the seventeenth-century attitude to the Eucharist looks paradoxical. On the one hand, the emphasis on the Offices and the accepted infrequency of celebrations implies that Holy Communion was undervalued. On the other hand, when we look at the popular devotional manuals of the time, this judgement must be revised. *The Whole Duty of Man* and *Holy Living* both contain long chapters —and plenty of common sense—on preparation for Communion. Robert Hill's *Pathway to Piety* is a long eucharistic instruction that leaves no doubt about its centrality in Christian living. And there are many more: Patrick, Nelson, Comber, Ken, all compiled such instructions, while Hooker, Andrewes, Cosin, Beveridge, and Ussher made important contributions to eucharistic theology of a pastoral kind. Apart from historical interest, this seeming paradox is important.

As is to be expected, the Caroline divines offer sound apologetic in favour of "frequent" Communion, and against the Puritan preoccupation with "unworthy reception". William Smythies called his book by the succinct title *The Unworthy Non-Communicant*, and stresses the proposition, "There is generally more danger in unworthy neglecting than in unworthy receiving". And there is something of a summary in all this teaching in Isaac Barrow's terse little epigram, "is any man unworthy to obey God's commands?"[1]

But this attempt to revive eucharistic worship seems to have been, by modern standards, singularly unsuccessful. The Offices—the "daily prayers" of the Church—and personal devotion of a mainly recollective sort flourished, while monthly Communion was considered about the norm. Three pastoral points arise out of this situation.

1. The Caroline teachers faced the old dilemma of trying to make Communion more frequent while safeguarding its veneration; they tried to beat the old bogy of "unworthy reception" while insisting on the need for devout preparation. But they defeated their own

[1] This kind of argument becomes far more impressive when supported by Julian of Norwich; cf. Ch. 17, III, above.

end by an ascetical error we still make: while seriously wishing
for more frequent Communion, they taught a rigorous system of
preparation which was only suited to very occasional use. They
said, in other words, that the long, devout preparation suitable for
thrice-yearly Communion should be made much more frequently:
an ideal unattainable by any but the greatly gifted and saintly, who
did not really need it. Their error, and ours, is a failure to see that a
Christian life based on, say, monthly Communion, is one legitimate
thing, while a life based on thrice-weekly Communion is something
quite different: two separate ascetical techniques are involved.

When we think of our own laxity and casualness in preparation,
and then read a Caroline instruction, we feel rightly condemned;
yet the answer is not simply to copy the seventeenth-century
method. Presupposing much more frequent Communion, we need a
different approach altogether; like, for example, that begun by
W. H. Longridge in his valuable retreat addresses published as
*Some difficulties in the practice of frequent Confession and Com-
munion.*[1] He boldly departs from the Caroline pattern, as such, yet
remains one with its general ethos in putting much emphasis on
habitual recollection and far less on "immediate preparation".

Modern spiritual guidance, especially in preparation for Confirmation, makes the same mistake as the Caroline writers. All are
exhorted to frequent Communion, while teaching on preparation
follows the seventeenth-century pattern, which, as the layman
Robert Nelson saw better than the clergy, is oppressive to the faithful and meaningless to the lax.[2]

2. We must further realize that very frequent Communion for the
laity is a peculiarly modern and Anglican idea. Infrequent Communion does not arise with the Protestant Reformers but with
medieval Catholicism; the principle of communicating only at
Easter after the annual confession is the idea of "unworthy reception" gone mad! Margery Kempe needed permission from no less
than the Archbishop of Canterbury to receive weekly.

The principle is that frequent Communion is right only for those
fully embracing the Church's Rule, which itself forms the habitual
preparation, as Longridge suggests. In the Middle Ages this meant
daily Communion as a priestly prerogative; the laity were logically

---

[1] Obtainable from The Society of St John the Evangelist, The Mission
House, Marston St., Oxford.

[2] See C. J. Stranks, *Anglican Devotion* (1961), pp. 168 foll.

excluded since they were divided from priest and Rule by the widest
of gulfs. It is difficult to count the errors contained in the late
Tractarian idea whereby Mattins and Evensong formed the
"priest's Office" while the laity were encouraged to daily Communion!

I would add the reminder that, so far as a pastoral–theological
justification for frequent Communion is required, no Caroline or,
so far as I know, modern authority, has reached anything like the
depths of Julian of Norwich: "the dearworthy Blood of Our Lord
Jesus Christ, as verily as it is most precious, so verily it is most
plenteous". Had the Carolines paid more attention to her and her
contemporaries, they, and we, would suffer less from pious but
heretical tension. Julian's important message here is that, like
freedom of approach to the Sacred Humanity in colloquy, very
frequent celebration and Communion may *feel* a little irreverent but
it is theologically correct. Whatever our feelings and deserts,
baptismal incorporation into the humanity of Christ gives us liberty
of prayer; whatever our pious scruples, the redeeming Blood is not
restricted to a few precious drops but is a still more precious never-
ending torrent. The case cannot be argued in terms of worldly
economics.

3. It is easy to exaggerate both the influence of the Caroline Church
on its social environment, and the ability of that environment to
receive Christian ideals. Even if theology was a general topic of
conversation, social history leaves little doubt that vice and brutality
everywhere abounded. To-day we get a little sick of "X" certificate
films, but most of them are not so very different from the more
rollicking examples of Restoration comedy: seventeenth-century
England was no ecclesiastical paradise. And yet, dangerous as are
generalizations, the Caroline Church seemed to make more
Christian impact upon it than does the Church to-day. It is
impossible to compare personalities, but we will have done
well if history grants the twentieth century a comparable body
of saints, both clerical and lay, with that which the seventeenth
produced.

The curious conclusion forced upon us is that, as creative ascetical
practice, the daily Office, recollection, and *monthly* Communion,
forms a more constructive pattern of Christian life than our own
ideal of very frequent Communion, much formal devotion, and a

comparative disregard of the Office. Or, in the face of St Benedict, is that so strange?

Needless to say, this is no argument against frequent Communion but against a lack of ascetical balance. If the daily Office and deeper recollection are added to our Eucharistic practice to-day—as they are beginning to be—then we may look forward to a third golden age of English spirituality.

THE POST-CAROLINE
DISINTEGRATION

William Law died in 1761, just a hundred years after the final
revision of the Book of Common Prayer. That was nearly, but not
quite, the end of the development of Spirituality within the English
Church. This is not to say that, during the eighteenth and nineteenth centuries, the Church was dead, or that its worship and
devotion were necessarily unhealthy. Caroline influence continued
after 1761 just as fourteenth-century influence continued after the
death of Margery Kempe. But the best of English religion during
these centuries was either a continuation of an earlier tradition
or a purposeful return to it. The technical point, within the
context and purpose of this study, is that, granting a true
greatness to the leaders of the Evangelical Revival and the Oxford
Movement, they teach us little that we have not already learned
from the medieval and Caroline periods. The best in William
Law is Caroline; the Evangelicals return us, in ascetical ethos,
to St Francis and St Bernard; and the best of pastoral
Tractarianism looks back to medieval English Catholicism. The
example and writings of John and Charles Wesley, of Froude,
Pusey, and Keble, may inspire us, but if we seek a solid basis of
ascetical theology upon which a twentieth-century spirituality can
be built, then I think we must regard the fourteenth- and
seventeenth-century systems as our most recent sources. Some
facets of the modern spiritual temper are more akin to the fourteenth
century than to the age of Victoria. Within our narrow context, then,
the post-Caroline period is one of disintegration; of ascetical emphases
and omissions which overthrew system, synthesis, and balance.

I. WILLIAM LAW

William Law was a transitional figure, looking back to the Caroline age and forward to the disintegration; the seeds of which are

inherent in his paradoxical position. He attacked Deism in 1731 through *The Case of Reason*, aimed at Tindall's notorious *Christianity as old as Creation*, yet the *Serious Call*, published some two years earlier, is in places so vigorously transcendental that one wonders if he was not something of a Deist himself. Sometimes there are shades of the ascetic renunciation of Rolle, but in other places this famous book reads very differently; hinting at an almost Barthian distrust for all such "works". In *Three Letters to the Bishop of Bangor*, Law attacks the Latitudinarianism of Hoadly, yet, as Non-juror, he remained outside the Church, riding very lightly to the principles of the Prayer Book system. It is explained that the *Serious Call* pays little attention to the daily Offices and public worship because it is an attack on prevailing formalism, but the answer to "formal church-going" is not to stop going to church! Here is the right Caroline emphasis on moral integrity in recollection, but torn away from the ascetical system which nurtures it.

The *Serious Call* has the rigour of the best Caroline moral theology without the domestic optimism of Julian or the gaiety of Rolle. It attacks rationalism with an extreme affectiveness derived from the worst facets of the German Dominican mystics. And it returns to the Middle Ages with something akin to a fivefold "office" (morning, 9, noon, 3, and evening prayer) thus overthrow-ing the established twofold pattern. This book contains great ideas, great affective passages, great literature, yet is might almost be subtitled "ascetical dualism" for its complexity and contradiction. Like so much pastoral and ascetical theory to-day, the *Serious Call* contains little that can bluntly be called "wrong", but it is a muddled mixture, not a system.

I may be biased, and the *Serious Call* invites bias; but my practical advice is that, if a busy parish priest wants to study English spirituality with a view to pastoral guidance, this book must be given very low priority.

II. THE EVANGELICAL REVIVAL

"Rationalism" is the speculative strain in religion cut loose from affectiveness, contemplation, and mystery. "Enthusiasm" is affective spirituality uncontrolled by theological discipline. The fact that these two words have become descriptive of eighteenth-century religion, itself points to the overthrow of the speculative-affective synthesis. During this period the two joined battle as, seven centuries before, Abelard and St Bernard had fought over the same issue. That this battle drags on, with "pure scholarship" on the one hand and a good deal of superstitious pietism on the other, supports the thesis that not since the Caroline era has English religion fully achieved its central quality.

The Evangelical Revival was the affective reaction against rationalism and laxity; it was the English renaissance of the Franciscan spirit, with much of its glory and some of its dangers. It is tragic that Wesleyan spirituality could not have been incorporated into Anglicanism, as Franciscanism—after similar struggles and embarrassments—managed to become absorbed into the medieval Church. When we look back on this distressing struggle, with John Wesley and his zealous followers on the one hand, Parson Woodforde with his "fat piggs, plumb puddings and contraband rumm" on the other, no serious Churchman can be anything but deeply penitent. And yet penitence is not just weakly sorrow; it is a bold assessment of all the facts. Within our special context and study, there is something to be said on the other side.

The itinerant Wesleyan preacher would have deep faith and burning pastoral zeal of a kind that Woodforde had never known; he may also have had unorthodox idiosyncrasies. Whatever the sanctity of their founders, Franciscan-type movements are inclined to attract curious camp-followers. Parson Woodforde also had his good points, which were necessary support to missionary preaching, and which, in the long run, have proved to be of more ascetical importance. These are the Benedictine principles, even if Woodforde would not have recognized them as such: love and generosity to a stable little flock, a deep sense of Divine Providence recollected in nature, and continuity of regular, if not very inspiring, devotion: "read prayers and preached . . . administered the H. Sacrament at Weston this morn". On 18 October 1766 he "entirely forgot that this was St Luke's Day, and therefore did not read Prayers at C. Cary which I should have done otherwise. As it was not done willfully, I hope God will forgive it." His penitence may not have been very deep or his standards very high; the Methodist preacher would not have forgotten his religious responsibilities so easily, but would the liturgical observance of St Luke's Day have been among them? If not, we must conclude that, all things considered, Woodforde's ascetical theology was the more orthodox. The point that may be missed is that, had

Methodism and the Church managed to come to terms, the gains would not have been all on one side. Woodforde and his kind needed more priestly discipline and zeal, but not at the expense of liturgical stability, domesticity, and optimism. The Methodist class meeting, in part reviving the English empirical tradition, would have been still more creative had Parson Woodforde presided.

III. THE OXFORD MOVEMENT

The Oxford Movement presents different problems, or perhaps the same problem in a different form. At bottom it is still the old dualism of speculative theology and affective devotion, but taking the form of that divorce between scholarship and pastoral practice from which Anglicanism still suffers. The villains of the piece were not the Oxford scholars, who kept to the doctrine–devotion ideal (learned men like Keble and King could be as affective as any), neither the great parish priests that the Movement produced; but a host of lesser men who allowed their pastoral zeal to run away from their theological integrity. They failed to see that true Catholicity means spiritual continuity in a tradition, and that, following my introductory quotation from Maisie Ward,[1] true Catholicity must imply locality. These Tractarian followers became the past-masters at taking as many excellent things from as many diverse—"Catholic" —sources as possible and mixing them into the biggest ascetical muddle yet: liturgy from modern Rome, mental prayer from the Spanish Carmelites, mysticism from the Rhineland, priestly ideals from the French Oratory, confessional practice from Jesuit moral theology, and church furnishings from the southern Mediterranean. All these things have their peculiar excellences, but none play much part in the 1500 years of English ascetical development, and by no ingenuity could they be harmonized into a new spirituality. They only make a mob that would lynch the Book of Common Prayer.

These Tractarian pastors also proved past masters at doing the right things for the wrong reasons, frequently in the wrong order. Eucharistic vestments and sacred images were reintroduced into parish churches, but not because of Victorine symbolism; auricular confession was expounded and practised, but not according to the tradition of either Celtic or Caroline theology; spiritual direction

[1] See p. 44.

again came to the fore, but it had little in common with the practice of Margery Kempe and Master Aleyn. Affective homage was paid to Jesus Christ in his redeeming Passion, but it bore little resemblance to St Francis and none at all to Julian of Norwich. Popular penitential devotions arose after the post-Bernardine pattern which William of St Thierry and Aelred of Rievaulx had once rejected. A sense of true priesthood returned—which was very necessary—but it was not the priesthood of Robert Spryngold, vicar of St Margaret's, Lynn, in Margery's time, nor of George Herbert, nor, for that matter, of St Aelred or St Anselm. Eucharistic worship increased in a manner for which the Carolines had vainly hoped, but at the expense of the daily Office which they had taken for granted. The Church split again into priesthood and laity, habitual recollection and formal religious exercises changed places, ascetical and moral theology suffered a second divorce.

All that has been said often enough before, and it is more important than ever to remember the particular, and narrow, context of this study. The Oxford reform revived, and perhaps saved, the English Church. Its theological renaissance was essential, sound, and overdue. Not a few of the Tractarian pastors were men of sanctity and heroism. Politically, liturgically, ecclesiastically, and socially, it was a glorious movement; but in terms of spiritual theology, it was a failure.

Now that its more unfortunate experiments are over perhaps we can rebuild upon the gains: the centrality of the Eucharist is established and the Offices are returning to support it. There is a reaction against Counter-Reformation spiritual techniques; the Parish Communion movement, despite its dangers, is helping to reunite priest and people; modern church architecture, also with its dangers, supports this unity. Most significant of all is the influx of adult converts, and a deepening spirituality amongst the faithful, which demands serious guidance in true spirituality. Such guidance demands a new interest in ascetical theology; sacerdotal authority no longer pretends to be a substitute for ascetical competence. My thesis remains that, whatever the general value of the Evangelical Revival, the Oxford Movement, and indeed the Christian social movement of Maurice and Kingsley, the sources of this necessary ascetical knowledge are still the English Schools of the fourteenth and seventeenth centuries, understood in the light of their biblical and patristic progenitors.

Let H. R. McAdoo have the last—or last but one—word on the subject:

> Caroline theology was to a large extent nourished by the liturgy, itself formed on the same principles. To substitute for the Book of Common Prayer a version of the Roman Missal is emblematic of a severance from that approach to theology which is distinctively Anglican and which has its liturgical counterpart in the public worship of the Church of England. If we would regain theological self-consciousness we must recapture the spirit of Anglicanism and cease to be camp-followers of other traditions. This does not mean reproducing models of Caroline sanctuaries with the zeal of museum curators, nor does it imply that we are tied to the theological findings of an earlier age. We are not concerned with antiquarian revivals either in parish-church or in study, but we lose more than our inheritance, we lose a noble presentation of Catholic truth, if we lose the spirit of Anglicanism which is perennial and of universal value, stressing as it does the vital importance of the fusion of authority and freedom in the realm of theological research and investigation. "We are freed", says Taylor, "from the impositions and lasting errors of a tyrannical spirit, and yet from the extravagances of a popular spirit too".[1]

It is not difficult to translate that into ascetical terms: only our ancient spiritual principles plus experiment can lead us on. Meanwhile it is useless to cry for "a modern spirituality in accord with contemporary life", for there is no such thing and nothing less than a genius compounded of Benedict, Bernard, Anselm, and Aquinas is likely suddenly to invent one.

To McAdoo goes the "one but last" word because, in this context, the substitution of the Book of Common Prayer by the Roman Missal could be, if barely excusable, comparatively unimportant. The real disaster is to split the Prayer Book into Missal, Breviary, and Prymer.

IV. SUBMERGED CONTINUITY

As there was (so I believe) a submerged continuity of tradition linking the fourteenth and seventeenth centuries, so a similar undercurrent of orthodoxy continues to this day. During the period

---

[1] *The Structure of Caroline Moral Theology* (1949), p. 3.

of disintegration, men like Dean Church and Dean Hook kept the true tradition alive.

Church discriminated between the deeps and shallows of pastoral Tractarianism: in an age of undisciplined liturgical enthusiasm, his innovations at St Paul's were strictly in line with Benedictine, Caroline and Prayer Book ascetic, and for pastoral reasons alone.[1] To Church, spiritual guidance was an adult and, in the right sense, "worldly" thing; based on serious discipline but not of the pietistic kind which was becoming fashionable. None of this was "moderation", the expedient middle course; it came from the central synthesis of St Anselm. If Anselm could inspire and guide Church through the complexities of his time, there is every reason to believe that he is still the right guide to-day.

Hook, too, is thoroughly patristic and thoroughly English in both doctrine and devotion. His pastoral sense may still inspire us, and whatever history's verdict, English ascetical theology must support him against Pusey in the "ritualist" controversy at Leeds.[2] Described by a learned friend as "the most gloriously, boisterous, richly genuine English thing since Chaucer; one of the great 'jolly' men of English Church history"; one feels that Church, Hook, Donne, and Margery Kempe, would have understood one another.

Deprived of cohesion and swamped by a too zealous enthusiasm for alien techniques, the English tradition continued—and still continues—to manifest its great characteristics: they peep out from unexpected places. The controversy between Pusey and F. D. Maurice about post-baptismal sin is Aquinas versus William of St Thierry in a new dress.[3] In terms of ascetic and devotion, the incarnational theology of *Lux Mundi* is a return to St Bernard. Without apparently realizing it, Bethune-Baker groped after an approach to the God through the Sacred Humanity which Margery Kempe and Julian of Norwich had practised with rather more success and much more orthodoxy. And in *Reality*, B. H. Streeter discusses the Incarnation as "symbol" in a way reminiscent of the School of St Victor, but again without its fuller orthodoxy.

The many-sided genius of William Temple forms itself into a

[1] B. A. Smith, *Dean Church* (1958), p. 158.
[2] W. R. H. Stephens, *The Life and Letters of Dean Hook*, II, pp. 190–204.
[3] See A. R. Vidler, *Witness to the Light* (1948), p. 100.

theocentric pattern that is thoroughly Anselmic: theology, philosophy, and devotion are in both men inseparable. The Bible and the Creeds were to be not "believed" but *used*; of Temple's *Readings in the Gospel of St John*, Reinhold Niebuhr said: "I think it represents a new medium in the combination of scholarly and devotional treatment."[1] There is the speculative–affective synthesis, but is it so new?

The nineteenth and twentieth centuries offer a certain parallel to the fifteenth and early sixteenth: the true tradition remains alive, but it is an underground current, buried beneath more spectacular modes and events. Our task is to recognize and rediscover this true tradition, and to work and pray that, by God's grace, it may lead us into our third golden age.

[1] See A. M. Ramsey, *From Gore to Temple* (1960), pp. 153f.

SPIRITUAL GUIDANCE TO-DAY

The Conclusion, which attempts to summarize a book of this kind, is useful but tedious. The object might be better served if we attempt a synopsis in more practical terms: given a directorial relationship, how exactly does an Anglican spiritual guide go about the job? What is his, or her, attitude to a spiritual child in Christ, what body of knowledge is required for competent guidance, and how should it be applied? There are seven headings under which these questions may be answered, and the book summarized.

I. EMPIRICAL GUIDANCE

Anglican direction is traditionally empirical rather than dogmatic or authoritarian. It consists of a mutual working out of ways and means to attain the particular perfection of a unique soul, and it is qualified by a sane yet real love between two people knit in Christ.[1] The relation is "domestic" or "homely" in the fourteenth-century sense, but it springs from the fundamental characteristics of English spiritual theology; empirical guidance is no Anglican pleasantry, or amateurism, no vaguely anti-clerical ideal; it is far more than just a nice friendly way of conducting pastoral relations.

1. It is demanded by, and springs from, the speculative–affective synthesis. Purely affective schools of spirituality are not condemnable because their guidance is dogmatic and authoritarian; affective devotion may well be inculcated and nurtured by the giving and receiving of direct orders. But Anglicanism insists on a place for reason in all devotion, so English Christians must ask *why* particular disciplines and devotions are suggested; they must make the attempt to understand the theology behind their prayer. And the human soul is unique; that is the fact, springing from the doctrine of creation, underlying a right responsibility and a right individualism. Empirical guidance, therefore, implies mutual discussion, interchange

[1] See further my *Christian Proficiency*, pp. 32–7.

of opinions, argument and experiment. It means "holy" but not blind obedience:[1] in Taylor's great passage, "such in our proportions is the liberty of the sons of God: it is a holy and amiable captivity of the spirit: the will of man is in love with those chains which draw us to God, and loves the fetters that confine us to the pleasures of the kingdom".[2] The service of God is perfect freedom.

It follows that the spiritual guide should try to nurture the gifts and graces found in a particular soul and not attempt to infuse others. He must try to improve a person's prayer in the state in which he is, rather than to push him up some hypothetical spiritual ladder. Empirical guidance is, in Fr Patrick Thompson's terms, both "art" and "science";[3] ascetical theology is quite properly theoretical, to be adapted and applied to individuals in particular situations. The "science" is absolutely indispensable if direction is to be safe and creative, but all theory is apt to appear tidier than experience: the "art" is to interpret its designs and patterns to unique persons and occasions.

It must also be remembered that "spirituality" is the totality of Christian life guided by prayer. There is thus a sense in which all decisions and factors of human life come under the influence of "spiritual" guidance. On the other hand, spiritual guidance should be firmly limited to the development of the controlling prayer; it must consist in "counsel" not "advice".[4] That is the Caroline position, in which all moral decisions in a recollective life depend on a well-trained conscience: the conscience is trained by spiritual direction, but it is that conscience, not the director, which makes its own practical decision in daily life.

For this, amongst other reasons, modern Anglican guides should absorb by prayer, the spirit as well as the doctrine of the great exponents of affective–speculative spirituality: Augustine, Anselm, William of St Thierry, Bonaventure, Hugh of St Victor, the fourteenth-century English asceticists and the Caroline divines. Fully to appreciate this synthesis it is also necessary to form some acquaintance with the complementary systems from which it is compounded: the Cistercian and Franciscan schools on the one hand, and scholasticism on the other.

[1] Ibid., pp. 29ff.
[2] See Thomas Wood, *English Casuistical Divinity* (1952), p. 140.
[3] *Priesthood*, ed. H. S. Box, ch. 10.   [4] *Christian Proficiency*, pp. 42ff.

2. Empirical guidance is the expression of the unity of the Church Militant in which priest and layman, learned guide and beginner, are closely knit into one Body of Christ and embrace a common ascetical system: "Common Prayer". The theological emphasis is on Baptism rather than on Holy Order, and therefore on the principle that the Church, not the priest as such, offers its praise to God through the Eucharist and the Office. To fulfil this ideal, the whole Church is concerned with eucharistic and ascetical doctrine, so that all members may take their full, responsible and intelligent part in the Church's activity. Again, purely affective traditions are not to be condemned for making attendance at Mass a question of directorial command, beginning with duty, leading into affective devotion, and bothering little with theological understanding. But it is ironical that, in such traditions, eucharistic worship tends to become personal devotion for the individual, whereas in the English tradition, stressing individuality, the emphasis is on the corporate worship of the Church itself. In post-Bernardine affective spirituality, the Christian was a regimented individual because he "heard the priest's Mass"; in the English tradition the individual becomes absorbed into the corporate whole because he is part of the Church which offers the Holy Sacrifice.

3. We have seen that empirical guidance, with its mutual give and take, its discussions, arguments, and experiments, is not merely valid but essential to English spirituality because it is our traditional source of ascetical theology. Such guidance becomes the duty as well as the privilege of all serious Anglicans, for only from such empiricism, based on tradition, can a truly contemporary spirituality evolve. Such devout experiment means a sane degree of trial and error; but guidance based on orthodox spiritual theology should make sure that it is only a sane degree. So long as fundamentals are secure (and the threefold Rule of the Prayer Book guarantees that) neither guide nor guided should be distressed by the occasional failure of spiritual experiment. This, too, is no pious game, no light-hearted amateurism set against the more authoritative systems of direction, but a deep-seated principle of our heritage. If we are, in McAdoo's phrase, to "regain theological self-consciousness", empirical guidance is essential. It is intensely personal yet more than personal, for it is the activity of the Church searching adventurously for love, truth, and wisdom: it is a bold and serious search for

God, neither a mere keeping of the rules nor a morbid self-culture.

To practise such guidance, and indeed to receive it, it is necessary to gain some insight into both spirit and letter of the English fourteenth-century teachers, backed up by Caroline pastoral thought. For here the principle is seen in action as well as in theory.

4. A difficulty confronting the single-handed parish priest should be mentioned. It is that spiritual guidance, in any tradition or context, demands an attitude exactly opposite to that required by evangelism and pastoral apologetic. Even if the tub-thumping, brass-band type of evangelism is now abandoned, the evangelist must be reasonably forceful; direction demands much self-effacement. In pastoral practice, the Christian apologist has to expound and defend the faith with speed, vigour, and certainty. The good director is often slow, seldom vigorous and frequently uncertain. Time and care are needed, decisions must often be postponed, and authorities prayerfully consulted. Jeremy Taylor, a learned man in a learned age, never intended the *Ductor Dubitantium*, or even its conclusions, to be carried in the head: it was a work of reference to be consulted as each situation arose. The apologist is slick and sure, repartee may be a legitimate part of his technique; but the director must be prepared to admit ignorance and bewilderment in some situations.

It is nevertheless paradoxical that self-effacement is more necessary to the authoritative director than to the empirical guide. Human beings are the most precious things in creation, and responsibility for their spiritual—in the proper sense—well-being is the greatest burden that anyone can be asked to bear. The authoritative director is therefore forced to be dogmatic rather than despotic; he must, in other words stick fast to the safety of dogma and eschew risk and experiment. He is self-effacing because the situation forbids him to risk a personal, unconventional—but probably creative—viewpoint. In empirical direction, the responsibility is still very great, but it is shared. Self-effacement is still necessary if people are to develop their unique gifts under the guidance of the Holy Spirit, but decisions are arrived at mutually, by equally responsible partners in Christ.

II. ASCETICAL-THEOLOGY AS BACKGROUND PATTERN

The spiritual guide is concerned with a Christian person *as he is*; with the gifts and graces pertaining to a unique individual in the state at which they have developed. We are not concerned with pushing a soul up a theoretical scale or ladder, but we must know the phase he has, in fact, reached. This is the first purpose of ascetical systems in the narrower sense; plans like the Three Ways are not so much ladders to climb as maps against which the spiritual state of a particular person may be judged, and his needs competently assessed.

Although we are not to fear postponement of counsel for reference and prayer, some of these basic patterns of ascetical theology, however, must be known with some familiarity. One respects the doctor who admits uncertainty in a complicated case and consults other authorities, yet his competence is in doubt if this procedure is overdone; one expects him to diagnose common ailments without reference to the book.

To Anglicans, Hilton's *Scale of Perfection* will supply as much of this "background" knowledge as is needed, but, in view of the rather difficult arrangement, or lack of arrangement, in Hilton, he will need to be supported by basic text-books like Harton, Scaramelli, or Guibert. This teaching implies some direct acquaintance with its sources: psychology from the School of St Victor, and the fundamental ascetical schemes of Thomism; grace and nature, the progression from sense experience to life in Christ, the infused virtues, the gifts of the Spirit, and the patterns in which they arrange themselves. The moral and psychological teaching of St Thomas on concupiscence, the appetites and passions, and the capital sins, also come under this general heading of "background" ascetic. Here too, a book like Harton's *Elements of the Spiritual Life* is useful. It is still "background" knowledge—ascetical-theology in the narrower sense—and as such it cannot but be technical and a little dull. Yet once its place in the total scheme of Christian guidance is understood, it becomes apparent that much criticism levelled against it is due to misunderstanding. As a "system", Harton is unsatisfactory, un-English and inadequate; as foundation knowledge to a study of the English School, as a "text-book" in the literal sense of that term, he can be very useful.

Empirical guidance requires free conversation and argument; it should be conducted in unhurried comfort, qualified by informality and spiritual friendship: "full homely dalliance". But such a technique is ever in danger of degenerating into pious small talk, and only familiarity with ascetical patterns and maps can defeat this danger. As a competent doctor can diagnose a man's general health by a simple examination and two or three straight questions, so a spiritual guide should be able to place a person on his particular rung of the spiritual ladder with similar expeditiousness.

III. ASCETICAL-THEOLOGY AS FRAMEWORK

The English emphasis on habitual recollection means Christian life understood as something integrated, continuous, and contemplative: "religious experience", wrote William Temple, "is the total experience of a religious man." But such integration and continuity demand a fundamental framework, pattern, or ascetical system. To Anglicans this can only mean the threefold Rule of the Church embodied in the Book of Common Prayer. This is the practical key to the whole situation, and, if we are true to our ancient heritage of proved worth, if we are to regain theological and spiritual self-consciousness, it must be insisted upon.

Because of the ascetical disintegration of the last two centuries, spiritual direction has become confined to private prayer and morals. This, indeed, is that personal aspect of Christian living which mostly requires guidance, but our error has been in isolating this from its essential roots in the liturgy. And defiance of the Prayer Book principle is nothing less than defiance of the total Catholic ascetic stemming from St Benedict and the Bible, proven and never rejected in the whole history of Christendom.

But Anglicanism is still bound to the speculative–affective ideal wherein mere obedience, even to so impressive a tradition, is not enough. Empirical guidance implies the right and duty to ask for reasons and counsel in all things, however acceptable and inviolable they are in terms of duty. *Why* is the threefold Rule so important? *How* should it be used? Even in cases of a healthy non-intellectualism, in the guidance of "simple" people—in the best and deepest sense of that word—the *why* may sometimes be dispensed with but the *how* always remains.

By the kind of tentative theology I have put forward and summarized in the sixth section of Ch. 20, we must try to explain why Eucharist and Office take precedence over formal private prayer, and how recollection in a fully Christian life flows from them. A great deal of theological thought is still needed on the whole subject.

Just as important, and even more neglected, is the answer to the practical question, *how*? Were a devout Hindu to listen to the recitation of Evening Prayer by a religious community, by a theological college on a weekday, and by a parish congregation on Sunday, he would assume that they were three completely different things. Which method of recitation is right? And why? What are the attitudes and techniques required to say an Office correctly? Exhortation to embrace the Rule of the Church, and theological explanation of its importance, must be completed by guidance in technique. Until we are quite clear what Mattins and Evensong are for, and how they should be used, revision is impossible.

The Caroline pattern, we have seen, is comprehensive but too complex for modern needs; the Breviary plan is monastic and clerical rather than the prayer of a united Church. The layman's *how* and *why* remain unanswered in any authoritative sense. Fr Patrick Thompson has made an important contribution to the subject in the essay referred to; E. S. Abbott discussed the matter at the Chelmsford diocesan conference in 1949.[1] Following the Benedictine approach of Augustine Baker, and to some extent reproduced by William Beveridge, I have made a plea for a right "mechanical" approach to the Office, which has engendered some legitimate criticism. But that is a drop in the ocean compared with the thought, study, and experiment still required on this question.

IV. *ASCETICAL* THEOLOGY

Spiritual direction is more usually concerned with private prayer and recollection, which in the English system here propounded, falls naturally into fourth place. This does not make it unimportant, yet to give it first place would overthrow many principles fundamental to the English School.

Formal private prayer, moreover, is subservient to recollection, about which much teaching and guidance is needed but which is often neglected. Spiritual direction in the English tradition will, therefore, place the principles of recollection before meditative techniques and methods. We have seen that English recollection is mainly of two types: the Caroline type stressing right action in daily life based on divine moral law, and the fourteenth-century type of affective recollection of the presence of Christ. Neither method is completely adequate and a combination of both is desirable, while

[1] *The Doctrine, Discipline and Devotional Quality of the Book of Common Prayer*, privately printed.

in support of such a synthesis three subsidiary methods of recollection all have their part. These are:

1. Recollection in, and of, the Holy Trinity, which gives a creative tension to life between transcendence and immanence. Here Christian life enters a mature balance between a calm acceptance of the rule of Divine Providence and a continuous co-operation with the indwelling Spirit. The first suggests divine law, the second depends on inspired conscience, thus supplementing the Caroline scheme.[1]

2. Recollection in, and of, creation, interpreted as Victorine symbolism. In so far as created things and daily circumstances remind us of the Sacred Humanity manifested in the Gospel narrative, this links up with the fourteenth-century pattern exemplified in Margery Kempe.

3. Both schemes are deepened and expanded by recollection in the Church; a habitual awareness of the Christian status gained by Baptism, its links with the threefold Church, and its daily manifestation in the Kalendar.[2] Such a technique has obvious connections with Office and Eucharist, dependent on the Church's seasons.

Our ultimate need, therefore, is a synthesis of Jeremy Taylor and Margery Kempe, supported by Hugh of St Victor. Spiritual guidance according to the Caroline pattern takes the form mainly of the training of conscience; in moral theology and casuistry and in the acquisition of divine knowledge in "intellectual" meditation. The needs relating to fourteenth-century affective recollection are different, and it is here that some of the Counter-Reformation methods and techniques may usefully be incorporated into the English system. Julian and Margery, and indeed some of the Caroline writers, give us sublime meditations on the Person of Christ. But, apart from the principle of seeking the adorable divinity through the Sacred Humanity, there is little detailed instruction. St Ignatius and the Carmelites fill this small gap in the English scheme and offer enrichment to habitual recollection through formal meditation. Yet care must be taken not to allow such methods and formal techniques to swamp the recollective principle, or, worse still, to overthrow the Prayer Book pattern.

It follows that, in Anglicanism, the real basis of personal guidance is not so much the methods and techniques of ascetical-theology— they are but useful incidentals—but *ascetical* theology in the wider

[1] See *Christian Proficiency*, pp. 64ff.   [2] Ibid., pp. 67ff.

sense of applied dogmatics. The knowledge required in an English director is not primarily the first, second, and third methods of St Ignatius, or the psychological progressions of St John of the Cross— they make a valuable background—but an ascetical interpretation of the Creeds. The knowledge needed for guidance in prayer, is, in other words, the doctrines of the Trinity, the Incarnation, Atonement, and the Church, but looked at in a special, ascetical, way.

Before considering the remaining three subsidiary points, the basic pattern of Anglican guidance can be summarized in this way: confronted with a person seeking direction, the guide should:

1. Enter an empirical relationship with freedom, mutuality, and self-effacement. Out of a reasonably brief conversation of this type, he should:

2. Gain an adequate idea of the state of the person, his gifts, needs and difficulties, by seeing him against a fundamental ascetical map, pattern, or background.

3. He should explain both meaning and method of Eucharistic devotion and the use of the daily Office; and insist upon their fulfilment.

4. Recollective technique, from actual to habitual and contemplative, should come next, according to any of the five methods just discussed, or a combination of them, according to the capacity and *attrait* of the person in question.

5. Formal private prayer only comes in at this point to support recollection; methods and techniques will again depend on temperament and *attrait*. And here especially a man's work and circumstances must be carefully considered. Long periods of private prayer "morning and evening" may be valuable in some cases, but this pious ideal has no great authority in English ascetical theology, and in no case can it be given priority over recollection and the Offices. Much confusion is caused by the fact that when Caroline writers stress "Morning and Evening Prayer" they refer to the daily Offices, but to Counter-Reformation teachers, "prayers, morning and evening" mean formal periods of private meditation and devotion. After the Offices, and in the context of habitual recollection, Anglicans are free to make their private prayers

whenever they like: there are no sacred hours. Here is room for much freedom and experiment. Three points remain:

V. SPIRITUAL READING

To Anglicans, spiritual reading means, predominantly, the Bible. Like the problems of the daily Office, and linked with them by the Lectionary, this presents us with another aspect of spiritual theology which demands much new thought and bold experiment. I have pleaded for a clear distinction between "Bible study" and meditation, which, in some ways, are opposed: the first is intellectual, speculative, and demands much disciplined training, the second is imaginative, affective, and free. The first seeks doctrinal truth, the second a relation with Jesus Christ. After the nineteenth-century biblical upheaval, pastoral need, not to say common sense, supports the meditative approach as the most creative for ordinary people; by which I mean everyone except trained biblical scholars. Not only has "Bible study" become extremely complex but scholarship supports the view that "revelation" means God's self-disclosure to the world rather than his utterance in a string of propositional and moral truths in Holy Scripture. If this is true, then a meditative approach to the Sacred Humanity is likely to be more accurate, apart from being more devotionally useful. What must be avoided as incompatible with modern standards is the glib exhortation to "read the Bible" (or "say the Office") with no answers to the right and inevitable "why?" and "how?".

If the meditative approach is accepted, Anglicanism cannot be content with mere affectiveness; theological reading must be brought in to support it. Simple expositions of the Creeds, a grappling with the eternal verities of the faith, according to the capacity of individuals, is likely to be more creative—and ultimately more "Biblical"—than amateurish attempts at "Bible study".[1] Here the great synthetic works of the English School, like the *Revelations* of Julian, have an obvious place in helping to solve the difficult "Bible problem".

As to the rest of spiritual reading, it need hardly be mentioned that, without narrow insularity and with due regard to personal attraction, the English devotional classics should be given their proper place. I do not think one need be a bigoted patriot to judge *Holy Living* to be a comparable book to the *Imitatio Christi* or the

[1] See *Christian Proficiency*, pp. 121f.

Devout Life. In the English tradition, the Caroline devotional writings come before, but not necessarily instead of, those from Spain and the Rhineland. St Anselm comes before St Bernard; William of St Thierry and Aelred of Rievaulx before Bonaventure and François de Sales. Wider reading is important and enriching; here personal attraction and liberty can have no limit. But it is of no small importance to understand just where such reading falls in relation to the tradition in which we live. The Catholic mind may be inspired by Protestant devotion, Christians can learn much from non-Christian theology, but we must recognize the position clearly and know *what* we are reading. The Anglican spirit may be inspired and edified by Tauler and Eckhart, by St Ignatius and the Little Flower, but guidance and discrimination is needed. A loyal Anglican can directly use Anselm or Julian, and live according to their teaching, but he cannot directly use Ruysbroek in quite the same way. No one wants an Anglican Index, but when it is remembered that the modern layman is short of reading time, and that he constantly seeks advice on this matter, very serious consideration must be given to it. Great harm is done by the indiscriminate use of a heterogeneous heap of "holy books", and it is alarming that, while libraries and bookshops carefully distinguish between "Anglican", "Roman", and "Nonconformist" theology, these all jostle one another on the shelf marked "devotion".

VI. PENITENCE AND CONFESSION

As there is significance in giving fourth place to formal private prayer, so is there further significance in placing confession sixth. This does not imply any lack of importance, but it counters the not uncommon idea that confession and spiritual direction are virtually the same thing, and it supports the Anglican view that makes sacramental confession voluntary and but a small part in the much wider context of direction.

Anglican guides should, therefore, insist on the value of confession while keeping it in perspective. This is no weak compromise but the logical outcome of the interpretation of penance as generous oblation rather than as a juridical tribunal, consonant with Anglican moral theology: compulsion is fundamental to the juridical outlook and incompatible with generosity. Practice and experience, however, suggest that, for those truly intent on spiritual growth, the old adage "none must, all may, some should" virtually translates itself into "none must, all should". The English emphasis is on repentance, and if this is instilled in general guidance, confession is usually desired at a comparatively early stage.

Our fourteenth-century writers stressed confession in accordance with the theology and discipline of their age, but the great meditative stress on the Passion, intended to inspire affective penitence, is not incompatible with the Caroline view. Nor is this later ideal in conflict with the older teaching that use of the Sacrament itself implies repentance, or makes up for the shortcomings of human frailty in its honest search for contrition. Under the voluntary English system we can safely assume that the flagrantly impenitent will not go to confession, and that sincere effort can be imputed to those who do. Once more a synthesis of our two golden periods is proved to be our need.

This points to the necessity of administering the Sacrament in the Anglican way: for the penitent it is an act of worship, for the confessor it is the administration of a sacrament of grace to a beloved partner in the one mystical Body. It follows that an objective expeditiousness in the administration of the sacrament is more in line with Anglican pastoral theology than long and intricate moral discussion. If a confession lasts longer than ten minutes it probably means that English moral, ascetical, and pastoral theology is being overthrown for that of another tradition.

The "penance" is essential to the rite, but its relation to the content of a confession remains very loose. The idea that certain penances fit certain sins is entirely juridical: two psalms for venial sins and four for mortal sins! The use of such orthodox things as the penitential psalms is sensible, but the confessor who was reputed to give the same penance all through a long ministry could find considerable support from English penitential theory.

Moral theology itself presents us with another example, possibly the most serious of all, where much research, study, and thought is urgently required. The scholastic system is neither wholly satisfactory nor well-suited to the English pastoral tradition, yet it remains the only safe foundation. The Caroline reinterpretation points to a more valuable approach, but it is defective as a modern system. Probabiliorism and rigorism are generally discarded in favour of a guarded and qualified probabilism, and with their intricate casuistry and analyses of conscience the Carolines were in danger of defeating their own ends. A new juridical complexity tends to replace an older one and to be equally incompatible with a pastoral emphasis on generous penitence.

To these two sources must be added a third: modern psychology, though doubtless exaggerated in some pastoral circles, has much to teach us, especially with regard to the influence of environment, heredity and upbringing on the moral act. If we take Dr Kirk's mortal–venial distinction as being "real and valuable from the confessor's point of view", the new psychology can enlighten us on the true voluntariness of moral decision.

We need new thought, based on St Thomas, interpreted by the Carolines, and illuminated by modern psychological research. Meanwhile we must play safe by an attempt to interpret orthodoxy in an English way.

VII. HUMILITY AND "IRONY"

That Anglican guides should avoid, and if possible forbid, spiritual "tension" is worth a heading to itself. This evil is very prevalent, yet completely inconsistent with almost everything for which English spirituality stands. Empirical guidance, not dogmatic direction; affectiveness curbed by doctrine; recollection, continuous and gentle, not set periods of stiff devotion; domesticity not militarism; optimism not rigour; all leads naturally into a balance, a sanity into what Julian called "full and homely" and what Taylor meant by "an amiable captivity of the Spirit".

This is not laxity, but what might be called speculative humility and what I think E. J. Tinsley means by "irony". It is that developed sense of creaturehood springing from faith in the divine transcendence, a creaturehood that rejects that pernicious sort of pride which takes itself too seriously.

It really returns to the doctrine of prevenient grace, to the firm assumption that all depends on God. That is not Quietism. We have our part to play in our response to divine Love and in co-operation with grace: that is what ascetical theology and spiritual guidance are all about. But our duties are to be taken seriously but gently, as befits a redeemed race of gloriously comic beings. Thus must we seek a right relation of means to end, with an ever-growing concept and an ever-growing wonder of what that end really is. That is the greatest secret of all.

APPENDIX

APPENDIX

A COURSE OF STUDY IN ASCETICAL THEOLOGY FOR PARISH PRIESTS AND THEOLOGICAL STUDENTS OF THE ANGLICAN COMMUNION

After the delivery of lectures on this and kindred subjects, I am invariably asked for a "reading list" by those of my audience whose interest has been stirred, or more likely, by those whose politeness and charity wish to give that impression. It is an immensely difficult request: we are not dealing with a "subject" with its own clearly defined literature, but with an approach to theology springing from, and leading back to, prayer. Neither are we dealing with scholars for whom theological study is their main job, but with busy parish priests and students whose burdensome curriculum does not include ascetics as such. This practical point is frequently forgotten by the compilers of such reading lists or courses of study; nothing is more frustrating to serious students and parish priests than to be given prescribed reading at the rate of twenty tomes a month, or to be exhorted to such scholarly ideals of sticking to original sources and eschewing simple commentaries. Since those giving this advice frequently spend their lives writing commentaries, one is forced to wonder what is the point of them all.

The following scheme is an attempt to avoid such impractical ideals. It is, I think, the sort of scheme that a serious reader of this present book—itself no more than an introduction—might naturally compose for himself. Spread over two years, in eight quarterly periods, the scheme suggests ten books to be seriously studied, which is possible to a parish priest giving only five hours a week to it. These books are listed in the first column. Column 2 lists twenty more books which might be "read through" rather than pored over: almost bedside books; or which may be referred to casually at odd free moments. The third column contains a selection of "devotional" books for use in private prayer, which fit in with the reading and which should give a fair picture of English Spirituality in action.

My scheme is obviously suggestive: details may vary with personal choice, and it is not meant to be adhered to rigidly. The daily Office is of course assumed, as is meditative use of the Bible throughout. Anyone who finds difficulty with the Office might well bring in some of the Caroline devotional teaching much earlier than the last six months of the two-year period. I have omitted the fundamental "background" books like Harton, Pourrat, and Scaramelli: these might be regarded as general works of reference. I have also kept rather too strictly to the English School: we have seen how St Ignatius Loyola and the Carmelites can be usefully incorporated, while slight acquaintance with, say, the Rhineland Dominicans brings English spirituality into relief by contrast.

I have tried to keep only to books currently in print, and have included devotional books most of which are now available cheaply in paperback form. A few visits to a good theological library, however, would reveal extra riches, particularly in the form of seventeenth-century manuals of private devotion.

If five hours a week of serious study (column 1) are backed up by a similar period of mental prayer or spiritual reading, I think we might have a creative scheme not unduly arduous to the type of reader in mind. Remembering the central speculative–affective synthesis, the main columns also tend to become interchangeable: Anselm and Julian can obviously either be studied or prayed. With a little fluidity and ingenuity it will be found that the four yearly quarters more or less fit with the liturgical season (Advent–Septuagesima, Septuagesima–Easter, Easter–Trinity 10, Trinity 10–Advent). I do not think a parish priest following such a scheme need spend much time on sermon preparation or devotional addresses: nor do I think these would be sub-standard!

My own scheme here appended is neither perfect nor invariable, but as a pattern I hope it may be practical and of use.

To Study seriously	To Read or Refer to	For Mental Prayer
St. Augustine *Enchiridion* [1]	*An Augustine Synthesis* Przywara and Martindale [2] or *A Companion to the Study of* *St Augustine* Battenhouse [3]	*Enchiridion* [1] Hugh of St Victor *The Divine Love* [4]
St Benedict *Regula* (with Commentary)	*Ways of Christian Life* Cuthbert Butler [2] *Benedictine Monachism* C. Butler [5] or *The Via Vita of St Benedict* Bernard Hayes [6]	St Benedict *Regula* William of St Thierry *Meditations* [4] *Mirror of Faith* [4]*
The Mystical Theology of St Bernard Etienne Gilson [2] St Bernard *On Grace and Freewill* ed. W. Williams [1]	St Bernard *Letters, Sermons* *The Cistercian Heritage* Louis Bouyer [4]	St Bernard *On the Love of God* [4]* *The Steps of Humility* [4]* St Aelred *Letter to His Sister* [4] *On Jesus at twelve years old* [4]*
St Anselm *Monologion* *Cur Deus Homo?*	St Thomas *Compendium of Theology* ed. Cyril Vollert (Herder Books 1958) *Morals and Man* Gerald Vann [5]† G. K. Chesterton *St Thomas Aquinas*	St Anselm *Proslogion* *Meditations and Letters* William of St Thierry *On the Nature and Dignity of Love* [4]*

To Study seriously	To Read or Refer to	For Mental Prayer
Walter Hilton *Scale of Perfection*	*The Ancrene Riwle*[6] Richard Rolle *Works* *The English Mystical Tradition*	St Bonaventure *The Mystical Vine*[4]*
		Rolle
	M. D. Knowles[6]	Hilton *Minor Works*[7]
Walter Hilton *Scale of Perfection*	*The Book of Margery Kempe*[3] (commentary *Margery Kempe* M. Thornton)[1]	Julian of Norwich *Revelations of Divine Love*
The Structure of Caroline Moral Theology	Anglican Devotion C. J. Stranks (S.C.M.)	*Whole Duty of Man*
H. R. McAdoo *English Casuistical Divinity* Thomas Wood[1]	*Anglicanism* More and Cross[1]	Various 17th-century Prayer Manuals at choice
E. L. Mascall *Christ, The Christian and The Church*[5]	M. Thornton *Christian Proficiency*[1]	Anselm at choice
	K. E. Kirk *The Vision of God*[5]	Julian *Revelations*
		Taylor *Holy Living*
		Lancelot Andrewes *Preces Privatae*

PUBLISHERS
[1] S.P.C.K.   [2] Sheed & Ward.   [3] Oxford University Press.   [4] Mowbrays (*denotes *Fleur de Lys* series).
[5] Longmans.   [6] Burns Oates & Washbourne.   [7] Faber & Faber.   † also available in paperback.

BIBLIOGRAPHY

AND INDEX

BIBLIOGRAPHY

CHAPTER ONE

Barry, F. R., *Vocation and Ministry*. Nisbet, 1958.
Demant, V. A., *God, Man, and Society*. Faber & Faber, 1933.
——*Christian Polity*. Faber & Faber, 1936.
——*The Responsibility and Scope of Pastoral Theology To-day*. Faber & Faber, 1961.
Herbert, A. G., *Liturgy and Society*. Faber & Faber, 1935.
Iremonger, F. A., *William Temple*. O.U.P., 1948.
Ramsey, A. M., *Durham Essays and Addresses*. S.P.C.K., 1956.
——ed., *Christian Spirituality To-day*. Faith Press, 1961.
Reckitt, M. B., *Faith and Society*. Longmans, 1932.
Temple, W., *Christianity and Social Order*. Penguin, 1942.
Thornton, M., *Pastoral Theology: A Reorientation*. S.P.C.K., 1956.
——*Christian Proficiency*. S.P.C.K., 1959.
——*Essays in Pastoral Reconstruction*. S.P.C.K., 1960.
Vidler, A. R., *Essays in Liberality*. S.C.M. Press, 1957.
——*Christian Belief and This World*. S.C.M. Press, 1956.

CHAPTER TWO (AND GENERAL)

Box, H. S., ed., *Priesthood*. S.P.C.K., 1957.
Cant, R. E., *Christian Prayer*. Faith Press, 1961.
Frost, Bede, *The Art of Mental Prayer*. S.P.C.K., 1940.
Goodier, A., *Ascetical and Mystical Theology*. Burns Oates, 1925.
Guibert, J. de, *The Theology of the Spiritual Life*. Sheed & Ward, 1954.
Hardman, O., *The Ideals of Asceticism*. S.P.C.K., 1924.
——ed., *The Christian Life*. 2 vols. S.P.C.K., 1932.
Harton, F. P., *The Elements of The Spiritual Life*. S.P.C.K., 1932, 8th imp., 1947.
Hayman, E., *Prayer and The Christian Life*. S.C.M. Press, 1948.
Heiler, F., *Prayer*. O.U.P., 1938.
Hugel, F. von, *Essays and Addresses on The Philosophy of Religion*. Dent, 1st series 1921, 2nd series 1926.
Kirk, K. E., *The Vision of God*. Longmans, 1931.
Lercaro, Cardinal, *Methods of Mental Prayer*. Burns Oates, 1957.
Mascall, E. L., *Christ, The Christian and The Church*. Longmans, 1946.
Northcott, H., *The Venture of Prayer*. S.P.C.K., 1950.
Pourrat, P., *Christian Spirituality*, tr. W. H. Mitchell and S. P. Jacques. 3 vols. Burns Oates, 1922.

Poulain, A., *The Graces of Interior Prayer.* Routledge, 5th imp., 1950.
Pym, T. W., *Spiritual Direction.* S.C.M. Press, 1928.
Scaramelli, J. B., *Directorium Asceticum.* St Beuno's College. Burns Oates, 7th edn., 1917.
Sharpe, A. R., *Perfection and the only Alternative* (after Scaramelli). Simpkin Marshall, 1921.
Stewart, G. S., *The Lower Levels of Prayer.* S.C.M. Press, 1939.
Temple, W., *Christus Veritas.* Macmillan, 1924.
——*Nature, Man and God.* Macmillan, 1934.
Underhill, E., *Worship.* Nisbet, 1936.
Underhill, F., ed., *Feed My Sheep.* Mowbray, 1927.

CHAPTER THREE

Bowman, J. W., *The Intention of Jesus.* S.C.M. Press, 1945.
Nineham, D. E., *A New Way of Looking at the Gospels.* S.P.C.K., 1962.
Richardson, A., *The Biblical Doctrine of Work.* S.C.M. Press, 1952.
——*An Introduction to the Theology of The New Testament.* S.C.M. Press, 1958.
Temple, W., *Readings in St John's Gospel.* Macmillan, 1939.
Tinsley, E. J., *The Imitation of God in Christ.* S.C.M. Press, 1960.
Verity, G. B., *Life in Christ.* Longmans, 1952.

CHAPTER FOUR
(see also under chapters 15 and 19)
Butler, C., *Ways of Christian Life.* Sheed & Ward, 1932.
Carpenter, S. C., *The Church in England.* Murray, 1954.
Hart, A. Tindal, *The Country Priest in English History.* Phoenix, 1959.
Malden, R. H., *The English Church and Nation.* S.P.C.K., 1952.
Moorman, J. R. H., *A History of the Church in England.* A. & C. Black, 1952.
Morgan, D., ed., *They became Anglicans.* Mowbray, 1959.
Pepler, C., *The English Religious Heritage.* Blackfriars, 1958.
Sykes, N., *The English Religious Tradition.* S.C.M. Press, 1953.
Wand, J. W. C., *Anglicanism in History and To-day.* Weidenfeld & Nicholson, 1961.
Ward, M., ed., *The English Way.* Sheed & Ward, 1934.

CHAPTER FIVE

Augustine, St, *Works,* ed. and tr. M. Dods. 15 vols. T. & T. Clark, 1872.
    see also: *Enchiridion,* ed. E. Evans. S.P.C.K., 1953.
        City of God, Everyman nos. 982–3.
        Confessions, Everyman no. 200.

Battenhouse, R. W., ed., *A Companion to the Study of St Augustine*. O.U.P., 1955.
Burnaby, J., *Amor Dei*. Hodder & Stoughton. 1944; 3rd. imp., 1960.
Cassian, J., *Conferences*, ed. and tr. E. C. S. Gibson. O.U.P., 1894.
Chadwick, W. O., *John Cassian*. C.U.P., 1950.
——ed., *Western Asceticism*. S.C.M. Press, 1958.
——ed., with J. E. L. Oulton, *Alexandrian Christianity*. S.C.M. Press, 1956.
Gilson, E., *The Christian Philosophy of St Augustine*. Gollancz, 1961.
Mascall, E. L., *Grace and Glory*. Faith Press, 1961.
Przywara, E., and Martindale, C. C., eds., *An Augustine Synthesis*. Sheed & Ward, 1936.
Sheed & Ward, ed., *A Monument to St Augustine*. Sheed & Ward, 1936.

CHAPTER SIX
Benedict, St, *The Rule*, ed. Gasquet. Chatto & Windus, 1925.
Butler, C., *Benedictine Monachism*. Longmans, 1919.
Hayes, B., *The Via Vita of St Benedict*. R. & T. Washbourne, 1908.
Hunter-Blair, D. O., *The Rule of St Benedict*. Sands, 1906.

CHAPTER SEVEN
Bernard, St, Works. *Patrologia Latina*, ed. Mabillon-Migne, vols. clxxxii-clxxxv. Paris, 1879.
——see also *Letters* (including some treatises), ed. D. J. Mabillon, tr. S. J. Eales. Hodges, 1889.
——*On the Twelve Degrees of Humility and Pride*, tr. B. R. V. Mills. S.P.C.K., 1929.
——*Concerning Grace and Freewill*, tr. W. W. Williams. S.P.C.K., 1920.
——*Sermons on the Canticle*. Methuen, 1903.
——*De Diligendo Deo*, Cambridge Patristic Texts; tr. W. W. Williams in *St Bernard, the Man and his message*. Manchester University Press, 1944.
Coulton, G. G., *Two Saints*. C.U.P., 1932.
Gilson, E., *The Mystical Theology of St Bernard*. Sheed & Ward, 1940.
Merton, T., *The Last of The Fathers*. Hollis & Carter, 1954.
Morison, J. C., *The Life and Times of St Bernard*. Macmillan, 1894.
Sparrow-Simpson, W. J., *Lectures on St Bernard of Clairvaux*. Masters, 1895.
Watkin Williams, W., *St Bernard of Clairvaux*. Manchester University Press, 1935.
——*Studies in St Bernard of Clairvaux*. S.P.C.K., 1927.

CHAPTER EIGHT

Aelred of Rievaulx, St, *On Jesus at Twelve years Old*. Mowbray, 1957.
——*Letter to His Sister*. Mowbray, 1958.
Bouyer, L., *The Cistercian Heritage*, tr. E. Livingstone. Mowbray, 1958.
William of St Thierry, *Meditations*, tr. a Religious of C.S.M.V. Mowbray, 1954.
——*On The Nature and Dignity of Love*, tr. Webb and Walker. Mowbray, 1956.
——*On Contemplating God*. Mowbray, 1957.
——*The Mirror of Faith*, tr. Webb and Walker. Mowbray, 1959.
——*"The Golden Epistle"*, tr. W. Shewring and J. McCann. Sheed & Ward, 1930.

CHAPTER NINE

Dickenson, J. C., *The Origins of the Austin Canons*. S.P.C.K., 1950.
Hugh of St Victor, Works, *Patrologia Latina*, vols. clxxv–clxxvii. *The Divine Love*, tr. a Religious of C.S.M.V., Mowbray, 1956.
Richard of St Victor, Works, *Patrologia Latina*, vol. cxcvi. *Selected Writings on Contemplation*, ed. and tr. C. Kirchberger. Faber & Faber, 1957.
Robert of Bridlington, *Dialogue*, ed. a Religious of C.S.M.V. Mowbray, 1960.

CHAPTER TEN

Adderley, J. (from P. Sabatier), *Francis of Assisi*. Arnold, 1900.
Bonaventure, St, Works, *The Mystical Vine*, tr. a Friar of S.S.F. Mowbray, 1955.
Chesterton, G. K., *St Francis*. Hodder & Stoughton, 1923.
Francis of Assisi, St, *Works*, tr. a Religious of S.S.F. R. & T. Washbourne, 1882.
The Little Flowers of St Francis, ed. J. Rhoades. O.U.P., 1925.
Gilson, E., *The Philosophy of St Bonaventure*. Sheed & Ward, 1940.
Hallack, C. and Anson, P. F., *These Made Peace*. Burns Oates, 1957.
Hutton, E., *The Franciscans in England*. Constable, 1926.
Moorman, J. R. H., *Church Life in England in the Thirteenth Century*. A. & C. Black, 1945.
——*St Francis of Assisi*. S.C.M. Press, 1950.
Sherley-Price, L., *St Francis of Assisi*. Mowbray, 1959.

CHAPTER ELEVEN

Aquinas, St Thomas, *Summa Theologica*, tr. the English Dominicans. 22 vols. Burns Oates, 1920.

——*Compendium of Theology of St Thomas Aquinas*, ed. and tr. C. Vollert. Herder Books, 1947.
——*Selected Writings*. Everyman no. 953.
Bedoyere, M. de la, *Catherine*. Hollis & Carter, 1947.
Catherine of Siena, St, *Dialogue*. E. Cartier, Paris, 1855.
——*Letters*, ed. and tr. V. Scudder. Dent, 1905.
Chesterton, G. K., *St Thomas Aquinas*. Hodder & Stoughton, 1933.
——*Orthodoxy*. Bodley Head, 1922.
Copleston, F. C., *Aquinas*. Penguin, 1955.
D'Arcy, M. C., *Thomas Aquinas*. Benn, 1930.
Emmet, D. M., *The Nature of Metaphysical Thinking*. Macmillan, 1949.
Fahey, D., *Mental Prayer according to the Teaching of St Thomas Aquinas*. Gill, Dublin, 1927.
Hawkins, D. J. B., *A Sketch of Medieval Philosophy*. Sheed and Ward, 1946.
Jarrett, B., *The English Dominicans*. Burns Oates, 1921.
Maritain, J., *True Humanism*, tr. M. R. Adamson. Bles, 1938.
——*The Angel of The Schools*. Bles, 1936.
Mascall, E. L., *Existence and Analogy*. Longmans, 1949.
——*The Importance of Being Human*. Longmans, 1959.
Pieper, J., *Scholasticism*. Faber & Faber, 1961.
Vann, G., *Morals and Man*. Collins, Fontana, 1959.

CHAPTER THIRTEEN

Allison, T., *English Religious Life in the Eighth Century*. S.P.C.K., 1929.
Browne, G. F., *Theodore and Wilfrith*. S.P.C.K., 1897.
——*Alcuin of York*. S.P.C.K., 1908.
——*The Venerable Bede and His Writings*. S.P.C.K., 1919.
Bede, The Venerable, *Works*, tr. J. A. Giles. Bohn's Library, 1849.
Deanesly, M., *The Pre-Conquest Church in England*. A. & C. Black, 1961.
Meissuer, J. L. G., *The Celtic Church*. Hopkinson, 1929.
Overton, J. H., *The Church in England*. 2 vols. Gardner Darton, 1897.
Robinson, J. A., *The Times of St Dunstan*. O.U.P., 1923.
Telfer, W., *The Forgiveness of Sins*. S.C.M. Press, 1959.
Watkins, O. D., *A History of Penance*. 2 vols. Longmans, 1920.

CHAPTER FOURTEEN

Anselm, St, Works. *Patrologia Latina*. Gerberon-Migne, vols. clviii–clix.
——*Devotions* (including *Proslogion*) ed. and tr. C. C. J. Webb. Methuen, 1903.
——*Cur Deus Homo?* tr. E. S. Prout. Religious Tract Society, 1886.
——*Meditations and Prayers*, tr. "M.R". Burns Oates, 1872.
Church, R. W., *St Anselm*. Macmillan, 1892.

Foley, G. C., *Anselm's Theory of the Atonement.* Longmans, 1909.
Rigg, J. M., *St Anselm of Canterbury.* Methuen, 1896.
Rule, M., *Life and Times of St Anselm.* 2 vols. Kegan Paul, 1883.
Welch, A. C., *Anselm and His Work.* T. & T. Clark, 1901.

CHAPTER FIFTEEN

Ancrene Riwle, The, ed. M. Day. Early English Text Society, original
　　series, no. 225. Modern tr. M. B. Salu. Burns Oates, 1955.
Capgrave's *Life of St Gilbert of Sempringham,* ed. J. J. Munro. Early
　　English Text Society, original series, no. 140.
Clay, R. M., *The Hermits and Anchorites of England.* Methuen, 1914.
Cutts, E. L., *Parish Priests and Their People in The Middle Ages in England.*
　　S.P.C.K., 1898.
Darwin, F. D. S., *The English Medieval Recluse.* S.P.C.K., 1940.
Ford, B., *The Age of Chaucer.* Penguin, 2nd imp., 1955.
Gasquet, F. A., *Parish Life in Medieval England.* Methuen, 1909.
Graham, R., *St Gilbert of Sempringham and the Gilbertines.* Elliot Stock,
　　1901.
Hodgson, G. E., *English Mystics.* Mowbray, 1922.
Inge, W. R., *Studies of English Mystics.* Murray, 1906.
Knowles, D., *The English Mystics.* Burns Oates, 1927.
——*The Monastic Order in England.* C.U.P., 1940.
——*The Religious Orders in England.* 3 vols. C.U.P., 1948, 1955, 1959.
——*The English Mystical Tradition.* Burns Oates, 1961.
Kendall, E. L., *A City Not Forsaken.* Faith Press, 1962.
Lay Folk's Mass Book, The, ed. T. F. Simmons. Early English Text
　　Society, original series, no. 71.
Pantin, W. A., *The English Church in The Fourteenth Century.* C.U.P.,
　　1955.
Piers the Plowman, The Vision of, ed. W. W. Skeat. Early English Text
　　Society, original series, nos. 28, 30, 54.
Prymer, The, ed. H. Littlehales. Early English Text Society, original
　　series, nos. 105, 109.
Robert of Brunne, *Handlyng Synne,* ed. F. J. Furnivall. Early English
　　Text Society, original series nos. 119, 123.
Toovey, J., *Lives of The English Saints* (from Dugdale). 4 vols. 1844.

CHAPTER SIXTEEN
(see also under ch. 15)

Hilton, Walter, *The Scale of Perfection,* ed. E. Underhill. Watkins, 2nd
　　imp., 1948. (For other editions, see text ch. 16.)
——*Minor Works,* ed. D. Jones. Burns Oates, 1929.
——*The Goad of Love,* ed. C. Kirchberger. Faber & Faber, 1952.

CHAPTER SEVENTEEN
(see also under ch. 15)
Julian of Norwich, *The Revelations of Divine Love*, ed. G. Warrack.
    Methuen, 13th, edn, 1949.
——*A Shewing of God's Love* (The "Shorter Version of the Revela-
    tions"), ed. A. M. Reynolds. Longmans, 1958.
Molinari, P., *Julian of Norwich*. Longmans, 1958.
Thouless, R. H., *The Lady Julian*. S.P.C.K., 1924.

CHAPTER EIGHTEEN
(see also under ch. 15)
Cholmeley, K., *Margery Kempe*. Longmans, 1947.
Cloud of Unknowing (after A. Baker) ed. and tr. J. McCann. Burns Oates,
    5th edn, 1947.
Deonise His Diuinite, ed. P. Hodgson. Early English Text Society,
    original series, no. 231.
Kempe, Margery, *The Book of Margery Kempe*, ed. S. B. Meech and
    H. E. Allen. Early English Text Society, original series, no. 212.
    ed. and tr. (modern version) W. Butler-Bowden. World's Classics,
    O.U.P., no. 543, 1936.
Rolle, Richard, *The Fire of Love and The Mending of Life* (from R.
    Misyn) ed. R. M. Harvey. Early English Text Society, original
    series, no. 106.
——Also ed. and tr. (modern version) F. M. M. Comper. Methuen, 2nd
    edn, 1920.
——*The Amending of Life*, ed. and tr. H. L. Hubbard. Watkins, 1922.
——*English Prose Treatises of Richard Rolle*, ed. G. G. Perry. Early
    English Text Society, original series, no. 20.
——*The Form of Perfect Living* (and other treatises), ed. and tr. G. E.
    Hodgson. Baker, 1910
——*Selected Works of Richard Rolle*, ed. G. C. Heseltine. Longmans,
    1930.
——*The Officium and Miracula of Richard Rolle*, ed. R. M. Woolley.
    S.P.C.K., 1919.
——*Minor Works*, ed. and tr. G. E. Hodgson. Watkins, 1923.
Thornton, M., *Margery Kempe*. S.P.C.K., 1960.

CHAPTER NINETEEN

I. SELECTED CAROLINE THEOLOGY

Andrewes, L., *Works*. 11 vols. Library of Anglo-Catholic Theology,
    1841–54.
Baxter, R., *The Reformed Pastor*, ed. H. Martin. S.C.M. Press, 1956.

Baxter, R., *Chapters from a Christian Directory*. Bell & Son, 1925.
Beveridge, W., *Works*, ed. J. Bliss. 12 vols. L.A.C.T., 1842–6.
Cosin, J., *Works*. 5 vols. L.A.C.T., 1843.
Hall, J., *Works*, ed. P. Hall. 12 vols. Oxford, 1839.
Herbert, G., *Life and Works*, ed. G. H. Palmer. 3 vols. Harvard, 1915.
Hooker, R., *Works*, ed. J. Keble. 4 vols. O.U.P., 1836.
Ken, T., *Prose Works*, ed. J. T. Round. Rivingtons, 1838.
Laud, W., *Works*, ed. W. Scott. 7 vols. L.A.C.T., 1847–60.
Patrick, S., *Works*, ed. A. Taylor. 9 vols. Oxford, 1858.
Sanderson, R., *Works*, ed. W. Jackson. 6 vols. Oxford, 1854.
Taylor, J., *Works*, ed. R. Heber and C. P. Eden. 10 vols. Longmans, 1861.
White, F., *The Orthodox Faith and Way to the Church*. Burnet, 1624.

II. CAROLINE LAY MANUALS AND DEVOTIONS
(see also under ch. 20, section I)

Andrewes, L., *Preces Privatae*.
Anon., *The Whole Duty of Man*. Garthwaite, London, 1661.
    (attributed to Author of *The Whole Duty*; *The Ladies Calling*. Oxford, 1720).
Baily, L., *The Practice of Piety*. 1656.
Donne, J., *Collected Poems*, ed. H. J. C. Grierson. 2 vols. O.U.P., 1929.
——*Devotions*. C.U.P., 1923.
Herbert, G., *The Temple and A Priest to the Temple*, ed. E. Thomas. Everyman, undated.
Hill, R., *The Pathway To Piety*. Pickering, London, 1847.
Horneck, A., *The Happy Ascetick*. Chapman & Ware, London, 1724.
——*The Sirenes*. Mortlock, London, 1690.
Nelson, R., *Address to Persons of Quality and Estate*. Smith, London, 1715.
Patrick, S., *A Discourse Concerning Prayer*. Pickering, London, 1848.
——*The Parable of The Pilgrim*. 6th edn, R. Chitwell, London, 1687.
Taylor, J., *Rules and Exercises For Holy Living, and Rules and Exercises For Holy Dying, On the State of Man*. Newman-Smith, London, 1699.
Traherne, T., *Poems of Felicity*, ed. H. I. Bell. O.U.P., 1910.
——*The Way to Blessedness*, ed. M. Bottrall. Faith Press, 1962.
——*Centuries of Meditations*, ed. G. I. Wade. Dobell, 1932.

III. MODERN COMMENTARY

Addleshaw, G. W. O., *The High Church Tradition*. Faber & Faber, 1941.
Blackstone, B., ed., *The Ferrar Papers*. C.U.P., 1928.
Bourne, E. C. E., *The Anglicanism of William Laud*. S.P.C.K., 1947.
Lewis, G., *Robert Sanderson*. S.P.C.K., 1924.

McAdoo, H. R., *The Structure of Caroline Moral Theology*. Longmans, 1949.
Maycock, A. L., *Nicholas Ferrar*. S.P.C.K., 1938.
——*Chronicles of Little Gidding*. S.P.C.K., 1954
More, P. E., and Cross, F. L., eds. *Anglicanism*. S.P.C.K., 1935.
Overton, J. H., *Life in The English Church. 1660–1714*. Longmans, 1885.
Sharland, E. C., ed., *The Story Books of Little Gidding*. Seeley, 1899.
Staley, V., *Hooker*. Masters, 1907.
Stranks, C. J., *The Life and Writings of Jeremy Taylor*. S.P.C.K., 1952.
——*Anglican Devotion*. S.C.M. Press, 1961.
Thornton, L. S., *Richard Hooker*. S.P.C.K., 1924.
Trevor-Roper, H. R., *Archbishop Laud*. Macmillan, 1940.
Welsby, P. A., *Lancelot Andrewes*. S.P.C.K., 1958.
Wood, T., *English Casuistical Divinity During The Seventeenth Century*. S.P.C.K., 1952.
Woodhouse, H. F., *The Doctrine of The Church in Anglican History*. S.P.C.K., 1954.
Wordsworth, C., *Bishop Sanderson's Lectures on Conscience and Human Law*. Rivingtons, 1877.

IV. MODERN MORAL THEOLOGY

Davis, H., *Moral and Pastoral Theology: a Summary*. Sheed & Ward, 1952.
Dewar, L., *A Short Introduction to Moral Theology*. Mowbray, 1956.
Dewar, L., and Hudson, C. E., *Christian Morals*. University of London Press, 1945.
Kirk, K. E., *Conscience and its Problems*. Longmans, 1927.
——*Some Principles of Moral Theology*. Longmans 1920; 8th imp., 1948.
Mortimer, R. C., *The Elements of Moral Theology*. A. & C. Black; 2nd imp., 1953.
Slater, T., *Cases of Conscience*. R. & T. Washbourne, 1919.

CHAPTER TWENTY

I. CAROLINE WORKS

Beveridge, W., *The Great Necessity of Public Prayer*. Smith, London, 1708.
Durel, J., *The Liturgy of The Church of England.**
Hopton, S., *Devotions in the Ancient Way of Offices.**
Nelson. R., *Fasts and Festivals.**
——*The Practice of True Devotion*. 13th edn, B. Dod, London, 1753.
Patrick, S., *A Book for Beginners: A Help to Young Communicants.**
Smythies, W., *The Unworthy Non-Communicant*.

Sparrow, A., *A Rationale on The Book of Common Prayer*, ed. J. H. Newman. Oxford, 1839.
White, F., *Treatise on the Sabbath Day.**

  * Caroline Theology has been published in a great many editions; Lay Manuals and Books of Devotion are frequently available at second-hand.
See also Bibliography to ch. 19, sections I and II.

II. MODERN WORKS

Abbott, E. S., *The Doctrine, Discipline and Devotional Quality of The Book of Common Prayer*. Chelmsford Diocesan Conference, 1949.
Clarke, W. K. L., ed., *Liturgy and Worship*. S.P.C.K., 1932.
Dix, G., *The Shape of The Liturgy*. Dacre Press, 1943.
Dugmore, C. W., *The Mass and The English Reformers*. Macmillan, 1958.
Harrison, D. E. W., *The Book of Common Prayer*. Canterbury Press, 1946.
Longridge, W. H., *Some Difficulties in the Practice of Frequent Confession and Communion*. S.S.J.E., undated.
Mascall, E. L., *Corpus Christi*. Longmans, 1953.
Perry, M. C., *The Pattern of Matins and Evensong*. Hodder & Stoughton, 1961.
Proctor, F., and Frere, W. H., *A New History of The Book of Common Prayer*. Macmillan, 1901.
The First and Second Prayer Books of Edward VI. Everyman, no. 448.
  See also Thornton, M., Hebert, A. G., Ramsey, A. M., under Bibliography to ch. 1; Underhill, E., under Bibliography to ch. 2.

CHAPTER TWENTY-ONE

Briscoe, J. F., and Mackay, H. F. B., *A Tractarian at Work* (Dean Randall). Mowbray, 1932.
Butler, J., *Works*, ed. W. E. Gladstone. O.U.P., 1896.
Carpenter, S. C., *Eighteenth-Century Church and People*. Murray, 1959.
——*Church and People*, 1789–1889. S.P.C.K., 1933.
Church, R. W., *The Oxford Movement*. Macmillan, 1891.
Clark, W. K. L., *Eighteenth-Century Piety*. S.P.C.K., 1944.
Creed, J. M., and Boys-Smith, J. S., *Religious Thought in the XVIII Century*. C.U.P., 1934.
Donaldson, A. B., *Five Great Oxford Leaders*. Rivingtons, 1900.
Ingram, K., *Keble*. Allan, 1933.
Jones, D. M., *Charles Wesley*. Skeffington, 1919.
King, E., *Spiritual Letters*, ed. B. W. Randolph. Mowbray, 1910.
Knox, E. A., *The Tractarian Movement*. Putnam, 1933.
Law, W., *A Serious Call to a Devout and Holy Life*. Methuen, 7th. edn, 1950.
——*Liberal and Mystical Writings*, ed. W. S. Palmer. Longmans, 1908.

Mansbridge, A., *Talbot and Gore*. Dent, 1935.
Overton, J. H., *Life and Opinions of The Reverend William Law*. Longmans, 1881.
——*The Anglican Revival*. Blackie, 1897.
——*John Wesley*. Methuen, 1891.
Oxford Lent Sermons, 1865–71, Parker. Oxford, 1865–71.
Pusey, E. B., *Letters*, ed. and pub. Parker. Oxford, 1839.
Ramsey, A. M., *From Gore to Temple*. Longmans, 1960.
Russell, G. W. E., *Dr Liddon*. Mowbray, 1905.
Smith, B. A., *Dean Church*. O.U.P., 1958.
Stephens, W. R. W., *The Life and Letters of Dean Hook*. 2 vols. Richard Bentley, 1878.
Stranks, C. J., *Dean Hook*. Mowbrays, 1954.
Tracts for the Times. 6 vols. Rivington-Parker, 1834–41.
Webb, C. C. J., *Religious Thought in the Oxford Movement*. S.P.C.K., 1928.
Wesley, J., *Works*, ed. J. Benson. 16 vols. Jones, London, 1809–13.
——*Journal*, ed. N. Curnock. 8 vols. Culley, 1909–16.
——*Letters*, ed. A. Birrell. Hodder & Stoughton, 1915.
Whyte, A., *William Law*. Hodder & Stoughton, 1893.
Woodforde, J., *Diary*, ed. J. Beresford. 5 vols. O.U.P., 1924–31. Also abridged edn, World's Classics no. 514.

OTHER WORKS CONSULTED

Cambridge Medieval History, C.U.P.
Cross, F. L., ed., *The Oxford Dictionary of The Christian Church*. O.U.P., 1957.
Coulton, G. G., *Five Centuries of Religion*.
D'Aygalliers, A. W., *Ruysbroek the Admirable*. Dent, 1925.
François de Sales, St, *Introduction To The Devout Life*, ed. and tr. A. Ross. Burns Oates, 1943.
Garrigou-Lagrange, R., *Providence*. Herder Books, 1937.
——*Christian Perfection and Contemplation*. Herder Books, 1937.
Gore, C., ed., *A New Commentary on Holy Scripture*. S.P.C.K., 1928.
——ed., *Lux Mundi*. Murray, 15th edn, 1904.
Ignatius Loyola, St, *Spiritual Exercises*, ed. W. H. Longridge. Mowbray, 4th edn, 1950.
Imitation of Christ, The, attributed to Thomas à Kempis. Chapman & Hall, undated.
Inge, W. R., ed., *Light, Life and Love* (Selections from the German Mystics). Methuen, 2nd edn, 1919.
John of the Cross, St, *Works*, ed. E. A. Peers. Burns Oates, 1947.
Martensen, H. L., and Hobhouse, S., *Jacob Boehme*. Rockliff, 1949.

Peake, A. S., *A Commentary on the Bible*. Jack, London, 1920.
Selwyn, E. G., ed., *Essays Catholic and Critical*. S.P.C.K., 1929.
Tanquerey, A., *The Spiritual Life*. Desclee & Co., 1930.
Tauler, J., *The Inner Way*, 36 Sermons, ed. and tr. A. W. Hutton. Methuen, 1904.
——*Meditation on The Passion*, ed. A. P. J. Cruikshank. London, 1904.
Teresa of Avila, St, *Works*, ed. E. A. Peers. Sheed & Ward, 1944.
——*Letters*, ed. Stanbrook Benedictines. 4 vols. Baker, 1919–23.
Tennant, F. R., *Philosophical Theology*. 2 vols. C.U.P., 1928–30.
Theologica Germanica, ed. S. Winkworth. Macmillan, 1907.

INDEX

Cowley Publications is a work of the Society of St. John the Evangelist, a religious community for men in the Episcopal Church. The books we publish are a significant part of our ministry, together with the work of preaching, spiritual direction, and hospitality. Our aim is to provide books that will enrich their readers' religious experience and challenge it with fresh approaches to religious concerns.